Arthur Young, William Richardson

Travels During the Years 1787, 1788 and 1789

Vol. 2, Second Edition

Arthur Young, William Richardson

Travels During the Years 1787, 1788 and 1789
Vol. 2, Second Edition

ISBN/EAN: 9783337266813

Printed in Europe, USA, Canada, Australia, Japan

Cover: Foto ©Andreas Hilbeck / pixelio.de

More available books at **www.hansebooks.com**

TRAVELS,

During the Years 1787, 1788, *and* 1789.

UNDERTAKEN MORE PARTICULARLY

WITH A VIEW OF ASCERTAINING

THE

CULTIVATION, WEALTH, RESOURCES,

AND

NATIONAL PROSPERITY,

OF THE

KINGDOM OF FRANCE.

THE SECOND EDITION.

VOL. II.

BY ARTHUR YOUNG, Esq. F.R.S.

SECRETARY TO THE BOARD OF AGRICULTURE; HONORARY MEMBER OF THE SOCIETIES OF DUBLIN, BATH, YORK, SALFORD, ODIHAM, AND KENT; THE PHILOSOPHICAL AND LITERARY SOCIETY OF MANCHESTER; THE VETERINARY COLLEGE OF LONDON; THE ECONOMICAL SOCIETY OF BERNE; THE PHYSICAL SOCIETY OF ZURICH; THE PALATINE ACADEMY OF AGRICUL-TURE AT MANHEIM; THE IMPERIAL ECONOMICAL SOCIETY ESTABLISHED AT PETERSBURGH; THE ROYAL AND ELECTORAL ECONOMICAL SOCIETY OF CELLE; ASSOCIATE OF THE ROYAL SOCIETY OF AGRICULTURE AT PARIS; AND CORRESPONDING MEMBER OF THE ROYAL ACADEMY OF AGRICULTURE AT FLORENCE; AND OF THE PATRIOTIC SOCIETY AT MILAN.

BURY ST. EDMUND'S:

PRINTED BY J. RACKHAM, FOR W. RICHARDSON, ROYAL-EXCHANGE, LONDON.

1794.

TRAVELS, &c.

CHAP. X.

Vines.

THE number of notes I took, in moſt of the provinces of the kingdom, relative to the culture of vineyards, was not inconſiderable; but the difficulty
of reducing the infinite variety of French meaſures, of land and liquids, to a
common ſtandard, added to an unavoidable uncertainty in the information itſelf,
renders this the moſt perplexing inquiry that can be conceived. It was an object to aſcertain the value given to the ſoil by this culture; the amount of the
annual produce; and the degree of profit attending it; inquiries not undeſerving
the attention even of politicians, as the chief intereſts of a country depend, in
ſome meaſure, on ſuch points being well underſtood. Now there is ſcarcely
any product ſo variable as that of wine. Corn lands and meadow have their bad
and their good years, but they always yield ſomething, and the average produce
is rarely far removed from that of any particular year. With vines the difference
is enormous; this year they yield nothing; in another, perhaps caſks are wanted
to contain the exuberant produce of the vintage; now the price is extravagantly
high; and again ſo low, as to menace with poverty all who are concerned in it.
Under ſuch variations, the ideas even of proprietors, who live by the culture,
are not often correct, in relation to the *medium* of any circumſtance: nor is it
always eaſy to bring individuals to regard rather the average of a diſtrict, than
the particular one of their own fields. In many caſes, it is more ſatisfactory
to rely on particular experience, when it appears tolerably exact, than to demand ideas, ſo often vague of what is not immediately within the practice of
the man who ſpeaks. Theſe difficulties have occurred ſo often, and in ſo many
ſhapes, that the reader can hardly imagine the labour which it repeatedly coſt

 B

me to gain that approximation to accuracy, which I was fortunate enough fometimes to attain. But, after all the inquiries I have made, with attention and
induftry, I do not prefume to infert here an abftract of my notes as intelligence
that can be *entirely* relied on : I am fatisfied, that it is impoffible to procure
fuch, without application, time, and exertions, which are not at the command
of many travellers. Contenting myfelf, therefore, with the probability of being
free from grofs errors, and with the hope of giving fome information on the
fubject, not to be found in other books, I venture to fubmit the following
extract to the public eye, though it be a refult inadequate to the labour, variety,
and expected fuccefs of my inquiries. It is neceffary farther to premife, that the
reader muft not contraft the circumftance of one place with thofe of another,
under the idea that a confiderable difference is any proof of error in the account.
The price of an arpent is fometimes out of proportion to the produce ; and the
profit at other times unaccounted for by either :—this depends on demand,
competition, the divifion of properties, the higher or lower ratio of expence, and
on various other circumftances, which, to explain fully in each article, would
be to enlarge this fingle chapter into a volume ; I touch on it here, merely to
guard againft conclufions, which are to be made with caution. The towns
named in the following table, are the places where I procured intelligence.—
None are inferted in which I did not make the inquiry, as I was at every place
mentioned in the margin.

The rents of vines are named but at few places ; for they are very rarely in
any other hands than thofe of the proprietor ; even where rent is named, there
is not one acre in an hundred let.

The price of the product is every where that of the fame autumn as the
vintage : thofe who can afford to keep their wine have much greater profits :
but as that is a fpecies of merchandize as much in the power of a dealer as of a
planter, it ought not to be the guide in fuch accounts as thefe.

Isle of France.—*Arpajon.*—Rent of fome to 80 liv. ; in common 25 liv.
Expences in labour, exclufive of vintage, 60 liv. (2l. 10s. 9d. per Englifh acre).
Produce, 6 pieces, of 80 pints, each 1¼ bottle.

Eftampes.—Meafure 80 perch, of 22 feet. Produce, 10 to 22 pieces. Rent to
90 liv. Labour, 60 liv. (2l. 13s. 9d. per Englifh acre), vintage excluded.

Orleans.—Price in the town, 150 liv. the piece, of 240 bottles, and retail 6 to
10f. the pint, of 1¼ bottle. Rent, 45 liv. Labour, 40 liv. vintage excluded
(1l. 13s. 9d. per Englifh acre.) Arpent of 40,000 feet.

S. of ditto.—Meafure 100 perch, of 20 feet. Produce, 7 pieces, and in a good
year 12. Rent, 36 liv. Labour, 40 liv. (1l. 13s 10d. per Englifh acre).

Sologne.—*Verfon.*—Rent in common, 35 to 50 liv. of the beft 60 liv. the
fétérée. Produce, 10 to 12 pieces, and to 22.——Account here,

Rent,

Rent,	-	60 liv.		Produce, 11 pieces, at 20 liv.	220 liv.
Tailles, about	12			Expences, - -	156
Vingtieme,	5			Profit, - -	64
Labour, -	40				
Props, -	6	10 f.			
Vintage,	33			Price, 220 liv. (9l. 6s. 4d. per Englifh acre.)	
	156	10			

They renew fome of the vines every year, by laying down fhoots, called generally *provins*, but here *fauffes*, five hundred per annum, at 50 f. the hundred. They manure to the amount of thirteen fmall cart loads, not reckoned in the above account. Twenty people neceffary for gathering an arpent, at 12 f. a day, and food. Vines are fometimes much damaged by frofts in the fpring.

BERRY.—*Vatan.*—No props; give four hoeings. *Fauffe* 1 liv. 15 f. the hundred. Rarely let. Produce, 3 pieces per fétérée, fome 6 or 8; price now 24 liv. Rent, 60 liv. Produce, 168 liv. (6l. 13s. 10d. per Englifh acre.) To plant a fétérée, for fetting only, 45 liv. to 48 liv.; for two years produces nothing; the third a little. All agree it is the moft profitable hufbandry, if one be not obliged to fell in the vintage, for want of capital to keep the wine.

Chateauroux.—Very few let. Earth them four times. Produce, 3 poinçons, or pieces, a fétérée. Rent, 60 liv.

Argenton.—Produce 5 or 6 pieces the fétérée, each piece 160 bottles. Planted about 2 feet 6 inches fquare. Ufe props of quartered oak.

QUERCY.—*Brive.*—A journal one-fourth of a fétérée, 0,4132 (*Pauëlon.*) In a good year produce 2 muids, of 242 pints of 2 bottles, but not general. Price, 3 to 6 f. the pint. Labour, 15 liv. vintage excluded.

Pont de Rodez.—The plants at 4 feet fquare; very old and large. Every where quite clean, and in fine order, worked four times. Price, 6 liv. for 96 Paris pints. Cartona about half an acre.

Pellecoy.—Pafs vineyards, of which there are many fo fteep, that it is ftrange how men can ftand at their work. One-third of the country under vines, which are planted on abfolute rocks, but calcareous.

Cahors.—Nineteen-twentieths under vines; in regular rows, at 4 feet; many more than two hundred years old. The true *vin de Cahors*, which has a great reputation, is the product of a range of rocky vineyards, that are upon hills hanging to the fouth, and is called *grave* wine, becaufe of the ftoney foil. Much fubject to ftorms of hail. Meafure the fétérée, not quite an arpent. Produce, 4 barriques, each 210 common bottles. Price, 50 liv.; fometimes at 20 or 30 liv.; and if two or three plentiful years together, the price of the wine does not exceed the cafk; laft year 12 liv.; 50 liv. the barrique, is 3 liv. the

dozen.

dozen. Price, 800 liv. the meafure (33l. 18s. 1d. per Englifh acre); fome at at 150 liv. (6l. 6s. 10d.); alfo at 300 liv. (12l. 13s. 8d. Labour, exclufive of vintage, 30 liv. (1l. 5s. 4d.) Their wines all bear the fea well. The inhabitants and proprietors have little to do in the wine trade; dealers buy up for the merchants at Bourdeaux, who mix thefe wines with their own thin bodied ones, and fell them for claret to the Englifh, Dutch, &c. They make much brandy; five barriques make one of brandy. I drank this wine of three and ten years old; the latter 30f. the bottle, and both excellent. I imported a barrique, three years old, at 100 liv. prime coft and charges; and it coft me into my cellar in Suffolk 15l. more, in freight, duty, carriage, and charges of all forts. Monf. Andoury, aubergifte at the *Trois Rois*, with whom I fettled a correfpondence, might fend me good wine; but not putting it into a double barrel, which he promifed, it came to me much too weak; for the *vin de Cabors* is full bodied as port, but much better. A barrique I had alfo of another fort of wine, from the Chev. de Cheyron, near Leyborne; and, for want of being cafed, it turned out fuch poor ftuff, that it is hardly good enough for vinegar. Without double cafing (and with it, for what I know), wines, *on a private account*, are tapped, and filled up with water.

Ventiliac.—See them, for the firft time in going fouth, ploughing between the rows of vines, at 5 feet and 5½ feet afunder.

Noé.—Ox-hoeing the vines on a plain; each ox walks on an interval, with a row between them; and yoked with a fliding yoke, to vary the diftance from ox to ox. Many young plantations of vines.

ROUSILLON.—*Pia.*—Vineyards not reckoned profitable, on land that will do well for other produ&s: a minatre (1200 cannes, about 40,000 feet), from five to ten charges, each 128 bottles, or pints of Paris. Good wine, of laft vintage, 6 liv. to 10 liv. the charge; but old at 72 liv.

Sejean.—The charge contains 60 pots, and weighs 360 lb.; five charges the muid, and the muid four tonneaux of Bourdeaux; price 10 liv. or 12 liv. the charge; freight from Cette to Dunkirk, 50 liv. 10f. the ton, and 20f. gratification; duty on export 7 liv.

Beziers.—Vineyards planted by Abbé Rozier, four feet four inches, by three feet ten inches, but not regular; fet in a deep foffe, and covered with flints only.

Méze.—New vineyards planted in all parts. A fétérée, in a common year, gives two muids, or four tonneaux; 576 pots to the muid, or 768 bottles, each a Paris pint. Four tonneaux of wine, give one quintal of brandy, which fells, at prefent, at 122 liv. 12f. the quintal. Produce in money 96 liv. (8l. per Englifh acre), labour exclufive; vintage 15 liv. (1l. 6s. per Englifh acre). Examined a vineyard, planted 1250 plants per fétérée; they were four feet nine inches one

way,

way, by four feet fix inches the other ; each plant therefore occupied 21½½ feet fquare : rejecting the fraction, there would be 2073 in an Englifh acre ; thus the fétérée is fomething better than half an acre. They are worked twice a year by hand ; the expence 15 liv. the fétérée : the cuttings pay the expence of taking. Taille 30 f. and making the wine 20 /. the muid ; common price of the wine 24 liv. the tonneaux.

Pijan.—Produce, 1½ muid per fétérée, at 50 liv. 640 bottles, or 2 f. the bottle. Within two leagues, Frontignan, fo famous for its mufcat wines, a fétérée of land has there yielded 500 liv. and half as much in a common year. Montbafin is alfo noted for its mufcats, which fells as dear as thofe of Frontignan : three barriques make one muid, or 640 bottles : price in a common year, embarked at Cette, 300 liv. : the red wine of Montbafin, 100 liv. the three barriques.

To Nimes.—Several thoufand acres of vines on a level plain.

Nimés.—For feveral leagues around, the vineyards yield from one muid to fix per faumée ; three, on an average ; and the mean price 60 liv. : meafure, 1715 cannes in a faumée, or 61,740 feet.

Plaifance.—An arpent of wheat, one year with another, yields more than an arpent of vines ; but an arpent of vines fells for near double one of arable.

Auch to Fleuran.—Many vines. Price, 500 liv. (21l. 17s. 6d. per Englifh acre).

Leitour.—Ditto on the ftoney hills. Meafure a fack, that land fown with a fack of 145lb. wheat. Price, 400 liv. (17l. 10s. per Englifh acre).

La Morte.—Landron.—Vines on the hills. Meafure the journal, and further ditto, in the rich vale on the Garonne : props of willow. Price, 1000 liv. (50l. per Englifh acre).

Langon.—Yellow wine famous. Meafure, arpent. Produce, 5 or 6 barriques. Price, 1000 liv. the arpent (50l. per Englifh acre). Produce, 300 liv. (15l. per Englifh acre).

Barfac.—Sell at 5 f. or 6 f. the pas of 2 feet 6 inches ; 90 pas the auln ; and price 100 liv. Four rows of vines, or 4 aulns, make the breadth, and 90 pas long ; are dreffed four times a year, for 3 liv. : 45 rows a journal ; but fell the fpace planted at one price, and the interval at another. The vines 20 liv. to 22 liv. the auln ; the fpaces between at 3 liv. Ninety by 2½, or 180 feet multiplied by 2½, for the breadth 450, and by 45, the number of rows, gives 20,250 fquare feet for a journal : 45 rows, at 22 liv. are 990 liv. : but 45 by 3, the price of the interval 135 liv. : average 562 liv. on the fuppofition of half vines, half intervals. Hills that hang to the Garonne, on the N. fide, an immenfe range of vines.

Caftres.—In a journal, the half only planted as above, will give, in a good year, 4 tonneaux, average 1½. Two years ago, 35 liv. the tonneaux ; this year, 60 liv. to 70 liv. at 40 liv. it is 90 liv. per journal. Cafks from the N. of Europe.

Europe, much inferior to French ones, becaufe the ftaves are larger and thicker; price of them, 240 liv. the dozen. Journal of Bourdeaux, to arpent de France, as 0,6218 to 1.

Bourdeaux to Cubfac.— This country, part *palus* and part high: **produce 5 to 6** barriques on the latter, **and 2½ to 3** tonneaux on the other: 1200 liv. (61l. 8s. 6d. per Englifh acre) a common price; but fome journals rife to 3000 **liv.** (153l. 11s. 3d. per Englifh acre), and even to 4000 liv. (191l. 19s. 3d.)

To Cavignac.—Produce wine 5 to 6 barriques the journal: **make much** brandy; 5 or 6 for 1; 220 bottles are fold at 120 liv.: their white wine for export is now at 150 liv. the tonneaux. The fogs and rains this year, when the vines were in bloffom, damaged them fo much, that the crop will be very poor; which they are not forry for, fince another great vintage or two would have ruined them, by the low price which is the confequence. They have a fabric of tartar.

ANGOUMOIS.—*To Petignac.*—*Roulet.*—The journal of 200 laft each, 12 feet fquare, gives 1½ tonneaux; **on** good land, 4 to 6 barriques the journal of **200** carreaux of 12 feet fquare, 28,800 feet; an arpent 1½; on worfe land 1½ **to 3.** A journal of wine not equal to **the** value of one of wheat: **make much very** fine brandy.

To Angoulême.—A journal, vines and arable land, of an equal price; 200 liv. common (10l. per Englifh acre); produce 40 liv. (2l. per Englifh acre).—An immenfe range of vines: produce, 3 to 4 barriques; common price, 10 liv.: **make** a great deal of good brandy, which fells now at 150 liv. **the barrique, but has** been at 60 liv.; beft vineyard 300 liv. to 400 liv.

Verteuil.—Price, 10 liv. to 15 liv. **the** barrique: **proportion of brandy varies** from 4 to 9 of wine for 1; in general 6 for 1.

Caudec.—Give 2, 3, and 4 barriques per journal.

POITOU.—*Chateaurault to Les Ormes.*—Poor hills, **with vines, fell equally** with their beft vale lands. Meafure the boiffelée.

TOURAINE.—*Tours.*—Produce, 5 to 30 pieces per arpent; average 10; and mean price, 15 liv. (150 liv. is 4l. 0s. 3d. per Englifh acre): meafure 100 chainé of 25 feet, 62,500 feet.

Amboife.—An arpent 8 pieces, at 4 liv. 192 liv. (5l. 12s. per Englifh acre): meadows a better eftate and fell higher: **the vines are 1500 liv. (43l. 15s. per.** Englifh acre).

Blois to Chambord.—Almoft all the country vines, and many new plantations, on a blowing fand; 2000 acres under the eye at once. Arpent 1600 toifes: produce 12 poinçons, and, in good years, to 36, each 240 bottles; moftly **made** into brandy: in one village, laft winter, they made 3000 poinçons: **in fome**

years

years 3 of wine make 1 : an arpent requires 7200 props, which laſt about eight years ; the price 18 liv. to 20 liv. the thouſand.

Chambord.—Same meaſure : average produce 12 pieces.

To Petiviers.—Produce, 12 pieces on good land, at 36 liv. now ; but average 10, at 24 liv. or 240 liv. (8l. 8s. per Engliſh acre). Meaſure 100 perch, at 22 feet : price 1000 liv. (35l. per Engliſh acre).

Petiviers.—Price of an arpent 700 liv. (24l. 10s. per Engliſh acre) : produce, 4 to 20 pieces ; average 10 : price now 50 liv. ; but average 24 liv. or 240 liv. (8l. 8s. per Engliſh acre). labour, excluſive of vintage, 30 liv.

Isle of France.—*La Chapelle La Reine*—Produce, 10 pieces, at 20 liv. 200 liv. (7l. per Engliſh acre) labour, excluſive of vintage, 30 liv. : meaſure 100 perches, 22 feet : price 600 liv. (21l. per Engliſh acre).

Liancourt.—A bad arpent 300 liv. ; a good 600 liv. (450 liv. is 15l. 13s. 3d. per Engliſh acre): the meaſure 100 perches, at 22 feet. Produce, 3 muids, at 60 liv. 180 liv. (6l. 6s. per Engliſh acre) the muid, of 360 Paris bottles ; yet bad, and not drank by gentlemen. Props, laſt five or ſix years, 10 liv. the thouſand ; to keep an arpent in order, 2000 every year.

Bretagne.—*Auvergnac.*—A ſcattering of them from Guerande hither, and no where elſe N. except a few on the coaſt at Piriac and St. Gildas. Meaſure the journal of 1280 toiſes. Price, 800 liv. (29l. 3s. 10d. per Engliſh acre). Produce, 6 to 8 barriques, each 240 pints of Paris Common price, 15 liv. to 20 liv. This for a good year. They reckon, that if they have no crop, they loſe 60 liv. per journal.

Nantes to Ancenis.—Produce, ſix barriques, now 25 liv. All promiſcuous, and no props.

Ancenis.—Boiſelée, the fifth of an arpent de Paris ; ſells, per arpent, at 750 liv. Produce, in a common year, 1½ barrique, or 7½ per arpent : and common price 22 liv. 165 liv. (8l. 8s. 10d. per Engliſh acre) : ſometimes let, at three-fourths and one-half produce, to metayers. Labour, 6 liv. the boiſelée, and 6 liv. the vintage ; in all, 60 liv. the arpent. Great region of vines along the river ; they extend not far from it : dung very little ; many not once in fifteen years.

Varades.—Meadows ſell at double the price of vineyards, yet theſe 600 liv. (30l. 14s. 3d. per Engliſh acre).

Anjou.—*St. George.*—Boiſelée, ¼ of an arpent, or 10,000 feet. An arpent, 40,000 feet, of the worſt vines ſells at 200 liv. ; beſt 500 liv. (350 liv. is 14l. 9s. 7d. per Engliſh acre). Produce, 1½ to 5 barriques.

Angers.—On the Loire, vineyards are various ; ſome produce very little of the beſt wine ; and others, by manuring, much of an inferior quality. Four barriques of good wine, on an arpent of 100 cords, of 25 feet, or 62,500, is

a common

a common produce, but not a medium. The price, in a plentiful year, 35 liv.; and in one of scarcity, 50 liv. the barrique: this year it is 25 liv. but the wine bad, the grapes not being ripe. Four barriques, at 40 liv. make 160 liv. Expences—labour in digging 24 liv.; vintage 3 liv. the barrique, or 12 liv. the arpent; casks, at 5 liv. 20 liv.; tythe $\frac{1}{11}$th; besides taxes. The assertion general, that vines are the worst of all estates. Why? Because, for one year in five or six, they yield nothing; and sometimes little, for two or three years together. But admitted, at the same time, that if a man has money to enable him to keep his wine, two good years pay more than the fee simple. An arpent of the best vines on the Loire, sells from 3000 to 4000 liv. Now, to gain from hence some facts by combination, call this 3500 liv. and that it pays only 5 per cent.—it is 175 liv.; labour 36 liv.; casks 25 liv.; and here is 236 liv. without a penny for the king, or any *profit* to the proprietor: at 5 barriques, this makes 47 liv. each; a sure proof, either that the produce must be more than 5 barriques,—or that the price must be more than 47 liv.; probably 9, at 40 liv. (360 liv. is 9l. 13s. 4d. per English acre), for a mean arpent, at 1750 liv. (47l. 5s. 3d. per English acre).

Duretel.—Vines sells higher than arable, and meadow higher than vines.

La Roche Guyon.—Vines the worst estate in the hands of poor proprietors only.——Account of an arpent of Paris. Price, 1200 liv. (61l. 8s. 4d. per English acre.)

	Liv.		Liv.
Rent; the interest of the price, at 4 per cent.	48	Produce, 6 muids, at 50 liv. -	300
Labour, } 68 liv. (3l. 9s. 2d. English acre) { 60		(15l. 7s. 1d. English acre.)	
Vintage, } { 8			
Manure, - - - -	40	Expences, - - -	227
Six casks, - - - -	36		
Props, - - - -	30	Profit, - - -	73
Taille, - - - -	5		
	227	The muid 240 pints de Paris.	

An extraordinary good year is 10 muids; a middling one six; and a bad one three. As to no produce at all, or so little as one, no such thing is known, not even in forty years. But query, hail?

In 1785, the crop was 12 muids, at 27 liv.			324 liv.
1786,	5	70	350
1787,	3	90	270
1788,	4½	75	337

The labour consists in carrying of dung, pruning, trimming, four diggings, staking, tying, budding, &c.

How

How this hufbandry can be efteemed unprofitable, as it is generally in France, furpaffes my comprehenfion : in the hands of a man without a fufficient capital, it certainly is fo ; but thus alfo is that of wheat and barley.

Neuf Moutier.—In one of the richeft diftricts in France, vines on the flopes fell at 2000 liv. to 2500 liv. (2250 liv. is 78l. 13s. 3d. per Englifh acre) the arpent of 100 perches of 22 feet ; where the rich vales let at 40 liv. to 60 liv. ; and land of 40 liv. fells not higher than 1500 liv. or 1600 liv.

CHAMPAGNE.—*Epernay, &c.*—Two-thirds of all the country around, about Ay, Cumiere, Piery, Dify, Hautvilliers, &c. &c. under vines ; and here all the famous Champagne wines are made. The country producing the fine white wine is all contained in the fpace of five leagues: and three or four more include Avife, Aungé, Lumenée, Crammont, &c. where they make the white wine, with white grapes only. At Ay, Piery, and Epernay, the white wine is all made with black grapes. La Montagne de Rheims, Bouzé, Verfeé, Verznée, Teafe, Airy, and Cumiere, for the *bon rouge de la Marne*. At Airy the firft quality of the white alfo made. With the black grape they make either red or white wine, but with the white only white wine.

The price of the land is very high ; at Piery 2000 liv. ; at Ay 3000 liv. to 6000 liv. ; at Hautvilliers 4000 liv. The worft in the country fells at 800 liv. (3000 liv. is 105l. 9s per Englifh acre ; 6000 liv is 210l. 18s.)

The produce, as may be fuppofed, varies much ; at Ay, two to fix pieces, and four the average ; at Reuil and Vanteuil, to twenty pieces ; at Hautvilliers, a convent of Benedictines, near Epernay, eighty arpents that yield two to four ; and the price varies equally : at Ay, the average is two, at 200 liv. ; one at 150 liv. ; and one at 50 liv. By another account, 200 liv to 800 liv. the queue, of two pieces ; average 500 liv. the queue. At Reuil and Vanteuil it is 60 liv. to 100 liv. The vines of Villiers 700 liv. to 900 liv. the queue. Red wine is 150 liv. to 300 liv. —— Account of a confiderable vineyard, an average one, given me at Epernay.

	For an Arpent.			Liv.	*Per Englifh Acre.*		
Intereft of purchafe, 3000 liv.	-	-		150	£. 6	11	3
Labour,	-	-	-	55	2 8	1¼	
Renewal *(provins)* ditto,	-	-	-	24	1	1	0
Tying,	-	-	-	8	0	7	0
Props,	-	-	-	30	1	6	3
Manure, 1 part dung to 14 earth,	-	-	20	0	17	6	
Vintage, 12 liv. a piece,	-	-	-	48	2	7	0
Cafks,	-	-	-	15	0	13	1¼
Taxes—— taille, vingtieme, and capitation,		9	0	7	10¼		
Carry forward,	-	-	-	359	15	14	1½

C

For an Arpent.	Liv.	Per English Acre.		
Brought forward, - -	359	£. 15	14	1½
Aides, 15 the queue, - - -	30	1	6	3
Cellar, vaults, prefs, refervoirs, tubs, &c. and building to hold them, 8000 liv. for 20 arpents, or 400 liv. per arpent, the intereft, - -	20	0	17	6
	409	17	17	10½
Product.——Two pieces, at 200 liv. -	400	17	10	0
One ditto, - - -	150	6	11	3
One ditto, - - -	50	2	3	9
	600	26	5	0
Expences, - -	409	17	17	10½
Profit, - - -	191	8	7	1½

Which, with the intereft charged, makes 10 per cent. on 3000 liv. land, and 400 liv. buildings; **the** general computation, and which feems admitted in the country. Sixty women are neceffary to gather the grapes for four pieces, by reafon of the attention paid in the choice of the bunches; a circumftance to which much **of** the fine flavour of the wine is owing, as well as to fingularity of foil and climate; the former of which is all ftrongly calcareous, even to being white with the chalk in it. A fine lengthened flope of a chalk hill, hanging to the fouth, between Dify and Ay, which I examined, is entirely covered with vines, from top to bottom, and is the moft celebrated in the province. It is indeed rather a marl than a chalk; in fome places white, in others much browner, and may properly be called a calcareous loam on a chalk bottom. This marl is, in fome places, very deep, and, in others, fhallow. I was fhewn pieces worth 6000 liv. the arpent, and others worth 3000 liv. but the difference of foil was not perceptible; nor do I credit that this difference depends on foil: none of it approaching to pure chalk. It is impoffible to difcover, in the prefent ftate of knowledge and information, on what depends the extraordinary quality of the wine. The people here affert, that in a piece of not more than three arpents, in which the foil is, to all appearance, abfolutely fimilar, the middle arpent only fhall yield the beft wine, and the other two that of an inferior quality: in all fuch cafes, where there is fomething not eafily accounted for, the popular love of the marvellous always adds exaggeration, which is probably the cafe here. Attention in gathering and picking the grapes, and freeing **every** bunch from each grape that is the leaft unfound, muft tend greatly to infure wine of the firft quality, when the difference of foil is not ftriking.

The

The vines are planted promiscuously, 3 or 4 feet, or 2½ from each other: are now about 18 inches or 2 feet high, and are tied to the props with small straw bands. Many plantations are far from being clean, some full of weeds; but a great number of hands spread all over the hill, farcling with their crooked hoe.

As to the culture, in the middle of January they give the cutting, *taillé:* in March dig the ground: in April and May they plant the provins: in June tie and hoe the seps: in August hoe again: in October, or, in good years, in September, the vintage.

To plant an arpent of vines, costs in all 50 louis **d'or: there are 8000** plants on an acre: and 24,000 seps and the props cost 500 liv.: to keep up the stock of props 30 liv. a year. It is three years before they bear any thing, **and six before** the wine is good. None are planted now; on the contrary, **they grub** up.

Very few persons have more than twenty or thirty arpents, except the Marquis de Sillery, near Rheims, who has two hundred and fifty arpents. At Piery there are twenty arpents now to be sold; a new house, a good cellar, magazine, a good press, and every thing complete, for 60,000 liv.: the vines a little, but not much, neglected. For this sum I could buy a noble farm in the Bourbonnois, and make more in seven years than by vines in twenty.

Those who have not a press of their own, are subject to hazards, which must necessarily turn the scale very contrary to the interests of the small proprietor. They pay 3 liv. for the two first pieces, and 25 *s.* for all the **rest:** but, as they must wait the owner's convenience, their wine sometimes is so damaged, that what would have been white, becomes red. Steeping, before pressing, makes red wine.

As to pressing, to do it very quickly and powerfully, is much the better way; and they perfer turning the wheel of the press by six, seven, or eight men, rather than by a horse.

In regard to the aides, or tax, on the transfer of wine, the proprietor who sells a piece worth 200 liv. pays   -   -   -   10 liv.

Ten sols per liv. - - - -	5
Augmentation ; *gauge,* constage, &c. -	5
Octroi de la Ville and du Roi, - -	5
	25

The merchant, when he sells it, pays the same; and every person through whose hands it passes. **The** duty at the **port,** on exportation, is **about** 15 liv. each **piece.** The cabareteer and aubergiste pays 30 or 40 liv. more retail duty. The wine trade with England used to be directly from Epernay; but now the wine is sent to Calais, Bologne, Montreuil, and Guernsey, in order to be passed into England, they suppose here, by **smuggling.** This **may** explain our Champagne

pagne

pagne not being fo good as formerly. Should the good genius of THE PLOUGH ever permit me to be an importer of Champagne, I would defire Monf. Quatrefoux Paretclaine, merchant at Epernay, to fend me fome of what I drank in his fine cellars. But what a pretty fuppofition, that a farmer, in England, fhould prefume to drink Champagne, even in idea! The world muft be turned topfyturvy before a bottle of it can ever be on my table. Go to the monopolizers and exporters of woollens—— go to——and to—— and every where——except to a friend of the plough!

The ecclefiaftical tithe is a heavy burthen. At Hautvilliers the eleventh is taken for a dixme; at Piery the twentieth, or in money 4 liv. 10 f.; at Ay, 48 f. and at Epernay 30 f.; at Dify $\frac{1}{14}$; but with all this weight of tax, nothing is known or ever heard of like the enormities practifed in England, of taking the actual tenth.

The idea of the poverty attending vines is here as ftrong as in any other part of France: the little and poor proprietors are all in mifery. The fact is obvious, that a hazardous and uncertain culture is ridiculous, for a man with a weak capital. How could a Kentifh labourer be a hop-planter? But no difcrimination is found commonly in France—the affertion is general, that the vine provinces are the pooreft; but an affertion without explanation is utterly ridiculous. To render vines profitable, it is a common obfervation here, that a man ought to have one-third of his property in rents, one-third in farm, and one-third in vines.

It is eafy to conceive, that the moft fuccefsful cultivators are thofe who have the largeft capitals. It is thus that we hear of the exertions of merchants; men who not only have many arpents of their own vines, but buy the wine of all their little neighbours. Monf. Lafnier, at Ay, has from fifty to fixty thoufand bottles of wine always in his cellar; and M. Dorfé from thirty to forty thoufand.

Rheims.—Average price of an arpent 2400 liv. (84l. per Englifh acre.)

Account.

	Liv.		Liv.
Intereft, - - - -	120	Produce, 3 pieces, at	
Culture by contract, - - -	40	240 liv. -	420
Manured every fifth year, 60 liv.; and 1000 men or women's		(14l. 14s. per Englifh	
loads of earth to mix, 36 liv. - -	96	acre.)	
Props, 20 bundles, - - -	12		
Extra hoeing, - - - -	6		
Taxes, - - - -	8		
Cafks, - - - -	13		
Vintage, at 20 f. a day, - - -	18		
Prefs, four men, at 20 f. and 20 f. food, -	8		
Carry forward, - - -	326	Carry forward, -	420

	Liv.		Liv.
Brought forward, - - -	326	Brought forward,	420
Intereſt of buildings, cellar, magazine, preſs, and utenſils,	30		
The cellar-man, 200 liv. for 20 arpents, per arpent,	10		
	366	Loſs, - -	24
Labour, 64 liv. (2l. 4s. 7d. per Engliſh acre) : intereſt of which for firſt year, - - -	18		
	384		
Droit d'aides, 7¼ per cent. on value, three pieces groſs, beſides conſtage, &c. &c. - - -	40		
	424		424

But inſtead of loſs, every one I talked with, and the gentleman himſelf who gave me this account, Monſ. Cadot L'Ainé, who has a conſiderable vineyard, aſſured me, that they pay, on an average of ten years, 7¼ per cent. on the capital; this will make a difference of 75 liv. which, with the 24 liv. loſs in this account, is 99 liv. which muſt be partly deducted from theſe expences, and partly added to the produce. On an average, the manuring is, I ſuſpect, eſtimated too high. The vines this year promiſe to yield not a piece per arpent; not by reaſon of froſts laſt winter, but of the cold, being ſo late as laſt week (in July).

The little proprietors here alſo are generally very poor, and many are ruined by not being able to wait for a price. The wine trade at Rheims amounts to four or five millions per annum (175,000l. to 218,700l.)

Sillery.—The Marquis has a hundred and ſixty arpents under vines, and not two hundred and fifty, as I had been informed; he has cellar room for two hundred pieces; this was mentioned as an extraordinary circumſtance, but it ſhews that he is very deficient in a power of keeping his wines: a hundred and ſixty arpents, at three each, are four hundred and eighty pieces; ſo that his cellar, inſtead of containing the crop of three years, will not hold half the crop of one year. It is evidently a buſineſs that ought to have a large capital, and even an apparently ſuperfluous one, or all the profit goes to the merchant.

LORAINE.—*Braban.*—Price, 175 liv. (25l. 10s. 1d. per Engliſh acre). Meaſure, 80 perches, at 11½ feet.

Verdun.—Meaſure, 480 verges, of 8 feet 2 inches, equal 66 perches of Paris: higheſt ſell to 2400 liv.; not uncommon 1100 liv. (84l. per Engliſh acre).

Metz.—Meaſure, journal, equal to 69½ perches of Paris. Price, 1200 liv. (89l. 14s. per Engliſh acre).

Account.

	Liv.		Liv.
Culture, 6 liv. per monée, 8 monées in the journal,	48	Produce, 40 hottes, each 44	
Props, 20 *f.* the monée, - - -	8	pints of Paris, at 6½ liv.	260
Two loads of dung, at 3 liv. - - -	6	(20l. 9s. 6d. per English	
Repairs of casks, - - - -	6	acre.)	
Taxes, taille, and capitation, - - -	13	Expences, - -	111
Ditto vingtieme, - - - -	4	Profit, - -	149
Pressing, one-thirtieth of the crop, - -	9		
Vintage, - - - - -	16		
	111		

 Labour, 64 liv. (5l. 0s. 7d. per English acre).

But interest of 1200 liv. is 60 liv. and the tithe here is from the twentieth to the thirtieth to be deducted. The general assertion, which seemed to admit no doubt, was that the profit is 7 per cent.

Pont au Mousson.—Measure a journal, 10 hommeés, or 250 verges of 10 feet, the foot of 10 inches.

Account.

	Liv.		Liv.
Labour, - - - - -	30	Produce, 400 hottes, on 13	
Manuring, 64 liv. but once in eight years, -	8	arpents, 30 per journal,	180
Vintage, twenty-five persons for 13 journals, at 12 *f.* fed,	3	(14l. 11s. 3d. per English	
Press, - - - -	2	acre.)	
Casks, - - - - -	16	Expences, - -	121
Taxes, no droit d'aides, - - -	3	Profit, - -	59
Props, - - - - -	4		
Arpent, 800 liv. (66l. 2s. 1d. per English acre), ⎫			
Buildings, 60 ⎬ - 45			
860 ⎭			
Interest of ditto, - - - -			
Droit de gabelle, and gauge, 13 *f.* per hotte, -	10		
	121		

 Labour, 33 liv. (2l. 9s. 10d. per English acre.)

But some little error here, for the common calculation is, that they pay 10 per cent.

 Vines are planted more and more, the culture augmenting every day; they plant the land proper for wheat as readily as any other.

Nancy.—Measure, 19,360 feet. Price of the best, 1000 liv.; the worst, 500 liv. (at 750 liv. 65l. 12s. 6d. per English acre). They have what they call the *gross race*, and the *petite race* of vines; the first gives much in quantity, but of a bad quality; the latter wine of a good quality, but in quantity small.

The

The medium produce is twenty meaſures per journal, of eighteen pots of two pints of Paris, of the grofs race, and ten of the petite. The mean price of the firſt 5 liv.; of the latter 10 liv. (at 100 liv. it is 8l. 15s. per Engliſh acre).

Luneville.—The journal 15,620 feet. Produce, 40 meaſures of the grofs race, of all ſorts; average, twelve meaſures, 6 liv. 15ſ. Price, per journal, 550 liv. (56l. 17s. 6d. per Engliſh acre). Produce, 80 liv. (8l. 12s. per Engliſh acre).

ALSACE.—*Wiltenheim.*—Meaſure, 100 verges, at 22 feet. Price, 900 liv. (31l. 10s. per Engliſh acre).

Straſbourg—Meaſure, 24,000 feet. Price, 800 liv. (55l. 7s. 9d. per Engliſh acre). Produce, thirty meaſures, of twenty-four pints of Paris. Good price, 6 liv. the meaſure; middling, 4 liv. 10ſ.; low, 3 liv. (at 150 liv. produce, it is 10l. 7s. 4d. per Engliſh acre).

Scheleſtadt.—Produce, forty meaſures. Price, 6 liv. the meaſure, 240 liv. (16l. 12s. 6d. per Engliſh acre).

Iſenheim.—Some ſo high as 3000 liv. but few that yield a hundred meaſures, at 6 liv. but by no means common.

FRANCHE COMPTE.—*Beaume.*—Meaſure, an œuvre. Produce, a muid, at 40 liv. to 60 liv.

Beſançon.—Meaſure, a journal, of 8 œuvres; the œuvre 45 perches, of 9½ feet. Price, 40 liv. to 400 liv. the œuvre. Produce, a quarter of a muid to one muid, or eight per journal. The grape, called the *gammé*, yields the moſt wine, but of the worſt quality. Common Price, 60 liv. the muid.——Account of a journal, 32,400 feet.

	Liv.		Liv.
Intereſt of 2400 liv. (123l. 6s. Engliſh acre), at 5 per cent.	120	Produce, 4 muids, at 60 liv. (12l. 6s. per Engliſh acre,	240
Culture, 5 liv. the œuvre,	40	Expences,	214
Props, 1 liv. ditto,	8	Profit,	26
Vintage, 5 liv. ditto,	40		
Tonneaux. 12 liv. the muid new; but reparation a trifle,	0		
Taille, capitation, and vingtieme 8ſ.	3 4ſ.		
No droit d'aide.			
Never dung, thinking it ſpoils the wine.			
Fauſſe, renovation 3 liv. per 100,	3		
Tythe, none in common; but, where found, only from one-twelfth to one-twentieth.			
	214		

Labour, 83 liv. (4l. 4s. per Engliſh acre.)

The common idea is, that the produce of an œuvre is	30 liv.	
And the expence	12	
	18	
Or profit per journal	144	
Intereſt	120	
Remains net	24	

They

They are alfo generally fuppofed to yield but five per cent. profit on capital, and fometimes not fo much.

The vines here are in double rows, at about two feet, and the props placed in an inclining pofition, fo as to join over the centre of that fpace, and are there tied to a horizontal prop; by which means any fmall fticks anfwer the purpofe of props.

BOURGOGNE.—*Dijon.*—Meafure, journal of 900 toifes. Price of common vineyards, 1000 liv. to 1500 liv. (at 1250 liv. it is 63l. 19s. 2d. per Englifh acre), the beft about Dijon. Produce, about feven or eight pieces, or muids, at 36 liv. (at 270 liv. it is 13l. 16s. 6d. per Englifh acre): pay fix per cent. But the fine vineyards of Veaune, Romané, Tafh, &c. fell at 3000 liv.

Clos de Veaujeau.—This is the moft famous of all the vineyards of Burgundy, the wine felling at the higheft price; it contains above an hundred journals, walled in, and belongs to a convent of Bernardine monks. This reminds me of Hautvilliers, near Epernay, one of the fineft vineyards in Champagne, having reverend mafters alfo. There are no trees in that at Clos de Veaujeau, though in all the more common ones. The vines are now not more than two or three feet high, the props being fhort alfo; they are not in rows, but planted promifcuoufly. The foil a brown loam, inclining to reddifh, with ftones in it, which, on trial, proved calcareous. It is not like the fine vineyards of Champagne, on a declivity, but flat, at the foot of a hill, which is rocky. The produce, 1½ muid, at 600 liv. the muid, 900 liv. (46l. 1s. 4d. per Englifh acre). The vineyard would, it is faid, fell for 10,000 liv. the journal (511l. 17s. 6d. per Englifh acre). They make white wine alfo, of a quality and price equal to the red.

Nurs—The fineft vineyards fell up to 7000 liv. and 8000 liv. a journal; but in common about 100 liv. (5l. 3s. 9d. per Englifh acre). The produce of the fine vines never great; four pieces, or muids, of half a queue, or two hundred and forty bottles, is a great produce; 1½ middling; and, in bad years, none at all, which happens fometimes, as at prefent, after a very fine appearance; but the frofts at the end of May cut them off fo entirely, that there is not a grape to be feen. Such wine as the poor people drink, fells commonly at 60 liv. or 70 liv. the queue, now 120 liv.——Account of a journal:

	Liv.		Liv.
Intereft, - - - -	50	Produce, 1½ piece, at	
Cu ture, by contract (fome at 60 liv.) -	72	100 liv. (8l. 19s. 4d.	
Props, called here, not *ecbalats*, but *paifeaux*,	6	per Englifh acre),	175
Cafks repaired, - - -	6	Expences, -	148
Taxes, - - - -	8		
Vintage, - - - -	6	Profit, -	27
	148		

One

One vigneron, with his wife and four children, muſt all work very well to do four journals ; for which, if at 60 liv. they receive 240 liv. but have the winter for other work. The vineyards which bear the greateſt reputation here, after the Clos de Veaujeau, are thoſe of St. George, Romané, La Taſhé, de Vaume, Richebourg, Chambertin, and Côte roté. The beſt is 25l. the piece, or 3 liv. the bottle ; but this is the price of the vintage ; kept three or four years it ſells for 4 liv. and even 5 liv. the bottle in the country.

In 1782, the crop was ſo great, that they gave 12 liv. for very miſerable caſks, and ſold them full at 20 liv. but the wine not good. 1785 was the laſt great crop, when the price of a caſk, a tonneau, which commonly is 12 liv. new, was 36 liv. to 40 liv. but the wine bad : they never dung for fine wines, only for bad ones, but they manure ſometimes with earth. New vineyards give a larger quantity of wine than old ones, but the wine of the latter the beſt quality. There are here, as in all the other wine provinces, many ſmall proprietors who have but patches of vines, and always ſell their grapes ; but there is no idea of their being poorer than if they did not purſue this culture.

Beaume.—The ſtones in the vineyards here calcareous. An œuvre coſts 400 liv. 3200 liv. per journal (163l. 16s. per Engliſh acre). Produce, two or three pieces, at 15 liv. this common wine ; but there are fine ones vaſtly higher. The wines of greateſt name here, after the *Clos de Veajeau,* are Volny, Pomar, Aloes, Beaume, Savigné, Mulſo (white), and Maureauché, which laſt ſells, ready to drink, at 4 liv. the bottle ; new at 1200 liv. the queue. They give here great accounts of the profit attending this culture ; but, on being analyzed, they are found all to turn on the ſuppoſition of having good cellars, and keeping for a price, which is mere merchandize, and not cultivation ; for the merchant who buys at the vintage, to fill his cellars, is exactly in the ſame predicament ; and to enjoy this profit, it is not neceſſary to cultivate a ſingle acre.

Chagnie.—Price of an œuvre 100 liv. ; eight of them to a journal, 800 liv. (40l. 19s. per Engliſh acre). Common produce, one piece per œuvre : the price now 60 liv. the piece, but 20 liv. more common (160 liv. is 8l. 3s. 7d. per Engliſh acre.)

Couch.—An œuvre, the eighth of a journal, ſells at 100 liv. ; but there is more at 80 liv. Produce, one piece, at 36 liv. common price, but now 60 liv. ; uſually one piece at 25 liv. : half the produce, by contract, for labour (at the price of 640 liv. it is 32l. 15s. 4d. per Engliſh acre.)

BOURBONNOIS.—*Moulins.*—Sell to 1000 liv. the arpent (34l. 12s. 1d. per Engliſh acre) of eight boiſeleés, each 168 toiſes, 48,384 feet. In a good year, produce eight poinçons, at 30 liv. ; common year five or ſix, at 30 liv. for common vineyards : half the produce is paid, by contract, for labour. Very rarely dung : props 7 liv. : tithe the eleventh.

Vov. II.   D   *Riaux.*

Riaux.—Common produce, half a piece per œuvre, or boifelée; one-fourth for proprietor, and one-fourth for labour.

St. Ponerin.—Vineyards on hills, 100 liv. the boifelée; 800 liv. the arpent (27l. 13s. 10d. per Englifh acre).

Auvergne.—*Riom.*—Sell at 200 liv. the œuvre; fometimes 1 f. the bottle, or 15 f. the pot; now 3 liv.; middling price 20 f. to 30 f.

Clermont.—Meafure, 800 toifes: beft 300 liv.; worft 100 liv.; midling 150 liv. an œuvre; 1200 liv. the arpent (70l. per Englifh acre); medium ten pots, each fixteen pints of Paris; on the beft land fifteen, and the mean price 30 f.; at prefent 3 liv.: tie them with willow branches, *falix viminea.*

Izoire.—In common fell at 500 liv. or 600 liv. the fétérée, but in good fituations 800 liv. (46l. 12s. 9d. per Englifh acre): the œuvre of the beft yields two fommes; middling one and a half; bad one: the fomme fix pots, each fixteen pints of Paris: the common price after the vintage, 25 f. to 30 f. the fix pots (at 168 liv. it is 9l. 16s. per Englifh acre).

Account of an Œuvre.

	Liv.	Sols.		Liv.
Labour,	8	0	Produce, 1¼ fomme, at	
Props,	2	10	30 f. the pot, 12 liv.	
Intereft buildings, 100 liv. 50 œuvres,	2	8	the fous,	21
Intereft of 100 liv. purchafe,	5	0	Expences,	19
Taille, &c.	0	11	Profit,	2
Provins,	0	8		
Dung ditto,	0	2		
	19	1		

By which we are only to underftand that they pay little more than common intereft.

Briude.—Price, 10 liv. to 100 liv. (55 liv. is 25l. 12s. 9d. per Englifh acre): the worft are on rocks, where a ftorm drives foil and crop away. It is very remarkable that the rocky declivities, which are fo natural to the vine, here yield a wine far inferior to the rich plain of the Limagne. This deferves remark, and a further attention from the naturalifts, who examine this very curious and interefting country. They have thirty-five forts of vines here; the *Lange dit de chien* is the firft.

Dauphine.—*Montelimart.*—Price of a fétérée, half an arpent of Paris, 168 liv. to 480 liv. and produces feven meafures of wine, called charges, each of a hundred bottles, the common price 15 liv. or 75 liv. per fétérée.

Account

Account.

		Liv.			Liv.
Interest of 300 liv. (44l. 12s. 6d. per English acre) mean price, - - - - -		15	Produce, (7l. 17s. 6d. English acre), -		75
Culture, 1st, - - 20 liv. }			Expences, - -		58
2d, - - 10 } - 30					
3d, paid by cuttings, - 0 }			Profit, -		17
No props.					
Vintage, - - - - -		6			
Casks, - - - - -		3			
Taxes, - - - - -		2			
No droit d'aides.					
Cellar, &c. &c. - - - -		2			
		58			

PROVENCE.—*Avignon.*—Price 70 liv. the eymena, and produce three barrels: price at present, 6 liv. the barrel, or 3 ſ. the bottle; common price 2 ſ. The best vines give 8 per cent. on capital.

Aix.—The carterée 800 liv. (63l. per English acre). Measure, six hundred cannes for the carterée; the canne of eight pans, the pan of nine inches and three lines.

Tour d'Aigues.—The produce of a somma is a hundred coup, each 60 lb. 3 lb. a pot; and the common bottle 2¼ lb.: 100 lb. of grapes give 60 lb. of wine. Mean price 30 ſ. the coup, or per somma 150 liv. Measure, 50,400 feet.

Account.

		Liv.	Sols.			Liv.	Sols.
Culture, - - - -		48	0	Produce, (4l. 19s. 6d. per English acre),		150	0
Hoeing and pruning, - - -		12	0	Expences, -		126	12
Vintage and carriage, - - -		10	0				
Interest of buildings, &c. - - -		15	0	Profit, -		23	8
Taille, by the cadastre (but this varies every year, by reason of provincial expence), - -		10	0				
Seigneural duty, - - - -		1	12				
Price, 600 liv. (20l. 2s. 6d. per English acre), interest,		30	0				
		126	12				

Hyeres.—Usually planted in double rows, at three or four feet, with intervals of different distances, ploughed, or hoed for corn; and this method they call *maysivere.* Two hundred and eighty plants produce one bout of wine, of six barrels, each barrel twenty-eight pots, and each pot 3 lb. Common price per bout 50 liv.

Observations.

Obſervations.

It is merely for curioſity I obſerve, that the average of all the prices per
meaſure, in the purchaſe of theſe vineyards, amounts to 61l. 8s. per acre; ſuch
a medium demands very little attention, unleſs the minutes were exceedingly
numerous, and equally ſo in every province. Rejecting thoſe in which the
prices exceed 100l. an acre, as going certainly much beyond what can poſſibly
be the medium of the kingdom, the average of the reſt is 41l. 1s. 6d. per acre.
But I ſhould wiſh that attention were rather given to another mode of calculating the price and produce of theſe vineyards; there are twenty-three minutes
that include both price and produce; the average of theſe excluſive of ſuch as
riſe above 100l. purchaſe, and 21l. produce, is

For the price per Engliſh acre,   -   £.45   1   0
For the produce,   -   -   -   9   2   0*
Which is in French money, per arpent of Paris,—Price,   -   871 liv.
Produce,   175

From which it appears, that vines, in theſe provinces, give, in annual produce,
one-fifth of their fee ſimple.

The amount of labour per acre, on an average of thoſe minutes, in which it
appears to be ſatisfactorily noted, and rejecting the higher articles as before, is
2l. 12s. 6d.

The net profit appears, from ſeveral of the minutes, to vibrate between 7 and
10 per cent. on the capital employed.

How nearly theſe averages, noticed in my route, approach the real medium of
the whole kingdom, it is impoſſible, with any degree of accuracy, to conjecture;
but I am inclined to believe, that the difference may not be conſiderable. This,
however, muſt be left, with a proper diffidence, to the well informed reader's
ſuperior ſagacity.

The importance of this branch of cultivation to the kingdom, and the idea ſo
common there, I may almoſt ſay univerſal, that the wine provinces are the
pooreſt, and that the culture is miſchievous to the national intereſts, are ſubjects
too curious to be diſmiſſed haſtily: as my opinion is directly the reverſe of the
prevalent one in France, it is neceſſary to explain the circumſtances on which it
is founded.

* The Marquis de Mirabeau obſerved, that an arpent of vines is, on an average, worth double the
beſt arpent of corn. *L'Ami des Hommes.* 5th edit. 1760. tom. vi. p. 137.   This agrees pretty well
with my notes.

It

It appears, by the preceding minutes, that the value of the foil thus employed was probably higher than it could be in any other application, good meadows (valuable from their fcarcity) alone excepted : that the produce much exceeds all others; and laftly, that the employment depending upon it is very confiderable. Under fuch leading and powerful circumftances, and connected as they are with another not lefs effential, that vaft tracts of the land thus employed are rock and declivities, too fteep for the plough,—it fhould feem aftonifhing, how an idea could ever be entertained that fuch a cultivation could be prejudicial to a country : it is, however, very general in **France.**

The queftion ought to be put folely on this iffue—Would the fame land, under any other culture, fell at the fame price ? 45l. per acre, amounting to thirty years purchafe, at 30s. an acre, is fuch a value as France, in the richeft vales, knows nothing of (meadows alone excepted, which will always be valuable according to fcarcity and heat of climate), and we in England as little. But this greater value arifes not by any means from the richeft lands, but from thofe which, confidered on a medium, are certainly very inferior to the reft of the kingdom. Great tracks could be applied to no other ufe than that of fheep-walk or warren; much is fituated, in fome of the pooreft foils in the kingdom, on fands, fharp gravels, and lands fo ftoney, as to be inapplicable to the plough : to poffefs a climate that gives the power of raifing fuch land to the value of 30l. or 40l. an acre, is beyond all doubt or queftion, a fuperiority that cannot be too much valued.

The amount of the produce is not lefs ftriking : rich paftures fell every where at high prices, becaufe they are attended wih no expences; and thus a fmall product may be claffed with a large one; but it is not fo with vines. The average of 9l. an acre, on a mean of good and bad years, is fuch as no other plant will equal that is cultivated in France, watered lands alone excepted. It is only on fingularly fine foils, in certain peculiar diftricts, that any thing approaching fuch a product is to be met with. There is no part of Europe, in which a crop of wheat, of fuch value, is not exceedingly large, and much beyond the average. That of all the wheat, in any of the richeft counties in England, vibrates between 6l. and 7l. an acre, prepared for, perhaps, by a barren and expenfive fallow,—at leaft by fomething much lefs profitable than itfelf. What then are we to think of a plant which covers your land with a rich crop of wheat every year ?

There are many men, however, in France, who will fay, YOUR REASONING MUST BE ERRONEOUS; *for there is not a vine proprietor in France, who would not give you his vineyard for your ideal wheat of every year.* The obfervation may be perfectly juft; but it is no anfwer to me, who am not fpeaking of *net profit,* but of *produce.* To him who confiders the fubject in a national light, and as a politician, the former is not the object ;—the great point is to fecure a large produce. The prince may levy fuch heavy taxes on the produce ; and

it

it may be gained by fuch an operofe culture, that the poor may levy a much heavier for their labour; the confequence to the cultivator may be a low profit, but to the nation at large the importance of the product remains the fame, and unimpeached. And in this light I look upon that of vines as fo confiderable, that fhould the fact of the real average of the whole kingdom prove lefs than I make it—even fo little as 7l. per acre, I fhould ftill efteem the culture an object of infinite national confequence. It is more than fugar pays in the Weft Indies, which is ufually fuppofed the moft profitable cultivation in the world.

In regard to the net profit, which on the minutes vibrates from 7 to 10 per cent. it does not feem to fome to be adequate to the peculiar happinefs of the climate, and the reputation of the wines throughout the world; or to the price of the land, or amount of the product. But, in this refpect, it muft be confidered, that the minutes, fo far as they concern the returns in money, are the prices of the vintage only: whereas every man that has a capital fufficient, by keeping his wine for three months only, adds confiderably to the profit.—If a proprietor be merely able to ftore his crop in cafks in his cellar, long enough to avoid the immediate neceffity of felling for want of cafks, he has an advance of price, which will greatly augment the ratio of his profit: it is very fair to give the cultivator of vines the fame time that is taken by moft of his brethren with whom corn is the object, that is to fay, fix months from the harveft. The difference of profit is exceedingly great between the fale in the vintage, and that of fix months after. But it is ftill of more confequence to obferve, that the rate per cent. here-mentioned, is not on the mere bufinefs of the cultivator, but on the purchafe of the eftate upon which the culture is carried on. This makes an enormous difference. If agriculture, in England, yield 15 per cent. and landed property three, throw the two together, and the mean is not more than 5½ or 6; and thofe who, in England, buy an eftate, and ftock, and cultivate it, and make 6 per cent. will not think they are fuffering, notwithftanding the accumulated advantages of a century of freedom.

It is this large annual product which in the vine provinces gives bread to fuch numbers of people; befide the direct object of common labour, which amounts, as we have feen, to 2l. 12s. 6d. per acre, and confequently is above thrice as high as that of common arable crops; and if they are not in very complete culture, the fuperiority is much more confiderable, there is the trade of cafks, which, independent of the employment of coopers, gives a value to the woods of a country, as well as an activity to foreign commerce, by the import of ftaves and hoops. The props have the fame effect as our hop-poles, and render willow plantations, as well as common under-woods, much more valuable than they would be otherwife. Befides, there is the circumftance, that fo many politicians

cians

cians regard alone, the exportation of the wine, and the cafk or the bottle; forming, whether in the fhape of wine or of brandy (as I fhall by and by fhew), one of the greateft trades of export that is to be feen in Europe; as much the export of French labour, as that of the filks of Lyons, or the cloths of Louviers. And after all this, if I be allowed to place laft, what in truth ought ever to be regarded firft, that is, the home confumption, there is the invaluable **advantage** of a whole people being well and amply fupplied with a beverage, **the effect of** their own induftry, and the refult of their **own labour; and** it furely **will not be** thought a fmall advantage, that a nation **has recourfe, for fupplying this con-** fumption, to her fands, gravels, declivities **and rocks; that** fhe demands it not of her rich plains, but of thofe lands which **her lefs fortunate neighbours are** forced to cover with copfe or rabbits.

But here we are not to forget, that argument is always **to give** way to fact. From what I have juft faid, the reader is not to conclude that fuch lands *only* are under vines in France, the contrary is the fact; I found them on the noble and fertile plain of the Garonne; on the richeft lands in the **vale** which extends from Narbonne to Nimes; in the vales of Dauphiné and **of the** Loire; and, in **a** word, indifcriminately on every fort of land in all the **wine** provinces; but I found them alfo on fuch rocky and bad foils as I have defcribed, **and in fo great** quantities as to fhew how well adapted they **are to fuch foils and fituations.** There are two reafons why vines are fo often found **in rich plains**; the firft **is,** the export of wheat being either prohibited, or allowed with fuch irregularity, that the farmer is never fure of a price: but the export of wine and brandy **has** never been ftopped for a moment. The effect of fuch a contraft **in policy muft** have been confiderable, and I faw its influence **in every** part of France, **by the** new vineyards already planted, **or begun to be planted, on corn** lands, while the people were ftarving for want **of bread; of fuch** confequence, in the encouragement of any culture, is a *fteady unvarying policy!* The **fact** is the more ftriking in France, becaufe the vine culture is very much **burthened in taxation;** but, always poffeffing a free trade, it thrives. The fecond **reafon is, that the** culture of this plant is much better underftood in France **than that of corn.** An advantageous rotation of crops, and that arrangement of a farm which makes cattle neceffary to corn, and corn neceffary to **cattle, on which** the profit of arable land fo much depends, is what the French have **hardly an idea of.** In their practice it is never to be feen, and in their books it **is never to be read.** But their vineyards are gardens; the turnips of Norfolk, **the** carrots **of Suffolk, the** beans of Kent, and the cabbages of an Englifh gentleman, **are not fo clean as** the vines of France, while the whole œconomy of the **plant is perfectly** underftood, both in theory and practice.

It is a queftion which I have heard often ftarted in converfation, **whether it** **be** nationally more **advantageous** that wine fhould be, **as in** France, the com-

mon-

mon beverage, or beer, as in England? How it should ever become a question
I cannot underſtand. We are, of neceſſity, *obliged* to have recourſe to our beſt
lands to ſupply our drink; the French, under a good government, would have
all theirs from their worſt ſoils. The ſands of Sologne, which are paſſed in
the way from Blois to Chambord, &c. &c. are as bad as ours in Suffolk and
Norfolk, which feed only rabbits. The French ſands, by means of vines,
yield 8l. or 9l. an acre, and thoſe of Suffolk not ſo many ſhillings. Through
nine-tenths of England, the land that yields wheat in every rotation yields alſo
barley. If our hills, rocks, ſands, and chalky declivities gave us our liquor,
could we not apply theſe richer ſoils to ſomething better than beer? Could we
not, by means of rotations, that made potatoes, tares, beans, and artificial
graſſes, the preparatives for wheat alternately, contrive to raiſe infinitely more
bread, beef, and mutton, if barley did not of neceſſity come in for an attention equal to what we give to wheat? Wheat, rye, barley, and oats exhauſt,
every other crop we raiſe, either actually or conſequentially, ameliorates. Would
it be no advantage to ſtrike out one of theſe exhauſters, and ſubſtitute an improver? Would it be no advantage to feed all the horſes of Britain on beans
inſtead of oats? Your populouſneſs may be proportioned to your quantity of
bread, mutton, and beef. With one-fourth of your land under barley, can you
have as much bread, mutton, and beef, as if you were not under the neceſſity
of having any barley at all? How few agricultural combinations muſt there be
in a mind that can entertain doubts on ſuch queſtions? There is a common
idea that wine is not a wholeſome beverage, I take this to be a vulgar error;
bad wine, or wine kept till ſharp and acid, may be unwholeſome, but ſo is
bad beer, or beer kept till acid: but this has nothing to do with the queſtion.
If the lower people be forced, through poverty, to drink bad liquor, the complaint ought not to be that wine is unwholeſome, but that a bad government is
unwholeſome: the beer drinkers under ſuch a one, will not have much to boaſt.
There may be more ſtrength and vigour of body among the common people in
England than among the ſame claſs in France; if this be true, it proves nothing
againſt wine. Are the French poor as well fed as ours? Do they eat an equal
quantity of animal fleſh? Were they as free? Theſe common prejudices, for
or againſt certain liquors, are uſually built on very inſufficient obſervation.

But the enemies of vineyards recur to the charge; *the vine provinces are the
pooreſt of the kingdom; and you always ſee miſery among the poor proportioned to the
quantity of vines* *.—This is the main hinge on which the argument turns; it is

* So lately as in the Journal Phyſique for May 1790, Monſ. Roland de la Platiere, a gentleman
with whom I had the pleaſure of ſome agreeable converſation at Lyons (in the happier period of his
life, before he was involved in the miſery and guilt of revolutions), ſays, that of all countries the
vine ones are the pooreſt, and the people the moſt wretched! And in the *cahier* of the clergy of
Auxerre, it is demanded, that the ordonances againſt planting vines on land proper for corn be
executed. P. 19.

an

an obfervation that has been made to me a thoufand times in France, and converfation never touches on the fubject but you are fure to hear it repeated.—
There is fome truth in it as a fact—there is none as an argument.

There is ufually a confiderable population in vine provinces; and doubtlefs it
is not furprifing, that where there is a great population there fhould be many
poor, under a bad goverment. But there is another reafon, much more fatisfactory, which arifes not at all from the nature of the culture, but from the
abufe of it.

It is the fmallnefs of the property into which vineyards are ufually divided; a
circumftance carried to fuch excefs, that the mifery flowing from it can hardly
be imagined by thofe who are whirled through France in a poft-chaife. The
nature of the culture depending almoft entirely on manual labour, and demanding no other capital than the poffeffion of the land and a pair of arms; no carts,
no ploughs, no cattle, neceffarily leads the poor people to this fpecies of property; and the univerfal practice of dividing it between the children, multiplies
thefe little farms to fuch a degree, that a family depends on a fpot of land for
fupport that cannot poffibly yield it; this weakens the application to other induftry, rivets the children to a fpot from which they ought to emigrate, and
gives them a flattering intereft in a piece of land, that tempts them to remain
when better interefts call them elfewhere. The confequence is, their labouring as much as they can for their richer neighbours; their own little vineyards
are then neglected; and that culture, which to a more able proprietor is de-
cifively advantageous, becomes ruinous to infufficient funds. But a misfortune,
greater even than this, is the uncertainty of the crop; to a man of a proper
capital, and who confequently regards only the average of feven years, this is of
no account; but to the poor proprietor, who lives from hand to mouth, it is
fatal; he cannot fee half a year's labour loft by hail, froft, cold, or other in-
clemencies of the feafon, without feeing, at the fame time, his children in want
of bread; before the ample produce comes, which certainly will come on the
average account, he finds himfelf in the hofpital.

This I take to be the origin of that general and too indifcriminate condemnation of vineyards in France. The poverty is obvious; it is connected with vines,
and for want of proper diftinctions, it is confidered as neceffarily flowing from
vineyards; but, in fact, it is merely the refult of fmall properties amongft the
poor: a poor man can no where be better fituated than in a vine province,
provided he poffefs not a plant. Whatever may be the feafon, the poor are fure of
ample employment among their richer neighbours, and to an amount, as we
have above feen, thrice as great as any other arable lands afford. That culture
which demands 2l. 12s. in hand labour only, whether there be crop or no crop,
and which employs women and children of all ages, ought not furely to be con-

demned as the origin of diftrefs among the poor. Attribute the fact to its true caufe, the defire and fpirit of poffeffing landed-property, which is univerfal in France, and occafions infinite mifery. This circumftance, fo prevalent in that kingdom, and (comparatively fpeaking) fo little known in ours, where the poor are fo much more at their eafe than in France and moft other countries, is very curious to a political obferver. What an apparent contradiction, that property fhould be the parent of poverty, yet there is not a clearer or better afcertained fact in the range of modern politics. The only property fit for a poor family, is their cottage, garden, and perhaps grafs land enough to yield milk; this needs not of neceffity impede their daily labour; if they have more, they are to be claffed with farmers, and will have arable fields, which muft, in the nature of things, be ill cultivated, and the national intereft confequently fuffer.

The explanations I have given of the wine fyftem in France will be received, I truft, with candour. To inveftigate fuch queftions fully, would demand differtations exprefsly written on every fubject that arifes, which would be inconfiftent with the brevity neceffary to the regifter of travels: I attempt no more than to arrange the facts procured; it belongs to the political arithmetician fully to combine and illuftrate them.

C H A P. XI.

Of the Culture of Silk in France.

QUERCY.—*Cauffade.*—IN the avenue leading to this town, two rows of the trees are mulberries, and thefe are the firft we have feen.

Montauban.—Many mulberries here, in rows; and under fome of them four rows of vines, and then fix or feven-times the breadth of corn. When the leaves are not in time for the worms, or are deftroyed by frofts, they are fed with lettuce leaves; and if no lettuce, with cabbage, but the filk is fo worthlefs, that the failure is reckoned nearly equal to having none at all.

Touloufe to Noé.—Mulberry trees are here worth from 6 *f.* to 20 *f.* and 30 *f.* each per annum, according to their fize.

Noé—Mulberries worth up to 3 liv. per tree, per annum. But filk worms have miffed much for three years paft.

Narbonne.—Many mulberries; all with pruned flat heads.

Pinjean.

Pinjean.—Olives are a beneficial article of culture, but they prefer mulberries, becaufe they yield a crop every year. On four fétérées of land they have fixty trees ; and at the fame time the land yields barley or oats, mown for forage, of which the four fétérées gives 60 quintals, that fell at 33 *f.* the quintal. Single mulberries have paid as far as two louis each, and many one louis. If four fété-rées equal two acres, there are thirty trees on an acre, and the acreable produce of forage will be 52 liv. or 2l. 5s. 6d.

Nifmes to Sauve.—Seven mulberries on an Englifh rood.

Quéfac.—Mulberry leaves fell commonly at 3 liv. the quintal. A tree yields from one to eleven quintals: two, three, and four are common. Gathering the leaves cofts 12 *f.* the quintal. Fifteen quintals of leaves are neceffary for one ounce of *grain* (the feed or eggs of the worm): 20 liv. the mean price of filk per lb.: reckon that an olive-tree pays as well as a mulberry.

Many mulberries about Quéfac, and fome on very poor dry land. In grafs fields the ground is kept dug around them, as far as the branches extend. Remark fome ftones laid around many trees, for fome diftance from the ftem.

Eight trees in fomething lefs than an Englifh rood.

By information, almonds, in Rouverge, pay better than mulberries, and with much lefs expence and attention ; 3, 4, 5, and 6 liv. a tree.

Gange.—Many fine mulberries about this place, which yield from 3 liv. to 8 liv. a tree in common, young ones excluded. They yield to twelve quintals of leaves ; in general, three, four, or five. The price varies from 3 liv. to 10 liv. the quintal. They are much more valuable than olives. This year the great cold in April deftroyed the young buds and hurt the crop greatly. They never think of giving any thing to worms but the leaves ; have heard of twenty things, but treat the idea with the greateft contempt, knowing as they do, by the fabric, the worthleffnefs of filk, if the worms are fo fed.

Lodeve.—Mulberries are more profitable than olives ; yield three, four, and five quintals of leaves, which fell, in common, at 3 liv.

Mirepoix.—Mulberries are here, but none after, in going from Carcaffonne to St. Martory.

Auch.—A few mulberries near the town.

It is here to be noted, that from Mirepoix to Bagnere de Luchon, and from thence by Pau to Bayonne, and back by Dax to Auch, a line of much more than 300 miles, I faw no mulberry trees.

GUIENNE.—*Leyrac.*—Some few mulberries.

Aiguillon.—A few trees for fome miles before this place. Behind the chateau, in the town, is a large plantation, formed by the late duke ; which, being in the fine vale of the Garonne, the land is cultivated as the reft, under hemp and wheat; but both thofe crops are lefs than middling, the expreffion of the perfon who gave us the information, on account of the roots and fhade of the trees. The duke gives the leaves to the people in the town, furnifhing alfo the wood, boards, grain, and whatever elfe is neceffary for the bufinefs, and he has in return the third part of the filk they make. Every one in the place, and all round the country, fay that he lofes confiderably by it; afferting, that the land thus occupied is worth 500 louis a year; that the crop of filk is fo precarious that he has had eight quintals, and in other years only three, two, and even one; fo that on an average, his third part gives only 150 louis, and the crops under the trees cannot make up one-half of the deficiency. They alfo maintain, that the land is too rich for mulberries; and, to prove that they are right in their ideas, they quoted many gentlemen in the neighbourhood, who have grubbed up their mulberries.

Tours.—They have in the neighbourhood of this city many mulberries, infomuch, that the value of the raw filk has amounted, as they affert, in a good year, to a million of livres. I walked feveral times into the country to view the trees and make inquiries. Many of the corn fields are regularly planted all over; the gardens are furrounded with them; and the roads and lanes have rows of them. The large good trees, in a favourable year, give to the value of 4 liv. but not in common. I viewed feveral plantations; containing old, young, good, and bad, that gave on an average, one with another, 30 f. which feemed, from various accounts, to be a general medium; it, however, excludes very bad years; fuch, for inftance, as laft fpring, in which they had no crop at all, the frofts in April (note, this is certainly one of the fineft climates in France) having entirely deftroyed it. I faw feveral trees which gave to the amount of 10 f. to 15 f. at ten years old, and 30 f. at the age of fifteen years. Plants, at two years old, are fold at 3 liv. the hundred: at three years old, 4 liv.: and good trees, proper to plant out in an arable field, 20 f. each. In regard to the diftance, at which the trees are planted, they have no general rule. I meafured many diftances, in a large corn field, and found them at two rod fquare, at an average: in another they were fix yards by nine; which trees gave 40 f. on a medium: round a garden they were at five yards from tree to tree: a field, entirely cropped with mulberries, had them in rows at one and a half rod; and between the rows another of fmall plants, in the manner of a hedge. If fixty fquare yards are allowed per tree, there will be eighty on an acre, and if they give 30 f. each, it will amount to the vaft produce of 5 l. per acre, befides what can be gained under them; it would, however be a queftion, whether this under-crop would make up for bad years, that yield nothing? Around fields, in roads, corners, &c. the profit will be greater. It is remarkable,

able, however, that with all this profit attending them, they do not increase about Tours, yet not one acre in an hundred adapted to the culture, is fo employed, which fhews either a very uncommon want of capital, or doubts whether the cultivation is fo profitable as it appears to be from fuch information.

In order to fpread the cultivation, government eftablifhed nurferies, and gave the trees gratis, until private nurferies were opened; and in winding the filk much affiftance was alfo given to the lofs to government, of 20ƒ. per lb.; but now the bufinefs is carried on without any premium of that fort. Probably fuch encouragements were of very little ufe; the abufes incident to all governments would direct fuch affiftance to be given where it was not wanted; and in that cafe it would, by raifing difguft, do mifchief.

They plant no mulberry but the white; the black they think very bad.

NORMANDIE.—*Bizy.*—Having read, in the Memoirs of fome of the Agriculture Societies in France, that the marfhal duke de Belleifle made a very confiderable and fuccefsful experiment on the introduction of the culture of filk in Normandie, on his eftate at Bizy, I had long ago made a note of it, for examining, as the fteps which proved fuccefsful in fuch an attempt in Normandie, might probably have the fame effect, if applied in a climate fo fimilar as that of England. I went to Bizy with this view, and did what I could to find out the proper perfons, concerned in this undertaking, to give me the information that was neceffary.

Five-and-thirty years ago, the duke began by making fome extenfive plantations of mulberries, to the amount of many thoufand trees: they fucceeded well; and, in order to draw all the advantage poffible from them, as the people in the neighbourhood were ignorant and awkward in the procefs, the duke, by means of a friend in Provence, procured a man, his wife, and all his children, well fkilled in the whole bufinefs of the filk-worm, and eftablifhed them at Bizy, in order to inftruct his own people in it. By thefe means, he made as much filk as the produce of leaves would admit. I wifhed to know to what amount, but could not afcertain it; but the duke continued his plantations of mulberries during nine or ten years. I tried hard to find out fome defcendant or remains of this provençal family, but in vain; the man was dead, the woman gone, and the children difperfed; the eftate, on the marfhal's death, having been fold, and coming into the poffeffion of the duke de Penthievre, made all thefe circumftances the more difficult. The great object was, the fuccefs of the experiment; this inquiry was uniformly anfwered by feveral perfons:—it had no fuccefs at all. It was a favourite project of the Duke's; and fupported, with perfeverance, for many years, until his death; but the filk did not pay charges: and though he very liberally

berally

berally offered leaves to the poor people, on eafier terms than they are fupplied with them in the fouth of France, and even gave trees; yet nothing more was done than what his influence and authority forced: and the Provençal family, after ten years experience, pronounced that the climate would do to make filk, but not with profit. To his laft hour, the duke had filk made, but not an hour longer; the practice had taken no root: the country people, by whom alone fuch an undertaking could profper, faw no inducement to go into the fcheme, and the whole fell at once into utter ruin and neglect on the duke's death; fo that the trees themfelves were by degrees condemned, and the number remaining at prefent inconfiderable. Certainly no pofitive phyfical proof, that filk will not do in Normandy, but it is a prefumptive one, pretty ftrongly featured. Go into Languedoc, Dauphiné, and Provence, and the poor people do not want the exertions of marfhals of France to induce them to breed filk-worms; they have a much more powerful inducement,—the experience that it is their intereft: had this inducement been prefent at Bizy, the culture would, in more than ten years, have taken root.

BOURBONNOIS.—*Moulins.*—Monf. Martin, gardener of the Royal Nurfery here, who is from Languedoc, cultivates filk with great fuccefs; he was fo obliging as to be as communicative as I could wifh. Trees of two or three years old, yield a few leaves, but to be ftripped cautioufly: at eight to ten years, they come very well into yielding. One ounce of *grains*, that is, of the eggs of the worm, requires twenty quintals (one hundred weight Englifh) of leaves, and yields from 7 lb. to 9 lb. of filk. He has made as far as 300 lb. in a year, the produce of 3000 lb. of cocoons; and the worms that year eat 12000 lb. of leaves every day, for four or five days together, and fifty perfons were employed for eight days. The whole bufinefs of hatching and feeding employs a month; the winding is afterwards done at leifure. For care and attendance of the worms, gathering the leaves, and winding the filk, he gives one-fourth of the produce, or about 6 liv. the pound of filk; for fpinning 3 liv.; in all, 9 liv.; refts profit, 15 liv. The men earn 20f. to 24f. a day, and the women 8f. to 10f. He prefers this climate for the bufinefs to that of Languedoc, though ftoves are here neceffary for keeping the room to the temperature of 18 degrees, Reaumur; whereas in Languedoc they do without fires. The feafon here varies from fifteen to twenty days; the earlieft is the 24th of April, and the lateft the 15th of May. If the leaves are not ready, he keeps the hatching back, by lodging the *grains* in a cool cellar. He has known one tree in Languedoc yield 80 liv. a year in filk. Moulins and its environs make to the value of 60 or 80,000 liv. a year. Monf. Martin fells trees, of two years old, at 20 liv. the thoufand. The diftance of planting, if for crops, under the trees, thirty feet;

if

if no crops, twenty feet. Of the writers that have treated of this subject, he prefers Monf. Sauvages.

In the particulars of an eftate to be fold, was one article relative to the produce of filk ; mulberries enough for 12 oz. of grain, yielding 60 lb. of filk.

VIVARAIS.—*Maiffe to Thuys.*—Firft meet with mulberries in going fouth from Auvergne. They yield very largely here; I am affured, that many trees, in a good year, reach 12 liv. each. That in four years after planting, they begin to produce leaves enough for ftripping. The beft of them are all grafted. Trees, fifteen years after planting, have, in a very good year, yielded 6 liv. I was fhewn a fmall field that yields, one year with another, 120 liv.; I ftepped, and found it 50 yards by 70 yards, or 3500 fquare yards (2l. 4s. 4d. per Englifh acre); yet the trees were not regularly planted, nor fully; and this befides the other produce of the ground.

Aubenas.—The filk mills here, which are confiderable, purchafe the cocoons of the farmer, at 28f. to 32f. the pound. The mulberry-trees here are very large.

Villeneuve de Bergue.—Twenty quintals of leaves give one quintal of cocoons, and one quintal of cocoons 10lb. of filk. They reckon that the wafte, *débris & dechet*, pay the fpinning. Eighteen trees, of feven years age, pay 28 liv. a year; but fome trees, of ten years old, have been known to give 3 liv. each. Three-fourths of an arpent de Paris have been fold for 400 liv.; the foil all rock and ftone, but calcareous. The trees are grafted before tranfplantation, which is at three years old; price, 12f. and 15f. each. The fecond year after planting they begin to gather. The price of the leaves 3 liv. the 100 lb.; and of gathering 10f. the quintal. The culture is reckoned more profitable than vines, which are fometimes grubbed up, to make way for mulberries. Of the forts, the *rofe fuille* is beft. In the road to Viviers, I remarked a tree 2½ feet in diameter; and very large ones are in the bed of a torrent, where no earth (only ftones) is vifible.

DAUPHINE.—*Montélimart.*—Silk is the great produce of the country; they have mills, where the cocoons are bought, at 27f. the pound. An ounce of *grains* gives 60 lb. of cocoons, and 12 lb. of cocoons 1 lb. of filk : forty middling trees, each yielding a quintal of leaves, being required to feed that proportion of worms. The *grains* are hatched by artificial heat, and the operation demands wood to the amount of 24 liv. to each ounce of grains. A common method of conducting the bufinefs is, for the proprietor of the land to find trees and half the *grains*; the poor people the other half and all the labour; and the parties divide the produce between them. The impediments in the culture are, —1. climate; frofts in the fpring deftroy the leaves, and, if at a critical time, there is no remedy. I demanded if they had no fuccedaneum, in fuch cafe, in
feeding

feeding the worms with the leaves of some other plants? The answer was, that experiments had been made upon that point, without any success; that the idea, however, was nonsense, for the quantity of food was so great, as to render it absurd to think of providing it, not for a certain want, but merely a contingent one; the expence of such a conduct would absorb all the profit. Nor is it frosts only that are dreaded—great and sudden heats make the worms fall, and they labour very poorly.——2. The extreme labour of attending the worms, is a great objection to the business; it is, for the last fifteen days, so severe, as to kill many; and, for the last eight days, they are cleaned every day.

Upon a comparison of the culture of the olive and the mulberry, it was remarked to me, that one great advantage of the olive, was the contracted space in which the roots feed, consisting chiefly of a tap-root and fibres, which made the crops sown under them good; but a mulberry threw out a profusion of roots, fifteen or twenty feet around, in every direction.

They have been known, at eleven years growth, to yield 200 lb of leaves each tree.

The mulberry is found not to like water; for there is in the watered meadows a mound of earth, to keep the water from the roots of these trees.

When silk-worms are ready to spin the cocoon, if they are cut in halves and thrown into vinegar, each worm gives two transparent ligaments, very strong, for making fishing lines, &c. &c.

Loriol.—Monf. L'Abbé Berenger, curé of this place, has given an uncommon attention to this culture; he was so obliging as to give me the result of many years experience on this interesting subject.

Time of Sowing.—There are two seasons; the first, with the fruit, fresh, at the end of June:—the second in May, with the seed of last year, dry; and this is better, because the June sowing suffers sometimes, if frosts are severe, or the weather is both cold and humid. When sown dry, if too early and cold weather succeeds, they are apt to fail. They are often watered.

Transplantation.—In April following, those that were sown in May are transplanted, three feet every way, into the nursery; only half the plants (the best) being drawn, the rest are left till the year after. They are never transplanted a second time. ·

Sort.—The *feuille rose*, with white or grey fruit, is the best; black fruit not known here, but said to be good for leafing late, and escaping frosts in the spring.

Grafting.—It is best to graft, in the nursery, in May, when they are three years old, at the head, with grafts cut in February preceding, and preserved in sand in a cellar: these grafts are branches three feet long, which are buried in sand, except four inches at the end, for three or four knots to shoot; if all

are

are buried in the fand, all the knots will fhoot. At grafting cut off thofe knots that have fhot out, and ufe the reft. The time is after gathering the leaves of the ftandard to be grafted, when the plants are 5 feet, or 5½ feet high. One year after grafting tranfplant, that is, about April. Graft three or four branches.

Soil.—Good and humid fands, and fandy loams are the beft: warm, forward, rich, and friable: rocky and ftoney foils do well; but all clays are bad. On the lighteft ftoney lands, the trees come into bearing much fooner than in the rich vale, but thefe laft vaftly longer; on the rich vale land, two hundred years are a common age for them.

Planting.—In bad land plant at eighteen feet fquare, in moderate at twenty-four, and in very good at thirty-fix; and, after feven or eight years, there can be no crops under them, if at thefe diftances. There are two forts of trees, the one large ftandards; and the others dwarf ones, which they call *murier nain*; an arpent contains, of courfe, many more in number of thefe than of the others; and they yield, for the firft ten or fifteen years, a larger produce, but afterwards the greater trees are more productive. The dwarfs are beft for being fet in rows, for ploughing between; they are grafted at 1½ feet high; are never watered. The price of trees 25 f. the hundred, at the age of one or two years; the great trees, at four or five years, for grafting, 20 f. each, at prefent 15 f. each, and grafted. The operation of planting is performed by digging a hole 6 feet fquare, and 2½ or 3 feet deep; and they commonly lay dung upon the roots.

Cultivation.—The attention with which they manage the trees after planting, merits the higheft commendation:—after they have been planted two years, a trench is dug around each tree, about two feet deep, which is left open all winter, and filled up again in the fpring; the year following another is dug, more removed from the tree, which is managed in the fame manner; and fo on every year a trench, till the whole land is ftirred as far as the roots extend. This appears to be a moft excellent fyftem, and preferable to trenching the ground at firft; as in that way much of it is confolidated again, before the roots of the voung trees reach it.

No crops whatever to be fown on the land after the trees are of a fize to have their leaves gathered; as much is loft in leaves as is gained by fuch crops.

The trees fhould never be pruned at any other feafon than March, and but once in two years; the wood pays the expence: they receive one digging per annum, at 6 liv. and a hoeing, at 3 liv. per arpent.

There is another admirable practice known here, and ufed by all fkilful cultivators, which is, that of wafhing the ftems of the trees every year, in May, for four or five years after planting. Monf. L'Abbé Berenger always practises this with great fuccefs.

Produce.—For the benefit of the young trees, they ought not to be ftripped for feven or eight years after planting into the field; they will pay well afterwards for this forbearance; but the practice is not common. I viewed a young plantation of Monf. Blanchard, at prefent in the National Affembly, who is famous for his attention to his mulberries; the trees were fix, feven, and eight years old, and none of them had ever been ftripped, and their appearance was very flourifhing. Monf. L'Abbé Berenger approves the practice, but has not adhered to it; his trees, however, are very fine, and do not complain; one plantation, of eight or ten years growth, that have conftantly been ftripped, are, notwithftanding, very fine. There are forty on 400 toifes of land, that this year produced, each tree, 8lb. of leaves. The beginning of February he planted the land under them with potatoes, which were dug in Auguft, and produced 40 quintals; among thefe potatoes maiz was planted in April, in fquares of five or fix feet, and the produce of that will be five or fix quintals, at 8 liv. the quintal. He fhewed me another plantation, of an arpent, of very fine and flourifhing dwarf trees, which yielded this year 8 lb. of leaves each tree, and 300 lb. on the arpent. They are ten years old; no crops have ever been fown under them.

The produce of leaves may be eftimated at 50 lb. from a tree of a toife fquare. The greateft produce known is 10 quintals, from a tree of fifty years old. At twenty years the medium is two quintals. They increafe till fixty years old; but are in good perfection at twenty.

The eggs.—A paper of nine inches by fifteen inches, covered with fmall leaves, ftuck full of worms, gives one quintal of cocoons; and this is what they call one ounce of *grains.* But proportions will not hold, for the produce is not increafed proportionably to an increafe of quantity.

Hatching.—Retarding the hatching of the worms with particular views, is, in many circumftances, impoffible. When once the heat of the atmofphere is come to a certain pitch, the hatching cannot be retarded by cellars. Monf. Faujas remarked, that in June they would hatch in an ice-houfe; which fhews that at a certain age they will hatch in fpite of cold. They never, however, truft to the natural heat for hatching them, which always does it too flowly; it is done with the affiftance of fire, and in the month of May. They begin to hatch at 20 to 22 degrees (Reaumur); but artificially it is done at 24 degrees. When the eggs happen to have been put in a cellar, at 10 degrees, their common temperature, they afterwards hatch with difficulty, and never well; always beft when they have to undergo but a moderate change.

Feeding.

Feeding.—In this bufinefs all forts of food, except the mulberry-leaf, is rejected, at the firft mention, as the moft ridiculous, impracticable, and impoffible idea, that ever entered the head of a vifionary; and never could be conceived but by thofe only who amufe themfelves with a few worms, without taking the the trouble of calculating quantity, expence, and quality of filk.

For one ounce of grain, a room of 10 feet by 14 feet, and 12 feet high, is neceffary; but the larger the better, and with windows only to the north. There fhould be ten tables, or fhelves, 6 feet long, and 4½ feet broad, one 18 inches above another; the firft expence of which 60 liv.

Till the 18th of April there is here no fecurity againft frofts. Two years ago there were many leaves before that day, and moft people began their operations; the leaves were all cut off, and they loft the year entirely, for it is three weeks before the leaves come again. Monf. L'Abbé Berenger would not truft appearances; did not begin till after that day, and had as good a year as at any other time.

The expences are ufually borne between the parties, and amount to half the produce, not including the keeping the utenfils in repair. But if they are paid by the owner of the mulberries, fome of them amount to as follow:—gathering the leaves, 12f. to 15f. the quintal; for gathering the dwarfs, only half the price of the others; wood, 15 liv. for 1, 2, or 3 oz. of eggs in one room; 30 liv. for 6 oz. becaufe in two rooms; 22 liv. 10f. for labour in the houfe; fpinning, 40f. per lb. of filk. The wafte is worth 20f. therefore the expence is 20f.

For the laft four or five days, eight men are neceffary to gather leaves for 20 oz. of grain, their voracity being incredible the latter part of the time.

The price of the leaves, if bought, is 4 liv. to 5 liv. the quintal, never at 3 liv. but has been at 10 liv. From 15 to 18 quintals of leaves give one quintal of cocoons, and one of cocoons gives 9 lb. of filk. Cocoons are fold at 26f. the pound; filk, on an average, at 19 liv. The leaves, diffected by the worms, are dried, and kept for hogs, fheep, &c. being worth 4 liv. the quintal; and an ounce of grain yields two quintals of fuch: and the dung of the worms, from an ounce, is worth 4 liv. more, being excellent; the beft indeed of all others.

Two brothers here, Meffrs. Carriers have had as far as 80 quintals of cocoons. Monf. Berenger's three hundred trees on an arpent, at 8 lb. of leaves each, are 24 quintals; and, at 4 liv. the quintal, amount to 96 liv.; and as 16 quintals of leaves give 9 lb. of filk, at 19 liv. it is 171 liv. and for 24 quintals 256 liv. the half of which is 128 liv.; hence, therefore, to fell the leaves at 4 liv. the quintal, does not anfwer equally with half the produce (128 liv. per arpent de Paris, is 6 l. 4 s. 3 d. per Englifh acre).

PROVENCE.—*Avignon.*—At ten years growth the mulberries yield a confiderable produce; at that age they give 100 lb. to 150 lb. of leaves, but not

common.

common.   For one ounce of grain, five or fix very large trees are neceffary; or, if the leaves are bought, to the amount of 24 liv. to 30 liv.   The ounce will give from 40 lb. to 50 lb. of cocoons, or 5 lb. of filk; but more commonly 12 lb. of cocoons for 1 lb. of filk.   Gathering the leaves, 10f. or 12f. the quintal, one with another, dwarfs and ftandards.   The wafte pays the fpinning.

Aix.—Mulberries, beyond all comparifon, more profitable than olives; will give 3 liv. or 4 liv. per tree, more regularly than olives will 10f.; but the great plantations of olives are on barren rocks that will not do for mulberries.

Tour d'Aigues.—One ounce of grain requires 15 quintals of leaves, and gives 50 lb. of cocoons; that is, 50 lb. in a fmall undertaking, like the houfe of a poor family; but not more than 30 lb. in a large building.   Monf. the Prefident has, however, had 75 oz. of grain that gave 40 lb. one with another: 14 lb. of cocoons give 1 lb. of organzine filk.

On good land, twenty trees, of ten years old, will give 15 quintals of leaves. The wafte, with the addition of 10f. per lb. will pay the fpinning.   Wood is 12f. the quintal, and 1½ quintal will wind and fpin 1 lb. of filk : and one quintal of charcoal will make 3 lb. of filk.   The common calculation is 10 quintals of charcoal for 1 oz. of grain.

Labour and fuel, 40f. per lb. of filk, exclufive of gathering the leaves; but the common method is to find the trees and the grain, and give half the produce for all the reft.   The whole bufinefs, exclufive of winding and fpinning, employs exactly a month.

Hyeres.—This article is here but little regarded; the number is not confiderable, nor do they pay nearly the fame attention to them as in Dauphiné. A tree of twenty years pays about 30f.; and fome, of a very great fize and age, 6 liv.

Frejus.—Clofe without the town, on the banks of a fmall canal of irrigation, are five or fix of the largeft mulberries I have feen, growing clofe to the water's edge; from which it fhould appear, that they have here none of that objection to water which was mentioned to me at Montélimart.

Eftrelles.—At the inn here there is a mulberry-tree which yields black fruit, and leaves of a remarkable fize.   I afked the mafter, if he ufed them for filkworms? *Never,* he replied, *they are no better for them than elm, oak, or pine leaves: it is the white mulberries that are for worms.*   So inaccurately underftood is this point, even in the filk countries; for in Languedoc they told me, all forts were given indifcriminately.   This tree would be worth 2 or 3 louis a year.

To these notes, taken by myfelf, I fhall add a few others, for the more general elucidation of the fubject.

Languedoc

Languedoc yields, in a common year, from 500 to 1200 quintals of filk*. I have fearched books in vain for information of the quantity of filk produced in all France; but I find the number of looms which work it, by one account, 29,000†, of which 18,000 at Lyons; but by a later and more authentic account, there were at Lyons only 9335 looms, which worked about 2,000,000lb.‡ and in all France 17,500 looms; which, in the fame proportion, would work about 3,763,000lb. In 1784, fhe imported raw filk to the value of 29,500,000liv. and in 1787, to 28,220,000 liv.; call it 29 millions, and 20 liv. the mean price per lb. it is 1,450,000lb.‖; which will leave about 2,310,000lb. for the home produce, or 46,200,000liv. which is fo grofs an impoffibility, as to afcertain to a certainty, the exaggeration of the number of looms, and confirms, in a frefh inftance, the many errors in the new Encyclopædia. If Languedoc produces only 100,000lb. all the reft of the kingdom cannot produce twenty times as much; for the culture is confined to three or four provinces, except fmall quantities, that enter for little in a general account. I was informed, at Lyons, that the home growth was about a million of pounds weight, of two-thirds of the value of the imported per lb. or about 20 liv. This makes the growth to the value of 20,000,000liv. or 875,000l. If fo, Languedoc muft produce more than 100,000lb. for that province muft be at leaft one-fourth, if not one-third of the whole. I muft confefs I have my doubts upon this point, and think that even one million of pounds much exaggerated, for I croffed the filk country in more than one direction, and the quantity of trees appeared inconfiderable for any fuch produce. But admitting the authority, and ftating that the kingdom does produce to the amount of 8 or 900,000l. fterling, I muft remark, that the quantity is ftrangely inconfiderable, and feems to mark, that the climate has fomething in it vaftly inferior to that of Italy, for the production of this commodity; in which country there are little principalities that give more than the whole kingdom of France;—yet, to human feelings, there is no comparifon between the climate of France and that of Italy; the former is better, beyond all queftion. But the fpring frofts (found in Italy alfo) are what bring the greateft deftruction on this culture, and will for ever retard its progrefs greatly in countries expofed to them. In 1788, there was a general failure in the fouth of France, yet acrofs the Pyrenees, in Catalonia, the crop was abundant, merely becaufe the fpring frofts did not pafs thofe mountains.

* *Confiderations fur le Commerce de Bretagne*, par Monf. Pinczon du Sel des Monf. 12mo. p. 5.

† *Lettre fur les Muriers & Vers a foie Journal Oeconomique.* 1756. vol. ii. p. 36.

‡ *Encyclop. Methodique Manuf.* tom. ii. pt. 2. p. 44.

‖ A very late writer was ftrangely miftaken, in faying, that France imports 20,000,000 of pounds weight. *Mr. Townfhend's Journey through Spain*, vol. i. p. 52.

In

In the districts and spots of the southern provinces, where the climate has, from experience, been found favourable to silk, there is no want of exertion in following it ; and about Loriol and Montélimart, it is cultivated with more energy than in any part of Lombardy, yet at small distances there are no mulberries, though the proprietors are as rich and as industrious as where they are found. The same observation is to be made every where, and seems to mark a great dependence even on the locality of climate, if I may hazard such an expression. Where the culture succeeds well, it appears, from the preceding minutes, to be highly profitable, and to form one of the most beneficial objects that can attract the attention of the industrious.

The Society of Arts at London, have, for many years, offered premiums for mulberries and silk in England; and much has been written and argued in favour of the scheme, which I take to be a great, but harmless folly: it may mislead and decieve a few ingenious speculative people, who may, for what I know, in the course of a century, arrive at such success as the late King of Prussia boasted, that of making a few thousand pounds of miserably bad silk, after forty years exertion. Such success is a real loss; for the same attention, time, capital, and encouragement, given to productions natural to the climate, would have made twenty times, perhaps an hundred times, the return. That silk may be made in England I have no doubt; but it will be made on the same principles, and attended by the same dead loss. The duke of Belleisle made silk, in Normandy, and if he had been a great sovereign, his hundreds would have been thousands of pounds; but all was loss, and, therefore, the sooner it dropped the better Another duke failed, not quite so much, in the Anguomois; and a third planted mulberries to loss on the Garonne ; his neighbours did the same, but grubbed them up again because they did not answer. At Tours, the finest climate of France for fruits, and by consequence well adapted for mulberries, they succeed tolerably, but the culture does not increase, which carries with it a presumption, that more steady heat in spring is wanted than the nothern provinces of France enjoy. Such circumstances bear with great force against any ideas of silk in England, where the heat is never steady; and least of all in spring, where late frosts cut off vegetables much hardier than the mulberry; even so late as the end of May and beginning of June; and where I have seen potatoes turned black by them, even on Midsummer day.

The minutes are invariably decisive, on the question of feeding worms with any thing but mulberry leaves ; the utter impracticability of that scheme is shewn in a manner too satisfactory for any doubts to remain ; and the difficulty of retarding the hatching of the worms beyond a certain period, though not proved with equal decision, is yet placed in a light not a little questionable. It is upon these two modifications of the common practice, that silk in England confessedly depends;

one

one of them is a vague groundlefs theory; and the other too uncertain to be relied on. But I muft further remark, that frofts, in fuch a climate as England, as well as abroad, are to be looked for *after* the leafing of the mulberry; and confequently, that the power of retarding the hatching of the eggs would be ufelefs; the worms in that cafe muft be put upon other food, which, with fmall parcels, would make bad filk, and with large ones would demand an expence impoffible to fubmit to every year for a mere contingency that might be demanded only once in three or four. To urge the example of Brandenbourg is idle: in the firft place, all continental climates are more regular than infular ones, and therefore the climate of the King of Pruffia's dominions may be better for the bufinefs; yet with this advantage Normandy failed. In 1788, that is, after forty years exertion, they made, in all the Pruffian territories, 11,000 lb.* of pounds lighter than French ones. And the author I quote on this fubject, who commends the project, informs us, that in Brandenbourg, to make a pound of filk, demands one-fourth more cocoons than in the fouth of France †; and that the filk thus made, is fo bad, that it will do only for certain objects ‡; of the climate he fays, that it is not favourable enough § for the bufinefs. What encouragement is to be collected from this detail, when it is confidered that forty years effort of the firft talents in the world, feconded by boundlefs power, forcing plantations and lavifhing premiums, have been able to drive this nail, that will not go but againft nature, to no greater extent than 11,000 lb. of bad filk in all the Pruffian dominions? In my opinion, the refult of fuch an experiment yields a more complete condemnation, than if it had never been tried at all in fuch a climate, and ought to be a leffon to us in England, not obftinately to perfift in fuch foolifh attempts, calculated only to bring ridicule on focieties, and difappointment to individuals. In all probability, the filk made in Pruffia coft every year ten times more than it is worth; that is to fay, the fame royal attention, the fame premiums, the fame favours, as giving trees and filk eggs,—the fame powerful inftigations to rectors and cureés of the crown livings, &c.—had they been exerted to people the heaths of Brandenbourg with fheep, would have yielded, in *wool alone*, ten times the value of 11,000 lb. of filk; which, if we value it 12s. a pound, being fo inferior, amounts only to 6600l.; —a pretty article of produce for forty years efforts of the moft energic government in Europe! 50,000 fheep, at 3s. a head in wool, go much beyond it, throwing mutton out of the queftion.

An idle error in England, is the idea that this culture demands the labour only of women and children, and old and infirm perfons: the contrary appears

---

* *Mirabeau Monarch. Pruff.* tom. i. p. 180.   † Tom. ii. p. 166.
‡ Tom. i. p. 180.   § Tom. ii. p. 166.

the fact; eight men are neceffary for gathering the leaves for twenty ounces of grain, during four or five days, when the worms are moft ravenous: and the work of gathering is that of men at all times; for the leaves are not *picked*, but *ftripped* along a branch, by force and hardnefs of hand. And even the feeding and cleaning worms is fo far from being light work, that it is, on the contrary, very fevere, fo as even to kill fome of the poor people that follow it up; as the induftrious will follow up all work feverely. The culture is therefore very far from what it has been reprefented in England, as being all net profit, demanding only women, children, and the infirm; on the contrary, it would demand many able men, at a bufy feafon of the year, when they could be ill fpared; and if a propofal was to be made at fuch a feafon to a farmer, that he muft fpare men enough to gather all the leaves of many hundred pollard trees of any fort, he would probably fay the price of mulberry leaves in the filk countries would not pay him; and that double that price would not be an inducement to him, at fuch a feafon, to derange his bufinefs, and take his men from neceffary work, for employing them on fuch a bufinefs. If it is afked, how the fame thing can be done in filk countries? I anfwer, that labour is but half the price of Englifh labour, owing to caufes explained in other chapters; that the multiplied fubdivifion of landed property fills many of thofe countries with hands,—many idle, and many not half employed. To them the culture is highly valuable; but to introduce it in a country, even if the climate would permit, conftituted and politically arranged, in a manner and upon principles abfolutely contrary, would be attended with difficulties and expences, not in the contemplation of people very ingenious, perhaps, who have amufed themfelves with filk-worms, and paid an attention to them, being a pleafure, which, if commercially valued, would poffibly amount to fifty times the value of all the filk they make.

CHAP.

CHAP. XII.

Of Cattle in France.

EVERY part of agriculture depends fo immediately on the quantity of live ftock, that a farming traveller cannot give too much attention to fo material a part of his purfuit. The candid reader will not, however, look to any traveller, that does not refide long in a place, for fuch information, as is alone to be acquired by fuch refidence. He who ftays a week will gain knowledge beyond the attainment of a day; and the attention of a month will produce fruits beyond the reach of him whofe obfervations are limited to a week, and yet remain very fuperficial, when compared with the refearches of others who live on the fpot. A mere traveller fhould gain what his opportunities allow, and what he is thus able to gain is not the lefs valuable, becaufe larger powers would have commanded a greater harveft.

PAYS DE BEAUCE.—*Toury, &c.*—Their beft cows fell at 150 liv.; they give twelve or thirteen bottles a day.

Orleans.—They have a remarkable cuftom of letting chick-weed get a head in their vineyards, which they pluck in May and dry. This they boil in water with bran for their cows, giving it thrice a day, and find that it makes them give double the quantity of milk they would do on any other food. This application of a common plant, that might eafily be cultivated, and got off time enough for a crop of turnips, probably improving the land, deferves a trial. The fact is curious.

SOLOGNE.—*To La Ferté.*—Make hay of the weeds of their vineyards, and are the chief fupport of their cows; do not boil, but give them in bran and water. In fummer feed with grafs and vine cuttings.—A cow, that gives one to three bottles a day, fells at 90 liv.

La Fuzelier.—The cows fmall, and very like Alderneys. Plough bullocks of the fame breed.

BERRY.—*Verfon.*—A pair of oxen, ready to work, fell at 400 liv. (17l. 10s.); and when old and paft labour, but lean, 300 to 340 liv.

Argentan.—A good pair of oxen fell at 400 liv.; common ones 300 liv.; very fine to 600 liv. (26l. 5s.) All the cattle here are cream coloured, as well as the droves we have met going to Paris.—A cow, not the largeft, fells at 150 liv. (6l. 11s. 3d.)

LA MARCHE.—*To Boifmandé.*—Very fine bullocks, well made, and in great order, 600 liv. (26l. 5s.) the pair. Thefe oxen are of a beautiful form; their backs ftrait and flat, with a fine fpringing rib; clean throat and leg; felt well; and are in every refpect fuperior to many breeds we have in England.

La Ville Aubrun.—Work their cows, but they do not give us much milk as if not worked. A good one fells, with its calf, at 150 liv. (6l. 11s. 3d.) They fatten oxen here with *raves,* a fort of turnip; begin to ufe them in October or November, and laft generally about three months. To fatten a pair of good oxen would take 45 cart loads, cut in pieces, and 20 quintals of hay: when the raves are done, they give the flour of rye or other corn, with water enough added to form a pafte; this they leave four or five days to become four, and then they di- lute it with water, thicken it with cut chaff, and give it to the oxen thrice a day; when fed with raves the oxen do not want to drink. Such a detail would imply a turnip culture of fome importance, but though hoeing is not abfolutely un- known, yet the turnips may be conjectured, from the common management, being never to hoe, fearing to cut up the crop by it. The young plant is fome- times eaten by the fly, in which cafe they fow again; froft fomtimes damages the roots, but never deftroys them entirely. Often fow wheat after them, and do not cultivate clover; thus three-fourths of the merit of the culture is loft.

Baffie.—Their raves yield, according to the year, two or three cart loads per boiferée of land, about eight of which make an Englifh acre. A pair of good oxen will eat a cart load in two days, but have hay with them: they are as fond of this root as horfes are of oats: they finifh with flour of rye, mixed as before-mentioned: they affert that the oxen like it the better for being four, and that it anfwers better in fatting them. They eat about a boifeau a day (weighs 22lb.) and never give this acid liquor without chopped hay. It is pro- per here to remark, that, in coming to Paris, we have met a great many droves of thefe oxen, to the amount, I guefs, of from twelve to fifteen hundred, and that they were, with few exceptions, very fat; and, confidering the feafon, May, the moft difficult of the year, they were fatter than oxen are commonly feen in England, in the fpring. I handled many fcores of them, and found them an excellent breed, and very well fattened.

LIMOUSIN.—*To Limoges.*—A pair of good oxen will eat a cart load of raves a day; begin to feed the end of October: after the raves, give rye-pafte as de- fcribed above, but with the addition of a *leven (levain)* to the pafte, to quicken the fermentation, and make it quite four: at firft the oxen will not drink it, but they are ftarved to it; ufually take it the fecond day, and after they have begun like it much, and never leave a drop. Saw a pair bought laft winter for 1100 liv. (48l. 2s. 6d.); but fuch as are ready for work, fell as dear as fat ones, which is remarkable. An arpent of raves yields forty cart loads; and a pair of good oxen

will

will eat one load a day. They have two kinds; one very large and flat; the other more round, and with a root that enters the ground deeply. They generally manure thoroughly for them, in March, and plough in so early, that the dung may be quite rotten and mixed with the soil by the end of June. Begin to sow a fortnight after Midsummer: they are not hurt by the frost when it thaws with rain, but are apt to rot when it thaws with the sun. About Christmas they plough up the part eaten, and sow rye, the rest for oats.—They plough their cows, milking them once a day, from three to five bottles.

Limoges.—The great staple of the whole province is fat cattle, sent to Paris and other towns, as well as hogs, that go for salting to the sea ports. The cattle are all of a yellow cream colour, with no other distinction than having, one in an hundred perhaps, a tendency to a blood red: all have horns of a medium length; legs short in proportion to their carcasses, which are deep and heavy; the shape in general very good; the back strait and broad; the rib springing, and consequently well arched; the hips and rumps very fat; the tail rising high from the rump; which I note, not because such points are of *real* importance, but because it is esteemed by some as a proof of a bad breed: the weight I guess to be from sixty to seventy stone (14lb.); some rise to eighty, and a very few may be so low as fifty. Their hogs are many of them large: some with lop ears like our old Shropshire's.

St. George.—The same breed of oxen continues here, but hardly so large; they are always kept in high order: a pair draws the weight commonly of 2000lb. and supports such labour well. They rear calves by keeping them eight or ten months with the cows.

Usarch.—Fatten their oxen with raves, as above, and then with rye-flour, made into a paste with leaven, and given four, as before described. They also fatten some with potatoes, mixed with chestnuts, and also alone; but in either case boiled thoroughly, and given fresh as boiled every day. They have a great opinion of their fattening quality: they feed their cows also with this root, and find that it gives a great increase of milk.—Calves reared, either for oxen or cows, suck ten or twelve months, which is the universal practice.

Quercy.—*Brive to Cressensac.*—A practical farmer, that has the largest oxen I had met with, gave me the following account:—they fatten with maiz, but, in order to render it tender, pour boiling water on it, cover it up close, and give it to the cattle the same day; and in this method it is a most excellent fattener, both of oxen and poultry. But, in order to make them fatten sooner and better, this farmer gives them, every night, and sometimes of a morning, a ball of pork-grease, as large as an apple; he says this is both physick and food, and makes them thrive the better.

To

To Soulliac.—Fat their oxen here alfo with raves, and give them alfo to lean beafts; the mafter of the poft town were we ftopped fays, that he fent laft year to Paris, four raves that weighed 100lb. They foil their oxen with crops of the *vicia latharcides,* and of the *lathyrus fetifolius;* of thefe plants he fpoke fo highly, when given in the foiling way, in the ftable, that he faid the oxen became fo fat, that they could not get out of the ftable if they were not worked. He fhewed me fome oxen that did not allow a doubt of the truth of what he faid, for they were as fat as bears. The fact of hog's greafe being given, was here confirmed; it is given to increafe the appetite, and anfwers fo well, that the beafts perfectly devour their food after it, and their coats become fmooth and fhining. The moft fattening food they know for a bullock, is walnut oilcake. All here give falt plentifully, to both cattle and fheep, being but 1*f.* a pound. But this practice is, more or lefs, univerfal through the whole kingdom.

Cahors.—Nearly all the draft cattle are mules, and yoked as oxen in England, only collars to the yoke inftead of bows. Cows and oxen all cream-coloured; very good, and in fine order.

LANGUEDOC.—*Toulouse.*—Very fine cream-coloured horned oxen; a pair good working ones fell at 25 louis.

St. Gaudents.—Price 120 liv. (5l. 5s.); in the winter kept in ftables, and fed upon hay.

Bagnere de Luchon.—Every parifh in thefe mountains has common paftures for their cattle and fheep, and each inhabitant has a right to fend as many as they can feed in winter. They are on the mountains three or four months, under the care of people who milk the cows, goats, and ewes, and give the proprietor, at the end of the period, two cheefes, of 18lb. for each cow; or four goats; or ten ewes; the price of the cheefe is 5*f.* the lb. but 10*f.* at a year old, and the overplus, if any, is their reward. A cow is reckoned to pay above 2 louis a year, valuing the calf, as they do, at a louis. A pair of cows, ftout enough to be worked, fell at 10 to 12 louis; and a pair of oxen 12 to 15 louis.

BASQUE.—Informed by a gentleman, at Bagnere de Luchon, that the mountains in this province afford a very great fupply of food, in fummer, for cattle, which are fent to winter on the *landes* of Bourdeaux, where they juft get a living on weeds, rough grafs, branches of trees, &c.; and that they pay only 5*f.* a head for wintering thefe cattle, which is perfectly incredible; but I note it as reported. He alfo informs me, that thofe mountains of Bafque, and alfo of Navarre, breed moft of the oxen that I faw in Limoufin; they are fold thither calves; and are all cream-coloured, or yellowifh.

LANGUEDOC.—*Pinjean to Montpelier.*—Ploughing with fine large oxen, in good order; fome cream-coloured, others deep red; middling horns. The
                                                                    fame

fame breed has been found all the way, almoſt from the Loire to Barcelona;
and from Calais to the Loire, variations of the ſhort-horned Alderney, or
Norman cow.

BEARN.—*Navarens.*—Cream-coloured cows, 100 liv. to 120 liv.

GASCOIGN.—*St. Palais to Anſpan.*—In 1786, on theſe mountains, the ſcarcity
of forage being very great, they cut much fern and made hay of it, and it anſwered well; horſes, mules, and young cattle, eat it freely; but it was cut early.
Through this country, and nearly to Bayonne, they fatten oxen with raves,
which they cultivate carefully for an after-crop. They anſwer perfectly well,
without other food being given; when the raves are done, they ſometimes give
maiz-flour, but dry, knowing nothing of the Limouſin method.

Port St. Marie.—Very fine cream-coloured oxen.

Aguillon.—Ditto, very fine and beautiful.

Tonnium to La Morte Landron.—As we advance on the Garonne, the oxen
are yet finer; meet common ones at 600 liv. and 700 liv. the pair; but ſome
very fine that riſe to 1000 liv. and 1200 liv. (52l. 10s.) as they are in the plough;
all are, however, in fine order, and many fat. Breed their own cattle; a pretty
good cow ſells at 250 liv.; harneſs and work them as oxen, but gently while
they give milk.

La Réole.—Work their cows: put oxen to work at three years old, and keep
them to it four, eight, and even ten years, according as they are found fit for it.
Riſe in price to 1200 liv. the pair. The leaſt weight they are put to draw, is
20 quintals (a ton Engliſh) a pair; but good oxen draw 30 quintals with eaſe: all
harneſſed by the horns; they are fed now upon maiz leaves, which are ſo excellent
a food for them, that it is ſown in ſucceſſion thickly for mowing for ſoiling.
Give alſo at preſent vine leaves, which are very good food. See them ſhoe an
ox; they are faſtened by the horns in a ſhoeing ſtall, and lifted from the ground,
if wanted, by two broad bands of hemp, that paſs under the belly. The ſhoe turns
over the toe, or hoof, as in England; ſhoe for ploughing as well as for the road.

Barſac.—Oxen, through all this country, where they are found fine, are
dreſſed as regularly every day as horſes.

ANGOUMOIS.—*Barbeſieux to Petignac.*—Cream-coloured oxen; 20 louis to
25 louis the pair.

POITOU.—*Poitiers.*—Red-coloured oxen, with a black tinge in the head;
the ſign of the Poitou breed.

Chateaurault.—Good cream-coloured and red oxen, but they have declined
ſince Bourdeaux. The good ones here ſell at 25 louis the pair. They plough
with a pair, without driver or reins.

Amboiſe.—Cream-coloured, and ſome blackiſh; and, which ſhews we are
got to the Loire, ſome Norman ones, with mixtures. This great river is the
ſeparation

feparation of breeds in a remarkable manner. All the way from Tours, to Blois, they raife raves for cows and oxen, but never hoe them ; and the fcale not at all refpectable.

Petiviers.—Cows quite the Norman breed, and the earth tilled by horfes.

Isle of France.—*Liancourt.*—Exceedingly deficient. Some poor ill fed cows upon the commons were all that I faw, except the Dutchefs of Liancourt's dairy of Swifs cows. Of oxen and fatting beafts they have none. Very fine fat beef appeared at table, which came from Paris, I think.

Braffeufe.—Madame la Vifcounteffe du Pont's dairy of cows fed entirely with lucerne, and the butter excellent; I admired it much, and found the manufacture quite different from the common method. The milk is churned inftead of the cream. Her dairy-maid is from Bretagne, a province famous for good dairymaids. The evening's milk and the morning's are put together, and churned as foon as the latter is milked; the proper quantity of falt is added in the churn, and no wafhing or making in water, which thefe dairy-maids hold to be a very bad method. Finer butter, of a more delicate flavour, was never tafted, than procured by this method from lucerne.

Comerle en Vexin.—This part of the province is famous for fatting calves for the Paris market. I had gathered fome circumftances at Marenne, and they were confirmed here. All is known at Paris under the name of Pontoife veal, but it comes chiefly from this country. The farmers here are moftly, if not all, in the fyftem of fuckling. The cows are of the Norman fhort-horned breed, nearly refembling our Alderney; thofe of three confiderable farmers, whofe herds I viewed, were fo unexceptionably. The management of their cows is to keep them tied up conftantly, as far as food is concerned, but turned out every day for air and exercife, during which time they pick up what the bare paftures yield. Their food is given in the houfes, being foiled on lucerne, fainfoin, or clover, mown frefh every day, while they give milk, but hay and ftraw in winter. The calves alfo are, in general, tied up in the fame houfe; thofe I faw, both cows and calves, were all littered; but they feemed to have fo little attention to keep them clean, that I enquired the reafon; and was told, that they are fometimes fuffered to reft on their dung till it rifes high, by the addition of frefh ftraw, but that no inconvenience is found from it. Having been affured that they fed their calves with eggs, for giving reputation to the veal of Pontoife, I enquired into the truth of it, and was affured that no fuch practice was known ; and that the reafon of the fuperiority of the veal of Pontoife, to that of Normandy, from which province moft of the other calves come, was fimply that of making them fatter by longer fucking ; whereas the Norman cuftom was to feed them with fkim milk. In this country of the Vexin, they are in the cuftom of keeping them till they are of a large fize: I faw fome of

four

four months old, valued at 4 louis each, and that would be worth 5 louis in another month; fome have been fold at 6 louis; and more even than that has been known. I felt one calf that fucked the milk of five cows. It was remarkable to find, that the value of many fatting calves I examined was nearly what it would be in England; I do not think there was 5 per cent. difference. They never bleed them to whiten the flefh, as is done with us. Some of the farmers here keep many cows; Monf. Coffin, of Commerle, has forty, but his farm is the largeft in all the country; the country people fay it is 20,000 liv. a year.

PICARDIE.—*St. Quintin.*—All the way from Soifons hither, the cattle are fome black, and black and white, which is very uncommon in France.

Cambray to Bouchaine.—Feed their cows, and fatten oxen and cows, on carrots. They reckon that no food is fo good, for giving much and excellent milk. For fattening an ox they flice them into bran: but they remarked, that in fattening, the great object was to change their food; that a middling one, with change, would go further than a good one without; but in fuch change, carrots rank very high.

FLANDERS.—*Valenciennes to Orchies.*—Finding that they fed cattle with linfeed-cakes, I inquired if they ufed any of their immenfe quantity of colefeed-cakes for the fame ufe? And was affured that they did; and that a beaft, with proper care, would fatten on them, though not fo well as on linfeed-cake; alfo that they feed their fheep with both. For fattening beafts and for cows, they diffolve the cake in hot water, and the animal drinks, not eats it, having various other food given at the fame time, as hay, bran, &c.; for there is no point they adhere to more than always to give variety of foods to a fattening beaft. Their cows, of which they are very proud, are Dutch; not large, though bigger than the Norman breed; they are red, or red and white, with a few black; the horns fhort and curled inwards, forward. They are fed in the houfe the whole year round, but kept clean with the greateft attention. They boaft of their butter being equal to any in the world; and I was affured of a cow that gave 19 liv. (16s. 7½d.) in butter every nine days. They feed them with potatoes, which give excellent butter; and with turnips, which give as bad. Cows fell at 150 liv.

To Lille.—All the cattle tied up in houfes, as they affured me, the year round; I inquired into their motives for this, and they afferted, that no practice is, they think, fo wafteful as letting cattle pafture abroad, as much food, or perhaps more, being fpoiled than eaten; the raifing dung alfo is a great object with them, which ftands ftill, to their great lofs, when cattle are abroad.

Their cows were now (November 4,) feeding on turnips and cabbages. In every cow houfe I faw a tub of bran and water, which is their principal drink;

boiled

boiled with bran in it is greatly preferred, but some give it without boiling. Such minutiæ of practice feems only poffible on a little farm, where the hands are very numerous compared with the quantity of land ; but it merits experiment to inquire, how far boiling all the water drank in winter can anfwer. Without experiment, fuch queftions are never underftood. All the cows I faw were littered, but the floors being flat, and without any ftep at the heel, they were dirty.

NORMANDIE.—*Neufchatel.* There are dairies here that rife to fifty cows, the produce of which in money, on an average, rejecting a few of the worft, is 80 to 100 liv. including calves, pigs, butter, and cheefe. In winter they feed them with ftraw ; later with hay ; and even with oats and bran ; but not the leaft idea of any green winter food. The vale from hence to Gournay is all full of dairies, and fome alfo to Dieppe. One acre of good grafs feeds a cow through the fummer.

To Rouen.—Good cows give three gallons of milk a day ; they are of the Alderney or Norman breed, but larger than fuch as come commonly to England.

Pont au Demer.—Many very fine grafs inclofures, of a better countenance than any I have feen in France, without watering ; grazed by good Norman cows, larger than our Alderneys, but of the fame breed : I faw thirty-two in one field. In the height of the feafon they are always milked three times a day ; good ones give three Englifh gallons of milk a day. A man near the town that has got cows, but wants pafture, pays 10*f.* a day for the pafturage of one, which is a very high rate for cattle of this fize.

Pont l' Eveque.—This town is fituated in the famous Pay d'Auge, which is the diftrict of the richeft pafturage in Normandy, and indeed of all France, and for what I know of all Europe. It is a vale of about thirty-five miles long, and from half a mile to two miles over, being a flat tract of exceedingly rich land, at the bottom of two flopes of hills, which are either woods, arable, or poor land ; but in fome places the pafture rifes partly up the hills. I viewed fome of thefe rich paftures, with a gentleman of Pont l'Eveque, Monf. Beval, who was fo good as to explain fome of the circumftances that relate to them. About this place they are all grazed by fatting oxen : the fyftem is nearly that of many of our Englifh counties. In March or April, the graziers go to the fairs of Poitou and buy the oxen lean at about 240 liv. (10l. 10s.) : they are generally cream coloured ; horns of a middle length, with the tips black ; the ends of their tails black ; and tan coloured about the eyes, which are the diftinctions of the Poitou breed. At Michaelmas they are fat ; and fent to the fair at Poiffy, that is Paris : fuch as are bought in at 240 liv. lean, are fold fat at 350 to 400 liv. (15l. 6s. 3d. to 17l. 10s.) An acre of good pafturage carries more than one

of

of thefe beafts in fummer, befides winter fattening fheep. This acre is 4 verges,
each 40 perches, and the perch 22 feet, or a very little better than 2 Englifh
acres. The rent of the beft of thefe paftures (called *herbages* here) amounts to
100 liv. (4l. 7s. 6d.) per Norman acre, or nearly 2l. 3s. 9d. the Englifh; the
tenant's taxes add 14 liv. (12. 3d.) or 6s. 1½d. per Englifh acre. The expences
may be ftated thus:

Rent, - - - -	100 liv.
Taxes, - - - -	14
Suppofe 1½ ox fattened, bought at 240 liv.	360
	474
Intereft of that total, - -	23
	497
Say, - - -	500
Ox and an half fat, at 375 liv. -	562
Expences, - - - -	500
Profit, - - - -	62

Which is about 1l. 6s. 6d. per Englifh acre profit; and will pay a man well, the
intereft of his capital being already paid. As thefe Norman graziers are generally rich, I do not apprehend the annual benefit is lefs. In pieces that are tolerably large, a ftock proportioned to the fize is turned in, and not changed till
they are taken out fat. Thefe Poitou oxen are for the richeft paftures; for land
of an inferior quality, they buy beafts from Anjou, Maine, and Bretange. The
fheep fed in the winter do not belong to the graziers, but are joifted; there is
none with longer wool than five inches, but the pafture is equal to the fineft of
Lincoln. In walking over one of thefe noble herbages, my conductor made me
obferve the quantity of clover in it, as a proof of its richnefs; it was the white
Dutch and the common red: it is often thus—the value of a pafture depends
more on the *diadelphia* than on the *triandria* family.

To Lifieux.—This rich vale of the Pay d'Auge, fome years ago, was fed almoft entirely with cows, but now it is very generally under oxen, which are
found to pay better. Whatever cows there are, are milked three times a day in
fummer.

To Caen.—The valley of Corbon is a part of the Pay d'Auge, and faid to be the
richeft of the whole. In this part, one acre, of 160 perches of 24 feet, or about
(not exactly) 2½ acres Englifh, fattens two oxen. Such rents are known as
200 liv. (3l. 17s. per Englifh acre) but they are extraordinary: the proportions

here are rather greater, and more profitable than in the former minute. They buy fome beafts before Chriftmas, which they keep on the pafturage alone, except in deep fnows; thefe are forwarder in fpring than fuch as are bought then, and fatten quicker; they have alfo a few fheep. There are graziers here that are landlords of 10,000 liv. and even 20,000 liv. a year, yet 100 acres are a large farm.

Bayeux.—The rich herbages about this place are employed in fattening oxen, of the Poitou breed, as before; bought lean, on an average, at 200 liv. and fold fat at 350 liv. Their cows are always milked thrice a day in fummer; the beft give 12 pots a day, or above 4 gallons, and fell at 7 or 8 louis each.

Ifigny to Carentan.—Much falt marfh, and very rich; they fat oxen; but I was furprifed to find many dairy cows alfo on thefe very rich lands. A cow, they fay, fometimes pays 10 louis in a year; giving 8 lb. of butter a week, at 20*f.* to 30*f.* a pound at fome feafons, but now (Auguft 25) only 10*f.* which, they fay, is ruinoufly cheap. All are milked thrice a day. Others informed me that a cow gives 10. lb. a week, at the average price of 15*f.* Thefe cows refemble the Suffolk breed, in fize and brindle colour, round carcafe, and fhort leg; and would not be known from them but by the horns, which are of the fhort Alderney fort. The profit on fattening a cow here they reckon at 72 liv. and an ox of the largeft fize 300 liv. They have alfo a common calculation, that dairy cows feed at the expence of 8*f.* a day, and yield 2 o*f.* leaving 12*f.* profit. It is remarkable, and cannot be too much condemned, that there are no dairies in this country: the milk is fet, and the butter made, in any common room of a houfe or cottage.

Carentan.—Many oxen are bought at Michaelmas, and kept a year. They eat each in the winter 300 bottes of hay, or 50 liv. but leave 150 liv. profit, that is, they rife from 300 liv. to 450 liv. Cows pay, on an average, 100 liv. and are kept each on a vergé of grafs, the rent of which is from 30 liv. to 40 liv. As the vergé is 40 perches, of 24 feet, or 23,040 feet, it is equal to 96 Englifh fquare perches, which fpace pays 100 liv. or per Englifh acre 7l. 5s. 3d.; but all expences are to be deducted, including what the wintering cofts. Here they have milk-rooms. They work oxen all the way from Bayeux, in yokes and bows, like the old Englifh ones, only fingle inftead of double.

Advancing; cows fell fo high as 10 and 12 louis. Many are milked only twice a day; good ones give 1¼ or 1½ lb. of butter a day. They remark, that cows that give the largeft quantity of milk do not yield the largeft quantity of butter. Fat cows give much richer milk than others.

Again; a good cow gives 6 pots of milk a day, which pays in butter 24*f.* Three thoufand livres profit has been made by fatting thirty cows. A great number of young cattle all over the country, efpecially year olds.

BRETAGNE.

BRETAGNE.—*Rennes.*—Good oxen of Poitou, 400 liv. to 600 liv. the pair; they are harnessed by the horns.   A good cow, 100 liv.   Milk but twice a day.

Landervisier.—I was at the fair here, at which were many cows; in general of the Norman breed, but small: one of the size of a middling Alderney, 4 louis, but said to be dear at present.   Colour, black and white, and red and white.

Quimper.—Many black and white small, but well made, cows on the wastes here; a breed somewhat distinct from the Norman; different horns, &c.

Nantes.—Many Poitou oxen; cream coloured; black eyes, tips of horns, and end of tail; about 50 or 60 stone fat; all yoked by the horns.

Nonant.—Much rich herbage; an acre of which feeds two oxen, to the improvement of 160 liv.   Many cows are fattened also; and some milked always three times a day in summer.

To Gacé.—Some very fine cream coloured oxen, of 60 stone or more; but, in general, red and white, not Poitou.

ISLE OF FRANCE.—*Nangis.*—Cows sell at 4 louis or 5 louis; oxen, half fat, from 8 louis to 11 louis.   They come from Franche Compté.

CHAMPAGNE.—*Mareuil.*—Monf. Le Blanc's Swifs cows give 18 pints, of Paris (the Paris pint is an English quart) of milk per diem, and hold their milk remarkably long.   He gave 40 louis for a bull and a cow.

LORAINE.—*Braban.*—A small cow, 75 liv.

ALSACE.—*Strasbourg.*—A cow, 6 louis; an ox the same.

Issenheim.—Cows improve as you approach Franche Compté.

Befort.—Good oxen, red and cream coloured, to 25 louis a pair

Isle.—Here much smaller; and they say the fine ones I have seen are from the mountains on the frontiers of Swifferland.

BOURGOGNE.—*Dijon to Nuys.*—Small oxen in this country, and yoked by the horns.

Autun to La Maison de Bourgogne.—Good oxen drawing by the horns.

AUVERGNE.—*Clermont.*—Salt given twice a day to cows that give milk.   In the mountains the price of cows, 150 liv. to 200 liv.; a few, 300 liv.; an ox, from 200 liv. to 450 liv.

Izoir.—A pair of good oxen, 16 louis to 18 louis, which will draw 2000lb. The Poitevins will buy only red cattle in Auvergne, having remarked that they fatten easier.*

VIVARAIS.—*Costerons.*—A small cow, 4 louis.

PROVENCE.—The cities of Aix, Marseilles, and Toulon, are fed by oxen, cows, and sheep, from Auvergne, which come every week; and a few from Piedmont.

* *See also Voyage D'Auvergne, par Monf. Le Grand D'Aussy.* 8vo. 1788. P. 273.

H 2

Tour

Tour d'Aigues.—A pair of good oxen, 18 louis or 20 louis. When they have done working, they are fattened with the flour of the *lathyrus fativus,* &c. made into pafte, and balls given frefh every night and morning ; each ox, two or three balls, as large as a man's fift, with hay.

Observations.

FROM the preceding notes it appears, that in Normandy, the Bas Poitou, Limoufin, Quercy, and Guienne, the importance of cattle is pretty well underftood ; in fome diftricts very well ; and that in the pafturage part of Normandy, the quantity is well proportioned to the richnefs of the country. In all the reft of the kingdom, which forms much the greater part of it, there is nothing that attracts notice. There would, in eighteen-twentieths of it, be fcarcely any cattle at all, were it not for the practice of ploughing with them. There are fome practices noted, which merit the attention even of Englifh farmers.—1. The Limofin and Quercy methods of fattening, by means of acid food.——It is remarkable, that I have found hogs to fatten much better with their food become acid, than when ufed frefh.* But in England no experiments, to my knowledge, have been made, on applying the fame principle to oxen ; it is, however, done in the Limoufin with great fuccefs. The fubject is very curious, but the brevity neceffary to a traveller will not allow my purfuing it at prefent.——2. The practice in Flanders, and, in fome degree, in Quercy, &c. of keeping cows, oxen, and all forts of cattle, confined in ftables the whole year through.—This I take to be one of the moft correct and probably one of the moft profitable methods that can be purfued ; fince, by means of it, there is a conftant accumulation of dung throughout the year, and the food is made to go much farther.——3. Milking well fed cows thrice a day, as in Normandy.—Experiments fhould be made on the advantages of this practice, which will probably be found not inconfiderable ; it is never done, either in England nor in Lombardy.

Except in the provinces I have named, the management of cattle in France is a blank. On an average of the kingdom, there is not, perhaps, a tenth of what there ought to be: and of this any one muft be convinced, who reflects, that the courfes of crops throughout the kingdom are calculated for corn only ; generally bread corn ; and that no attention whatever is paid to the equally important object of fupporting great herds of cattle, for raifing manure, by introducing the culture of plants that make cattle the preparative for corn, inftead of thofe barren fallows which are a difgrace to the kingdom. This fyftem of interweaving the crops which fupport the cattle, among thofe of corn, is the

---

* *Annals of Agriculture,* vol. i. p. 340.

pillar

pillar of Englifh hufbandry; without which our agriculture would be as miferable and as unproductive as that of France. The importance of grafs in fuch
views, is little underftood in France; but in proportion as corn is the ultimate
object, fhould be the attention that is paid to grafs. England, by the immenfe
extent of her paftures, has a prodigious preparation always ready for corn, if it
was demanded. He who has grafs can, at any time, have corn; but he who
has corn, cannot at any time have grafs, which demands one or two years accurate preparation. In proportion to your grafs, is the quantity and mafs of
your improvements; for few foils, not laid to grafs, are at their laft ftage of
improvement. The contrary of all this takes place in France; and there is
little appearance, from the complexion of thofe ideas which are at prefent
fafhionable there, that the kingdom will be materially improved in this respect:
the prejudices in favour of fmall farms, and a minute divifion of property, and
the attention paid to the pernicious rights of commonage, are mortal to fuch
an improvement; which never can be effected but by means of large farms, and
an unlimitted power of enclofure.

Horfes.

THIS is an animal about which I have never been folicitous, nor ever paid
much attention; I was very early and practically convinced of the fuperiority
of oxen for moft of the works of hufbandry; I may, indeed, fay for all, except quick harrowing: and if oxen trot fix miles an hour with coaches, in
Bengal, which is the fact, they are certainly applicable to the harrow, with
proper training. To introduce the ufe of oxen in any country, is fo important
an agricultural and political object, that the horfe would be confidered merely
as adminiftering to luxury and war. The very few minutes I took, I fhall infert
in the order they occurred.

LIMOUSIN.—This province is reckoned to breed the beft light horfes that
are in the kingdom; and fome capital regiments of light horfe are always
mounted from hence; they are noted for their motion and hardinefs. Some
miles to the right of St. George, is Pompadour, a royal demefne, where the
King has a *haras* (ftud): there are all kinds of horfes, but chiefly Arabian,
Turkifh, and Englifh. Three years ago four Arabians were imported, which
had been procured at the expence of 72,000 liv. (3149l.); and, owing to thefe
exertions, the breed of this province, which was almoft fpoiled, has been much
recovered. For covering a mare, no more is paid than 3 liv. which is for the
groom, and a feed of oats for the horfe. They are free to fell their colts to
whom they pleafe; but if they come up to the King's ftandard of height, his
officers have the preference, on paying the fame price offered by others; which,

however,

however, the owner may refuse, if he pleases. These horses are never saddled till six years old, and never eat corn till they are five; the reason given is, that they may not hurt their eyes. They pasture all day, but not at night, on account of the wolves, which abound so in this country as to be a nuisance. Prices are very high; a horse of six years old, a little more than 4 feet 6 inches high, sells for 70 louis; and 15 louis have been offered for a colt at one year old. The pastures are good, and proper for breeding horses.

Cahors.—Bean-straw they reckon excellent for horses, but not that of pease, which is too heating.

Agen.—Meet women going to this market, loaded with couch roots to sell for feeding horses. The same practice obtains at Naples.

SAINTONGE.—*Monlieu.*—Never give chaff to their horses, as they think it very bad for them.

ISLE OF FRANCE.—*Dugny.*—Monf. Cretté de Palleuel has found cut chaff one of the most œeonomical foods that can be given to horses; and his machine for cutting it is by far the most powerful one that I have any where seen. It is a mill turned by a horse; the cutting instruments are two small cylinders, that revolve against each other, circular cutting hoops being on their surface, that lock into each other; those of one, plain, but of the other, toothed: just above them is a large trough or tray, to hold a truss of straw, which weighs 12 lb. and the machine cuts it into chaff in three minutes, without putting the horse out of his pace; and in two minutes, by driving him quicker; a man attends to spread the straw equally in the tray, as it is sucked in by the revolving cylinders; a boy driving the horse. One of the machines common in England, for dressing corn, is at the same time turned: the whole is in a building of eight yards square.

NORMANDIE.—*Isigny.*—The rich herbages here are fed, not only with bullocks and cows, but also with mares and foals.

Carentan.—Colts, bred here, sell for very high prices, even to 100 louis, at three years old; but in general good ones from 25 to 30 louis.

BRETAGNE.—*Rennes.*—Good horses sell at 150 liv. The author of the *Considerations sur le Commerce de Bretagne*, says, p. 87. that he has seen many markets in the bishopricks of Rennes and Nantes, where the best horse was not worth 60 liv.

Morlaix.—See in this vicinity, for several miles, some fine bay mares with foals.

Auvergnat.—Informed that Bretagne exports 24,000 horses, from 12 to 25 louis each; and the country that chiefly produces them, is from Lamballe to the sea beyond Brest.

ALSACE.—*Strasbourg.*—A good farm horse, 12 louis.

To Scheleftadt.—Clover mown for foiling all the way.

The

The Norman horſes for draught, and the Limouſin for the ſaddle, are eſteemed the beſt in the kingdom. Great imports have been made of Engliſh horſes for the coach and ſaddle. It is no objeɛt to leſſen that import, for their own lands can be applied to much more profitable uſes than breeding of horſes. The *œconomiſtes* were great enemies to the uſe of oxen, and warm advocates for that of horſes becoming general; one of the many groſs errors which that fanciful ſeɛt were guilty of.

Hogs.

GASCOIGN.—*St. Palais to Anſpan.*—See many fine white, and black and white hogs; they are fed much on acorns, but are fattened throughout this country on maiz ground to flour, and boiled with water to a paſte, and given freſh, milk-warm, every day. Some on beans. They are turned a year old when put up to fatten; riſe to the weight of two or three quintals. Theſe are the hogs that furniſh Bayonne with the hams and bacon, which are ſo famous all over Europe. The hams ſell at 2*o.ſ.* the pound.

I have reſerved this minute, from ſome others of little conſequence, for the opportunity of remarking, that, in England, the old cuſtom of feeding hogs with warm food, is totally diſcontinued; but it well deſerves experiment, whether it would not anſwer in fattening, and alſo in the nouriſhment of ſows and pigs. Such experiments are difficult to make ſatisfaɛtorily, but yet they ought to be made by ſome perſons that are able. Warm food in winter, regularly given, I ſhould ſuppoſe, muſt be more fattening than that which is cold, and, in bad weather, half frozen.

CHAP.

CHAP. XIII.

Of the Culture of various Plants in France.

IN the courfe of my inquiries into the French agriculture, I made fome minutes on various articles, that do not merit a feparate chapter affigned to
each; I fhall therefore introduce them to the reader alphabetically. It may be
of ufe to future travellers to know what articles are cultivated in that kingdom,
that they may give to each fuch an attention as may fuit their purpofe.

Almonds.

PROVENCE—*Aix.*—More fubject to accidents than olives: fometimes three,
four, and five bad crops to one good. Olives flower in June, but almonds in
February, and confequently fubject to frofts. The produce of a good tree is
commonly 3 liv.

Tour d'Aigues.—Do not yield a good crop oftener than once in ten years.
Price, 36 to 40 liv. the quintal: four and a half quintals in the fhell yield one
clean: the price has been 70 liv. Price of the piftachio almond, 6 liv. the 15lb.
in the fhell. Some few fine almond trees will give a quintal in the fhell. They
are a moft hazardous culture, by reafon of the fog that makes them drop; the
worm that eats; and the froft that nips.

Beans.

SOISSONOIS.—*Coucy.*—In the rich lands cultivated, in the courfe of, 1, beans;
2, wheat, remark now (October 31) fome beautiful curled and luxuriant pieces
of wheat, which, from the beans among it, appear to have been fown after
this crop.

ARTOIS.—*Lillers to Bethune.*—Many beans through all Artois, in drills at
12 or 14 inches, very fine and very clean; the culture is as common and as good
as in Kent, and they have a much richer foil. Wheat is fown after muftard,
flax, and beans; and is better after beans than after either of the other two
crops.

ALSACE.—*Wiltenheim to Strafbourg.*—Many pieces; good and very clean.
Produce, fix facks (of 180 lb. of wheat) per arpent of 24,000 feet (28 bufhels per
Englifh acre).

Schelefladt.—Produce, fix to eight facks, at 7 to 12 liv. (7 at 9 liv. is 4l. 7s.
per Englifh acre).

The

The culture of beans is by no means fo common in France as it ought to be; they are a very neceffary affiftance on deep rich foils in the great work of banifh-ing fallows; they prepare on fuch foils better than any other crop for wheat, and are of capital ufe in fupporting and fattening cattle and hogs.

Broom.

BRETAGNE.—*Rennes.*—The land left to it in the common courfe of crops. It is cut for faggots; fold to the bakers, &c.

Morlaix.—Cultivated through all this country, in a very extraordinary fyftem; it is introduced in a regular courfe of crops, and left three or four years on the land; at which growth cut for faggots, and forms the principal fuel of the coun-try. It is a vaft growth, much fuperior to any thing I ever faw; fix or feven feet high, and very ftout; on regular lands, with intervals of two or three feet. Price fometimes of a cord of wood, 30 liv. Does this apologize for fuch a fyftem?

Breft.—The broom feed is fown among oats, as clover is in other places, and left four years, during all which time it is fed. The faggots of a good journal will fell for 400 liv. (14l. per Englifh acre). The faggots weigh 15lb. and fell fifty for 9 liv. to 12 liv. being a three-horfe load. It is only within the reach of Breft market that it is worth 400 liv.—elfewhere only 300 liv. the beft. Four years broom improves land fo much, that they can take three crops of corn after it.

BOURGOGNE.—*Luzy.*—When I left Bretagne, I never expected again to find broom an article of culture; but the rye-lands of all this country, and there is nothing but rye in it, are left, when exhaufted by corn, to cover themfelves with broom, during five years; and they confider it as the principal fupport of their cattle.

To Bourbonlancy and BOURBONNOIS.—*Moulins.*—Much broom through all this diftrict of rye-land.

Carrots and Parfnips.

FLANDERS.—*Cambray.*—See fome fine carrots taken up, which, on inquiry, I find are for cows. They fow ¼ lb. of feed per arpent; hoe them thrice: I gueffed the crop about four bufhels per fquare rod. An arpent fells, for cattle, at 180 liv. the purchafer taking up (5l. 5s. per Englifh acre). After them they dung lightly, and fow wheat.

Orchies to Lille.—The culture here is fingular; they fow the feed at the fame time, and on the fame land, as flax, about Eafter; that crop is pulled in July, the carrots then grow well, and the produce more profitable than any other application of the flax ſtubble. They yield, I gueſs, from 60 to 80 buſhels, and ſome more, per Engliſh acre ; but what I ſaw were much too thick.

Argentan to Bailleul.—Carrots taken up, and guarded, by building in the neateſt and moſt effectual way, againſt the froſt ; they are topped, laid in round heaps, and packed cloſe, with their heads outwards ; and being covered with ſtraw, in the form of a pyramid, a trench is digged around, and the earth piled neatly over the ſtraw, to keep out the froſt. In this manner they are found perfectly ſecure.

ARTOIS.—*Aſs to Aras.*—A ſprinkling of carrots, but none good.

BRETAGNE.—*Ponton to Morlaix.*—Many parſnips cultivated about a league to the left ; they are ſown alone and hoed. They are given to horſes, and are reckoned ſo valuable, that a journal is worth more than one of wheat. Nearer to Morlaix, the road paſſes a few ſmall pieces. They are on beds, 5 or 6 yards broad, with trenches digged between, and on the edges of thoſe trenches a row of cabbages.

Morlaix.—About this place, and in general through the biſhoprick of St. Pol de Leon, the culture of parſnips is of very great conſequence to the people. Almoſt half the country ſubſiſts on them in winter, boiled in ſoup, &c. and their horſes are generally fed with them. A horſe load, of about 300 lb. ſells commonly at 3 liv. ; in ſcarce years, at 4 liv. ; and ſuch a load is good food for a horſe fifteen days. At 60 lb. to the buſhel, this is 5 buſhels, and 2s. 7½d. for that, is 6½d. per buſhel of that weight. I made many inquiries how many loads on a journal, but no ſuch thing as information tolerably to be depended on ; I muſt therefore gueſs the preſent crop, by the examination I made of many, to amount to about 300 buſhels, or 350 per Engliſh acre. The common aſſertion, therefore, that a journal of parſnips is worth two of wheat, ſeems to be well founded. The ground is all digged a full ſpit deep for them ; they are kept clean by hand-weeding very accurately, but are left, for want of hoeing, be-yond all compariſon, too thick. They are reckoned the beſt of all foods for a horſe, and much exceeding oats ; bullocks fatten quicker and better on them than on any other food ; in ſhort, they are, for all ſorts of ſtock, the moſt va-luable produce found on a farm. The ſoil is a rich deep friable ſandy loam.

Landernau to Breſt.—The culture of parſnips here declines much, but I ſaw a few pieces ; one was weeding by five men, crawling on their knees. Fatten many horſes, by feeding them with cabbages and parſnips boiled together, and mixed with buckwheat-flour, and given warm. They have a great pride here in having fat horſes. Many other diſtricts in France, beſides Bretagne, poſſeſs the right ſoil for parſnips ; and many more, beſides Flanders, that for carrots ; but they are no where elſe articles of common culture. Parſnips are not cul-tivated in England ; but carrots are in Suffolk, with great ſucceſs, and all the

horſes

horfes in the maritime corner of that county fed with them. I have, in the *Annals of Agriculture*, given many details of their culture and ufes. Carrots fucceed well on all dry foils that are fix inches deep; but, for large crops, the land fhould be a foot deep, rich and dry. The extent of fuch in France is very great, but this general profitable ufe not made of them.

Cabbages.

FLANDERS.—*Orchies to Lille.*—The kale, called here *choux de Vache*, is common through this country; it never cabbages, but yields a large produce of loofe reddifh leaves, which the farmers give to their cows. The feed is fown in April, and they are tranfplanted in June or July, on to well-dunged land, in rows, generally two feet by one foot: I faw fome fields of them, in which they were planted at greater diftances. They are kept clean, by hoeing. They are reckoned excellent food for cows; and the butter made from them is good, but not equal to that from carrots.

NORMANDIE.—*Granville to Avranches.*—In the gardens of the cottages, many cabbage trees five and fix feet high.

BRETAGNE.—*St. Brieux.*—Many fown here on good land, on wheat ftubbles, for felling plants to all the gardens of the country, and to a diftance. I do not fee more than to the amount of a journal in one piece; which, in September, I muft have done, had they poffeffed any cabbage culture, as reprefented to me, worth attention. They firft clean, and then plough the wheat ftubbles, and chop and break the furface of the three-feet ridges fine, and then fow. The plants are now (September 7) about an inch high, and fome only coming up.

Morlaix.—They have fome crops that are much more produ&tive than their turnips, but planted greatly too thick: they are given to cows and oxen.

ANJOU—*Migniaine.*—The *chou d'Anjou*, of which the Marquis de Turbilly fpeaks, is not to be found at prefent in this country; they prefer the *chou de Poitou*, which is a fort of kale, and produces larger crops of leaves than the *chou d'Anjou*. Monf. Livonniere gave me fome feeds, but, by miftake, they proved a bad fort of *rave*, and not comparable to our turnips, as I found, by fowing them at Bradfield.

ALSACE.—*Saverne to Wiltenheim.*—Many cabbages, but full of weeds.

Strafbourg.—Crops to a great weight, but only for four-crout.

Scheleftat.—The quantity increafes between Benfeldt and Scheleftat. Their culture is, to fow the feed on a bed in March, covered with mats, like tobacco, and tranfplant in June, 2000 to 3000 plants on an arpent; they make a hole with a fpade, which they fill with water, and then plant: they never horfe-hoe, yet the diftance would admit it well. They are in fize 10 lb. or 12 lb. and fome

I 2

20 lb.;

20 lb.; the hearts are for four-crout, but the leaves for cows. An arpent is worth 303 liv. (20l. 15s. 10d. per Englifh acre); but carriage to a town is to be deducted.

The culture of cabbages, for cattle, is one of the moft important objects in Englifh agriculture; without which, large ftocks of cattle or fheep are not to be kept on foils improper for turnips. They are, in every refpect but one, preferable to that root; the only inferiority is, that of cabbages demanding dung on all foils, whereas good land will yield turnips without manuring. Great attention ought to be paid to the full introduction of these two crops, without which we may venture to predict, that the agriculture of France will continue poor and unproductive, for want of its due ftock of cattle and fheep.

Clover.

ISLE OF FRANCE.—*Liancourt.*—Never cultivate it for its place in a rotation, but merely for forage, like lucerne; have a barbarous cuftom of fowing it without tillage on wheat ftubbles, and it lafts fo fometimes two years.

ARTOIS.—*Recouffe.*—Monf. Drinkbierre, a very intelligent farmer here, af-fured me, that clover exhaufted and fpoiled the land, and that wheat after it was never fo good as after a fallow; but as the clover is fown with a fecond, and even a third corn crop, no wonder therefore that it fouls land.

I could add many other notes on this fubject, but will be content to mention, in general, that the introduction of clover, wherever I have met with it, has been commonly effected in fuch a manner that very little benefit is to be ex-pected from it. All good farmers in England know, from long experience, that the common red clover is no friend to clean farming, if fown with a fecond or third crop of corn. In the courfe, 1, turnips or cabbages; 2, barley or oats; 3, clover; 4, wheat: the land is kept in garden order. But if after that fourth crop, the farmer goes on and fows, 5, barley or oats; 6, clover; 7, wheat, the land will be both foul and exhaufted. In a word, clover is beneficial to the really good and clean farmer only to the extent of his turnips, cabbages, and fal-low; and never ought to be fown but on land previoufly cleaned by thofe hoeing crops, or by fallow. As to fallow, no Frenchman ever makes it but for wheat, confequently the culture of clover is excluded. I have often feen it fown in this courfe; 1, fallow; 2, wheat; 3, barley; 4, oats; 5, clover; 6, clover; 7, wheat; 8, oats; and the land inevitably full of weeds. I may venture to af-fert, that clover thus introduced, or even in courfes lefs reprehenfible, but not correct, will do more mifchief than good, and that a country is better cultivated without than with it. Hence, therefore, let the men, emulous of the character of good farmers, confider it as effential to good hufbandry to have no more

clover

clover than they have turnips and cabbages, or some other crop that answers the same end; and never to sow it but with the first crop of corn; by these means their land will be clean, and they will reap the benefits of the culture without the common evils.

I have read in some authors, an account of great German farmers having such immense quantities of clover, as are sufficient to prove the utter impossibility of a due preparation: these quantities are made a matter of boast. We know, however, in England, in what manner to appreciate such extents of clover.

Chefnuts.

BERRY.—*La Marche.*—First meet with them on entering La Marche.

Boifmandé.—They are spread over all the country; the fruit are sold, according to the year, from 5*f.* to 10*f.* and 15*f.* the boiseau, which measure will feed a man three days: they rub off the skin; boil them in water with some salt; squeeze them into a kind of paste, which they dry by the fire; they commend this food as pleasant and wholesome. The small ones are given to pigs, but will not fatten them so well as acorns, the bacon being soft; when fattened with acorns, they are finished with a little corn. A chesnut tree gives two boiseau each of fruit on an average; a good one, five or six. The timber is excellent for building; I measured the area spread by many of them, and found it 25 feet every way. Each tree, therefore, occupies 625 feet, and an acre fully planted would contain 70; at two boiseau each it is 140, which, at 10*f.* is 2l. 18s. 4d. and as one of these measures will feed a man three days, an acre would support a man four hundred and twenty days, or fourteen months. It must, however, be obvious, that land cannot be so exactly filled, and that an acre of land would not probably, in common, do for half that number.

La Villeaubrun.—They eat many chesnuts, but do not live upon them, eating some bread also; in which mode of confuming a boiseau, it will last a man five or six days. Price as above.

LIMOUSIN.—*Limoges.*—Price 7*f.* to 15*f.* the boiseau. This food, though general in the country, would not be sufficient alone; the poor eat therefore some rye bread. The comfort of them to families is very great, for there is no limit in the consumption, as of every thing else: the children eat them all day long; and in seasons when there are no chesnuts there is often great distress among the poor—The exact transcript of potatoes in Ireland. The method of cooking chesnuts here, is to take off the outward skin, and to put a large quantity into a boiler, with a handful of salt, and very little water, to yield steam; they cover it as closely as possible, to keep in the steam: if much water is added, they

lose

lofe their flavour and nourifhing quality. An arpent under chefnuts does not yield a product equal to a good arpent of corn, but more than a bad one.

To Magnac.—They are fpread over all the arable fields.

QUERCY.—*Brive to Noailles.*—Ditto; but after Noailles there are no more.

Payrac.—Boil them for their food, as above defcribed.

LANGUEDOC.—*Gange.*—Many in the mountains; and exceedingly fine chef-nut underwood.

POITOU.—*Ruffec.*—Yields a good crop, to the amount even of 10 liv. for a good tree's produce. The poor people live on them. A meafure of 45 lb. has been fold this year at 48 f.

BRETAGNE.—*Pont Orfon.*—On entering this province, thefe trees immediately occur, for there are none on the Normandy fide of the river, that parts the two provinces.

MAINE.—*La Fleche to Le Mans.*—Many chefnuts, the produce chiefly fold to towns; the poor people here not living on them with any regularity: three bufhels (each holding 30 lb of wheat) are a good crop for one tree, and fell at 40 f. the bufhel; this is more than a mean produce, but not an extraordinary one. The number here is very great; and trees, but of a few years growth, are well loaded.

VIVARAIS.—*Pradelles to Thuytz.*—Immenfe quantities of thefe trees on the mountains; it is the greateft chefnut region I have feen in France. The poor people live on them boiled; and they fell, by meafure, at the price of rye.

The hufbandry of fpreading chefnuts over arable lands muft unqueftionably be very bad; the corn muft fuffer greatly, and the plough be much impeded. It is as eafy to have thefe trees upon grafs land, where they would be compara-tively harmlefs: but the fact is here, as is fo general in France, that they have no paftures which the plough does not occupy by turns; all, except rich mea-dows, being arable. The fruit is fo great a refource for the poor, that planting thefe trees upon lands not capable of tillage by the plough, is a very confiderable improvement: the mountains of the Vivarais thus are made productive in the beft method perhaps that they admit.

Chicory.

ISLE OF FRANCE.—*Dugny.*—Monf. Cretté de Paleuel, 1787, had this plant recommended to him by the Royal Society of Paris; in confequence of which, he has made feveral very fuccefsful experiments on it. He has had it two years under cultivation. The feed is fown in March, 12 lb. per arpent (100 perches at 18 feet) on one ploughing, and is harrowed in. It rifes fo thick, as to cover the whole ground, and is mown the fame year once; Monf. Cretté has cut one

piece

piece twice the firſt year. The following winter he dunged it, at the rate of eight loads, of three horſes, per arpent. The year after, ſome was cut three times, and ſome four; and Monſ. Cretté remarks, that the oftener the better, becauſe more herbaceous and the ſtalks not ſo hard. He weighed the crop upon one piece, and found the weight, green,

		lb.
Of the firſt cutting,	- - -	55,000
ſecond,	- - - -	18,000
third,	- - - -	3,000
Per arpent,	- -	76,000

By making ſome of it into hay, he found that it loſt three-fourths of its weight in drying, conſequently the arpent gave 19,000 lb. of hay, or 10 tons per Engliſh acre. It is ſo ſucculent and herbaceous a plant, as to dry with difficulty, if the weather be not very fine; but the hay, he thinks, is equal to that of clover, though inferior to meadow hay. He has uſed much in ſoiling, and with great ſucceſs, for horſes, cows, young cattle, and calves; finds it to be eaten greedily by all, and to give very good cream and butter. Monſ. Cretté's fine dairy of cows being in their ſtalls, he ordered them to be fed with it in my preſence; and they ate all that was given, with great avidity. When in hay, it is moſt preferred by ſheep; cows do not, in that ſtate, eat the ſtalks ſo well as ſheep. A circumſtance which he conſiders as valuable, is its not being hurt by drought ſo much as moſt other plants; and he informs me, but not on his own experience, that it will laſt good ten years.

I viewed one of his crops, of ſeven or eight arpents, ſown laſt ſpring, and which has been mown once; I found it truly beautiful. He ſowed common clover and ſainfoin among it, and altogether it afforded a very fine fleece of herbage, about eight or nine inches high (October 28) which he intends feeding this autumn with his ſheep. He is of opinion that the ſainfoin will be quite ſuffocated, and that the chicory will get the better of the clover.

Provence.—*Vaucluſe to Orgon.*—In a very fine watered meadow, one-third of the herbage is this plant.

I liked the appearance of this plant ſo well in France, and was ſo perfectly ſatisfied with what I ſaw of it, cultivated by Monſ. Cretté de Paleuel, and growing ſpontaneouſly in the meadows, that I brought ſeed of it to England; and have cultivated it largely at Bradfield, with ſuch ſucceſs, that I think it one of the beſt preſents France ever made to this kingdom. I ſow it with corn like clover; but it pays well for occupying the land entirely. It will prove, without doubt, a very valuable plant for laying land permanently to graſs; and alſo for introducing, in courſes of crops, when the land wants reſt for three, four, or

five

five years. I am much miſtaken if we do not in a few years make a much greater progreſs in the culture of this plant than the French themſelves, from whom we borrowed it, will do.

Sheep are ſaid to be very fond of it*, a fact I have ſufficiently proved in Suffolk. From a paſſage in an Italian author, who ſpeaks of ſowing the wild chicory, I am in doubt whether the French have the honour of being really the firſt introducers of this plant†.

Coleſeed.

FLANDERS.—*Cambray.*—Near this town, I met firſt with the culture of coleſeed: they call it *gozá.* Sow the ſeed thick on a ſeed-bed, for tanſplanting; ſetting it out on an oat ſtubble, after one ploughing. This is ſo great and ſtriking an improvement of our culture of the ſame plant, that it merits the utmoſt attention ; for ſaving a whole year is an object of the firſt conſequence. The tranſplanting is not performed till October, and laſts all November, if no froſt ; and at ſuch a ſeaſon there is no danger of the plants not ſucceeding: earlier would however ſurely be better, to enable them to be ſtronger rooted, to withſtand the ſpring froſts, which often deſtroy them ; but the object is not to give their attention to this buſineſs till every thing that concerns wheat ſowing is over. The plants are large, and two feet long ; a man makes the holes with a large dibble, like the potatoe one uſed on the Eſſex ſide of London, and men and women fix the plants, at 18 inches by 10 inches ; ſome at a foot ſquare, for which they are paid 9 liv. per manco of land. The culture is ſo common all the way to Valenciennes, that there are pieces of two, three, and four acres of ſeedbed, now cleared, or clearing, for planting. The crop is reckoned very uncertain ; ſometimes it pays nothing, but in a good year up to 300 liv. the arpent (100 perches of 24 feet) or 8l. 15s. the Engliſh acre. They make the crop in July, and, by manuring the land, get good wheat.

Valenciennes to Orchies.—This is a more valuable crop than wheat, if it ſucceeds ; but it is very uncertain. All tranſplanted.

Lille.—The number of mills, near Lille, for beating coleſeed, is ſurpriſing, and proves the immenſe quantity of this plant that is cultivated in the neighbourhood. I counted ſixty at no great diſtance from each other.

Bailleul.—The quantity cultivated through this country immenſe ; all tranſplanted ; it occurs once in a courſe of ſix or ſeven years. Price of the cakes, 3½ſ. each ; they are the ſame ſize as ours in England.

---

* *Phytographie Oeconmique de la Loraine,* Par M. Willemet. 1780. 8vo. P. 57.
† *Ronconi Dizionario D'Agricoltura o ſia La Coltivazione Italiana.* Tom. ii. P. 148.

ARTOIS.

ARTOIS.—*St. Omers.*—Great ftacks of colefeed ftraw all over the country (Auguft 7th) bound in bundles, and therefore applied to ufe.

I fhould remark, in general, that I never met with colefeed cultivated in any part of the kingdom merely for fheep-feed; yet it is an object, fo applied, of great confequence, and would be particularly ufeful in France, where the operofe cultures of turnips and cabbages will be long eftablifhing themfelves. With this view colefeed fhould be thus introduced:

1. Winter tares, fown the begnining of September on a wheat ftubble; mown for foiling: then the land ploughed and colefeed harrowed in.
2. Barley, or oats.
3. Clover.
4. Wheat.

Fuller's Thiftle.

ISLE OF FRANCE.—*Liancourt.*—Very profitable: has been known to amount to 300 liv. or 400 liv. the arpent (about 1½ acre).

Furz.

GASCOIGN—*St. Palais to Anspan.*—A practice in these mountainous waftes, which deferves attention, is their cutting furz when in bloffom, and chopping them mixed with ftraw for horfes, &c.; and they find that no food is more hearty or nourifhing.

NORMANDIE.—*Vologne to Cherbourg.*—Throughout this country a fcattering of furz fown as a crop, with wheat or barley, as clover is ufually fown : the third year they cut it to bruife for horfes; and every year afterwards : and it yields thus a produce of 40 liv. the vergé, of 96 Englifh perch.

BRETAGNE.—*St. Pol Leon.*—Through all this bifhopric the horfes are fed with it bruifed, and it is well known to be a moft nourifhing food.

The practice here minuted is not abfolutely unknown in England; there are many traces of it in Wales, and fome other parts of the kingdom. I have been affured that an acre, well and evenly feeded, and mown for horfes every year, has yielded an annual produce, worth, on a moderate eftimate, 10l. but I never tried it, which was a great neglect, in Hertfordfhire, for I had there land that was proper for it.

Culture of Hemp and Flax.

PICARDIE.—*Montreuil to Picquigny.*—Small patches of flax all the way. At Picquigny, a good deal of land ploughing for hemp, to be fown in a week (May 22).

QUERCY—The hemp, in much of this province, is fown every year on the fame fpots; and very often highly manured. This appears to be an erroneous fyftem, wherever the lands in general are good enough to yield it.

Cauffade.—Vaft quantities near this place, now (June 12,) two or three feet high.

LANGUEDOC.—*Monrejeau.*—Flax now (Auguft 10) graffing.

Bagnere de Bigore to Lourd.—Never water their flax, only grafs it. I faw much with the grafs grown through it; if the land or weather be tolerably wet, three weeks are fufficient.

GUIENNE.—*Port de Leyrac.*—This noble vale of the Garonne, which is one of the richeft diftricts of France, is alfo one of the moft productive in hemp that is to be found in the kingdom.

Agen.—Hemp yields 10 quintals per carterée, at 40 liv. the quintal, *poid de table* (17l. 10s.), which carterée is fown with 217 lb. of wheat. This is probably about 1½ Englifh acre.

Aguillon.—The hemp is every where watering in the Garonne: they do not leave it in more than three or four days.

Tonneins.—The whole country, from Aguillon to this place, is all under either hemp or wheat, with exception of fome maiz; and its numerous population feems now employed on hemp.

La Morte Landron.—It yields 10 to 12 quintals, at 36 liv. to 45 liv. the quintal.

SOISSONOIS.—*Coucy.*—Hemp cultivated in the rich vales, in the courfe,— 1, hemp; 2, wheat. It yields 500 bottes, at 25 liv. the hundred, reckoned on the foot before watering.

St. Amand.—The carterée of land, of 100 verge of 19 feet (36,100 feet), under flax, has this year a very good crop, on account of the rainy weather; it has been fold at 1200 liv. or very near the fee fimple of the land (55l. 11s. 3d. per Englifh acre). This amazing value of flax made me defirous of knowing if it depended on foil, or on management. Sir Richard Wefton, in the laft century, who has been copied by many fcores of writers fince, fpeaks of poor fandy land as being the beft for that flax of which the fine Bruffels lace is made; confequently this is made from land abundantly different from what produces the Valenciennes laces, if that affertion were ever true. The foil at St. Amand is a

deep

a deep moist friable loamy clay, of vast fertility, and situated in a district where the greatest possible use is made of manures; it therefore abounds very much with vegetable mould. Flax is sown on the same land, once in twelve to fifteen years; but in Austrian Flanders, once in seven or eight years. Advancing, and repeating my inquiries, I was assured that flax had been raised to the amount of 2000 liv. the carterée (92l. 15s. 6d. per English acre). The land is nearly the same as above described, and lets, when rented, at 36 liv. the carterée (1l. 13s. 3d. per English acre). They sow 2 *raziere* of seed, each holding 50 lb. of wheat per carterée; and a middling crop of good flax is from 3½ to 4 feet high, and extremely thick. They water it in ditches, ten, twelve, and fourteen days, according to the season; the hotter the weather, the sooner it is in a proper state of putrefaction. After watering, they always grass it in the common method.

Going on, and gleaning fresh information, I learned that 1200 liv. may be esteemed a great produce per carterée; the land all round, good and bad, of a whole farm letting at 30 liv. and selling at 1200 liv. Nothing can shew more attention than their cultivation: besides weeding it with the greatest care, while young, they place poles, or forked stakes, amongst it, when at a proper height, in order to prevent its being beaten to the ground by rain, from its own length and weight; without this precaution it would be flat down, even to rotting.

Orchies.—A carterée of flax, of 40,000 feet, rises to the value of 1500 liv. and even more (63l. 18s. 9d. per English acre). They sow such as is intended for fine thread, as soon as the frosts are over, which is in March; but such as is for coarser works, so late as May. Never feed their own flax, always using that of Riga. They prefer for it, an oat-stubble that followed clover; and they manure for it in the winter preceding the sowing. Wheat is, in general, better after flax than after hemp.

Lille.—Flax, in common, is worth 90 liv. the *centier*, or 360 liv. the carterée (15l. 6s. 3d. per English acre): this is excluding uncommon crops.

ARTOIS.—*Lillers.*—Flax all through the country, and exceedingly fine. Sow wheat after it.

Betbune.—An arpent of good flax worth more than one of wheat; yet *good* wheat is worth 200 liv.

Beauval.—Flax sometimes worth 500 liv. the journal (25l. 17s. 11d. per English acre). Hemp does not equal it. They do not water flax here, only spread it on grass or stubbles.

NORMANDIE.—*Bolbec to Harfleur.*—Flax not watered, but spread on stubble.

BRETAGNE.—Throughout this province, they every where cultivate flax, in patches, by every family, for domestic employment.

K 2

Ancenis.

Ancenis.—The culture of flax is generally, throughout the kingdom, as well as in the greateſt part of Europe, that of a ſpring crop; but here it is ſown in autumn. They are now working the wheat-ſtubbles on one ploughing, very fine, with a ſtout bident-hoe, and ſowing them: ſome is up. It is pulled in Auguſt, and wheat ſown after it.

A N J O U.—*Migniame.*—They have winter-ſown flax all over the country. The value of the crop exceeds that of wheat. They do not water, only graſs it; yet admit that watering makes it whiter and finer.

Turbilly.—Hemp is ſown in patches every where through the country; ſells at 8ſ. the pound, raw; ſpun, at 26ſ. and 27ſ.; bleached, at 30ſ. to 36ſ. The crop is 30 to 40 weights, each 15 lb. or 16 lb. per journal, or about 210 liv.

M A I N E.—*Gueſceland.*—Through all this country there is much hemp ſown every year, on the ſame ſpot; ſpun; and made, by domeſtic fabrics, into cloth, for home uſes. Spinning is 10ſ. the pound; and it is an uncommon ſpinner that can do a pound in a day; in common but half a pound.

L O R A I N E.—*Luneville.*—Hemp is cultivated every where in the province, on rich ſpots; hence there is much of it; and ſome villages have been known to make a thouſand crowns in a year of their thread and linen. If it is wiſhed that the hemp be very fine, they do not water, but only ſpread it on the graſs; but, in general, water it. Uſe their own ſeed, and furniſh much to their neighbours; but have that of flax from Flanders. Sow beans among flax, for ſupporting it; others do this with ſmall boughs of trees. Some alſo ſow carrots among their flax; which practice, I ſuppoſe, they borrowed from Flanders. Hemp is always dunged, and always ſown on the ſame ſpots, which ſell at the ſame price as gardens; a common and execrable practice in France. A journal gives, on good land, 95 lb. and 103 lb. of *toup*; price laſt year, ready for ſpinning, 16ſ. the lb.; the *toup* 11ſ. now higher: alſo 2 *razeau* of ſeed (each 180lb. of wheat). The journal equals 65 Engliſh perches.

A L S A C E.—*Straſbourg.*—Product 3 quintals, at 27 liv. the quintal, the arpent (5l. 12s. per Engliſh acre).

Scheleſtat.—Produce 2 quintals, ready for ſpinning, at 36 liv. to 48 liv. the quintal (5l. 16s. 3d. per Engliſh acre). Water it for cordage, but not for linen; graſs it only, as whiter.

A U V E R G N E.—*Clermont.*—In the mountains; price of hemp, ready to ſpin, 15ſ. to 18ſ. the lb.; ſpun, 24ſ. fine, 30ſ.

Izoir.—Produce of hemp, per cartona, 150lb. rough, at 5ſ. the lb. which is 113lb. ready for ſpinning; but bad hemp loſes more. The ſeterée is 8 cartoni, of 150 toiſes, or 43,200 feet. Hemp grounds ſell equally with gardens (11l. 11s. 6d. per Engliſh acre).

Briude.

Briude.—Hemp yields a quintal, raw, per cartona ; female is worth 40 liv. the quintal, male, 30 liv. ; alfo 8 coups of feed, at 6 f. Average produce 35 liv. or 36 liv. in all.

DAUPHINE.—*Loriol.*—Chinefe hemp fucceeds well with Monf. Faujas de St. Fond, and perfects its feed, which it rarely does in the King's garden, at Paris. He thinks it an error to fow it, like other hemp, in the fpring ; for he is of opinion, that it would feed even in England, if fown in autumn. He has found, by experiment, that it is excellent for length and ftrength, if fown thick enough to prevent its fpreading laterally, and to make it rife without branching.

PROVENCE.—*Marfeilles.*—Price of hemp: Riga, firft quality, 36 liv. the quintal ; ditto, fecond quality, 33 liv. Ancona, firft quality, 33 liv. ; ditto, fecond quality, 30 liv. to 31 liv. Piedmont, 3 group, 26 liv.; 4 group, 28 liv.

From thefe notes it appears, that hemp or flax is cultivated in fmall quantities, through every part of France : generally for the ufes of domeftic manufactures among the lower claffes. A very interefting political queftion arifes on thofe diffufed fabrics, and on which I fhall offer a few obfervations under the chapter of manufactures.

Madder.

ALSACE.—*Srafbourg Fertenheim.*—Much of this plant is cultivated in various parts of Alface, where the foil is very deep and rich, efpecially on that which they call *limoneufe*, from its having been depofited by the river. They dig the land for it three feet deep, and manure highly : the rows are fix to nine inches afunder, and they hoe it clean thrice a fummer. The produce of an arpent, of 24,000 feet, is 40 quintals green, before drying, and the mean price 6 liv. the quintal (16l. 12s. 6d. per Englifh acre). Such is the account I received at Strafbourg ; but I know enough of this plant, by experience, to conclude, that fuch a produce is abfolutely inadequate to the expences of the culture, and therefore the crop is probably larger than here ftated ; not that the low rate of labour fhould be forgotten.

DAUPHINE.—*Piere Latte.*—Planted here in beds, ; but it is very poor, and apparently in a foil not rich enough.

To Orange.—Much ditto ; all on flat beds, with trenches between, but weedy and ill cultivated. The price is 27 liv. the quintal, dry. Some juft planted, and the trenches very fhallow: dig at three years old. Price 24 liv. the quintal, dried in the fun. The roots are fmall and poor.

Avignon.—Price 24 liv. to 30 liv. but there is no profit if it be under 50 liv. It is three years in the land. Sow wheat after it ; but if it were not well dunged

the

the crop is poor. A good deal on flat beds, 8 feet wide, with trenches between, two broad and two deep, which are digged gradually for spreading on it.

Lille.—An eymena in three years gives 5 quintals, at 20 liv. to 24 liv. the quintal, but a few years ago was 50 liv. to 70 liv. The expences are very high, 120 liv. At 4l. a cwt. which equals a French quintal, madder paid a proper profit for inducing many English cultivators to enter largely into it; but falling to 40s. and 50s. per cwt. some were ruined, and the rest immediately withdrew from it. But in France we find they carry on the culture; it is however weakly and poorly done; with so little vigour, that common crops, well managed, would pay much better.

Maiz.

The notes I took on the subject of this noble plant were very numerous; but as there is reason to believe that its culture cannot be introduced, with any prospect of advantage, in this island, I shall make but a few general observations on it.

In the paper on the climate of France, I have remarked, that this plant will not succeed, in common cultivation, north of Luneville and Ruffec, in a line drawn diagonally acrofs the kingdom; from which interesting fact, we may conclude, that a considerable degree of heat is necessary to its profitable cultivation, and that all ideas of introducing it into England, except as a matter of curiofity, would be vain. It demands a rich soil or plenty of manure, and thrives best on a friable sandy loam; but it is planted on all sorts of soils, except poor gravels. I have seen it on sands, in Guienne, that were not rich, but none is found on the granite gravels of the Bourbonnois, though that province is situated within the maiz climate. The usual culture is to give two or three ploughings to the land; sometimes one ploughing, and one working with the heavy bident-hoe;' and the feed is sown in rows at 2 feet or 2½, by 1½ or 2; sometimes in squares. Some I have seen near Bagnere de Bigore, in rows, at 3 feet, and 18 inches from plant to plant. The quantity of feed in Bearn, is the eighth part, by measure, of the quantity of wheat sown. It is universally kept clean by hoeing, in most districts, with such attention as to form a feature, in their husbandry, of capital merit. In August, they cut off all that part of the stalk and herbage which is above the ear, for feeding oxen, cows, &c. and it is perhaps the richest and most faccharine* provender that the climate of France affords; for wherever maiz is cultivated, no lean oxen are to be seen; all are in high order. The crop of grain is, on an average, double the quantity commonly

* A real fugar has been made from it. *Spec. de la Nature.* Vol. ii. p. 247.

reaped

reaped of wheat; about Navareen, in Bearn, more than that; and there the price (1787) is 54 *s.* to 55 *s.* the meafure, holding 36 lb. to 40 lb. of wheat; but in common years 18 *s.* to 20 *s.* Whether or not it exhaufts the land is a queſtion: I have been aſſured, in Languedoc, that it does not; but near Lourde, in Guienne, they think it exhaufts much. Every where the common management is to manure as highly as poſſible for it. In North America it is faid to exhauft confiderably * ; Monf. Parmentier contends for the contrary opinion + : whereever I found it, wheat fucceeds it, which ought to imply that it is not an exhauſting crop. The people in all the maiz provinces live upon it, and find it by far more nouriſhing than any bread, that of wheat alone excepted. Near Brive, in Quercy, I was informed that they mix one-third rye, and two-thirds maiz to make bread, and, though yellow and heavy, they fay it is very good food. A French writer fays, that, in Breſſe, maiz cakes coft 9¾ deniers the pound, but that a man eats double the quantity of what he does of bread made of wheat ‡. A late author contends, that it is to be claſſed among the moft wholefome articles of human food ‖.

Every one knows that it is much cultivated in North America; about Albany, in New York, it is faid to yield a hundred buſhels from two pecks of feed § ; and that it ſhoots again after being killed by the froft, even twice; that it withſtands the drought better than wheat *(this is queſtionable)*; does much better on loofe than on ſtiff foils, and not well at all on clay. In South Carolina it produces from 10 to 35 buſhels per acre ¶. On the Miſſiſſippi two negroes made 50 barrels, each 150 lb.** In Kongo, on the coaft of Africa, it is faid to yield three crops a year ++. According to another account, great care is taken to water it where the fituation will admit ‡‡; this I have feen in the Pyrennees; but moft of the maiz in France, even nineteen parts in twenty, are never watered. About Douzenac, in the Limoufin, they fow it thick to mow for foiling, and at Port St. Marie, on the Garonne, they do the fame, after the harveft of other grain, which is the moft profitable, and indeed admirable huſbandry. This is the only purpofe for which it can be cultivated in northern climates. It might be fown in England the firft week in June, and mown the end of Auguft, time enough to catch a late crop of turnips, or as a preparation for wheat.

* *Mitchel's Prefent State of Great Britain and N. America*, p. 157.   + *Memoire fur le Mais* 4to. 1785. P. 10.   ‡ *Obfervations fur l'Agriculture*, par M. Varenne de Fenille, p. 91. ‖ *Inftruction fur la Culture & les Ufages des Mais.* 8vo. 1786. P. 30.   § *Kalm's Travels in North America.* Vol. ii. p. 245.   ¶ *Defcription of South Carolina.* 8vo. 1761. P. 9. ** *Du Pratz Hiftory of Louifiana.* Vol. i. p. 306.   ++ *Modern Univ. Hift.* Vol. xvi. p. 25. ‡‡ *Mem. de l'Acad. des Sciences.* 1749. P. 471.

Muſtard.

Muſtard.

ISLE OF FRANCE.—*Petiviers.*—At Denainvilliers, near this place, I ſaw
them mowing muſtard, in full bloſſom, to feed cows with.

ARTOIS.—*Lillers.*—Much all the way to Bethune; ſow ſpring corn after it.

Orchards.

NORMANDIE.—*Falaiſe.*—Many apple and pear trees are ſcattered over the
country. They never plant them on the beſt lands, as they are convinced that
the damage to the corn, &c. is at leaſt equal to the value of the cyder; but on
the poorer ſoils they conſider it as an improvement, forming a fourth, or third,
and in ſome caſes even a half of the value of the land.

BRETAGNE.—*Doll.*—A cyder country; but reckon the trees at no real value
beyond that of the land, for they ſpoil as much as they produce.

Rennes.—A common proportion is to plant thirty trees upon a journal (about
five roods Engliſh), which, if well preſerved, will yield, on an average, 5 to 10
barriques of cyder every year; and the mean price 12 liv. the barrique, which is
120 pots; this year good orchards give 40 or 50 per journal, but they have
produced none, or next to none, for four years paſt. The damage the trees do
to the corn is ſo great, that, in common expreſſion, they ſay they get none.
The cyder is made by the preſs, which is of the ſame kind as Jerſey, I ſuppoſe,
brought from this country. The ground apples, and wheat or rye ſtraw, in
layers under the preſs, and reduced to ſuch a deſiccated ſtate that they will burn
freely immediately out of the preſs.

LORAINE.—*Blamon to Savern.*—The whole country ſpread with fruit trees,
apples, pears, &c. from 10 to 40 rod aſunder.

AUVERGNE.—*Vaires.*—The valley of this place, ſituated in the Limagne, ſo
famous in the volcanic hiſtory of France, is much noted for its fine apples, particularly the *rennet blanche*, the *rennet gris*, *calville*, and *apy*, all grafted on
crab ſtocks.

Olives.

ROUSSILLON.—*Bellegard to Perpignan.*—Reckoned to pay 1 liv. each tree.

Pia.—The land under them fallowed every other year, and ſown with corn:
they are pruned in the fallow year, yielding no fruit; a crop being only in the
corn year.

LANGUEDOC.—*Narbonne.*—Olives pay, in general, 3 liv. each tree per annum; ſome 5 liv. Many fields of them are planted in rows, at 12 yards by 10.

Beziers.

Beziers.—The trees on the farm, that was Monf. L'Abbé Rozier's, are 17 yards by 2.

Pinjean.—Some trees fo large and fine are known to give 84lb. of oil in a year, at 10*f.* the lb. or 42 liv.; but they reckon, in common, that good trees give 6 liv. one with another; this epithet *good,* fhews that the common average of all trees is much lower. In planting, if they mean to crop the land with corn, in the common manner, that is, one year in two, the other fallow, they put 100 trees on 8 feterées of land; but if they intend to have no corn at all, the fame number on 4 feterées: under corn, the 8 feterées yield 40 feptiers of corn, each 100 lb. at 9 liv. (7s. 10½d.). The feterée is about half an acre, as I con-clude, from the beft intelligence I could procure. This proportion is 100 trees on four Englifh acres, or 25 per acre: if they were all good, the produce in oil would be 150 liv. and of wheat 90 liv.—in all 240 liv. or 10l. 10s.; the half only of which is annual produce, or 5l. 5s. which feems not to be any thing very great, even fuppofing the trees to be all good, which muft be far from the fact.

Montpellier to Nifmes.—The trees are 3 rods afunder, by 1½; alfo 2 by 1½; both among vines; alfo 2 fquare; alfo 1 by 1½.

Pont de Gard.—Planted at 1 rod and 1½; their heads almoft join. They are all pruned to flat round heads, the centre of the tree cut out, cup-fafhion; and thefe formal figures add to the uglinefs of the tree.

VIVARAIS.—*Aubenas.*—In paffing fouth from Auvergne, here the firft olives are met with.

DAUPHINE.—*Piere Latte to Avignon.*—Many; but feven-eighths dead from the froft, and many grubbing up.

PROVENCE.—*Aix.*—Land planted with olives fells at 1000 liv. the carterée, whilft arable only 600 liv. but meadows watered 1200 liv. Clear profit of a carterée of olives, 40 liv. (21,600 feet, at 40 liv. it is 3l. 2s. 1d. per Englifh acre). Gathering the olives 40 liv. 10*f.* the quintal: preffing 2 liv.: cultiva-tion 18 liv. the carterée: the wood pays the pruning.

Tour d'Aigues.—The olive, pomegranate, and other *bard* trees, as they are called here, bear fruit only at the end of the branches; whence, they conceive, refults the neceffity of their being pruned every other year. Thirty years ago, the common calculation of the produce, per olive, was 5*f.*; but now, the price being double, it may be fuppofed 10*f.*

Toulon.—They have great trees in this neighbourhood that are known to yield 20 liv. to 30 liv. a tree, when they give a crop, which is once in two years, and fometimes once in three. Small trees yield 3 liv. 5 liv. and 6 liv. each, and are much more profitable than mulberries, for which tree the foil is too dry and ftoney. Olives demand as great an expence in buildings, preffes, coppers, backs, &c. as vines. Preffing comes to 3 liv. a barrel. Crop of a large tree, 8 to 10 pannaux. Olives, in Provence, never pruned into the hollow cup-form, which is fo general in Languedoc: they appear here in their natural form.

Hyeres.—They produce confiderably in twenty or thirty years, and fome have been known to be a hundred years old. I faw, going to *Notre Dame*, fome that refifted the froft of 1709. A good tree, of thirty years, gives, when it bears, 3 pannaux of olives; the pannaux holds 30 lb. to 32 lb. of wheat, and the common price is 24 f. the pannaux. They have great trees, that give a *mot*, or 20 pannaux, or 24 liv. each tree. When fields, planted with olives, are bought, they are meafured by the fquare canne or toife; a canne of good land, well planted, 30 f.; middling, 20 f.; bad, 10 f.; but there are fome that fell to 60 f.; confequently a middling arpent is 900 liv.

Antibes.—The largeft trees I have feen in France are between this place and the Var, as if the near approach to Italy marked a vegetation unknown in the reft of the kingdom.

The culture of this tree is found in fo fmall a part of France, that the object is not of very great confequence to the kingdom ; one fhould, however, remark, that in Provence, where the beft oil in Europe is made, there might be twenty trees to one that is found there ; whence we may conclude, that if it were fo profitable a hufbandry, as fome authors have reprefented, they would be multiplied more. The moft important point is, their thriving upon rocky foils and declivities, impenetrable to the plough ; in which fpots too much encouragement cannot be given to their culture.

Oranges.

Provence.—*Hyeres.*—This is, I believe, the only fpot in France where oranges are met with in the open air: a proof that the climate is more temperate than Rouffillon, which is more to the fouth; the Pyrennees are between that province and the fun; but Hyeres lies open to the fea; fo indeed does the coaft of Languedoc; and fo does Antibes; but there is a peculiarity of fhelter at Hyeres, from the pofition of the mountains, that gives this place the advantage. I always, however, doubt whether experiments have been made with fufficient attention, when thefe nice difcriminations are pretended, that are fo often taken on truft without fufficient trial. The dreadful froft of laft winter, which deftroyed fo many olives, attacked the oranges alfo, which were cut down in great numbers, or reduced to the mere trunk ; moft of them, however, have made confiderable fhoots, and will therefore recover.

The King's garden here, in the occupation of Monf. Fine, produced, laft year, 21,000 liv. in oranges only, and the people that bought them made as much by the bargain; the other fruits yielded 700 liv. or 800 liv.: the extent of
this

this garden is 12 arpents; this 1808 liv. per arpent, besides the profit (94l. 7s. 7d. per English acre). A fine tree will produce 1000 oranges, and the price is 20 liv. to 25 liv. the 1000, for the best; 15 liv. the middling; 10 liv. the small. There are trees here that have produced to the value of two louis each; and what is a more convincing proof of great profit, a small one, of no more than seven or eight years, will yield to the value of 3 liv. in a common year. They are planted from the nursery at two or three years old, and at that age are sold at 30*f.* each; and it is thought that the flowers, sold for distilling, pay all the expences of cultivation; they must, however, be planted on land capable of irrigation, for if water be not at command, the produce is small.

Pomegranates.

PROVENCE.—*Hyeres.*—The hedges are full of them, and they are planted singly, and of small growth: the largest fruit sell at 3*f.* or 4*f.* each; middling, 1*f.*; little ones, 1 liard. A good tree, of ten or fifteen years, will give to the value of 2 liv. or 3 liv. a year.

Pines.

GASCOIGN.—*Bayonne.*—The great product of the immense range of waste, as it is commonly called, *landes,* is resin: the *pinus maritimus* is regularly tapped, and yields a produce, with as much regularity as any other crop, in much better soils. I counted from fifty to eighty trees per acre, in some parts; but in others, from ten to forty; those with incisions for the resin are from 9 to 16 inches diameter. Some good common oak on this sand, 12 to 14 inches diameter, but with bodies not longer than from 8 to 10 or 12 feet.

St. Vincent's.—Here pines are cut for resin, at the age of fifteen to twenty years; the first year at about 2 feet from the ground, the second to 4 feet, the third to 6 feet, and the fourth to 8 or 9 feet; and then they begin again at bottom, on another side of the tree, and continue thus for 100 years: the annual value per annum in resin, 4*f.* or 5*f.* When they yield no longer, they cut into good plank, not being spoiled by tapping. Much tar also is made, chiefly of the roots. Cork trees are barked once in seven years, and yield then about 15*f.* or about 2*f.* per annum. Men are appointed, each to a certain number of trees, to collect the resin, with spoons, out of the notches, cut at the but-end of the tree to receive it.

Dax.—Pines pay 4*f.* a year in resin. Pine woods, with a good succession of young ones; from 1½ rod to 3 asunder.

Tartas.—Several persons united in asserting, that the pines give, one with [another, 4*f.* to 5*f.* each, from 15 to 100 years old, and are then sold, on an

L 2

average, at 3 liv. each ; that taking the refin was fo far from fpoiling the tree, that it was the better, and cut into better planks. This furprifing me, I fought a carpenter, and he confirmed it*. They added, that an arpent of pines was worth more than an arpent of any other land in the country ; more even than of vines: that it would fell, according to the trees, from 500 liv. to 1000 liv. while the inclofed and cultivated fands would not yield more than 300 liv. or, at moft, than 400 liv. The arpent, I found, by meafuring a piece of 2 arpents, to be 3366 Englifh yards (500 liv. is 31l. 10s. per Englifh acre).

St. Severe.—Pafs feveral inclofures of fandy land, refembling the adjoining waftes, fown with pines as a crop; they are now of various heights; and very thick. See fome very good chefnut underwood on a white fand.

Guienne.—*Langon.*—Many of the props ufed for their vines here, are young pines, the thinnings of the new fown ones; are fold for 36 liv. to 40 liv. the thoufand, or twenty bundles, each fifty pines.

Cubfac to Cavignac.—On the pooreft lands fow pines, which are not an unprofitable article of culture. At five years old they begin to thin them for vine props; and the fmall branches are fold in faggots. At fifteen years the produce is more confiderable; and at twenty-five the beft trees make boards for heading cafks. I faw a journal and half, the boards of which yielded 1200 liv. They fow 135 lb. of wheat feed on a journal. Several crops of fown pines very thick.

Bretagne.—*Quimperley to L'Orient.*—Pines abound in this country, and feem to have fown themfelves all around; but none are cut for refin.

To Vannes.—Such a fcattering of them, that I apprehend all this country was once pine land.

Auvergne.—*St. George.*—In the mountains, fee immenfe pine planks laid by way of fences, not lefs than 60 feet long, and 2 and 2½ broad.

Fix.—Dr. Coiffier has them in the mountains 80 feet high, and 10 feet round.

Provence.—*Cuges to Toulon.*—In the rocky mountains of this coaft, there are pines, and fuch as are of any fize are cut for refin; but they ftand too thin to yield an acreable produce of any account.

Cavalero to Frejus.—The mountains here are covered chiefly with pines, and have a moft neglected defert appearance.

To Eftrelles.—The fame; and hacked and deftroyed almoft as badly as in the Pyrennees.

Pines are juftly efteemed a profitable crop *for the landlord*, for they yield a regular and certain revenue, at a very little charge; no repairs, and no lofles, by

---

* M. Secondat makes the fame obfervation, *Mem. fur l'Hift. Nat. du Chene.* Folio. 1785. P. 35. The fame affertion is made in *Mémoire fur l'Utilité du défrichement des Terres de Caftelnau-ée-Médoc.* 4to. 1791. *Réponfe au Rapport,* p. 27.

failure

(failure of tenants. But, in regard to the nation, pines, like moſt of the poor woods of France, ſhould be reckoned detrimental to the public intereſt, ſince a kingdom flouriſhes by *groſs produce,* and not by *rent.*

Poppies.

ARTOIS.—*Lillers.*—Much cultivated for oil: they are called here *zuliette.* Get as good wheat after them as after colefeed.

Aras.—Many here; they are reckoned to yield more money per arpent than wheat; equal to colefeed; which, however, is a very uncertain crop.

LORAINE.—*Nancy to Luneville.*—Some fine pieces on a poor gravel.

ALSACE.—*Savern to Wiltenheim.*—Many poppies; ſome fine crops, and very clean.

Straſbourg.—Product three ſacks, at 24 liv. per arpent, of 24,000 ſquare feet (4l. 19s. 9d. per Engliſh acre). Manure for them, and ſow wheat after.

Our ideas of the exhauſting quality of certain plants, are, at preſent, founded, I believe, but upon that half-information which is ſcarcely a degree above real ignorance. It is a common obſervation, that all plants whoſe ſeeds yield oil, are exhauſters of ſoil; an obſervation that has ariſen, from the theory of oil being the food of plants. Experiments upon both have been ſo few and unſatisfactory, as to be utterly inſufficient for the foundation of any theory. Colefeed, ſeeded in England, is almoſt generally made a preparation for wheat; ſo it is in France, and we here find the ſame effect with poppies. It can hardly be believed, that wheat, which demands land in heart as much as almoſt any other crop, ſhould be made to follow ſuch exhauſting plants as the theory of oil would make one believe theſe to be; it is the organization of the plant alone that converts the nouriſhment into oil; which, in one plant, turns it to a ſaccharine ſubſtance, and, in another, to an acid one; but the idea that plants are fed by oil, and that they exhauſt in proportion to their oil, is abſolutely condemned by the olive, which yields more oil than any other plant, and yet thrives beſt on dry arid rocky ſoils, of abſolute poverty, as far as oil is concerned. We ſhall be wholly in the dark in this part of agriculture, treated as a ſcience, till experiments have been greatly multiplied.

Potatoes.

ANJOU.—*Angers to La Fleche.*—More than is common in France.

LORAINE.—*Pont a Mouſon.*—Throughout all this part of Loraine there are more potatoes than I have ſeen any where in France; twelve acres were at once under the eye.

To

To Nancy.—Many cultivated through all this country, but degenerated, by being sown too often on the same land; and for want of new sorts. A journal yields 20 toulins, or about 24 bushels English; and 2½ journals are equal to an arpent de France, which makes the acreable produce miserable. Price now, 3 liv. the toulin; was only 25*s.*

Luneville—More still; they plant them, after one ploughing, in April: for seed, cut the large ones only; but sell the smaller ones uncut. Always dung much. Every man that has a cow, keeps the dung carefully for this crop; and such as have no land, plant on other people's, without paying rent, that being the preparation for wheat: the crop of that grain is, however, very moderate, for the potatoe *pumps* much, to use the French expression,—*i. e.* exhausts greatly. Poor light soils answer best for them, as they are found not to do on strong land. Product per journal, 30 to 50 *rasaux*, which measure contains 180lb. of wheat. I found an exact journal, by stepping, to be 1974 English yards, or about 65 rods. At 40 *rasaux*, each 3 English bushels, it is nearly about 300 bushels English per acre. The price is now, 7 liv. the *razal*, heaped; when low, 3 liv.; and in common, 4 liv. 10*s.* The culture increases much.

ALSACE.—*Savern to Wiltenheim.*—Many, and good potatoes.

Strasbourg.—Produce of an arpent, of 24,000 feet, 75 sacks to 100, at 36*s.* to 60*s.* (at 2½ liv. and 90 sacks, it is 15l. 10s. 7d. per English acre). Sow wheat after them, if manured, otherwise barley. In the mountains they pare and burn for them.

Schelestat.—Produce 50 or 60 sacks, at 3 liv. but 4 liv. or 5 liv. sometimes (55 sacks, at 3½ liv. are 13l. 5s. 10d. per English acre). In planting, they think the difference is nothing, whether they be set cut or whole. The people eat them much.

Befort.—The culture continues to this place.

FRANCHE COMPTE.—*Besançon.*—And a scattering hither.

Orechamps.—Now lose the culture entirely.

AUVERGNE.—*Villeneuve.*—In these mountains they are cultivated in small quantities.

VELLAY.—*Le Puy to Pradelles.*—Ditto.

To Thuytz.—They are met with every where here.

DAUPHINE.—*St. Fond.*—Many are cultivated throughout the whole country; all planted whole; if sliced, in the common manner, they do not bear the drought so well. They are plagued with the curl.

These minutes shew, that it is in very few of the French provinces where this useful root is commonly found; in all the other parts of the kingdom, on inquiring for them, I was told, that the people would not touch them: experiments have been made, in many places, by gentlemen with a view to introduce

them

them for the poor, but no efforts could do it. The importance, however, would be infinite, for their use in a country in which famine makes its appearance almost periodically, arising from abfurd reftrictions on the corn trade. If potatoes were regularly cultivated for cattle, they would be ready for the poor, in cafe of very high prices of wheat; and fuch forced confumption would accuftom them gradually to this root; a practice in their domeftic œconomy, which would prevent much mifery, for want of bread. This object, like fo many others, can only be effected by the exhibition of a large farm, highly ftocked with cattle, by means of potatoes; and the benefit, in various ways, to the nation would make fuch an exhibition exceedingly advantageous. But fuch eftablifhments come not within the purview of princes or governments in this age: they muft be enveloped in the mift of fcience, and well garnifhed with the academicians of capitals, or nothing can be effected.

Racine de Difette.

Isle of France.—*Dugny.*—This plant, the *beta cycla altiffima* of Linnæus, Monf. Cretté de Paleuel has cultivated with attention: he has tried it by tranfplantation, as directed by Monf. l'Abbé de Commerell; alfo by fowing the feed broadcaft where it remains; and likewife feed by feed, in fquares of 15 inches; and this laft way he thinks is the beft and moft profitable. The common red beet, which he has in culture, he thinks yields a larger produce; but it does not yield fo many leaves as the other, which is ftripped thrice in the fummer by the hand, an operation which may anfwer where labour is exceffively cheap; but I have my doubts whether the value in England would equal the expence of gathering and carriage. Cows and hogs, Monf. Cretté has found, will eat the roots readily, but he has made no trial on it in fattening oxen or feeding fheep.

Alsace.—*Scheleftat.*—The culture is common in this country: I viewed three arpents belonging to the mafter of the poft, which were good and clean. They gather the leaves by hand for cows, and then return and gather again, and the roots are the beft food for them in winter; they come to 8 lb. and 10 lb. and are fown and planted like tobacco.

Rice.

Dauphine.—*Loriol.*—Sixty years ago the plain of Livron, one mile from Loriol, and half a league from St. Fond, more than a league long and a league broad, was all under rice, and fucceeded well, but prohibited by the parliament, becaufe prejudicial to health.

Saffron.

Saffron.

ANGOUMOIS.—*Angouleme.*—The beft land for this crop is reckoned that which is neither ftrong not ftoney, but rich and well worked; plant the rows fix inches afunder, and two inches from plant to plant; fow wheat over the planted land, and gather the Saffron among the wheat; bloffom at All-Saints, when they gather it. In a good year, and on good land, a journal yields 3 lb. which fells, when dear, at 30 liv. per lb. but is fometimes at 16 liv. : lafts two years in the ground, after which it is removed. They affert, that the culture would not anfwer at all if a farmer had to hire labour for it; all that is planted is by proprietors.

Tobacco.

FLANDERS.—Moft farmers, between Lille and Montcaffel, cultivate enough for their own ufe, which is now (November) drying under the eaves of their houfes.

ARTOIS.—*St. Omers.*—Some pieces of tobacco, in double rows, at 18 inches and 2 feet intervals, well hoed.

Aire.—A crop is worth three times that of wheat on the fame land, and at the fame time prepares better for that grain than any thing.

ALSACE.—*Strafbourg.*—Much planted in all this rich vale, and kept very clean. Product 8 to 10 quintals per arpent of 24,000 feet, at 15 liv. to 30 liv. per quintal (9 at 23 liv. is 14l. 6s. 2d. per Englifh acre). Sow wheat after it; and the beft wheat is after tobacco and poppies.

Benfeldt.—Great quantities here, and all as clean as a garden.

Schelcftat.—Produce 6 quintals to 8 per arpent, at 16 liv. the quintal (8l. 15s. 7d. per Englifh acre). This they reckon the beft crop they have for producing ready money, without waiting or trouble. There are peafants that have to 600 quintals. They always manure for it. They fow it in March on a hot bed covered with mats; begin to plant in May, and continue it all June and the beginning of July, at 18 inches or 2 feet fquare, watering the plants in a dry feafon. When 2 feet high, they cut off the tops to make the leaves fpread. Their beft wheat crops follow it.

Tobacco, as an object of cultivation, appears in thefe notes to very great advantage; and a refpectable author, in France, declares, from information, that, inftead of exhaufting the land, it improves it like artificial graffes*; which feems to agree with my intelligence; yet the culture has been highly condemned by others. Mr. Jefferfon obferves thus upon it; " it requires an extraordinary

* *De l' Adminiftration Provinciale par M. le Trone.* Tom. i. p. 267.

degree

degree of heat, and still more indispensably an uncommon fertility of soil: it is a culture productive of infinite wretchedness: those employed in it are in a continued state of exertion, beyond the powers of nature to support: little food of any kind is raised by them; so that the men and animals, on these farms, are badly fed, and the earth is rapidly impoverished. The cultivation of wheat is the reverse in every circumstance: besides cloathing the earth with herbage and preserving its fertility, it feeds the labourers plentifully; requires from them only a moderate toil, except in the season of harvest; raises great numbers of animals for food and service, and diffuses plenty and happiness among the whole. We find it easier to make an hundred bushels of wheat than a thousand weight of tobacco, and they are worth more when made*." This authority is respectable; but there are circumstances in the passage which almost remove the dependence we are inclined to have on the author's judgment. The culture of wheat preserving the fertility of the earth, and raising great numbers of animals! What can be meant by this? As to the exhausting quality of wheat, which is sufficient to reduce a soil almost to a *caput mortuum*, it is too well known, and too completely decided, to allow any question at this time of day; and how wheat is made to raise animals we must go to America to learn, for just the contrary is found here; the farms that raise most wheat have fewest animals; and in France, husbandry is at almost its lowest pitch, for want of animals, and because wheat and rye are cultivated, as it were, to the exclusion of other crops. Tobacco cannot demand an uncommon degree of heat, because it has been cultivated on a thousand acres of land successfully in Scotland: and as to the demanding of too great exertions, the free hands of Europe voluntarily addict themselves to the culture; which has nothing in it so laborious as reaping wheat. I take the American case to be this; ill husbandry, not tobacco, exhausted the land; they are now adopting wheat; and, if we may judge from the notions of the preceding quotation, that culture will, in a few years, give the finishing stroke to their lands; for those who think that wheat does not exhaust, will be free in often sowing it, and they will not be long in finding out what the result will prove.

Monf. Bolz, in Swisserland, says, that they are disgusted with the culture of tobacco, because it exhausts their lands: half an arpent gave 5 to 6 quintals of leaves†. Estimated grossly, this may be called a thousand weight per acre, which Mr. Jefferson compares with 100 bushels of wheat; a quantity that would demand, in England, four acres of land to yield; and, as American crops do not yield in that proportion, it is one acre of tobacco being as expensive as five or six of wheat, which surpasses comprehension.

* *Notes on the State of Virginia.* P. 278.
† *Mem. de la Société Oeconomique de Berne.* 1763. Tom. I. p. 87.

The Strafbourg produce of 9 quintals, in the notes above, equal 15 cwt. per English acre.   The Scheleftat produce of 7 quintals is about 12 cwt. per acre.

Dr. Mitchel, many years before Mr. Jefferson, gave the fame account of the exhaufting quality of tobacco *.

The cultivation is at prefent fpreading rapidly into countries that promife to be able to fupply the world.   In 1765, it was begun to be cultivated in Mexico, and produced, in 1778, to the value of 800,000l. and in 1784, 1,200,000l.†

Turnips.

GUIENNE—*Anfpan to Bayonne.*—*Raves* are, in thefe wafte tracts, at the roots of the Pyrennees, much cultivated; they manure for them, by burning ftraw, as defcribed under the article manure; weed, and, as they told me, hoe them; and have fome as large as a man's head.   They are applied entirely to fattening oxen.   Maiz is fown after them.   The people here knew of the orders given by the King, for cultivating this plant, but I could not find they had had any effect.   The practice obtained here before the two laft fevere years, which were the occafion of their increafing it, much more than any orders could do.

FLANDERS.—*Valenciennes to Orchies.*—Many fields of this root, but quite thick, though it was faid they have been hoed; thefe are all after-crops, fown after corn.

NORMANDIE.—*Caen.*—In going to Bayeaux, many, both flourifhing and clean, though too thick; but, on inquiry, found them all for the market, and none for cattle or fheep.   I thought the colour of the leaf differed from our own, and got off my horfe more than once to examine them.   They are the *raves* of the fouth of France; the roots, which ought to have been of a good fize, were carrot-fhaped and fmall.

BRETAGNE.—*Belle-Ifle to Morlaix.*—Here is an odd culture of raves amongft buckwheat; fown at the fame time, and given to cows and oxen, but the quantity is very inconfiderable.

Morlaix.—Get their beft turnips after flax, fometimes to a very good fize; but, for want of fufficient thinning the crops, in general, very fmall roots muft be produced; yet the leaves large, healthy, and vigorous.   They fow them alfo among buckwheat; but the product is trifling, and the ufe but momentary, as they plough the land for wheat.

ANJOU.—*Migniame.*—If one were to attend only to converfation, without going into the fields, a ftranger would be perfuaded that the culture of turnips

* *Prefent State of Britain and North America.* 8vo.   1767.   P. 149, 151.
† *Bourgoanne's Travels in Spain,* vol. i.   p. 368.

flourifhed

flourished here: they actually give some, and cabbages too, to their cows, for every man has a scrap: but sown quite thick, and the largest I saw not bigger than a goose egg; in general not a fourth of that size; and the largest piece I saw was half an English acre. They have, in like manner, patches of a sort of kale, which is the *chou de Poitou*; this **is instead of the** *chou d'Anjou*, of which the Marquis de Turbilly speaks so much; and which is quite neglected in this country now, in favour of this Poitou cabbage, that is found to produce many more leaves. To me it, **however**, appears inferior **to the** *chou de Vache* of Flanders.

To La Fleche.—A scattering of miserable *raves* all the way.

Alsace.—*Scheleftat to Colmar.*—Some scattered pieces, but in very bad order; and none hoed, which they ought to have been three weeks before I saw them.

Auvergne.—*Iſſoire.*—Raves are cultivated for cattle, but on so small a scale, that they scarcely deserve mention. They sow them also among buckwheat, which is *drawn by hand, when in bloſſom, for forage,* and the raves left. No hoeing, but some are weeded.

Brioude.—Many raves, and cultivated for cattle: common to 2 lb. weight.

St. George's to Villeneuve.—Many raves, but miserable poor things, and all weeds.

Perhaps the culture of turnips, as practised in England, is, of all others, the greatest desideratum in the tillage of France. To introduce it, is essential to their husbandry; which will never flourish to any **respectable extent, and** upon a footing of improvement, till this material **object be effected. The** steps hitherto **taken** by government, the chief of which is distributing the seed, I have reason to believe, failed entirely. I sent to France, at the request of the **Count** de Vergennes, above an hundred pounds worth of the seed; enough for **a small** province. When I was at Paris, and in the right season, I begged to be shewn some effects of that import; but it was all in vain. I was carried to various **fields,** sown thick, and absolutely neglected; too contemptible to demand a moment's attention. Not one acre of good turnips was produced by all that seed. It is with turnips, as in many other articles; a great and well cultivated English farm, of 700 or 800 acres, should be established, on an indifferent soil; and 200 acres of turnips cultivated upon it, and eaten on the land by sheep, should every year be exhibited; and a succession of persons educated on such **a farm, dispersed over** the kingdom, would do more to introduce the culture than all the measures yet attempted by government.

Walnuts.

Berry.—*Verſon to Vatan.*—Many of these trees spread over the **country,** which yield a regular revenue by oil.

M 2

Quercy.

QUERCY.—*Souillac.*—Walnut-oil cake the finest food of all for fattening oxen. They export pretty largely of this oil, the trees being every where.

ANGOUMOIS.—*Rignac.*—Walnuts spread over almost every field.

Ruffec.—A common tree yields a boisseau of nuts; sold at 3 liv. or 4 liv.; but a good tree 3 boisseau. All for oil, which the people eat in soups, &c.

POITOU.—Many through all parts of the province, which I passed in crossing it. Oil universally made from them. This year (1787) all were so frozen, that the crop will be very small; sometimes get 16 boisseau a tree, even to 20 boisseau; the boisseau sells generally at 20*f.* There is, on an average, one tree to an acre. One tree gives 5 or 6 measures of nuts, and each measure makes something more than a pint of oil, which sells at 18*f.* or 20*f.*

ANJOU.—Across this whole province they are found every where, but none through Bretagne.

ALSACE.—*Isenheim.*—Great numbers spread all over the country; for oil.

BOURBONNOIS.—*Moulins.*—Some estates have a good many scattered trees; the oil sells at 12*f.* the lb.

AUVERGNE.—*Clermont.*—Many in every part of the country; a prime tree will, in a good year, give 20 lb. and even 30 lb. of oil; one of ten years 6 lb.; common price 6*f.* per lb.

Lempde.—Here they finish; as we advance from this village, no more are met with.

Various Plants.

QUERCY.—*Brives.*—Figs we met with here for the first time; they are scattered over the vineyards, and wrapped up in mats, to preserve them from frosts.

Creissensac.—*Gieyse* much cultivated here; it is the *lathyrus setifolius.* Also *jarash*, the *vicia latharoides.* They sow them both in September and the spring, which are generally used, mown green, for soiling.

Souillac.—They have no meadows in many districts of this country, but supply the want by the above-mentioned plants, which are always used green. They do not answer equally in hay, as it is said that the leaf falls off in drying.

Cahors.—Near this place meet with four new articles of cultivation; one a *vicia sativa varietas*; another the *cicer arietinum*; the third the *ervum lens*; and the fourth the *lupinus albus.*

Caussade.—Here the *trifolium rubens* is cultivated, and continues through all the Pyrennees.——On all these articles I must, however, observe, that they do not seem to equal, for soiling, the common winter-vetch, which we cultivate so much in England; nor lucern, so successfully sown in France.

GUIENNE.

GUIENNE.—*Triticum Repens.* Upon the banks of the Garonne I met women loaded with the roots of this plant, going to fell it at market; and they informed me it was bought to feed horfes with. It is applied to the fame ufe at Naples. It grows with great luxuriance at Caygan Solo, in latitude 7 [*]; and being the great plague of Englifh hufbandry, may be called a univerfal grower. It feems, from a late account [†], as if they cultivated it in the ifland of Nantucket, in America.

ISLE OF FRANCE.—*Dugny.*—Monf. Cretté de Paleuel gave me fome notes of experiments he had made on various plants, in drying them for hay.

The *epilobium anguftifolium* makes hay that is readily eaten by fheep, and lofes half in drying. They are very fond of the hay of the *fpirea ulmaria*, the *lithum falicaria, thaliêtrum vulgaris, pucedanum filaus*, and *centaurea jacea*; all thefe lofe half, when made into hay; the *althæa officinalis* two-thirds. Monf. Cretté is of opinion, from his trials, that thefe plants may be very ufeful in cultivation, for hay. He found, at the fame time, that an arpent of wet meadow gave 13,200 lb. of green herbage, which loft two-thirds in drying. An arpent of winter-vetches 17,800 lb. green.

The common fun-flower he has alfo cultivated; he plants it in rows, at two feet afunder, and one foot from plant to plant; an arpent containing 16,200 plants; the leaves he gives to cows, the flowers may be ufed for dying; of the ftems he makes vine props, or for French beans, and afterwards burns them; and of the feed he makes oil, which leaves a cake good for fattening cattle. Six perch of land, each of 18 feet fquare, has given him 22 boiffeau of feed, the boiffeau $\frac{1}{14}$ of the feptier, that contains 240 lb. of wheat; but the crop exhaufts the land exceedingly, and fmall birds devour the feed greedily.

The fame gentleman compared cabbages and potatoes, in alternate rows an arpent gave (half the ground) 62 feptiers of potatoes, which weighed 14,880 lb.; the cabbages on the fame land, in number 5400, weighed 25,500 lb.

Dammartin.—Summer-vetches cultivated here, they are mown for hay, and yield 800 to 1000 bottes per arpent; 1100 have been known.

ARTOIS.—*La Recouffe.*—Winter-vetches are found on every farm, on the good land from Calais to St. Omer: oats are mixed, to keep them up; and every one foils his horfes in the ftable.

Afs.—Some hops here.

ANJOU.—In the way from Angers to La Fleche, the number of citroules is very great, even to acres, and the crop extremely abundant; the metayers feed their hogs with them.

[*] *Foreft's Voyage to New Guinea*, p. 16.
[†] *St. John's Letters of an American Farmer.* 8vo. 1782. P. 207.

AUVERGNE.

Auvergne.—*Brioude.*—Jarouſſe every where ſown, the end of Auguſt or beginning of September, for hay.

Dauphine.—*Loriol.*—The *melilotus ſibyrica*, from Monſ. Thouin, at the King's garden, at Paris, makes, in the garden of Monſ. Faujas de St. Fond, a moſt ſuberb figure; nobody can view its prodigious luxuriance without commending the thought of cultivating it for cattle. The *coronilla varia*, a common plant here, and of ſuch luxuriance, that it is hardly to be deſtroyed. The *hedyſarum coronarium* does well here.

Provence.—*Cuges.*—Capers are here met with, for the firſt time, in going from Marſeilles to Italy. It is a low buſh, planted in ſquares of about 5 or 6 feet. This year they yield nothing, becauſe damaged by the froſt; but, in common, more profitable than vines; they mentioned 1 lb. per tree, at 30 ſ.

Toulon.—Capers are not ſo profitable as vines. The buſhes here are planted at 6½ or 7 feet ſquare; and a good one will give 1½ or 2 lb. of capers; but the price varies prodigiouſly, from 30 liv. or 40 liv. to 120 liv. the quintal; average, 30 liv. or from 6 ſ. to 20 ſ. the pound.

Hieres [*].—Capers here are planted in ſquares, at 6, 7, and 8 feet; each good buſhel yields 2 lb. from 6 ſ. to 24 ſ. the pound; but, in a groſs eſtimate of a whole crop, are not ſuppoſed to pay more than 6 ſ. to 10 ſ. per buſhel.

Graſſe.—Here is one of the moſt ſingular cultures to be met with, that of plants for making perfumes; whole acres of roſes, tuberoſes, &c. for their flowers, and a ſtreet full of ſhops for ſelling them: they make the famous otter of roſes, as good and as clear as from Bengal; and it is ſaid now to ſupply all Europe.

Lyonnois.—The fromental of the French (*avena elatior*) is cultivated in this part of France, and in ſome diſtricts of Franche Compté. The ſeed is commonly ſold by the ſeedſmen, at Lyons, of whom I bought ſome to cultivate in England. The firſt perſon who mentioned it publickly was, I believe, Monſ. Miroudot, who wrote an eſſay upon it, in which he fell into an error, copied by many of his countrymen †, namely, that of calling it the ray-graſs of the Engliſh. The great botaniſt, Haller, was miſtaken in ſuppoſing it the *avena flaveſcens* ‡. King Staniſlaus made ſome experiments on it in Loraine. In Bretagne ‖ it has been found to yield ten times the produce of common meadows. That it is very productive cannot be doubted, but it is a very coarſe graſs: how-

---

* The natural hiſtorian of Provence mentions a ſingular profit by this plant, at Hieres, of 200 cannes ſquare giving 200 liv. net, while the ſame breadth, in common huſbandry, only 28 liv. *Mem. pour ſervir a l'Hiſt. Nat. de la Provence,* par M. Bernard. 8vo. Tom. i. p. 329.

† *Bomarre Dict. d' Hiſt. Nat.* Tom. ii. p. 565; v. p. 225.

‡ *Mem. de la Soc. de Berne.* 1770. P. 16.

‖ *Corps d'Obſerv. de la Soc. de Bretagne.* 1759, 1760. P. 44, 45.

ever,

ever, it merits experiments, and ought to be tried upon a large fcale, as the qualities of plants cannot be afcertained upon a fmall one.

Citroules, in this province and the neighbouring ones, are cultivated largely, and rarely fail. They may be preferved until the beginning of January: oxen, cows, and hogs eat them freely; for lean cattle they are given raw, but commonly boiled for fattening: from 10 lb. to 20 lb. a day, given to cows, foon fhews the effect in the quality of milk. For fattening an ox, in Breffe [*], with them, they mix the citroule with bran or pollard, or flower of buckwheat, and boil them together, and give 35 lb. to 40 lb. to each beaft per diem. In fome places they apply them to feeding carp. The poor people eat them in foup, in moft parts of the kingdom, but not in great quantities.

CHAP. XIV.

Of the Wafte Lands of France.

Sologne.—THERE is, in this province, fuch a large mixture of wafte, even in the moft cultivated parts, and cultivation itfelf is carried on upon fuch barbarous principles, that there will not be much impropriety in confidering the whole as wafte; to every fpot of culture called a farm, a much greater proportion of rough fheep-walk and wood (eaten down and deftroyed) is annexed; fo that any good farmer, who got poffeffion of 1000 or 1500 acres, would conclude the whole as wafte, and treat it accordingly: by much the moft unproductive and pooreft part of fuch a tract would, in every cafe, be the lands at prefent under the plough. I may, in confirmation of this general idea, add, that there are many abfolute waftes in France, that yield as good, and even a better produce than all Sologne, acre for acre. I know no region better adapted for a man's making a fortune by agriculture, than this; nothing is wanted but capital, for moft of the province is already inclofed.

Berry.—*Chateauroux.*—Leaving this place for the fouth, enter vaft heaths of ling and furz, but much mixed with trefoils and graffes. Some fmall parts of thefe heaths are broken up, and fo ill ploughed, that the broom and furz are in full growth. After this another heath, of feveral miles extent, where

* *Obferv. et Exp. par Fenille,* p. 86.

the

the landlords will not give leave either to build or break up, referving the whole for fheep, and yet not flocked; for the people affert, that they could keep twice the number, if they had them.

LIMOUSIN.—*To Limoges.*—The mountainous heaths and uncultivated lands are commons, and therefore every metayer fends his fheep in the common flock of the village.

BIGORRE.—*Bagneres de Luchon.*—The wafte tracts of the Pyrennees, by which are to be underftood, lands fubject to common pafturage, are fo much fubject to the will of the communities, that thefe fell them at pleafure. Formerly the inhabitants appropriated to their own ufe, by inclofure and cultivation, what portions they pleafed; but this obtains no longer; at prefent the communities fell thefe waftes, and fixing a price on them, nearly to their value, new improvements are not fo common as heretofore.

LANGUEDOC.—*Narbonne to Nifmes.*—This vale, which is by far the richeft of Languedoc, in productions, is of no confiderable breadth, yet the quantity of wafte neglected land in it is very great.

Monrejau to Lann-Maifon.—Vaft waftes, covered with fern; the foil good; and land projecting into it cultivated to advantage.

Bagneres de Bigorre.—Thefe immenfe fern-waftes continue for many miles, with many new improvements in them. They belong to the communities of the villages, which fell portions of them to any perfons willing to buy. The price moft common has been 20 liv. the journal, of 128 cannes fquare, the canne 8 pans; the pan 8 inches and 4 lines, 4 journals making an arpent. The method of improving has been, firft to burn all the fern and rubbifh, then to mattock it and fow rye, which is pretty good; then oats for fix, feven, or eight years, according to circumftances; after that they fummer-fallow and take wheat. Some they leave to grafs and weeds, after thofe eight crops of oats; a detail of the hufbandry of barbarians! They have all a right of commonage on the waftes, as long as thefe continue uninclofed; confequently can keep cattle, and efpecially fheep, to any amount in fummer; yet, in their inclofed improvements, they give not a thought to raife winter food! Such ftupidity is deteftable. The parifh of Cavare has 104,000 arpents of thefe waftes, without one metayer; all are peafant proprietors, who buy morfels as it fuits them. The improvements are exempted from tithes for ten years; but not at all from the King's taxes, which is fhameful.

BEARN.—*Pau to Moneins.*—Vaft waftes of rich foil, covered with an immenfe product of fern, to the amount of five or fix waggon loads an acre.

St. Palais to Arjpan.—Vaft waftes; belonging to the communities of the parifhes, that fell them to whoever will buy: a common price 120 liv. per arpent; but after they are brought into culture, they fell for at leaft 300 liv. The advantages

vantages of this fyftem, which extends through the whole region of the Pyrennees, is prodigious: it excludes the rights of commonage, becaufe all is inclofed as faft as bought; and enables every induftrious man, that faves a little money, to become a land proprietor, which is the greateft encouragement to an active induftry the world can produce; it has, however, one evil, that of too great a population.

Bayonne to St. Vincents.—In this line I came firft to the *landes* of Bourdeaux, becaufe they extend from the gates of Bayonne to thofe of Bourdeaux, and of which I had read fo much, that I was curious to view and examine them; they are faid to contain 1,100,000 arpents *. They are covered with pines, cork-trees (only half the value of pines), broom, whins, ling, and furz; the foil fand, but the growth of trees fhews a moift bottom. There is a good deal of cultivation mixed with the wafte this firft ftage. There is much land alfo under water, a fort of fandy fen. Pafs a great fpace, without trees, covered with dwarf furz, ling, and fern. Others before Dax; one of them of five or fix miles long, by two or three broad: much rough grafs and ling on it: but none of thefe tracts appear half ftocked.

Dax to Tartas.—This diftrict is a deep white fand, the whole of which has evidently been *lande*, but part of it inclofed and improved; much is, however, yet rough.—Singular fcene of a blowing fand, white as fnow, yet oaks growing in it two feet diameter; but a broken ground difcovers a bed of white adhefive earth, like marl, which explains the wonder.

Learn at Tartas, that thefe immenfe waftes, the *landes*, without pines or wood, are to be purchafed, at all times, very cheap indeed, of the King, the great lords, and of the communities of many parifhes, even fo low as 3 liv. per arpent, with an exemption from tithes, and from taxes for twenty years. But every one here reckons them fo bad, that all the money fpent would be fure to be loft; yet it is admitted, that there is a bed of marl or clay under all the country. This opinion is chiefly founded on the attempts of Monf. Rollier, of Bourdeaux, having made a trial of cultivating them, and fucceeded very ill. I guefled how fuch improvements had been attempted, and told my informants what I fuppofed had been done; and my guefs proved exactly right: corn—corn—corn—corn; and then the land pronounced good for nothing. It does not fignify telling fuch people, that the great objects, in all improvements of waftes, are cattle, and fheep, and grafs, after which corn will be fure. Nothing of this kind is comprehended from one end of France to the other.

As I fhall here take my leave of thefe *landes*, I may obferve, that, fo far as they are covered with pines, they are not to be efteemed waftes; but, on the contrary, occupied with a very profitable culture, that does not yield lefs than from 15s.

---

* *De la Neceffité d'Occuper tous les gros Ouvriers*, p. 8.

to 25s. an acre annual revenue. Of the very extenfive tracts not fo employed, and which are to be purchafed at fo cheap a rate, they are among the moft improveable diftricts in the kingdom, and might be made, at a very fmall expence, capable of fupporting immenfe flocks of fheep.

Cavignac to Pierre Brune.—Many fandy waftes, with white marl under the whole.

To Cherfac.—Great waftes, of many miles extent, covered with fern, ling, and fhrubby oak; all greatly improveable.

To Montlieu.—Ditto. Many of thefe waftes belonged to the Prince of Soubife, who would not fell, but only let them; the confequence has been, that no improvements have been wrought.

La Graule.—The waftes in this country are fold at 10 liv. the journal, and lefs; fome better at 30 liv. The journal here is to the Englifh acre as ten to thirty-eight; it confifts of 10 carraux, each 18 feet fquare.

NORMANDIE.—*Valogne to Cherbourg.*—Monf. Doumerc, of Paris, having bought of Monfieur, the King's brother, 3000 arpents, part of 14,000 fold at the fame time, being parcel of an ancient, but much neglected, foreft, has made an improvement here, which, fo far, deferves attention, as it fhews the principles on which French improvers proceed. He has brought into culture 700 verges, which form his prefent farm, around a houfe for himfelf, and another for his bailiff, all built, as well as many other edifices, in much too expenfive a manner; for thefe erections alone coft 2500 louis d'or. Such unneceffary expenditures in building is generally fure to cripple the progrefs in much more neceffary matters. The firft bufinefs in the improvement, was to grub up the wood; then to pare and burn; and manure with lime, burnt with the furz, fern, and heath of the land; the ftone was brought from Valogne: as foon as it was cleared, it was fallowed the firft year for wheat. Such infatuation is hardly credible! A man is commencing his operations in the midft of 3000 acres of rough ground, and an immenfe pafturage for cattle and fheep, begins with wheat; the fame follies prevail every where: we have feen juft the fame courfe purfued in England, and prefcribed by writers. Such people think cattle and fheep of no importance at the beginning of thefe improvements. This wheat, limed at the rate, per arpent, of 7 or 8 tonneaux, of 25 boiffeau, each 18 pots of 2 pints; 4 boiffeau of feed fown, and the crop 40 boiffeau. After this wheat fown 5 boiffeau of oats, the crop 40. Then barley, feed 4 boiffeau, produce 20 to 25 boiffeau. With this barley clover fown; mown the firft year twice, and paftured the fecond; being then ploughed for wheat, which is inferior to the original crops; then oats and fallow again. From all thefe crops it is fufficiently evident, that French farmers efteem corn, and not cattle, the proper fupport of a new improvement. The foil which has been thus reclaimed,

claimed,

claimed, is on a ftone quarry in general; a friable fandy loam, covered with a ftrong fpontaneous growth (where not foreft) of furz, fern, and, in fome places, heath; mixed with much grafs, and even clover and *millefolium*; which, if properly ftocked by cattle, well fed in winter, would be of confiderable value in its prefent rough ftate.

Though the methods purfued have not been calculated on the beft prin-ciples, yet there is certainly a confiderable degree of merit in the undertak-ing. Laft year's crop of wheat produced 40,000 gerbs: and this year (1787) there is one piece of oats, of 80 verges, which gives 12,000 gerbs, at 15 boiffeau per hundred; each boiffeau 40 lb. and the price at prefent 45*f*. The prefent ftock, 207 wethers, 10 horfes, 21 working oxen, 10 cows, 1 bull, 6 young cattle, are certainly fine, for a fpot where, ten years ago, Monf. Baillió, the bailiff, who has executed the whole, and who feems to be a truly excellent man, was in a hovel, with no other ftock than a dog. The whole improved, would now let at 15 liv. per verge, 2½ to the arpent.

BRETAGNE.—*Combourg to Hédé.*—Pafs an immenfe wafte for a league, but to the left a dead level, boundlefs as the fea; high lands at one part, feemingly 8 or 10 leagues off. Every part which the road paffes, has been under the plough, for the ridges are as diftinct as if made but laft year; and many ruined banks of hedges crofs it in various ways. The fpontaneous growth, furz, ling, and fern; the foil good, and equal to valuable crops, in a proper management. The King has part, Monf. de Chateaubriant part, and other feigneurs alfo; but every body I talked with fays, it is good for nothing. Would to heaven I had 1000 acres of it at Bradfield! I would foon put that affertion to the teft.

Rennes.—The wafte lands, which, in almoft every part of the province, extend for many leagues, are almoft every where to be bought, in any quantity, of the feigneurs, at 10*f.* the journal, which is to the Englifh acre as 47 to 38, with a fmall quit-rent per annum.

St. Brieux.—Inquiring here into the period of the cultivation which I every where remarked on the *landes* of Bretagne, I was told, that it was no antient culture, but common for peafants, who took them of the feigneurs, to pare and burn, with the *ecoubu*; exhauft; and then leave them to nature: and this for forty, fifty, and fixty years back. Rented for ever at 20*f.* to 30*f.* the journal.

St. Nazaire to Savanal.—Immenfe bog marked on all the maps of Bretagne, and filling the fpace of many leagues, covered with vaft growth of bog myrtle, and coarfe graffes, three or four feet high; what a field for improvement, in a climate that gives fuch a fpontaneous growth!

To Nantes.—In the *landes*, which, ftrange to fay, extend to within three miles of Nantes, there was an improvement attempted fome years ago: four good houfes of ftone and flate are built, and a few acres run to wretched grafs,

which

which have been tilled, but all savage, and become almost as rough as the rest: a few of the banks have been planted. This may be the improvement I heard of afterwards at Nantes, made by some Englishmen, at the expence of a gentleman, and all the parties ruined. I inquired how the *improvement* had been effected: pare and burn; wheat; rye; oats!!! Thus it is for ever: the same methods, the same failures, the same folly, the same madness. When will men be wise enough to know, that good grass must be had, if corn is the object?

Nantes.—I have now travelled round the vast province of Bretagne, and may observe, that so large a proportion of it is waste, as to be difficult to calculate: I have passed tracts of land, of three, four, five, and even eight miles in extent, without any cultivation, and I have heard of much more considerable, even to fourteen leagues in length. I have marked one district in the map which contains some hundred thousand acres. Three-fourths of the province are either waste, or so rough as to be nearly the same thing. This is the more surprising, as here are some of the first markets in France; that is to say, some of the most considerable commercial towns; and every where the vicinity of the sea. These enormous wastes, which are said to exceed two millions of arpents *, are found, as I have remarked, in my notes on the great road, within four miles of such a city as Nantes: vast districts are to be had on leases, or rather property for ever, on the payment of very slight fines. The soil is generally very improveable; I mean, convertible to cultivation, at a very small expence, and with great facility; contrary to the assertion of every body in the province, who have been so used to see it desolate, that they cannot readily believe it capable of a better husbandry than being burnt, exhausted, and left to nature. The means of improving these wastes are absolutely unknown in France, and not much better understood in England. The profit of the undertaking, however, when properly pursued, upon the never-failing principle of grass—sheep—cattle—corn; instead of the common blunder, which puts the cart before the horse (if I may use a vulgar proverb), will be found great and rapid.

ANJOU.—*Turbilly.*—In the journal-part of this work, I have explained the motives which carried me out of my road, to view the wastes of this vicinity, and particularly the improvements of the late Marquis of Turbilly, described at large in his *Memoire sur les Défrichemens*, which has been so often cited in almost every language.

The immense heaths, or *landes*, are, in general, a sandy or gravelly loam; some on a gravel, others on a clayey, and others on a marley bottom; and others, again, on imperfect quarry ones: the spontaneous growth would predominantly be every where forest, particularly of oak, if it were inclosed, and

* *De la Necessité d'Occuper tous les gros Ouvriers*, par Monf. Boncerf. 1789. P. 8.

preserved

preferved from depredation. At prefent, it is wood browfed and ruined, fern furz, broom, ling, &c. &c. In the defert ftate in which the whole country is left at prefent, the value is nothing elfe **but what it yields to a few** cattle **and** fheep; not the hundredth part of what might be **kept, if any well regulated** provifion were made for **their** winter fupport. I p.ffed **ten miles over thefe** heaths; they were, in fome **directions,** boundlefs to the **view; and my guide** affured me, I might continue travelling upon them **for many days. When at** Tours, **I was told of their extending** much in that direction **alfo. The climate is good. There are ftreams that pafs through thefe** waftes, **which might be employed in irrigation, but no ufe whatever made of** them; there are **marl** and **clay under them, for manure;** and **there** is every where to be found plenty of **pafturage, for the immediate** fummer food of large flocks.—In a word, there **are all the materials for making a** confiderable fortune——except fkill and **knowledge.**

Such was the country **in** which the late **Marquis of Turbilly** fat down, at an early period of life, determining to improve **his eftate of 3000** arpents in thefe deferts; with all the neceffary activity of difpofition; **every energy of** mind; and that animated love of laudable attempts, **to give** life **and efficacy to** the undertaking. **Some meadows** and plantations, **which he made, fucceeded well, and remain;** but, of all **his improvements of the heaths, to the** inconfiderable amount of about 100 arpents, hardly any other traces **are now to** be feen, except from the more miferable and worn-out appearance of the land; which, **after** cropping, was, **of** courfe, left in a much worfe condition than **if** it had never been touched. The fences **are quite deftroyed;** and the whole **as** much *lande* as before **improvement. This flowed from the unfortunate error, fo common, indeed fo univerfal,** among the improvers of wafte lands; **and unexceptionably** fo in France—that of improving, merely for the purpofe of getting corn. Pyron, the labourer who worked in all the Marquis' improvements, informed me, that he pared and burnt, which is the common practice of all the country, and **then took three crops of corn in fucceffion; that the firft was very** good, the fecond not good, and the third good for nothing, that is, not above three times **the** feed : from that moment there was an end of improvement; it only crawled, **during many years, to the** amount of 100 acres; whereas, if he had begun on **right principles, he would, in** all **probability,** have improved the **3000;** and, **others** copying **his modes, the** whole country might, by this time, **have been under** cultivation. **It was** reckoned a vaft effort in him to fold 250 fheep : **and this was** the beft engine he had in his hands; but giving the fold for corn, it **was** loft as foon as exerted. Inftead of 250 fheep, the Marquis fhould have **had 500** the firft year, 1000 the fecond, 1500 the third, and 2000 the fourth; **and all his** paring, burning, manuring, folding, exerted to raife turnips (not

their

their contemptible *raves*) to winter-feed them; with fo much burning, folding, and eating off the turnips, the land would have been prepared for grafs;
and when once you have good grafs, good corn is at your command. Thus
corn was the laft idea that fhould have entered his head: inftead of which, like
other French improvers, he rufhed upon it at once—and from that inftant all
was ruined.

The particular advantages of the fpot are confiderable, if ever an improver
fhould arife, with knowledge enough to purfue the methods that are adapted
to the foil and fituation. The hills of all the country are fo gentle, that they
are to be tilled with great eafe; offering the advantage of perennial ftreams,
that run at prefent to wafte in the vales. There are rich veins of white marl,
with an under-ftratum, in many places, of clay. There is a hill of fhell fand,
for improving the ftiffer foils and the moory bottoms. There is lime-ftone at
the diftance of half a league, and plenty of peat to burn it. The Marquis of
Galway's father fpread fome of the fhell fand on a fmall poor field, and had an
immediate luxuriance of crop in confequence. The prefent curé of the parifh
has tried the marl, with equal fuccefs. But both thefe manures, and indeed any
other, would be abfolutely loft, if a fucceffion of corn crops were immediately
to follow. It is this valuable under-ftratum of clay and marl which gives fuch
a growth to wood. In paffing from La Fleche to Turbilly, I was amazed, in
fome fpots, at the contraft between the apparent poverty of the furface foil,
and the oaks fcattered about it; they are, in general, eaten up by cattle, yet
the bark is clean and bright, and this year's fhoots four and even five feet long.
A common mode, and indeed the only one, of attempting improvements here,
is to permit the peafants to pare and burn pieces of the heath; to take five crops
in fucceffion, but to leave the ftraw of the laft; to fence the piece around; and
to fow whatever feeds of wood the landlord provides, ufually oak, for a copfe,
which, in this villainous way, fucceeds well; but as fuch copfes are fenced with
a ditch and bank only, and never any hedge planted, they are prefently open
and eaten.

MAINE.—*Gueffelard.*—The *landes* of Anjou extend over a great part of
Maine alfo. Here they told me, that the extent in that neighbourhood is
hardly lefs than fixty leagues in circumference, with no great interruption of
cultivation. The account they give of the foil is, that it is abfolutely good for
nothing but to produce wood, which it will do very well. The feigneurs fief it
out for ever, in any quantity, at the rent of half a bufhel of oats an arpent (the
bufhel 30 lb. of wheat), and fome at 10f. to 20f. The peafants pare and burn,
and get a very fine crop of rye; then another poor crop of rye; and after that
a miferable one of oats; reckoning, in common, that a burning will give juft
three crops; after which the land is ftrictly good for nothing, but is left to nature

ture to recover itself. The price of paring and burning 30 liv. per arpent. I can hardly record these instances of barbarism with tolerable patience—without dealing execrations, **not** against a poor unenlightened peasantry, **but against a government possessing, in demesne, immense tracts of these lands, without ever** ordering any experiments to **be made and published, of the best methods of im**proving them. But had it **come into any such project, and had those experi**ments had French conductors, **they would have been merely with a view of** getting corn! **corn! corn!**

To Le Mans.—Much **of these wastes here resemble the sands of Cologne;** upon a dead level, and water standing in many places; yet the soil a sand; and, in spots, even a running one: it arises from the same circumstance which makes them productive of oak timber, wherever preserved, viz. the bottom of clay and marl.

BOURBONNOIS.—*Moulins.*—**Three-fourths of the whole province waste, or** heath, or broom, or wood.

St. Pourçain.—**As** I quitted the Bourbonnois in this vicinity, entering Au**vergne, it** will not be improper to remark, that **the whole province,** as well as that **of** Nevernois, ought, respecting all the purposes **of improvement, to be** deemed waste. The culture that is carried on, without **any exception, on the** arable lands, is only fallowing for rye; and, **after two or three rounds,** the land is so exhausted by this blessed system, that it is **left** to weeds: broom is the prevalent spontaneous growth in such a case; and if the broom be left for a number of years, it becomes a forest. This rye-course produces the landlord, for his half (as all is in the hands of metayers), about 2s. 6d. **or 3s. an acre through the** whole farm, by corn, cattle, &c.; and at such **rates a vast pro**portion **of** the province is chiefly to be **bought. Considering that the lands** are all inclosed; that wood enough is every **where found; that the country is** furnished with a sufficient quantity of buildings; **that the roads are excellent;** that it enjoys a navigation to the capital; that markets are **good, and prices** high; that there is marl or clay under the sands and sandy gravels; that the climate is one of the finest in Europe; and the country highly pleasant and beautiful when all these circumstances are well weighed, it will be admitted that no part of France is so eligible to establish a great and profitable improvement; but, **as** I must again repeat it, the whole province appears waste to the eyes of an English farmer.

AUVERGNE.—*Brioude.*—The mountains in this neighbourhood too much cultivated; the earth is, by such means, washed away by **storms, and** torrents drive away every thing.

VIVARAIS.—*Pradelles.*—Pare and burn old turf in these mountains. Great **tracts burnt,** exhausted, and left to nature to recruit.

To

To Thuytz.—Cultivation is carried on in thefe mountains to an incredible height; and is all by hand. In fome cafes, earth is carried, by hand, in bafkets, to form the terraced beds, that yield a difficult and fcanty crop, that is brought away on the back. Nothing could poffibly fupport fuch exertions, but the whole being fmall properties; every peafant cultivates his own land.

PROVENCE.—*Tour d'Aigues.*—The mountains here are all calcareous, yet they are, from a vicious culture and management, deftroyed and abandoned, and yield fubfiftence to a few miferable goats and fheep only; fuch mountains in the Vivarais, the Prefident remarks, are covered with fuperb chefnuts, that yield a good revenue;—this country would do equally well for them, as appears from the very fine ones found in the park of Tour d'Aigues. The cutting of every bufh for burning the earth is the caufe; this fpecies of culture loofens the furface, and renders it a prey to torrents; fo that all is wafhed into the rivers, and becomes the deftruction of the plains. The Durance, in its whole courfe, of near 200 miles, has deftroyed, on an average, to the breadth of half a league.

General Obfervations.

In the preceding notes, mention is often made of great tracts of country, fo miferably cultivated, that the whole would, by a good Englifh farmer, be confidered as *wafte*. This is particularly the cafe in Bretagne, Maine, Anjou, Sologne, Bourbonnois, &c.; and it is this circumftance which reduces the general average product of France to fo low a pitch, as appears in the chapter which treats of it, notwithftanding the immenfe tract of twenty-eight millions of rich land, the products of which are, of courfe, very high. Here then ought to be the great effort of a new fyftem of government in France. The revolution has coft immenfe fums; and has occafioned a happy defalcation of the revenue, provided it be replaced, wifely and equally, on fome object of general confumption, *and not on land*; but the public burthens of the kingdom are fo heavy (proportioned to its confumption and circulation), that every attention fhould be exerted to increafe and improve the contributing income; and this can in no way, and by no methods, be effected fo well and fo eafily, as by fpreading improvements over thefe immenfe waftes, which are fuch a difgrace to the old government. The waftes alone are calculated, in thefe fheets, at 18,000,000 of Englifh acres; if to thefe we add the tracts, in the abovementioned provinces, which, though cultivated, are no more productive than waftes, and much of them not of equal profit, we cannot reckon for the whole less than 40,000,000 of acres that are in a wafte ftate: not abfolutely unproductive, but which would admit of being rendered four, five, fix, and even ten times more fo than they are at prefent. This extent is nearly equal to that

of

of the kingdom of England; whence we may judge of the immenſe reſources to be found in the improvement of the agriculture of France; and the wiſdom of the meaſures of the National Aſſembly ought to be eſtimated in proportion to their exertions in this reſpect, rather than in any other. If they give a ready, immediate, and abſolute right of incloſure; an exemption from all taxation whatever, for twenty-one years; and, by a wiſe ſyſtem of impoſts, the future proſpect of not being too much burthened; if ſuch be their encouragements, in addition to the great ones already effected, particularly in the abolition of tithes, they may expect to ſee, in a few years, great undertakings on theſe deſolate tracts. But the policy of a good government will not, in this point, do the whole; it may encourage buildings, incloſures, manuring, and the inveſtment of large capitals; but if theſe ſoils be attempted to be cultivated, as they have hitherto always been in France, failure, bankruptcy, and ruin, will be the conſequence; and the lands, after a few years, left in a worſe ſtate than they are in at preſent. The government ſhould therefore not omit taking the neceſſary ſteps, to have inſtructions well diffuſed for the cultivation of theſe immenſe tracts of country; not in the ſpirit of the old * ſyſtem, by printing memoirs, which, if followed, probably would ſpread more miſchief than benefit, but by the exhibition of a farm in each conſiderable diſtrict, under a right management, and in that degree of perfection of culture which is applicable to the practice of all mankind; of the poor farmers as well as of rich ones: every other ſpecies of perfection does well enough for gentlemen to commend, but is not adapted for farmers to imitate. One large farm, taken entirely from waſte, in Bretagne, another in Anjou, a third in Sologne, a fourth in Bourbonnois, and a fifth in Guienne, would be ſufficient. If theſe farms were cultivated on right

---

* The edict, exempting new improvements from taxation, was in the right ſpirit. We are informed by Monſ. Necker, that from 1766 to 1784, no leſs than 950,000 arpents were declared *defrichts. De L'Adminiſt. des Fin.* 8vo. T. iii. p. 233. There can be no doubt but the greater part of theſe are long ſince abandoned again to nature. I never met with a ſingle perſon in France who had half an idea of improving waſte lands; and I may add, that, of all other practices in **the** agriculture of England, this is the leaſt underſtood. See my *Obſervations on the preſent State of the Waſte Lands.* 8vo. In regard to the excellent edict above-mentioned, there occurs a proof of the groſs and conſummate ignorance which one meets ſo often in France on all agricultural ſubjects. In the *Cahier du Tiers Etat de Troyes,* p. 38, they demand the abrogation of this edict, as prejudicial to the nouriſhment and multiplication of cattle. Even the nobility of *Cambray, Cahier,* p. 19, are againſt cultivating commons. **The** nobility of *Pont-à-Mouſſon, Cahier,* p. 38, declare, that the encouragement of incloſures and *defrichemens,* is prejudicial to agriculture; ſhame on their folly! The clergy are wiſer; for they demand that the poſſeſſors of waſtes ſhall either cultivate them themſelves, or let **others** that are willing, on reaſonable terms. *Cahier de Melun & Moret,* p. 22; and that all commons ſhall be alienable for the proſperity of agriculture. *Bayonne,* Art. 51. And ſome of the *Tiers Etat* alſo; all commons to be divided. *Cotentin MS.* And new *defrichemens* to be exempted from all taxes for twenty years. *Nimes,* p. 19. *La Rochelle,* Art. 17, *MS.*

 practical

practical principles, on those of utterly disregarding corn till the ample support of sheep and cattle (but particularly the former) in winter, by means of green crops, and in summer by grasses, gave such a command and facility of action, that whatever corn was then sown, would, in its produce, be worthy of the soil and climate of France, yielding ten for one on these wastes, instead of five or six for one, the present average of cultivated lands in that kingdom. If this were done, I say, the profit of *such* improvements would be equally great and durable; the practice exhibited would take deep root in the respective provinces; and extensive and speedy improvements would be the consequence. By such a policy, the National Assembly would prove themselves genuine patriots; the kingdom would flourish; population, which, at present, is a burthen, would be rendered useful, because happy; and the consumption and circulation of these provinces increasing, would give a spur to those of the whole society; the weight of taxes would lessen, as the basis enlarged that supported it:—in a word, every good effect would flow from such undertakings, if properly executed, that can add to the mass of national prosperity; and consequently the most worthy of the attention of an enlightened legislature*.

Attempts have been made to improve these **wastes, but** always with ill success; I saw a neglected farm gone back nearly **to its** pristine state, not far from Nantes; the Marquis of Turbilly's, in Anjou, had no **better success;** and equal failures attended those that were tried on the heaths of Bourdeaux; and I heard of some others, similar undertakings, in different parts of the kingdom; but, in general, they were all equally unsuccessful; and **no wonder, for all were** conducted on the same **plan,** with no other **object in view than corn; but this is the** least important **of the products, as it hath been above** observed, that **should be found on new improvements.** A French writer†, who speaks from experience, as well as the Marquis of Turbilly, prescribes this course;—1, dig, at the expence of 20 liv. per arpent, of 46,000 feet, in winter, and summer-fallow, with many ploughings and harrowings, for—2, wheat;—3, oats;—4, fallow;—5,

---

　* At present (August 1793) we know what the blood-hound government of France have done for agriculture: COMPLETELY *ruined* all that was good in it.

　† *Experiences and Observations sur les Défrichemens.* Par Monf. le Docteur. *Lamballe.* 1775. 4to. P. 26, 28, 33. This gentleman tells us, that paring and burning should be practised only on a calcareous soil, for in Bretagne the peasants get but two or three crops of corn by it; and if more, much dung is requisite. But if they can have two crops of corn, cannot they have one crop of turnips? Cannot they have GRASS, which seems never to be in his contemplation, though almost the only thing that ought to be in view. De Serres knew better; he recommends paring and burning, describes the operation, and answers the objection of those who urged a short continuance of the profit, by shewing, that such cases proceed from improper management, and do not occur, if the laws of good tillage be pursued, *au cultiver & au reposer.* Le Théatre D'Agriculture, par D'Olivier de Serres. 4to. 1629. P. 64 to 70.

wheat;

wheat;—6, oats, &c. &c. This gentleman, who tells us he broke up and *improved* 450 arpents, has not explained how *real* improvement is to be made without fheep or cattle. Where is his winter food in this prepofterous courfe? If thefe 450 arpents be really improved, they have coft him five times more than they are worth; but I fufpect they are—improved *a la Turbilly*. It is mere romance to think of improving waftes profitably without a great flock of fheep. The ideas of French improvers feem rooted in a contrary fpirit; to the prefent moment, there is no other plan than the old one of corn. A publication of the year 1791, *Memoire fur l'Utilité du Défrichement des Terres de Caftelnau-de-Medoc*, fpeaks of the fame methods—*déraciner*—*labourer*—*herfer*—*enfemencer*—*froment*—*feigle*, p. 5. The fame views in every part of the kingdom; but when you inquire for cattle, you have, on fome hundreds of acres, feven cows, three mares, four oxen, and no fheep! (P. 4.)

As the fubject is one of the moft effential in French agriculture, I will very briefly fketch the right principles on which alone wafte countries can be improved to profit. The rapid view which is practicable for a traveller to take, will allow no more than an outline; fully to explain the procefs would demand a diftinct treatife.——1, The buildings, upon which fo much money is generally fo ufelefsly employed, fhould, in a private undertaking, be adapted to that fized farm, which lets in the country moft advantageoufly; but, in a public undertaking, they fhould be adapted to that fized farm which is moft favourable to a beneficial cultivation of the foil; in the latter cafe from 400 to 600 acres. This attention to the fcale of the buildings flows from the plan of the improvement, which is that of letting the land in farms, as faft as it is well improved, and brought into the cultivation in which it ought afterwards to remain. But whatever the fize of the future farms may be, the ftricteft attention ought to be had to keeping this part of the expenditure as low as poffible; it contributes little to the productivenefs of the land, except what arifes from convenient offices for cattle and fheep.—2, The next object is to buy a large flock of fheep, to feed on the lands in their wafte ftate, that are to be improved; five hundred would be a proper number to begin with. Thefe fheep fhould be, as nearly as poffible, fuch as the South Downs of England; of the French breed, the moft profitable, and the beft to procure, would be thofe of Rouffillon. It is of more confequence to have a breed not too large, and well clothed with a fhort firm fleece, than larger or more expenfive breeds.—3, The firft fummer fhould be entirely employed in paring and burning, and cultivating, at leaft, 100 acres of turnips and rape, for the winter fupport of the fheep and ploughoxen. After the turnip feafon is paft, the paring and burning to continue for rye, artificial graffes to be fown with the rye.—4, Begin, as early in the fpring as poffible, to pare and burn frefh wafte, firft for a crop of potatoes, on fifteen

or

or twenty acres, and then for 200 acres of turnips. The turnip land of laſt year to be ſown with oats, on three ploughings; and with the oats, over fifty acres, clover-feed to be ſown. After the turnip feaſon is paſt, continue paring and burning for rye, as before. The labourers employed in the ſummer on paring and burning, to work in the winter on ditching, for forming incloſures; the banks to be planted with white thorn, and willows for making hurdles.— This is ſufficient to ſtate the leading principles of the undertaking. Oeconomy in the execution demands that the labourers employed ſhould have work con- ſtantly; in ſummer paring and burning, and managing the hay and corn har- veſt; and in winter ditching; quarrying, if there be lime-ſtone on the premiſes, for burning lime for manure; and, if not, digging and filling marl, or chalk, or other manures which may be found under the ſurface. In like manner the number of maſons and carpenters ſhould be ſo regulated, in proportion to the works, ſo as to find conſtant employment through the building ſeaſon.

The courſes of crops will explain the whole buſineſs of tillage. On the land pared and burnt, and planted with potatoes in the ſpring, the following rota- tion: 1, potatoes;—2, oats:—3, turnips:—4, oats, and graſs feeds for laying down.

On the land pared and burnt, and ſown with turnips at midſummer:—1, tur- nips;—2, oats;—3, turnips;—4, oats, or barley, and graſs feeds for laying down.

On the land pared and burnt, and ſown with rye in autumn:—1, rye;—2, tur- nips;—3, oats;—4, turnips;—5, oats, and graſs feeds for laying down.

All the turnips to be fed on the land with ſheep, by hurdling, except the ſmall quantity that would be wanted for the plough oxen.

All the graſſes to be mown the firſt year for hay, and then paſtured by ſheep, for two, three, four, or more years, according to circumſtances. When they wear out, or betray indications of a want of renewal, they may be broken up with a certainty of yielding grain in plenty; but no two crops of white corn ever to be ſown in ſucceſſion: by white corn is underſtood wheat, rye, barley, and oats.

A very eaſy, and, in ſome caſes, effectual method of improving heaths, is by grubbing up the plants that grow ſpontaneouſly, and ſpreading lime upon the waſte without any tillage, ſowing graſs feeds and covering them by the ſheep- fold: it is ſurpriſing what a change is thus effected at the ſmalleſt poſſible expence; ſoils, apparently miſerable, have been made at once worth the rent of 20s. per acre.

It is not poſſible to give more than an outline in ſuch a ſketch as this; varia- tions, ariſing from a difference of ſoil, will occur; which, though not conſi- derable, muſt be marked with care, or uſeleſs expences will often be incurred. The method juſt hinted at is particularly applicable upon thoſe waſtes, which

are

are, in culture, steril, from abounding with the vitriolic acid; the case of many in Bretagne; where pudding stone is found in some districts at six to eight inches under the surface: cultivation on such, by the plough, may be so tedious and expensive, that the mere paring and burning, and application of a calcareous manure, lime or marl, with grass seeds, and told, as above-mentioned, would be much the best improvement, as I have myself experienced, in a country more vitriolic and steril than any wastes I saw in Bretagne.

The progress of the flock of sheep will, by its procreation, shew what may be the given progress of such an improvement, providing turnips, in the proportion of one acre to five sheep, which will allow enough for oxen and other cattle, and and supposing the losses upon a flock to be 5 per cent.

If the breed of sheep be good, all the ewes should be saved, for increasing stock, and the wethers should be kept until two years old and past, sold fat at from two to three years. On such a plan, a flock increases rapidly, perhaps more so than the capital employed. But the conductor of such an undertaking would of course proportion his flock to his money, so that all the works might be constantly going on, without stop or break; to effect which, would demand no inconsiderable foresight and knowledge of the business.

By the plan of letting the lands, as soon as brought into complete cultivation, the capital employed in the undertaking would be exerted to the utmost force and advantage, in spreading the improvement over the greatest possible breadth of waste. If the lands were all to be kept accumulating into one farm, it would grow too vast to be managed with profit; but, by letting, the principal attention, exertion, and force of capital would be always employed where most wanted and most useful; and it is hardly to be believed, by those not accustomed to such observations and inquiries, how great a tract of country might, in twenty years, be improved.

Planting colonies of foreigners upon wastes, has been a favourite method pursued in several countries, particularly in Spain and in Russia; such speculations have rarely answered the immense expences bestowed upon them. The lands are usually but half improved; the husbandry introduced is almost sure to be bad; and the jealousy, with which the new settlers are viewed by the natives, prevents their practice from ever being imitated. Such a mode of improvement, as is here sketched, would be infinitely more beneficial; what was done would be well done; all would be executed by natives; for the only foreigner employed in the business should be the director. There would be no probability of the improvement not being durable and spreading widely; for the lands not being let until the cultivation was completely in train, the profit as well as the method would be seen by every one.

By

By executing the improvement of a wafte on thefe principles, ten thoufand pounds would have an infinitely greater effect than an hundred thoufand expended in any other method: in the German colonies, eftablifhed in the Siera Morena in Spain, and in various others in different parts of Europe, much attention has been paid to the eftablifhing of little farms **only**. I do not want to view fuch, to know that the improvement is beggarly, **and** the hufbandry contemptible: **no wafte can** be really improved, and to the beft advantage, but by means of the fheep, powerfully applied; all other methods are coftly, flow, and of weak effect; but no little farmer can have a flock fufficient. **This** paltry idea of eftablifhing nothing but little farms, is the refult of moft impolitical ideas refpecting population, which ought never to be the object of a moment's attention. If it exift idle, or beyond the proportion of employment, it is the fource of poverty and wretchednefs; it is valuable only in proportion to regular and active employment; find that employment, and you will **have** an induftrious active population in fpite of every obftacle. But fmall farms and little divifible properties, increafing the people, without increafing employment, has no other tendency than to propagate idle beggars, and to diffeminate modes of **hufbandry, calculated** to exhauft the land, and keep its cultivators in mifery. This is not theory but fact, of which almoft every province, in France, **abounds** with glaring inftances. But of this more in another chapter.

There is another fort of wafte land, that abounds alfo very **much in France,** I mean marfhes: it is afferted, that there are from 1,200,000 to **1,500,000** * arpents of them in France. **The** improvement of thefe is vaftly more expenfive and more difficult than that of *landes*, heaths, moors, &c. The drains de**manded for** them require a confiderable capital. Thefe ought to be cônverted to meadow and rich pafture, by means of draining. Where they admit it, the cheapeft improvement **of fuch is by** irrigation; the general drainage of great marfhes, if not trufted by the affemblies of the departments to the conduct of fome one able director, fhould be done by commiffion; by conftituting a **company,** as in England, and paying the expence, by a tax **on the** lands drained. **If the rage** for fmall farms continue, thefe marfhes, in proportion as the foil **is boggy, will** admit of being divided into fmall portions, that is, of 30 to 60 **arpents, but it** fhould be under an abfolute prohibition of the plough. The bog, **which I faw** in paffing from Auvergnac to Nantes, **and** which feems, from its **appearance on** the map of Bretagne, **to** be of **a** vaft extent, **is highly fufceptible of improve**ment, **and every acre of** it might be converted **into rich meadow.**

* *Rapport du Comité d'Agriculture,* &c. 7 Fev. 1790, par M. de Lamerville, deputé de Berri. P. 3. *De la neceffité d'occuper tous les gros Ouvriers,* 1789, par M. Bonçerf. P. 3.

CHAP.

CHAP. XV.

Of Coals, in France.

LIMOUSIN.—*Limoges.*—I WAS here affured, that a vein of coal has been found at the depth only of 12 yards, which is 17 feet thick; but it is no where ufed, either in houfes or in manufactures; the iron forges are all worked with charcoal. If this is fact, what a want of capital it proves!

FLANDERS.—*Valenciennes.*—There are mines worked here. The manco of **240 lb.** fells for 23 *f.* 9 den. and the worft of all at 12½ *f.*; the largeft of all at 35 *f.* and 36 *f.*; they are more abundant at Mons. Wood is burnt here **at the** inns, and all the better private houfes, but the poor burn coal: the mines, they fay, are 700 feet deep; the coal is drawn up by four horfes; they have four **fteam engines.**

Lille.—**Coals, the** raziere, 3 liv.

Dunkirk.—Englifh, the raziere of 300 lb. 8 liv. Thefe **are burnt** in every **houfe in the** town, and are one-third cheaper than wood: there is a canal to the coal pits at Valenciennes, but the diftance too great, and locks **too** numerous and expenfive to rival the import from England.

Bethune.—Pits within a few leagues. Price here 44 *f.* to 46 *f.* the raziere, which, I have been told, holds about nine Englifh pecks; but the raziere of St. Omers holds 195 lb. of wheat.

Rouen.—The boiffeau of 22 pots, each 2 bottles, 3 liv. 10 *f.*

Ifigny.—A mine newly opened, at which the coals fell at 14 *f.* 1 liard, the boiffeau, of 90 lb. to 100 lb.

Carentan.—**Coals of the country only for blackfmiths, 14 *f.* the boiffeau of 80 lb. dry at the mine, but wet are 90 lb. or 100 lb. : they are not half fo good** as what is brought from England.

Cherbourg.—In the manufacture of blown plate glafs, a great quantity of Newcaftle coal is burnt; 13 keel, or 103 chaldrons, coft, all Englifh charges included, about 7500 liv.; the French duty 3600 liv.; and port charges, &c. make it in all about 11,000 liv. which being near 5l. a chaldron, feems an enormous price, at which to buy fuel for a manufacture. The coals of the Cotentin, they fay here, are good for nothing.

Granville.—The blackfmiths burn *Guernfey* coals.

Auray.—Englifh coals 3 liv. the boiffeau of about three Englifh pecks, which the blackfmiths ufe for particular purpofes.

Nantes.

Nantes.—French coal 300 liv. the 21 barriques, each double wine meafure, or 480 pints, but one barrique of Englifh is worth two of it.

A coal mine worked by a Monf. Jarry, at Langien, five leagues from Nantes. Another at Montrelais, near Ingrande; and at St. George, near Saumur. The French coals ufed in the foundry, near this city, come to 34 liv. the 2000 lb.

La Fleche.—Price 16 f. the boiffeau, of 30 lb. wheat; they are from Angers.

Rouen.—Monf. Scannegatty works the common borer, with a windlafs, in boring deep for coals, for which purpofe he has been employed by government he fhewed me the model of one made at Paris, 300 feet long; with this he has bored 160 feet, much of it in hard rock, without accident; his objection to fhafts, is the water rifing; he would ufe fhafts until he comes to water, but after that muft bore. He fays, the badnefs of the coal, in the mine near Cherbourg, arifes merely from being ill worked; they have got at prefent only to the furface coal, inftead of piercing through the bed. M. Scannegatty afferts, the confumption of Englifh coals, in the generality of Rouen, to be two millions a year. The price is 40 liv. for 6½ barriques, each barrique 150 lb. or 975 lb. or about 80 liv. a ton.

Elbœuf.—Confumes 200,000 liv. a year in Englifh coals.

Nangis.—Brought from Berri. Price 4 liv. the Englifh bufhel.

Lorraine.—*Pont-à-Mouffon.*—From Sarbruck 18 liv. the 1000 lb. At the mine 5 liv.

Alsace.—*Befort.*—Price at the mine, four leagues from this place, 12 f. the 100 lb.; here 16 f. They are ufed only by blackfmiths.

Bourgogne.—*Chagny.*—Coals from Mont Cenis; at the mine 6 liv. the the wine *queu*; here 10 liv. Nobody burns coals in their houfes.

Mont Cenis.—At the mine a *ban* 10 f. It is remarkable, that at the inn here, and at every houfe, except thofe of the common workman, wood is burnt; which fhews the abfurd prejudices of the French, in favour of that fuel, in fpite of price.

Bourbonnois.—*Moulins.*—Price 30 f. the *bachole*, of which 4 make a poinçon.

Auvergne.—*Clermont.*—Price 10 liv. the *raze* of 2 feet 2 inches, by 1 foot 6 inches, and nine inches deep. Ufed only in ftoves, or by blackfmiths; they are from Brioude.

Brioude.—The *raze*, of 150 lb. 16 f.; but the beft is 20 f.

Fix.—The *carton*, of 50 lb. 14 f.

Vivarais.—*Cofteros.*—The quintal 50 f.

Thuytz.—The blackfmiths here burn charcoal, yet are near the coal mine, which I paffed in the vale; it is a ftone coal; the price 7 f. the 100 lb.

Dauphine.

O

DAUPHINE.—*Montélimart.*—Large coal 1 liv. 15 *f.* the 155 lb. ; fmall, for blackfmiths and manufacturers, 22 *f.* the 155 lb. The mine is at Givors, near Vienne, at five leagues from Lyon ; there is a canal to Vienne, but with a toll. Coak, made of coal, for melting, 5 *f.* the quintal.

Pierre-Latte.—Coals 3 liv. the meafure of about 6 pecks ; none ufed but by blackfmiths.

PROVENCE.—*Tour d'Aigues.*—Price 40 *f.* the quintal. 16 *f.* or 18 *f.* at Aix. At the mine, three leagues from Aix, 5 *f.*

Marfeille.—Coals from Givors, in Dauphiné, near Lyon, 33 *f.* for 210 lb. of Faveau, in Provence, 40 *f.* to 42 *f.* for 300 lb. Of Valdonne, 41 *f.* ditto : ufed in the foap fabric and fugar refineries. Of England 42 *f.* to 45 *f.* on board the fhip, for 210 lb. ; on fhore 60 *f.* for 195 lb.

LYONNOIS.—*Lyon.*—Coals 30 *f.* the 130 lb. The mines are fix leagues off ; price there 24 *f.* for 160 lb. : there is a canal from the pits to the Rhone.

The want of vigour in working the coal-mines in France, is to be attributed to two caufes ; 1, the price of wood has not rifen fufficiently to force this branch of induftry ; and, 2, the want of capital, which affects every thing in that kingdom, prevents exertions being made with the neceffary animation. But thefe evils will correct themfelves ; the gradual rife in the price of wood, which, fo far from being an evil, as it is univerfally thought in France, is only a proof of national improvement, will by degrees force the confumption of coals ; and when thefe are in the neceffary demand, they will be produced in greater quantities.

CHAP. XVI.

Woods, Forests, Timber, and Planting, in France.

*Pyrennées—*A Confiderable proportion of thefe mountains is under wood, and a much larger has been; for the deftruction of them making every day, is not credible to thofe who have not viewed them. Paffed frequently through feveral woods near Bagnere de Luchon, in which the wood-men were at work, riving and cutting beech ftaves for cafks; I was fhocked to fee the deftruction they made, which could not have been more wafteful or lavifh if they had been in the midft of an American foreft. Large and beautiful beeches are cut off, 3, 4, and 5 feet high, and thofe noble ftumps left to rot; whole trees, which, on trial, would not rive well, left for years, and now rotting untouched; and in working thofe we faw, nothing but clean cuts taken, 3 or 4 feet perhaps in 50, and the reft left on the ground in the fame confufion in which it fell. The deftruction fo general in this noble foreft of Lartigues, that it is almoft deftroyed; there is no young growth for fucceffion; and in ten or twelve years it will be a bare mountain, with a few miferable fhrubs browzed by goats and other cattle. In fome tracts which I paffed, at a few leagues diftance, towards the walks of the Spanifh flocks, there are fome forefts deftroyed in fuch a fhameful manner, that to a perfon, from a country where wood is of any value, muft appear incredible; feveral fcores of acres fo utterly deftroyed that not a tree remains ftanding; yet the whole a foreft of ftumps, 3, 4, and 6 feet high, melancholy and fhocking to behold. The torrents every where roll down as much wood as ftone, and prefent a fpectacle of fimilar ruin; the roads are formed of fragments of trees, and are guarded againft the precipices by whole ones laid and left to rot; you no where pafs many yards without thrufting your cane into bodies, rotten, or rotting; all is ruin, wafte, and defolation; and the very appearance one would fuppofe a wood to carry, in which a foreign enemy had, with the moft wanton malice, deftroyed every thing.

Thefe woods are commons belonging to the communities of the parifhes, upon which every inhabitant affumes the right, and practifes the rage of depredation. So carelefs of the interefts of pofterity, or rather fo inflamed againft every idea but that of the prefent moment, that, in the general opinion, there will be an undoubted fcarcity in thirty years, amidft what have been, and yet are, in fome diftricts, very noble forefts. The communities fometimes fell woods; an inftance occurred lately, that of Bagnere de Luchon fold a *fall* for 14,000 liv. but worth, it is faid, 35,000 liv. in which fome pilfering might take place; this

was

was to pay their fhare of the new bathing houfe. Is it poffible that fuch a recital can be given of a country that imports pot-afh from the diftance of 2000
miles !

The number of faw mills, in thefe mountains, turned by torrents, is confiderable; they are of a very cheap and fimple conftruction, but exceedingly incom-
plete, having no mechanical contrivance for bringing the tree to the faw, a man
conftantly doing it by preffing with his foot on the cogged wheel.

LANGUEDOC.—*Lunel.*—At the Palais Royal inn there is one, among many
ftables, which is covered by twelve large beams, 16 or 18 inches fquare, and
45 feet long. The whole country is at prefent *quafi* fuch trees as thefe, de-
nuded.

GASCOGNE.—*St. Palais to Anfpan.*—An oak here fells for 30 liv. which
would, in England, fell for 45s. to 50s.

ISLE OF FRANCE.—*Lieurfaint.*—In the royal foreft of Senars, the oak copfes
are cut every twenty years, and fell at 600 liv. the arpent (the cord of wood felling, at Paris, at 50 liv.), which makes 30 liv. a year, but from this carriage
is to be deducted, and there will remain about a louis d'or.

Liancourt.—Woods here form a confiderable portion of the whole country.
They are in general cut at twelve years growth, but in fome parts at fifteen and
twenty; they fell at twelve years from 100 liv. to 200 liv. the arpent (about 1¼
acre): at 150 liv. it may be called 12 liv. per annum; as they are on the poorest
land this is much more confiderable than the fame land would let for, but it is
much inferior to what the *product* of the fame lands would be, under a tolerable
fyftem of cultivation. The quantity of foreft fpread over the country, in almoft
every direction, makes timber cheap: oak, afh, and elm fell at 30f. the cubical
foot, a larger foot than that of England. The poorest family 60 liv. a year
in wood.

Clermont.—Near this place, in the foreft of la Neuville eu Haye, belonging
to the king, there is an undertaking now (1787) going forward, which does
honour to government: it is a plantation of oak for timber. The land is inclofed with pales, wired to the rails, in the French manner, inftead of nailing:
the land is all trenched 2 feet deep, for which the workmen are paid according
to the foil, 20f to 40f. the fquare perch of 22 feet, and they earn about 22f. a
day: as it was an old foreft where they work, there are many roots, for extract-
ing which they are allowed fomething more. The foil in general is a good
light loam, except in fome parts, on a pure white fand. The whole expence,
by contract (fencing excepted), digging, planting, filling vacancies, and hoeing
twice a year, for five years, is 300 liv. the arpent, of about 1¼ acre. The fence
is 3 liv. the toife, or about 1s. 2d. a yard, running meafure: 60 arpents are
done, and they are ftill at work. I viewed the oaks with pleafure; they are

moft

moſt of them remarkably fine; they thrive well, and are very healthy; ſome are five years old from the ſeed, and others five years old from transplanting; the plants then three years old theſe are the largeſt, but not more ſo than three years difference in age ought to make them: they are in rows at about 4 feet. There is alſo a ſmall incloſure of cheſnuts and Bourdeaux pines (*pinus maritimus*), ſown four years paſt, which are now five feet high, which is a vaſt growth. The only enemy which the oaks have hitherto met with, is the cock-chaffer grub, which has killed ſome.

Dugny.—Monſ. Cretté de Paluel has planted many thouſands of the poplar, with ſucceſs, and has cut them when only twelve years old, large enough for building. Several of his farming offices, very well and ſubſtantially built, are of this wood, erected twelve years ago: and the timbers are now as ſound as at the time of uſing; but he has found, that when expoſed to the weather, it does not laſt.

Normandie.—*Bon.*—The ſeat of the Marquis de Turgot, elder brother of the celebrated controleur-general. A large plantation of foreign trees, in which nothing is ſo remarkable as the ſuperiority of the larch to every other plant.

Falaiſe.—Woods, at twelve years growth, pay 8 to 10 louis an acre, or 22 liv. a year.

Harcourt.—The larch and Weymouth pine, of eighteen years growth, have thriven beyond any thing. I meaſured a larch, of that age, 3 feet 6 inches in circumference, at 5 feet from the ground; and a Weymouth 2 inches larger. Woods throughout Normandie, on an average, pay 20 liv. the Norman acre (10s. 6d. per Engliſh acre).

La Roche-Guyon.—There is nothing in this country that pays better than plantations of willows for yielding vine props. The Dutcheſs D'Enville has a piece of 3¼ arpents, which yields 400 liv. a year, by being cut every third year. New ones are ſet as the old wear out; the heads are cropped at three years old, and the great product is from nine to eighteen years of age. Lombardy poplars, planted by the preſent Dutcheſs, of twenty-four years growth, are worth 11 liv. each, ſtanding only 6 feet aſunder: it would be uſeleſs to apply calculation to this fact, to ſee what the acreable produce would be; for if a man had a few acres to ſell every year, he would be able to get no more than the price of a very bad fire wood, not ſaleable till after every better ſort in a country was conſumed. Could a demand be found, the profit would be enormous. They grow on the level of the Seine. They are cut into boards 10 inches wide, which ſell at 2 ſ. the foot.

Isle of France.—*Columiers.*—Woods, at nine years growth, worth 180 liv. the arpent (9l. the Engliſh acre).

Champagne.

CHAMPAGNE.—*Mareuil.*—At twenty years growth, worth 300 liv. the arpent (10l. 10s. per English acre), at 1½ or 2 leagues from the Marne, but if further, 4 liv. per arpent per annum deduction.

Epernay.—It is possible to go from hence to Alsace, with no great interruption, through forest, all the way.

LORRAINE.—*Braban.*—Woods are cut, at twenty years growth, and the produce 12 liv. per arpent per annum (18s. 4d. per English acre).

Metz.—Woods cut, at twenty to twenty-five years growth, 120 liv the journal.

Luneville.—Woods cut, at twenty-five or thirty years growth, from 40 liv. to 100 liv. net the journal, 1974 English yards.

FRANCHE COMTE.—*Befançon.*—Cut, at twenty-five years growth, and yields 150 liv. to 200 liv. the cutting, or 8 liv. per annum per arpent; near the forges of the city, to 300 liv. (10l. 10s. per English acre).

Orchamps.—A little auberge confumes from twenty to thirty waggon loads, each 8 liv. in a year, at one fire.

BOURGOGNE.—*Auxonne.*—Pafs a wood felled and corded, 12 cords per English acre; the cord 8 feet by 4 feet, and two high; and the price 8 liv. A little aubergifte confumes to the amount of 200 liv. a year, one fire. It would coft a poor family 80 liv. a year, if they bought fairly all they burn. Calculate

Four millions of families, at one cord, and at ten per acre, 400,000 acres.

Cut, at twenty years,	-	-	-	-	8,000,000
At two cords,	-	-	-	-	16,000,000
At three ditto	-	-	-	-	24,000,000

Dijon.—Confumption of one fire, 5 or 6 *mœul* for the poor, the *mœul* 4 feet cubical. Of the whole town, of 24,000 people, 40,000 *mœul*. Beft oak timber, 3 liv. the cubical foot. Inferior to 20f. Elm dearer than oak; ufed for wheel carriages only. Pine one-third cheaper.

BOURBONNOIS.—*Moulins.*—Copfes cut, at fifteen years growth, and fell at 50 liv. the arpent, of 48,384 feet; no expence except cutting. Oak timber, 18f. to 20f. the cubical foot. Planks of 9, 10, and 11 inches wide, 45 liv. to 60 liv. the hundred toife (6 feet), ¼ inch thick. Laths 14f. the faggot, of 52, and 5 feet long.

AUVERGNE.—*Riom.*—One fire, and a very poor one, 80 liv. if bought.

Clermont.—A poor family, to fteal none, muft have ten cord, or 60 liv. and charcoal to the amount of 15 liv.; but, in general, they fteal, or collect as well as they can.

VIVARAIS.—*Pradelles to Thuytz.*—Great woods of pines in thefe mountains, with faw-mills for cutting them.

DAUPHINE.—*Loriol.*—Oak 12f. the 100 lb.

PROVENCE.

PROVENCE.—*Tour d'Aigues.*—Wood thrives greatly in this country. The President has a great many oaks, and some of a vast size ; also black poplar and beech. One by the farm-house, 13 feet 11 inches, French, in circumference, at 5 feet from the ground, and 80 feet high. Here also are evergreen oaks, 500 years old. He has *platanus* of a vast growth, in twenty-five years, and the *morus papyrifera*, of a great size. The poorest family in this country consumes 60 quintals of wood a year, stolen, or bought ; generally the former. A bourgeoise, that has soup every day at one fire, 150 quintals.

Fréjus to Estrelles.—The pines, &c. in these mountains, hacked, plundered, and destroyed, almost as wantonly as in the Pyrennees : and spots every where burnt by the shepherds, though prohibited, in order to produce herbage for their flocks.

		Price per Paris load of 140 ft. liv.
1787.—LIMOUSIN.—*Limoges.*—Charcoal 30 *s.* the quintal.		
ANGOUMOIS.—*Verteuil.*—Cord of wood 10 liv. near a navigation ; 3 liv. at a distance.		
ISLE OF FRANCE.—*Montgeron.*—Cord 44 liv.		
FLANDERS.—*Lille.*—Ditto 60 liv.		
Dunkirk.—Ditto 60 liv. the load of 100 measures.		
1788.—NORMANDY.—*Caen.*—Charcoal 20 *s.* the raziere, of 40 lb. of wheat.		
Cord of beech wood, 6 feet long, 4 broad, and 4 high, 24 liv.	-	35
Other woods 18 liv. to 20 liv.	-	27
Faggots of 3½ feet around, and 5 feet long, with large wood in them, 60 liv. to 80 liv. per hundred.		
BRETAGNE.—*Rennes.*—Cord 8 feet long, 4 high, and 2½ broad, 15 liv. to 17 liv.	-	28
Landernau.—Cord 8 feet by 4 feet, and 2½ high, 24 liv.	-	42
L'Orient.—Cord 8 feet by four feet, and 2½ high, 20 liv.	-	35
Auray.—Charcoal 3 liv. the barrique. Iron 5 *s.* the lb. A horse-shoe 12 *s.*		
Auvergnac.—Cord of wood, 28 liv.	-	49
Nantes.—Ditto 30 liv. to 36 liv.	-	57
Swedish iron 280 liv. the thousand pound. Hemp 50 liv. the hundred ditto.		
Ancenis.—Cord 24 liv.	-	42
ANJOU.—*Angers.*—Cord 8 feet long, 4 feet high, and 4 broad : a double cord, 40 liv.	-	42
Faggots 18 liv. to 24 liv. the hundred.		
La Fleche.—Cord 16 liv to 21 liv.	-	39
Charcoal 70 liv. to 80 liv. the 42 barriques.		

MAINE.

Price per
Paris cord
of 140 ft.

MAINE.—*Guefcelard.*—The cord, 6 feet by 3½ feet, and 3½ high, of   liv.

pine, 6 liv. - - - - - -   12

Ditto of oak, 14 liv. - - : - - -   26

NORMANDY.—*Gacé.*—Charcoal 52 *f.* the barrique. Iron 23 liv. the hundred pound, or 1 liard lefs than 5 *l.* the lb. They charge 8 *f.* the lb. for heavy work, and 32 *f.* for fhoeing a horfe.

Elbœuf.—The cord 8 feet by 4 feet, and 2½ high, 24 liv. - -   42

La Roche-Guyon.—Cord 8 feet by 4 feet, and 4 high, is 30 liv. -   32

ISLE OF FRANCE.—*Nangis.*—Cord 12 feet by 4 feet, and 4 high : price 24 liv. to 28 liv. - - - - - -   18

CHAMPAGNE.—*Mareuil.*—Cord 8 feet long, 5 feet high, and 3 feet 7 inches broad, fells, oak 36 liv. - - - -   31

White woods 24 liv. - - - . -   21

Charcoal 50 *f.* the tonneaux, of 200 pints of Paris (quarts).

Epernay.—The cord 40 liv. - - - -   40

St. Menehoud.—Cord 8 feet by 4 feet, and 3½ inches : 18 liv. 10 *f.*; in the town 19 liv. ; but twenty-five years ago it was 7 liv. 10 feet. -   24

LORRAINE.—*Braban.*—Cord 8 feet by 4 feet, and 4 high, is 19 liv. - 20

Mar-le-Tour.—Cord 8 feet by 4 feet, and 4 high, is 16 liv. ; the beft 21 liv. - - - - - -   20

Metz.—Charcoal 30 *f.* the fack : cord 8 feet by 4 feet, and 4 high ; is 32 liv. : of beach and hornbeam, - - - -   35

Of oak, 22 liv. - - - - -   24

Pont-à-Mouffon.—Cord 8 feet by 4 feet, and 4 high : in town 16 liv. 10 *f.*   18

In the foreft 12 liv.

Nancy.—Cord floated oak 20 liv. ; other forts 23 liv. - -   28

Not floated oak 26 liv. ; beech and hornbeam 34 liv. - -   37

Luneville.—Cord 8 feet by 4 feet, and 4 high : now 24 liv. to 28 liv.

Beech, - - - - - - -   28

Oak 22 liv. to 23 liv. - - - - -   24

ALSACE.—*Strafbourg.*—Cord 6 feet by 6 feet, and 3 high ; price 27 liv.   38

Schelefat.—Cord 6 feet by 6 feet, and 3 high ; price 24 liv.* -   31

Ifle.—Cord 8 feet by 4 feet, and 4 high ; price 12 liv. yet many iron forges, - - - - - -   14

FRANCHE COMTE.—*Befançon.*—Cord 8 feet by 4 feet, and 4 high, floated, 16 liv. 10 *f.* - -. - - - -   18

Not floated, 25 liv. : - - - -   27

* Some fold 6 feet by 6 feet, and 6 high.

Orchewfs.

Orchamps.—Iron; all used by blacksmiths; is of the country; 5 f. the
lb. Charcoal only used in making it, at 40 liv. the load of four horses,
about 50 or 60 bushels; there are forges spread over the whole country:
one within three leagues, which, with its furnace, uses 50 loads of wood
per diem. Shoeing a horse 40 f.

Dijon.—Cord 7½ feet by 4 feet, and 4½ high, at 26 liv. the mœul, a
cube of 4 feet, and the price 13 liv.   -   -   -   -   26
Price of carriage 20 f. per thousand pound for each league.

Chagny.—Mœul, cube of 4 feet, 13 liv. to 16 liv.   -   -   31
Iron: tier of wheels 7 f. the lb. and 8 f. for the nails. Price of iron
5 f. 1 liard.

Moulins.—Cord, 2 to a coche, 30 liv. Charcoal 3 f. to 3½ f. the English
peck. Iron 1 liard under 5 f. per lb. Cast ditto 3 f.

Clermont.—Cord 3 feet 11 inches, by 7 feet 4 inches circumference;
price 6 liv. about one-fourth of a Paris cord,   -   -   24
Charcoal 2 f. the lb.

Fix.—Iron 5½ f. the lb.

Montélimart. Charcoal 5 f. the hundred pound.

Pierre Latte.—Wood 20 f. the hundred pound.

Avignon.—Wood 18 f. to 20 f. the hundred pound. Charcoal 3 liv. the
hundred pound.

Tour d'Aigues.—Charcoal 45 f. the hundred pound.

Marseille.—Wood 3 liv. 17 f. for 300 lb. and 8 f. carriage from the ship.
In winter the same, 5 liv. Charcoal, by shipping, 50 f. the quintal,
120 lb.; by land 70 f.

Lyon.—Oak, the mœul, 3 feet 8 inches square, 23 liv.
                General average,   -   -   -   -   30

To these data may be here added, that the woods and forests of the kingdom
amount to 19,850,515 acres, and that the average annual produce may be reckoned
14s. an acre. It here appears, that the average price per cord, of 140 cubical feet,
is 30 liv.

The price of wood has risen considerably in France.—Price of the lignier,
equal to two Paris voies, at Bourg, in Bresse.

In 1688,	-	-	3 liv.	0 f.
1718,	-	-	3	12
1748,	-	-	7	10
1778,	-	-	9	0
1789,	-	-	21	0*

* *Observations sur l'Agriculture,* par Mr. Varenne de Fenille. 8vo. p. 141.

The

The fcarcity of wood in France, as marked in this rife of price, has occupied at leaft an hundred pens during the laft ten years: almoft all the cahiers complain heavily of it, and in that of the clergy of Meaux, they call it a **real calamity.** There is hardly a fociety of agriculture, in the kingdom, that has not offered premiums for memoirs that fhould explain the caufes **of fuch** an alarming want, **and point** out the beft means of remedying it. The opinion is univerfal; I have **met** but one mind upon the topic, which, confidering the talents for political œconomy, furprifed me a good deal; for I muft declare myfelf of **a** dire 'ly contrary opinion, and venture to affert, that the price of wood is too **low** in France; that it has not rifen fo rapidly as it ought to have done; **and that all** ideas **of** encouraging plantations, to prevent a further rife, are ignorant and mifchievous, and founded in a total mifconception of the fubject, for want of **combining** thofe circumftances **which bear** upon the queftion. The rent of arable **land, in** France, calculated **feparately,** and rejecting the parts left wafte, and in neglect, is 15s.7d. an acre; but the rent of woods is only 12s. How then in common **fenfe** can any one complain of a price of wood, which, inftead of being, at its **prefent** rate, an injury to the confumer, is actually a material one to the landed **intereft,** who do not make by their woods nearly what they would do by the land if it was grubbed, cleared, and converted to cultivation; and I am fo well perfuaded of this, that if I was the poffeffor of woods, in France, I would moft affuredly grub up every acre that did not grow upon land impracticable to the plough; and I fhould do this under the firmeft conviction that my fpeculation would be profitable. If tillage improves, and freed from tithes and inequality of **taxation,** no one can doubt but it will improve, the price of wood ought to rife very confiderably to prevent landlords, who are well informed, from grubbing up; and let it be confidered, how vaft a premium there is to induce them to fuch a conduct, in all woods where the growth is antient, as forty, fifty, fixty and **a** hundred years, at which age many are found in France: the money which the fale of fuch would produce, placed at intereft, and the land converted to tillage, would, in moft inftances, treble, and even quadruple, the revenue to be gained from the fame land, while cropped with wood. Nor is it to be forgotten, that frefh wood-land is generally fertile; poffeffing ftores that, with good management, in refpect to cropping, may be made to laft at leaft twenty years, and in fome meafure for ever. We may fafely determine that the price of wood is not rifen to a fair par with other land products, until it can no longer be the intereft of the land owner to grub up, and till woods yield as good a revenue as the lands around them, *well cultivated.* It is an undoubted fact, that the price is not yet rifen near fo fuch a par.

There is yet another, and equally unqueftionable, proof, that the price of wood is much too low in France, and that is the coal mines, found in almoft every part of the kingdom, remain, for the greater part, unworked; and that the people burn wood, even in the immediate vicinity of such mines; I was myself served with wood at all the inns, at and near the coal mines wrought, of Valenciennes, Mont-Cenis, Lyon, Auvergne, Languedoc, Normandie, Bretagne, Anjou, &c. &c. Is it possible to suppose that this would be the case if wood was risen to its fair par with other commodities?

The conclusion to be drawn, from this state of facts, is sufficiently clear, that the legislature ought not to take any steps whatever to encourage the production of wood, but leave it absolutely free to rise gradually to that fair price to which demand will carry it; and that the societies and academies of agriculture, composed of citizens, that is to say, commonly of mere consumers, uninterested in the production, ought to cease their unjust and impertinent clamour against the price of a commodity which is much too cheap. Whenever the price of wood rises too high, coal mines will every where be effectually worked, and the people in sight of them most assuredly will not burn wood.

We have of late had, in England, the same vulgar apprehension of a want of wood, especially for ship building, which has disgraced France. No wonder timber has been destroyed in both kingdoms, while the price was inadequate to the expence of raising it. Timber for ship building, as well as cord-wood, should at least bear a proportion with corn, meat, butter, wool, &c. which the ground might yield if not occupied in a different manner. The comparisons made are by landlords, who look only at *rent*, but the national interests require that *produce* should be consulted. The argument commonly used, by the proprietors of the *landes* of Bourdeaux, against cultivating them, is, that they yield at present, in pines, a better *rent* in resin than they would do for cultivation, which is certainly true, if the culture introduced was not good; but what a loss to the nation to have lands employed to yield, like all the woods of the kingdom, a gross produce of 16 liv. per acre, instead of 40 liv. the produce of arable land? Those who contend for encouragements to planting, because wood is dear, call for the marvellous improvement of converting land, which now yields 40 liv. to the state of yielding 16 liv.! It is just the same in England; our societies offer premiums for planting, and, as far as those premiums are claimed, or induce men to think planting an improvement, they are attended with the mischief and absurdity of preferring a small to a great produce. There are tracts of *impracticable* land, I will not say *waste*, because nine-tenths of our waste lands, like those of France, are susceptible of cultivation, and therefore it is a public nuisance to plant them: it may be profitable to the landlord to plant quick growing trees, because he considers only *rent*, but societies and the nation should look at *produce*, and consequently discourage all planting.

The

The common argument, that is founded on the fuppofed neceffity of a Royal Navy, I fhould be forry to beftow three words upon; for I hold every idea of a great naval force to be founded on very queftionable theories. Injurious to other nations in its object, which is that of extending to the moft diftant parts of the globe the mifchievous effects of ambition; and all the horrors that attend the fpirit of conqueft, when flowing from the worfe fpirit of foreign commerce. A great navy affords the means of fpreading what may to Europe be called a domeftic quarrel to the moft diftant regions of the globe, and involving millions in the ruin of wars, who are in juftice as unconcerned in the difpute as they are removed by diftance from the natural theatre of it. And whatever commercial neceffity, founded upon the worft principles, may be urged in the fupport of it, yet the expence is fo enormous, that no nation, it is now well underftood, can be formidable both at land and fea at the fame time, without making efforts, that throw our own burthens, by means of debts, on our innocent pofterity. Mr. Hume remarks, that the Britifh fleet, in the height of the war of 1740, coft the nation a greater expence than that of the whole military eftablifhment of the Roman Empire, under Auguftus, while all, that deferved to be called the world, was in obedience to his fceptre; but in the late war, the expence of our fleet amounted to more than the double of what attracted the notice of that agreeable and profound politician, for the naval expence of 1781 arofe to 8,603,884l.

The ambition of ftatefmen is ready at all times to found upon a great commerce the neceffity of a great navy to protect it; and the next ftep is, the fuppofed neceffity of a great commerce to fupport the great navy; and very fine arrangements, in political œconomy, have been the confequence of this mifchievous combination. The delufive dream of colonies was one branch of this curious policy, which coft the nation, as Sir John Sinclair has calculated, two hundred and eighty millions! Rather than have incurred fuch an enormous expence, which our powerful navy abfolutely induced, would it not have been better had the nation been without commerce, without colonies, without a navy? The fame madnefs has infefted the cabinet of France; a great navy is there alfo confidered as effential, becaufe they have in St. Domingo a great colony; thus one nuifance begets another. The prefent century has been the period of naval power. It will ceafe in the next, and then be confidered as a fyftem founded on the fpirit of commercial rapine.

But whatever neceffity there may be for navies, there is none for raifing oak to build them, which it is infinitely better to buy than to cultivate. There is no profpect of exhaufting the oak of the north, of Bohemia, Silefia, Poland, Hungary, and the territories on the Adriatic, for centuries to come; the price will rife as carriage becomes expenfive, but the fupply will remain for ages. So long

ago

ago as the beginning of the laft century, we ufed fir for building, from the
fcarcity of oak*; and notwithftanding the immenfe confumption, fince the
countries that fupply it promife to continue that fupply for five centuries to
come.

A veffel of the firft rank is faid, in France, to demand 60,000 cubical feet of
timber†; but a later account makes it much more confiderable.

	Quantity in a Ship of 116 Guns.		Quantity in a Ship of 74 Guns.
Cubical feet,—Firft fpecies,	77,520	—	47,356
Second ditto,	39,840	—	16,161
Third ditto,	5,896	—	12,300
Fourth ditto,	1,250	—	1,780
Fifth ditto,	180	—	19
Plank,	1,995	—	1,497
	126,681	—	79,113
Fir,	8,449	—	6,338‡

The common price of oak 3 liv. the foot.

I cannot quit the fubject of woods without remarking, that many of the nobility, in France, have given that attention to the introduction of exotic trees,
which would have been a thoufand times better applied to improving the agriculture of their diftricts: I faw many places, the owners of which affected to
make a reputation by their evergreens, and other plantations, while living in
the midft of lands, under a cultivation difgraceful to the kingdom, and the fame
even on their own farms.   For one fol that France will ever be improved by
their exotics, it was in their power to have improved her many louis, by very
different exertions.

* " And now of late, for want of other timber, we begin to ufe fir for building of houfes." *An
Old Thrift newly revived, or the Manner of Planting, &c. by R. C.* 4to. 1612.   Black letter. P. 7.

† *Recherches fur la Houille d'Engrais.*   Tom. ii. p. 25.

‡ *Encyclopédie Méthodique.* 4to. *Marine.*   Tom. i. part 1. p. 163.

CHAP.

CHAP. XVII.

On Some Œconomical Practices, in France.

SOME fcattered minutes, not abfolutely ufelefs, may, perhaps, better be thrown together than burnt; for ingenious men fometimes catch hints from a flight mention of practices, and apply them to ufes not at firft thought of.

Building.

LANGUEDOC.—*Montauban to Touloufe.*—At a brick-kiln, obferve that they burn only faggots of vine-cuttings.

Bagnere de Luchon.—For building the new bathing-houfe erecting here, by the ftates of Languedoc, they work the lime (burnt from a fine blue hard ftone) with gravel inftead of fand, of which they have none in the country; and, on examination, I found this gravel to be a true lime-ftone one, the fame fo often met with in Ireland. I could not find that the mortar was the harder or better for this; but, on breaking, rather fofter than that of fand. They have here a very effectual method of cementing ftone; when fquared blocks break, they join them very eafily, by applying this cement;—refin, three-fourths; fulphur and wax, one-fourth; powdered ftone, of the fort to be joined, enough to give it the right confiftence when melted. This holds the ftone fo firmly together, that the folid part will break rather than at the junction.

NORMANDIE.—*Carentan to Coutances.*—They build here the beft mud houfes I have any where feen; very good ones, of three ftories, are thus raifed: and confiderable offices, with large barns. The earth and ftraw well kneaded together, are fpread, about four inches thick, on the ground, cut in fquares of nine inches, and thefe toffed from a fhovel to the man on the wall, who builds it; it is finifhed, layer by layer, and left for drying, as in Ireland; the layers three feet high, and the thicknefs of the walls about two feet; they make them projecting about an inch, which they cut off, layer by layer, perfectly fmooth; if they had the Englifh way of white-wafhing, they would look as well as our lath and plafter houfes, and be vaftly better and warmer. In good houfes, the doors and windows are in ftone work.

Bernay.—Mud walls to inclofe gardens, and for fruit, well built and thatched at top.

CHAMPAGNE.—*Epernay.*—Monf. Paretclaine's new oak floor, which is the common fafhion of France, of fhort fcantlings, in a fort of Mofaic, cofts 40 liv. the fquare toife of 6 French feet, including joifts and all. They are dove-tailed

along

along the sides, but nailed at the ends; the nails knocked in, and a plug of wood driven in and plained off.

Lime.

LANGUEDOC.—*Bagnere de Luchon.*—The lime-kilns here, while burning, have a remarkable smell of burning sulphur, from the quantity of that mineral, with which the lime-stone is mixed. They build their kilns oval, swelling in the middle, with a mouth, not quite at the bottom, where they put in the wood: the upper part is covered with stones, in order to keep the heat in. They are 24 hours burning the lime. When burnt, stop the mouth close, and leave it to cool, which takes three days; after which, they take the lime out. A kiln holds 400 septiers, which may be supposed the septier of Paris. They carry, with a pair of oxen, but 2 septiers. Sell it at 40 *f.* to 45 *f.* the septier. Such a quantity of lime takes 600 faggots to burn, and a little other wood.

FLANDERS.—*Armentieres to Montcassel.*—Heaps are lying in some of the fields, ready for spreading. It is burnt in the country.

MAINE.—*La Fleche to Le Mans.*—Lime burning; the price 5 liv. the pipe, of 2 barriques.

Beaumont.—Lime-stone plentiful, yet lime 10 liv. the pipe.

Alençon to Nonant.—Lime-stone every where, yet lime 16 liv. the tonneaux, of 2 pipes.

BOURBONNOIS.—*Moulins.*—Lime 55 *f.* the poinçon, 30 inches high, and 22 diameter.

VIVARAIS.—*Pradelles.*—Lime 9 *f.* the measure of 32 lb.

Fences.

NORMANDIE.—*Pays de Caux.*—The fences here resemble more the double banks and ditches of Ireland than any I have seen: parapet banks are thrown up out of a double ditch, sloped; and upon them are planted a hedge, and one or two rows of trees; and the soil is so rich, that all thrive to such a pitch, as to form hedges 40 or 50 feet high, and perfectly thick. By means of some small inclosures of this sort, around every house, every habitation is a redoubt, and would make the country very defensible for a small army against a great one.

Pont L'Eveque.—Many of the rich pastures here are so well fenced, that one can no more see through a single hedge, than through a wood; yet there are many willows in them, with only a mixture of thorns and bramble; but they are so well trained, and of such a luxuriant growth, as to be impenetrable to man or beast.

In fencing little is to be learned in France, yet a considerable portion of the kingdom is inclosed. In England we have carried that art to a perfection of

which

which the French know little. It is only in a few diftricts, where gates and
ftiles are regular; in others, a few bufhes, put in a gap, fupply the place.
Whenever the French have invefted in their agriculture, the fums it ought to
attract, at leaft three or four thoufand millions of livres more than in it at prefent, thefe objects will receive an attention which they have not yet commanded.
They are, by no means, unimportant; and as far as connected with inclofing,
in general, are effential to profperity.

Fifh Ponds.

SOLOGNE.—This province abounds very much with ponds of all fizes, which
let at from 5 liv. to 12 liv. the arpent.

BOURBONNOIS.—*Moulins.*—Through every part of this province, which I faw
in croffing it, in two directions, the number of fifh ponds is very confiderable.
The country, though in extenfive views flat to the eye, is, on a nearer examination, found to fwell into a variety of gentle inequalities, which form val-
lies, with fmall brooks, fprings, or ftreams, in them, as eligible for a refidence,
and agreeable to the eye, as it would be beneficial to cultivation, if they knew
how to apply them. Mounds are made acrofs thefe little vales, to form ponds;
and there are mills at their heads, when the ftreams are confiderable enough.
Thefe ponds are from two or three to ten, twenty, and thirty acres, and fome
a great deal more. They are all fifhed regularly every fecond or third year, and
the fifh fold, at fo much a thoufand, to the merchants, who fend them, by the
Allier, Loire, canal of Briare, and Seine, to Paris. On one eftate, I faw eight
ponds, that paid 800 liv.; on another, four paid 800 liv.; and, on a farm of
about 400 acres, four ponds paid 1000 liv. Water deceives one fo much in
gueffing the fuperficies, that I may be erroneous (for nothing is meafured in this
province); but I fhould guefs, that land under water paid 20 liv. an acre at leaft,
inftead of 3 liv. which is the more common net produce of the country; and,
at the fame time that the proprietor receives this fuperior benefit, his table is,
by the terms of the contract with the merchant, who ftocks the ponds himfelf,
allowed to be amply fupplied.

BRESSE.—The ponds of this little province and Dombes, cover 66 leagues
fquare of country, and are found terrible to population, from the effect they
have on the climate*. In 1764, ponds in France generally let at 5 liv. to 7 liv.
per arpent †.

The management of ponds is vaftly better underftood in France than it is in
England, both as to ftocking, adapting the fort of fifh to the foil, clearing the

---

* *Obferv. fur L'Agricult. par Monf. Varenne de Fenille,* p. 270.

† *Chanvalon Manuel des Champs.* 12mo. P. 363.

ronds,

ponds, emptying, fishing, &c. &c. In all Catholic countries, fish is of more importance than in Protestant ones, and this occasions more attention being paid to them.

Leaves.

LANGUEDOC.—Gathering, the end of July, leaves of mulberries, for feeding cattle.

POITOU.—See them gathering elm leaves for cattle, particularly for mules, the first week in September.

TOURAINE.—Clipping elm trees to feed cows, in September.

Near Clarey, they gather the vine leaves in September; we saw them spread, in large quantities, by the sides of the roads, with many women, girls, and boys, gathering and drying; they are for winter provender for their cows; this custom is general through the country. They make an infusion of these leaves in hot water, by boiling them with some bran; which mixture they give to their cows, in snow or frosty weather, with straw. Was a cow fed with leaves alone, it would require 8 or 10 arpents to support a cow the whole winter; they reckon them very beneficial for this useful animal. Leaves are sometimes sold, in which case, such a heap dry as would equal 30 lb. of hay, sells for 20 *f.* but all this varies according to the year. An arpent produces seven or eight times that quantity.

ISLE OF FRANCE.—Among the winter provision which Monf. Cretté de Paluel, of Dugny, makes for his sheep, is that of faggots, cut in summer while in full leaf, and housed as soon as dry: these he has found to be of considerable use, and to answer the purpose perfectly well. When given to the sheep they pick off every leaf carefully. Such a practice well deserves attention in England.

DAUPHINE.—About Montélimart the leaves of all mulberry trees are gathered in November for feeding sheep. A gentleman, near the same place, feeds a flock of Spanish and half bred sheep, with faggots cut in summer from full leaved trees.

PROVENCE.—The president de la Tour d'Aigues making elm faggots, in September, for his sheep; a common practice: poplar also and oak; indeed all forts are thus applied. Olives are also excellent; one of twelve years growth will thus yield to the value of 12 *f.*; every second year, on good land, more than the expence.

For the better understanding this subject I beg to refer the reader to an excellent and useful memoir on the subject, by Mr. Professor Symonds, inserted in the *Annals of Agriculture*, vol. i. p. 207*.

This is one of the œconomical practices of France, which well deserves imitation in England: not gathering leaves, for I question whether it would answer the

* See also *Mem. de la Soc. Roy. d'Ag. de Paris.* 1785. *Trimestre d'eté.* P. 22.

expence

expence of labour, but cutting faggots in fummer inftead of winter; drying them like hay before binding, and then ftacking and thatching for feeding fheep. I made a ftack of them in 1789, but the two following winters were fo open and mild, that I could not experience the benefit. I fhall, however, make other trials on the practice, for I have not the leaft doubt of its anfwering as well here as in France. Leaves are very nourifhing, but aftringent, and wholefome for fheep, and fuch ftores might be got at eafily when the ground is covered with fnow, to the great faving of hay. Confidering the immenfity of leaves that fall to wafte, in a woodland country, it is certainly an object that well deferves attention.

Threfhing.

ROUSSILLON.—LANGUEDOC.—Through all the fouthern parts of this province, they tread out the corn with horfes and mules; a man in the centre of the threfhing floor, in the open air, drives them round, and other men fupply the floor, and clear away the ftraw. In fome converfation I had on this method, between Narbonne and Niffau, I was affured it was far preferable to the ufe of flails. That 24 mules or horfes, and 12 men, would *depiqué*, as they term it, 150 feptiers of wheat in a day. That fome farms produce 2000 feptiers of corn; what would flails do for fuch a quantity? I examined the wheat, and did not find it more damaged than with flails; but the climate is to be remembered, which makes the grain much harder than any with us. Seeing fome flails going alfo, I demanded the reafon, and was told that the mafter would fometimes have particular parcels of ftraw threfhed fo, to get the corn that was left in it, if he fufpected too much; at others the labourers defire to do it for themfelves, which is fometimes granted.

DAUPHINE.—*Loriol.*—But Monf. Faujas de St. Fond has tried threfhing the corn all at once with flails, and finds it much better than with horfes, &c.

Monrejeau to Lann-Maifon.—The oats are all mown to the ftanding corn; one woman follows each fcythe, gathers and lays them in gavels, ready to be bound afterwards in fheaves.

Orange to Avignon.—The fame method of threfhing with horfes, &c. prevails here; and they ftack their ftraw very neatly, plaftering at top with white clay, mixed with ftraw and water.

PROVENCE.—*La Tour d'Aigues.*—Seeing a large quantity of the Prefident's wheat fpread on cloths, for drying in the fun, and inquiring what it meant, I found it was wafhed, as all is, of which the beft bread is made; owing, beyond all doubt, to the mode of threfhing, which renders it fo foul that this operation is neceffary.

CHAP. XVIII.

Of Tillage, and the Implements of Husbandry, in France.

NOT an object of the first consequence, but of too much importance to be neglected by a farming traveller. In a climate in which the sun has power to burn up weeds, with only a scratching of the soil, and in a territory where harsh, obstinate, churlish clays are almost unknown, perfection of implements, and great powers of **tillage, are not so necessary as in the less favourable climate** and soil of England.

Of the Tillage, and Laying of Lands.

PICARDIE.—*Calais.*—Lands well and straight ploughed; three horses.

Montreuil.—All turn-wrest ploughs; which, from having two breasts, go alone almost as well as with holding; I saw a man leave his plough to chat with the driver of a load of bark, and the five horses went on and performed their work **as** well without as with him: the double breast occasions the cutting double work. The man, while I held it for a bout, told me that his master expected him to plough 30 measures thrice in the summer.

Bernay.—A pair of horses.

Abbeville.—Very badly, with four asses or two horses. Feed their asses with hay and oats.

Piquigny.—Women **ploughing with a pair of horses.**

PAYS DE BEAUCE.—*Toury.*—**Do not** give **the first stirring to their fallows** until **May.** Plough well, straight, and clean.

SOLOGNE.—*La Ferté.*—Plough their poor sands all on three feet ridges; and **assert that** without them they should get no corn, as they preserve the sand from **plastering in** rains: this is an **odd idea,** as plastering **such sharp sand is** usually a **means of** improvement; **but showers here** certainly **fall** with much greater violence than with us; **their crops,** however, are so beggarly as to give no weight to their opinions. Their teams of horses **are kept out all** the year, as they have the **pasturage of** the landlord's **woods for** them. What a barbarous system! **Plough an arpent a day** with three. **Plough** also with **six** oxen, and this in sand.

To La Motte Beuvron.—Plough with eight bullocks, and on sand! Buckwheat is given before winter, mixed with oats; if alone, before it has had a sweat, it gives the cholic; but afterwards, alone safely

Nonan de Fufilier.—For two years paft, chaff cut at the poft, of rye ftraw, mixed with buckwheat, for horfes, and found excellent: the fcarcity of forage alone drove them to this ufeful experiment.

La Loge.—Through all Sologne the land is ploughed on to the two-bout ridge of three-feet, and they never ftir it in any other way.

Salbris.—Plough their fandy gravels with fix to eight oxen, that are pretty good, felling for 6 or 7 louis each.

BERRY.—*Verfon.*—Tillage all done with oxen, harneffed by the horns; a pair draw a plough; fome are not bigger than our Alderney cows; the furrow about four inches deep, but hardly to be called a furrow, fo irregularly and ill cut. They are now ploughing up oat ftubbles for wheat; an Englifhman can hardly conceive what work they make; they give four of thefe wretched fcratch-ings for every crop.

NORMANDIE.—*Argentan.*—Wretched ploughs drawn by four oxen.

LIMOUSIN.—*Limoges.*—Plough throughout the province with oxen or cows, harneffed by the horns.

QUERCY.—*Pellecoy.*—Walked from the road to a peafant at plough with two cows, about as big as Alderney's; it is not poffible for an Englifh farmer to con-ceive how badly; trenches 3½ or 4 inches broad, and two deep, were fcratched parallel to each other, and the earth driven afide by two mould boards, fome one way, fome another; no coulter to the plough: they do about an Englifh rood a day. A fhim, where there are no ftones, and a Kentifh nidget, where there are, would do the work much more effectually, and ten times as quickly. But their burning fun deftroys weeds better than fuch tillage. Their hoeing is excellent and effective, and to this their crops are more owing than to their ploughing.

Cauffade.—The lands ploughed as ftraight as in Suffolk; all by oxen or cows.

LANGUEDOC.—*Montauban.*—Plough with oxen, without either reins or driver.

Touloufe to St. Lyce.—The ploughs better, the mould boards being larger. The fields are thrown into ftetches or flat lands. Ploughs are ox-hoeing the vines, each ox walking in an interval with a row between them, and yoked with a fliding yoke, to vary the diftance from ox to ox, and bafkets at their mouths to prevent their biting the vines. The rows at five feet, and the plants at two.

Bagneres de Luchon.—They ox-hoe the rows of their maiz. All oxen yoked by the horns.

ROUSSILLON.—*Bellegarde to Perpignan.*—Plough with mules yoked; alfo with affes in the fame way. Earth-boards of the ploughs are to the left.

Pia.—Day's work of a man, his plough and team, 3 liv.

R 2

LANGUEDOC.

LANGUEDOC.—*Narbonne.*—Of many ploughs now going (July), moſt are drawn by mules, in yokes ; the plough beam faſtened to the centre of the yoke ; earth-board to the left. They plough well.

Pezenas to Montpellier.—The oxen all yoked by the horns. Ploughing olive grounds with one horſe ; the plough of an odd conſtruction, the beam dividing and forming ſhafts for the horſe.

BEARN.—*Pau to Moneins and Navareins.*—All this country is ploughed with oxen that are good, and in good order.

GUIENNE.—*Agen to Aiguillon.*—Plough with very fine cream-coloured oxen, a pair to a plough. All draw by their horns.

Tonneins.—A pair of very fine oxen plough a journal a day ; that meaſure contains 33,750 ſquare feet, and is to the Engliſh acre as 33 to 38. The plough beams all faſten to the yokes.

To La Motte Landron.—They are now (Auguſt) ploughing for *jarouche* and forage (by the laſt is meant oats for ſoiling), and are very attentive in the order- ing and finiſhing their lands, and covering the ſeed ; breaking the clods with a wooden beetle and rake, ſo that the high ridges are brought down in ſuch a manner as to admit the ſcythe, and at the ſame time the furrows are kept open.

Barſac.—They are now ox-hoeing their vines quite clean ; and ſee one piece of oſiers ox-hoed.

POITOU.—A pair of oxen without either driver or reins.

TOURAINE.—*Montbazon.*—Horſe-ploughs ; ſaddles on the horſes with a bar like a curricle, one from ſaddle to ſaddle, to which the beam of the plough at- taches. A bad plan, as by this means the horſe does not draw from his ſhoul- ders, where his ſtrength and weight lie.

SOLOGNE.—*Chambord.*—The poor ſands of this country are laid on the three feet ridge of two-bouts, and rye and buckwheat ſown on them ; the furrows are as wide as the ridges, and yield nothing but weeds.

La Chapelle La Reine.—Plough with two horſes and no driver, yet the price per arpent is 5 liv. 100 perch 22 feet.

ISLE OF FRANCE.—*Mellun.*—Plough into broad flat lands, and very ſtraight. Many ploughs with three horſes, one before a pair ; no driver.

Liancourt.—In the general arrangement of their farms, they reckon three horſes to a plough, though they never uſe more than two at a time ; and a plough to 75 arpents (1¼ acre), 25 of which are fallow ; and a common calcula- tion here is 1500 liv. rent per plough, which makes 20 liv. per arpent. They never uſed oxen until the Duke of Liancourt introduced them from England.

Paris to Villers Coterets.—The whole way the lands are ploughed quite flat, with a turn-wreſt wheel-plough, and much of the wheat is overflowed, for want of furrows to carry off the water from the late rains.

PICARDIE.

PICARDIE.—*La Fere.*—Four horfes in the ploughs, and no driver.

St. Quentin to Cambray.—Thirty-five horfes to a farm of 800 feptiers; and twenty horfes on one of 400. The latter proportion is feventeen on 400 Englifh acres.

FLANDERS.—*St. Amand.*—This feafon (November 1, 1787) the wheat here, owing to the exceffive rains, is put in as badly as poffible. The loweft and wetteft fields are perfectly flat, and half of them, in parts, overflowed. Furrows are drawn, as marks for digging, which is doing, through all the country, with a narrow fpade, of 5 inches wide, and 8 long; thefe furrows are from 6 to 8 yards afunder, but done poorly, miferably crooked, and the whole unfightly.

Lille.—There is a minutia of labour and attention given to land in this country, which muft, in the nature of things, refult from that over-population, which is found every where in France, on fmall properties. I faw many men and women hoeing up the land with great mattock-hoes, almoft a foot fquare, with long handles; by which they are lifted high, that in the fall they may cut 4 or 5 inches deep. They work by lines that mark out beds, 5 or 6 feet broad, along which other men dig out trenches, a full fpit deep, fpreading the earth over the beds. Wheat feed is then fown, and covered by a man's drawing a wooden harrow over it: another follows with a hoe, to cut clods, and level inequalities. I calculated, in my mind, what this would coft me in Suffolk, and I made it amount to 3l. 10s. per Englifh acre. Such operofe methods are not in practice here, becaufe the labour which comes to market is cheap, fince fuch labour, like every thing elfe in Flanders, is what is commonly called dear: it fprings alone from the population that is attached to the poffeffion of land in property; and is, relative to any other country, a fyftem of trifling; a wafte of labour not greatly better than picking ftraws. Perhaps it is owing to this over-population of the fields, that Flanders, with the richeft foil in Europe, cannot feed her own towns, but is forced to import large quantities of wheat from Artois and Picardie, where large farms enable thofe provinces to fpare to the wants of their more fubdivided neighbour.

About four or five miles from Lille begins another method of laying their lands; it is that of ploughing them up, in very broad high arched beds, of all breadths, from four rods to ten or twelve. When inclofures are fmall, a whole one is formed into but one land; and in larger fields, there is a drain left at every parting furrow, which is either planted with a row of alders or willows, or dug into a trench and laid to grafs. In a land ten or twelve rod wide, the centres may rife four or five feet higher than the bottoms of the furrows; the flopes on each fide very gentle and regular; and fo equal, that all water is effectually drained off. I difcourfed with fome farmers on this method, ftating

objections

objections and hearing their anfwers. They infift, that no other method of laying land dry, is fo effective, cheap, durable, or commodious. That all the methods I mentioned, are known and practifed in fome part or other of Flanders, but that all the beft hufbandmen have one opinion, are united in thinking this mode fuperior to all others. That planting alders or willows (which are always kept low, by conftant cuttings), or having grafs in the furrows, are not neceffary parts of the fyftem, and that the furrows, in a few years after throwing up the lands, are as good as the reft of the field. The neatnefs and regularity with which the fyftem is executed, is extraordinary; the borders, headlands, and fides of fields, are fo dug away, that a fmall one has the form of a feather-bed, the feathers of which are driven towards the middle. I never faw this fyftem fo well executed as here, though I have known it copied in England; not in the highlands of many of our counties, which are, on comparifon, a barbarous method, but in the practice of a few individuals who had feen the effect in Flanders.

Armentieres.—Paffing this town, meet with another exertion of induftry, that deferves attention. Many ftubbles were ploughed into beds eight or ten feet wide, and the furrows digging out, and the earth fpreading on the beds. I fuppofed this was for wheat, but, on inquiry, found that thefe fields were intended for beans. They leave the land, thus prepared, till March, and then plant, without further tillage. As fpring tillage is thus avoided on wet land, the fyftem muft be admitted to be excellent.

Mont Caffel to Berg.—The lands not raifed fo high as thofe above-defcribed, nor with equal fkill or attention, and this wet feafon (November) fhews the confequence of it; they cannot get on to their lands to fow wheat, but moft of the high lands are fown, and fome of them green.

ARTOIS.—*Lillers to Bethune.*—The lands broad and arched; but gently. From Ardres to Bethune, all the way, the greateft attention to plough the land the moment the corn is carried, yet much is now uncut and ripe.

To Arras.—They are now (Auguft 8,) ploughing the ftubbles of fuch corn as is carried, with one horfe, that walks, not in the furrow, but on the unploughed land, by the fide of it: the plough beam very fhort, with a foot; no coulter; a well-curved breaft and throat; but too wide in the heel: ftir fhallow, and do not make good work; do about a meafure a day.

NORMANDIE.—*Rouen.*—All the harrowing is done in this country by men leading many horfes. I faw one man leading feven horfes, each drawing a harrow: the horfes are tied one behind another, obliquely, fo as to be out of danger of the harrows.

BRETAGNE.—*Rennes.*—Plough with four horfes and a driver; or two horfes and two oxen.

Vannes.

Vannes.—The common plough team, two oxen; always harneffed by the horns, and a little horfe, a mere poney, before them; if no horfe, the oxen are led by a woman. They ufe aukward, ill made, but light, wheel-ploughs.

Auvergnac.—The farmers (metayers) have here the Effex cuftom of digging away the borders and margins **of all** arable **fields, and** carrying them on to the land, which they practife very exactly, as it is done in that county.

ANJOU.—*Migniame.*—They plough deeper, in common, than ever I faw in any part of either England or France; eight or nine, and even ten inches deep; ufing fix or eight good oxen of the Poitou breed; but it is done, in one refpect, badly,—their depth obliges them to carry a furrow a foot wide, yet their fhare is not fix inches; and they do every thing on four-feet ridge-work. The great **ftrength of the** team is moft wanted for the roots of the fern, which **are now lying about the land in heaps.**

La Fleche to Le Mans.—They are now ploughing fand **land, very flowly,** with four bullocks and two horfes. Prepofterous!

NORMANDIE.—*Beaumont.*—Two bullocks and two horfes, to draw thirty bufhels of dung.

To Alençon.—Plough with four or fix bullocks, or horfes, and a driver.

Bernay.—Wheel-ploughs, with two horfes, and no driver. The rich loams here are on broad lands, very well arched.

Toftes.—Wheel-ploughs; three horfes, and no driver.

To Dieppe.—Ditto; well ploughed, flat, and deep.

BRIE.—*Neuf Moutier.*—Monf. Gibert, à confiderable farmer and proprietor, keeps fifteen horfes for 300 arpents of rich loamy clay (375 acres Englifh).

CHAMPAGNE—*Chalons to Ove.*—Plough with one horse.

To St. Menehould.—Plough with four horfes, without a driver; **turn-wreft** ploughs.

LORRAINE.—*Mars-la-Tour to Metz.*—Fallows dunged, after ploughing with fix horfes (July).

Luneville to Blamont.—Broad lands, and fome arched, but no water-cuts, confequently the crops much damaged, whenever rain falls. Plough with four, fix, and eight horfes, cows, and oxen; all mixed fometimes. I have feen women holding the plough, and a boy driving: wheels, but not turn-wreft.

ALSACE.—*Saverne to Wilteim.*—Here is a remarkable cuftom, of both waggons and ploughs being driven by poftillions.

To Strafbourg.—The lands broad and arched, as in Flanders.

To Scheleftat.—The fame lands on the flat rich vale.

Colmar to Ifenheim.—Oxen here improve much on the preceding country: they are harneffed by the horns, drawing fingly in lines, and alfo mixed with horfes.

To

To Béfort.—Plough with a pair of oxen, without line or driver. Arched broad lands.

BOURGOGNE.—*Dijon.*—Plough with fix horfes.

Bourbon-Lancy.—Plough with fix oxen, that draw by the horns. A level country; a fandy gravel.

BOURBONNOIS.—*Chavannes.*—All the arable thrown into one-bout ridges, about fixteen inches broad.

AUVERGNE.—*Riom to Clermont.*—Plough with a pair of oxen.

Clermont to Iffoire.—Ploughing with oxen only; fome of them good; all draw by the horns.

Fix to Le Puy.—Miferable ploughing; the plough has one long handle; and the man holds a long light pole in the other hand for a goad: a pair of little oxen.

DAUPHINE.—*Montélimart.*—Plough with two mules.

There is no part of England where lands are laid fo neatly as in Flanders; but the French have no other province that partakes of this perfection; Alface is in a fimilar fyftem, but not fo well executed. In general, the tillage of the king-dom is moft miferably performed; and many of the provinces are, in this refpect, fo backward, that, to Englifh eyes, they appear to be pitiably conducted.

The principal queftion that arifes upon tillage is the comparative advantage of ufing horfes or oxen. Both have had their advocates. The principal opponents to oxen were the œconomiftes, that fanciful fect, of very worthy and ingenious men, who, from their chambers at Paris and Verfailles, offered opinions upon every part of the farmer's bufinefs. They divided the arable lands of France into thofe managed in the great and little culture: in the former, the tillage done with horfes, and in the latter, with oxen; and as Flanders, Picardie, Normandie, &c. where horfes were in ufe, being alfo let at money rent, thofe provinces were neceffarily more at their eafe than Sologne, Berry, Limoufin, and others in the hands of metayers. This comparifon is often made in the writings of the œconomiftes, and abundantly more ftrefs laid on the nature of the team than it deferves; they gave many calculations to fhow, that horfes were more advantageous, but all founded on falfe data; for they allowed only two horfes to a plough, but four or fix oxen, forgetting that in Guienne, Quercy, part of Languedoc, &c. a pair of oxen plough as well as any pair of horfes; an omiffion this the more extraordinary, becaufe thofe provinces are among the beft cultivated in France the diftrict of the Garonne is like a garden, and the oxen, large, vigorous, beautiful, and in fine order, the very contrary of the miferable half ftarved beafts, defcribed by the Marquis de Mirabeau, Monf. Du Pont, Du Quefnay, and other œconomiftes. The comparifon has been made in England with great accuracy; and the opinion now is, that oxen are the moft

beneficial

beneficial and the moſt profitable, and that a pair of good oxen will plough as much in a day as a pair of good horſes. The other œconomical points of the compariſon are all in favour of oxen.

But though the ſuperiority, both in ſaving to the farmer, and in national benefit, is clearly in favour of oxen, yet there want improvements to be made in training and working them. Some ſtep well, and move with as much freedom and activity, on a walk, as horſes, but this is not the caſe with the generality; they are trained to go too ſlowly, and demand, *for light work*, more hours than horſes. This is certainly owing to negligence and idleneſs of workmen and farming ſervants, for I am well perſuaded, from circumſtances I have remarked in them, that they are capable of great activity and quick motion. I have had them of a large ſize, which have taken leaps that no horſe in the world would attempt, a proof not of activity only, but of great muſcular ſtrength.

Accuſtoming them to more ſpeed, even to a trot of five or ſix miles an hour, is certainly as practicable, in the cool climates of Europe, as it can be in the burning ones of Aſia. The fact that they draw coaches at that rate, in the Eaſt Indies, ſeems to have been long aſcertained. The Targuzinian Tartars ride on their oxen*: the Nogayan Tartars, of Koundour, do the ſame†: Mandelſloe‡ rode on an ox part of the way from Agra to Dehli, that carried him ſeven leagues in four hours: in Kachemire they ſaddle, bridle, ſhoe, and ride them as faſt as horſes‖; they alſo draw their coaches: at Surat, in riding them, they take care their horns are not more than one foot long, to avoid being ſtruck when flies bite; they never ſhoe them but in rough places: in the caravan from that city, they carry 300 to 350 lb.§: a camel **carries 900** to 1000 lb.¶: but in a late account, of great authenticity, 500 and 600 lb. **is mentioned** as the common load of a camel in croſſing the Arabian deſerts**: **the hackrees, a ſort** of coach, is drawn in Indoſtan by oxen; which, when well trained and managed, will maintain their rate againſt horſes at full trot; thoſe of Guzerat and Cambray are as **large** as Lincoln beaſts, and white ††: the oxen that are rode in Formoſa, go as well and as expeditiouſly as the beſt horſes, by being trained young ‡‡: the Hottentots train oxen to gallop and even run down an elk §§

If ſuch quickneſs of movement could be given to the oxen of France and England, it would be a very conſiderable object, for it would get over the principal objection to them, and would at the ſame time render them applicable to a great variety of uſes, to which at preſent they are never put.

---

* *Iſbrandt Ides. Harris' Voyages*, vol. ii. p. 936.   † *Ruſſia; an Account of all the Nations which compoſe that Empire.* 8vo. 1780. vol. ii. p. 85.   ‡ *Harris*, vol. i. p. 764.   ‖ *Ib.* p. 814. and *Le Blanc's Travels*, p. 54.   § *Harris*, vol. i. p. 827.   ¶ *Ib.* vol. ii. p. 883.   ** *Phil. Tranſ.* vol. lxxxi. part 2. p. 136.   †† *Groſe's Voyage to the Eaſt Indies*, p. 249.   ‡‡ *Grozier's General Deſcription of China.* 8vo. vol. i. p. 225.   §§ *Sparman's Cape of Good Hope*, 4to. vol. i. p. 230.

Of the Implements of Hufbandry.

PICARDIE.—The harrow teeth of wood, all the way from Calais to Clermont. Turn-wreft ploughs, and bad.

SOLOGNE.—The ploughs have all a broad double finned fhare, and double mould-boards, with wheels; the whole ill conftructed.

BERRY.—The plough very ill made; it has two fcraps of fomething like mould-boards, and a long ground-reft, at the end of which is an iron fhare, four inches wide, fomething like the fhim which they ufe in Kent for earthing up beans: a hole for a coulter, but I faw none ufed. Nothing can be worfe than its work. They have alfo turn-wreft ploughs, fomething like thofe of Kent, but bad. Beyond Argenton, the beam of the plough faftens to the yoke of the oxen; the plough has a chiffel-reft and point, and no other mould-board than two fmall fticks, fluck in it, with a circularly bent one behind; thefe fticks anfwered the purpofe of two mould-boards, but very badly; the handles fo low, that the body of the ploughman is in a bent pofition to hold them.

LIMOUSIN.—The ploughs which I faw near St. George, &c. have one mould-board on the left fide; the fhare long, and $1\frac{1}{2}$ inch broad; the beam reaches to the yoke, and confequently faves traices. They plough better than in La Marche.

QUERCY.—The fame long beams to ploughs that reach to the yoke; have two very bad mould-boards; the fhare long and narrow, with no coulter; but the land excefiively ftoney.

LANGUEDOC.—*Montauban to Touloufe.*—The **plough much better than** many **I have feen** in France; it has a broad coulter, and a fhort nofed fhare; one mould-board, and that to the left; the plough beam, like many others, fixes to the ox-yoke.

To Noe.—Meet waggons for the firft time; the wheels fhod with wood, that is, wood upon wood. The oxen all cloathed with linen againft the flies, one tape **under** the tail and another round the neck. The price of thefe waggons new is **60** liv. (2l. 12s. 6d.); they carry, with a pair of oxen, two cafks of wine, containing 4 barriques, which is 20 quintals, or about a ton Englifh. Some pairs of oxen will draw 40 quintals.

GUIENNE.—*Tonneins.*—The ploughs have very long hollow or fluted mould-**boards, for lifting the furrow,** in order to make fharp high two-bout ridges.

ANGOUMOIS.—*Barbefieux.*—Wheel-ploughs.

ISLE DE FRANCE.—*Melun.*—Large heavy wheel-ploughs, with breafts as wide and thick in the throat, as the heel is broad; muft go very heavy for the horfes.

Commerle.—Wheel-ploughs drawn by a pair of horfes.

Dugny.

Dugny.—One of the beft implements I faw in France, was the chaff-cutter of Monf. Cretté de Paleuel; it confifted of two cylinders, with edges that worked into the vacancies of each other, and, fucking in the ftraw delivered very rapidly, cut it into coarfe chaff; one man fed the machine, by fpreading the ftraw on an inclined plane; and a boy drove a fingle horfe, which turned the machine. A tolerable mechanic, improving on the idea, would produce a much more powerful cutter than any yet invented.

FLANDERS.—*Lille.*—Many waggons loaded with chalk ftones, &c. with the principal part of the load laid on the hind wheels, and a very fmall portion on the fore ones; a good fenfe that reproaches our barbarians in England.

ARTOIS.—The fhort fcythe which they ufe through this province, and all over Flanders, is one of the moft ufeful implements that can be feen: they call it the *pique:* it is much like the reprefentation given by Mr. Walker in the Annals of Agriculture; only the handle here is much fhorter: a man cuts an arpent a day in general with it, and fometimes more; he cuts and rolls into bottes an arpent of vetches (called here, mixed with oats, *dravin*); and he cuts an arpent of any fort of white corn, others following to bind with ftraw bands, made at home. This is a moft œconomical fyftem. The fhort handle of the pique is made to reft againft the elbow; he holds it with the right hand only, or rather hand and arm; and in his left he has a ftick, with a hook at the end of it, with which he draws or holds the corn in the right pofition to receive the ftroke. They ufe fcythes and cradles alfo for fome works.

St. Omer—That the pique is much eafier to work than a fcythe, appears from women and even girls cutting ftout crops of tares with it. They give 45 *f.* per meafure of oats for cutting, with the pique, and a man **does** three-fourths per day.

NORMANDIE.—*Harfleur.*—I noticed here, what I may have often paffed, perhaps, without feeing it, a pierced roller behind, and before a cart, which turns in the frame, or in the ladders, by which means a load is corded with a fmall handfpike, almoft in a moment; I have known fomething like it in the ladders of carts in England, but forget where; here they let down a cart behind, by raifing the fhafts in the air, fet it againft a cafk, and wind the cafk on to the cart, by means of the fore-roller, eafily and commodioufly.

Avranches.—Sea-fand is drawn in this country in carts, by a horfe in the fhafts, and another to lead, with two or three oxen between, and all in a line. About Carentan they attach the rope, by which they draw, to the yokes of the oxen, confequently the horfe draws them down to the line of his own draught; and their rope to the top of the pole between the two thillers (when they are two), confequently all draw the thill-horfes down. A team of five, thus harneffed, does not draw more than from 20 to 24 bufhels of fea-fand: the horfes are, however, poor fmall things; and no wonder, from the number of miferable

S 2

garran

garran (poney) ſtallions that infeſt every ſtable you enter. The oxen are better, but not large.

BRETAGNE.—*Varades.*—They are now working their ridges, of three and four feet acroſs, with a great timber triangular machine, drawn by oxen, to anſwer the treble purpoſes of harrowing, rolling, and levelling.

ISLE DE FRANCE.—BRIE—*Nangis.*—Wheel-ploughs, and very good, except ſingly the breadth, which is 16 or 18 inches, and in narrow lands loſes a fourth; it only wants to be taken in narrower, and left with the ſhare projecting more from the throat.

CHAMPAGNE.—*Mareuil.*—Bad turn-wreſt ploughs; but have the Brie one, which they prefer when there are root weeds to cut.

Rheims.—Very light ploughs, with a broad ſhare, and one earth-board, but ill ſet on; it has wheels on the beam, which is little more than a ſtick. Women are ploughing.

To Chalons.—Many rollers every where; an implement very uncommon in France.

St. Menehould to Verdun.—Wheel ploughs that are not turn-wreſts, with well turned mould-boards. This is among the beſt ploughs I have ſeen in France.

LORRAINE.—*Mars-la-Tour to Metz.*—Broad ſhare and good, but too wide at the heel; wheels.

Pont-à-Mouſſon to Nancy.—Here, for the firſt time, I met with waggons of a peculiar ſtructure, the fore wheels are within four inches as high as the hind ones, and are high enough to enable one horſe, for none are drawn by more, to convey 8oo lb. to 1ooo lb. **Ploughs ſo** wide at the heel, that they are drawn by eight horſes.

ALSACE.—All through the part of Alſace, which I have **ſeen, they uſe** ploughs with low wheels; the ſhare round and broad, and as wide on the land ſide as on that of the furrow, which is very erroneous, for they are not turn-wreſts; but with fixed breaſts, turning the furrow to the left.

BOURBONNOIS.—*Moulins.*—The common plough a turn-wreſt one; but they have another for ſtirring, called *areou*, without an earth-board.

AUVERGNE.—*Iſſoire.*—The plough only opens a ſlight furrow, into which the earth falls again, and buries nothing, and without a hot ſun would kill nothing; the ſhare a chiſſel point, one inch wide at one end, and three inches at the other end for ſtoney land, or for that which is free, turning it occaſionally end for end. An earth-board on each ſide, but not more than four inches high.

Upon the implements in general, I may obſerve, that they will in all countries be proportioned to the wealth of the farmers. There is nothing in the kingdom comparable to those which we ſee in every part of England, where the implements of huſbandry are carried to a perfection of which one ſees nothing

in

in any other country that I have viewed. The right form and powers of all inſtruments, uſed in agriculture, depending very much on the application of mechanical principles, were proper objects for the attention of thoſe ſcientific men that compoſe academies; I do not know, however, that they have done any thing in this reſpect in agriculture, though ſuch great exertions have been made in manufactures and ſhip-building. At one period, the ingenuity of mechanical genius in France was employed on agricultural tools; and then, as an ill ſtar would govern, nothing was-thought of but drill-ploughs and horſe-hoes. Fortunately all invented were abſolutely good for nothing, which threw ſuch a diſcouragement on the practice, that the folly was but of ſhort duration; had they been better it would have laſted longer, and would have done ſo much the more miſchief; for the drill huſbandry, at its beſt efforts, is fitter to amuſe very ingenious gentlemen, who aim at great products without attending to expences, than to become the ſteady ſtaple practice of a kingdom, in the hands of men who cannot eaſily underſtand refinements; and if they could underſtand, could much leſs afford them. Adopting beneficial courſes of crops, that will allow a great increaſe of cattle and ſheep; draining, irrigating, manuring; ſuch objects are applicable to common farmers, little and great; but the refinement of drilling, applicable but to certain crops and certain ſoils, is not adapted to the maſs of huſbandmen, by whoſe more plain exertions mankind muſt be content to be fed.

CHAP. XIX.

Of Manures and Manuring in France.

PICARDIE.—THROUGHOUT this province, moſt of the way from Calais to Clermont, the dung is now (May) carried out and ploughed in upon the fallows; it is in a long ſtrawy ſtate, and not one-fifth part rotten; nor half of it ploughed in.

PAYS DE BEAUCE.—*Toury.*—Many pits of white marl in this rich plain of Beauce, quite to Orleans; the fine loam four or five feet deep on it. They ſpread it on their lands, but the quantity very ſmall; nor did I ſee any ſigns of old pits.

SOLOGNE.—*La Motte Beuvron.*—The rye-ſtubbles are (May) collected in heaps on the land, having been left ſo all winter, to prepare it for rotting for manure. Surely they might find a better way of doing it; houſing their ſheep, as they do, at noon as well as night.

LIMOUSIN.

LIMOUSIN.—*Uſerch*.—Collect leaves to make manure with.

LANGUEDOC.—*Niſmes to Quiſſac*.—In cultivating waſtes, or old neglected pieces, they pare and burn; alſo collect turfs and clods in heaps, on faggots of box-wood, which they burn.

Lann-Maiſon to Bagnere de Bigorre.—Cut from their waſtes, much fern, which they ſpread on their cultivated lands, and, ſetting fire to it, find the aſhes equal to a dunging. They alſo cart much to their ſtables and farm-yards, to make dung with.

GASCOGNE.—*St. Palais to Anſpan*.—Paſs three or four lime-kilns, which, my guide aſſures me, are employed in burning for manure, to improve the waſtes that abound ſo much in this country; and I ſaw ſeveral heaps near houſes, without any ſings of building going forward.

A general practice through theſe mountains, and almoſt to Bayonne, is that of manuring for *raves*, with the aſhes of burnt ſtraw. I obſerved ſeveral fields quite black; and, demanding what it was, my guide told me of this common practice here; afterwards I ſaw them ſtrewing ſtraw thickly over land, part of which had been already burnt on. They do this on a wheat-ſtubble; but not thinking that ſtubble enough is left, they add much wheat-ſtraw; and, ſetting fire to it, burn the weeds as well as the ſtraw, and clean as well as manure the land. With ſuch quantities of fern on all their extenſive waſtes, I aſked why they did not burn that, and keep their ſtraw? The reply was, that fern makes much better dung than ſtraw, ſo they burn the ſtraw in preference. As ſoon as the operation is over, they plough the land, and harrow it in rave ſeed. One large field, thus treated, I ſaw ploughing for that crop. They both hoe and hand-weed the raves, and have them ſometimes very large; many as big as a man's head. Uſe them for oxen.

Fleurange to Leitoure.—Chop their ſtubbles axactly as in Suffolk, driving it on with their feet: they gather it for making manure.

TOURAINE.—*St. Maure*.—Here we found a greater exertion in huſbandry than is commonly found in France, that of marling. We ſaw ſeveral large heaps of white marl, and at one of them four or five carts at work, each with three horſes. It is found almoſt every where under the country, at the depth of three to five feet; the ſoil on which they lay it, is a good loam; adheſive, but not clay. They draw it up by buckets, which is a ſingular practice for ſuch ſlight depths. The marl is in ſome pits white, in others yellowiſh, which is reckoned the beſt; it is very ſoft and fat to the touch. They ſpread twelve cart loads per arpent, of 100 *chainé*, each 25 feet ſquare, 62,500 feet, or more than an acre and half; and it laſts good about 24 years. The landlords, on leaſes of nine years, pay the digging, and the tenants the carting. Of the yellowiſh ſort they do not ſpread quite ſo much as the white. The ſame account was given at

Montbazon;

Montbazon; they fpread it on the fallows, after two ploughings; and having ploughed in the marl, manure it with dung, and fow wheat. Make compofts alfo of marl and dung mixed.

Orleans to Petiviers.—Under the greater part of this country there is a bed of imperfect marl, which is over the calcarious ftone of which the roads are made. The farmers fpread this marl on their lands, at the rate of 10 *tomberaux* per arpent, which lafts twelve years; fome, better than the reft, has been known to laft thirty years.

Isle de France.—*Liancourt.*—Within two leagues of Liancourt, there is a navigation from Paris, but no idea, in any part of the country, of bringing manures; no wonder; for they carry flour thither by land carriage; even the millers, who fend it regularly, do the fame.

Soissonois.—*La Fere.*—A vaft excavation made in a hill, by digging and burning pate for manure: great heaps of the afhes now here. The price the farmers give is 22f. per meafure, that holds 60 lb. of wheat, fifteen of which they fpread upon an arpent. The effect is very great on all kinds of plants. This peat is unlike any I have feen, refembling an imperfect coal; and the being found, not on a plain, but on hills, for I faw feveral, and all equally on elevations, diftinguifh it remarkably from the peats of England. The mine of this hill is nearly exhaufted, as the common red loam of the country now appears nearly all around it.

Flanders.—*Lille.*—See many loads of urine and night-foil carrying into the country, by the farmers, for manuring their lands with. It is loaded in cafks: each waggon carries 10 *tonneaux* of about half an hogfhead Englifh. They lay from fixteen to twenty upon a *quartier* of land, at the expence of 7 liv.: ufe it for cole-feed, wheat, flax, &c. and find it equally excellent for all forts of crops.

Armentieres to Montcaffel.—Holes are dug in the fides and corners of many fields, for receiving the urine and night-foil, which is brought from every town, in cafks, and kept againft the feafon when it is wanted. Some have fmall roofs built over, to exclude the fun, wind, and rain; and others covered with ftraw. The moft correct and never-ceafing attenfion with which they procure and ufe this manure, deferves the greateft commendation.

To Berg.—A good deal of land chalked as well as dunged, and ready for wheat. The chalk is in large hard lumps, but broken and fpread moft curioufly; more evenly than ever I beheld any thing fimilar in England; where the rough and unequal manner in which marl is rather tumbled than fpread over the ground, is a reproach even to our beft farmers, who permit thofe labourers, whofe families are fupported by poor-rates, to execute their work in that manner, to earn ten fhillings a week inftead of eight.

Normandie.

NORMANDIE.—Throughout the part of this province which I have feen, they gather their wheat-ftubbles, and even bundle it in fheaves: they chop it with an inftrument fomething like a crooked fcythe, fixed at the end of a handle of fix or feven feet long; but do it much flower than in England, with a common fcythe.

Ifigny.—Here, for the firft time in France, I faw compofts of dung and earth made.

Carentan.—Ufe fea-fand for manuring their paftures, fpreading twenty loads per *vergé*, each load twelve to fixteen Englifh bufhels. The *vergé* equals 96 Englifh perches. Mix it alfo with dung.

To Coutances.—Manuring with fea-fand continues hither.

Avranches.—And hither; they have banked out half the river, which is a fmall arm of the fea, in order to build a bridge; and the countrymen are digging out the blue fea-mud, and carrying it away to confiderable diftances.

BRETAGNE.—*Dol to Combourg.*—Wheat-ftubbles gathered carefully; and a great deal of fern cut now (September 1), and in heaps.

Hedé.—From entering Bretagne, paring and burning every where practifed, but the heaps too large and too much burnt.

Rennes.—The farmers and gardeners buy the town dung, at 4 liv. the load.

Belle-Ifle to Morlaix.—The rough land of this country is reckoned to find fuel and manure: one of the reafons for almoft the whole of it being in fuch a rough favage ftate. They have an execrable cuftom, well adapted to perpetuate their deferts, that of burning parts for afhes, to carry to their good land.

Morlaix.—Heaps of fhell fand on lays, ready to fpread for fowing wheat; the fame hufbandry is practifed on our oppofite coaft, in Cornwall.

To Breft.—A moft excellent cuftom of going round all the inclofures with an inftrument between a fcythe and a wood-hook, for cutting up all grafs, weeds, and rubbifh, on the banks and in the ditches, leaving them in heaps, and then carting them away for making litter and dung; a practice that cannot be too much commended.

Chateaulin.—Paring and burning, the origin of all the culture there is in Bretagne; and the ruin of the province at the fame time. They pare $2\frac{1}{2}$ and 3 inches deep; and having exhaufted the afhed by three or four crops, leave it to weeds for twenty years before it is fit to burn again.

Quimperlay.—There is here a moft fingular hufbandry, of which I never faw any traces before. It is to pare the rough land, and not to burn, but to pile it up in heaps regularly fquare, of about 25 or 30 cubical yards in each, and about four of them to an acre; they are fquared up very neatly, and then the field is left for fome time, to cover itfelf with a new herbage, which is free from furze and broom, but not quite fo from fern; after a time, the heaps being rotten, they

are

are carted and fpread, and the land cultivated. Sometimes they cultivate the land before they are fpread, as I faw fome in pieces of buckwheat. Paring and burning is alfo practifed. This method is inferior to burning; it does not equally deftroy grubs, vermin, and weeds; and the double carting is a confiderable expenfe.

Vannes.—Thefe heaps formed in the fpring, and many will be fpread this year for rye. Here they confift of three-fourths or feven-eights of turf, pared off from every hole and corner from commons and bad fields, and carried to the good ones; and if this execrable practice is of any antiquity, it will account for the barren and wretched ftate of the country. Every poor field is made good for nothing, and the good one cropped, in confequence, till it is almoft as bad. Thefe heaps continue about Vannes in amazing quantities.

ANJOU.—*Migniame.*—The common manuring, ten loads of dung, each 3000 lb; but not more than four of Angers dung, night-foil, afhes, &c.

MAINE.—*Le Mans.*—Marl is here ufed; 100 pipes are laid on a journal.

NORMANDIE.—*Allençon.*—Fallows all dunged, with fquare lumps of dung, quite black, as if caft in a mould; and very thinly, not more than fix or feven loads an acre.

Leffiniole.—Marl employed here; or rather a hardifh imperfect chalk-ftone; drawn up in buckets; it lafts twenty years. Stubbles cut clofe and botted.

Bernay to Elbœuf.—Marl.

Rouen.—Monf. Scannegatty, Profeffor of Phyficks in the Royal Society of Agriculture here, having obferved, that, in calcining gypfum, it was apt, for various ufes, to be unequally burnt, part being partially reduced to lime, and the reft not fufficiently calcined, invented a furnace for the more equal diftribution of the heat; a vault pierced for the fuel, with a long channel beneath, for conveying air, and a door to the mouth of the furnace; at top, various holes, by way of chimnies, for the fmoak to iffue, and which he clofes alternately. He knows when the gypfum is fufficiently calcined, by applying a cold bright iron to thefe holes; it is infufficiently done while any humidity rifes.

La Roche Guyon.—Elm leaves are found to make good dung, but not oak ones; the latter take three years to rot fufficiently.

ISLE DE FRANCE.—*Nangis.*—There are afs-men, who take marling to do for the farmers, at 18 liv. per arpent (to Englifh acre as 32 to 38). Monf. De Guerchy, after water in a pond, nine crops of oats, and all good.

To Meaux.—Long dung fpread and fpreading now (July 2), for wheat next year.

Neuf Moutier.—Manure their rich clays with the white marl found under them; which has the appearance of confolidated pafte. They fallow for wheat, and manure the fallows in June, with long dung almoft in the ftate of ftraw; a me-

VOL. II. T thod

thod they contend warmly for; thinking that a greater degree of putrefaction would be lofs of quantity and virtue. But there is a circumftance which feems in fact much to condemn this method; it is, that while the wheat crops are to be ranked among the fineft in France, and would indeed make a capital figure in England, the oats and barley are wretched, indeed (foil confidered) below contempt. Does not this feem to prove, that the expofition of the manure, through the year of fallow, to the fun, exhaufts it to the amount of the benefit which one crop would receive from it, and that the wheat has it at fecond hand, and the fpring corn at the third.

ALSACE.—*Strafbourg*.—Gypfum ufed as a manure for clover with fuccefs; does beft on clayey lands; there are mills for pounding it. It is faid to laft good for fome time; 2 or 3 boiffeau, of 30 lb wheat per arpent of 24,000 feet between two and three bufhels per Englifh acre). If a quantity is ufed, it fpoils the land. What myfteries are thefe about this manure!

Befort.—Manure with blue marl.

To Ifle.—The dunghills here are the neateft fpectacles I have any where feen; the walls of them are twifted bands of ftrow, clofe and regular as a bee-hive, and fome are covered at top with leaves and branches of trees to exclude the fun. Admirable! Deferving univerfal imitation.

DAUPHINE.—*Loriol*.—Box, in this country, is cut on the mountains for manuring vines, by burying it frefh at their roots. For mulberries alfo it is excellent. Three trees were planted at the fame time, and in the fame foil, one with box, and the other without, and there is now no comparifon between them.

M. Foujas de St. Fond has tried gypfum, on a large fcale, on fandy land, for fainfoin, with great fuccefs.

PROVENCE.—*Salon to St. Canat*.—Dead olive branches and cuttings, are piled up with clods and rubbifh for burning, as in Catalonia.

Tour d'Aigues.—Paring and burning is practifed every where; and, as in Ireland, in corners, holes, waftes, and even ditches, to make heaps of manure for their cultivated lands. They are now (September) burning every where. The common opinion is very much againft it; but the Prefident remarks, that it has been practifed here uninterruptedly, probably, for 2000 years, yet the land is no worfe than it has always been.

The importance of manuring is well underftood in many of the French provinces; where faults are to be found, it is more for exhaufting the benefit as faft as poffible, than for want of knowing the operation and effect. The beft farmers in England fpread manures for ameliorating crops, in order that the hoe or the fcythe may cut off the weeds that are apt to rife in confequence; and as fuch crops fupport cattle, the more manure is fpread the more manure is made; it is

in

in arithmetical progreſſion: on the contrary, when it is given for exhauſting crops, as wheat or rye, the benefit is foon exhauſted, and the increaſe, fo valuable in the œconomy of a farm, does not take place. By means of fpreading the dung for thoſe crops that fupport cattle and ſheep, the live ſtock of a farm may be always gradually increaſing; and it is impoſſible they ſhould increaſe, without the farm improving, and corn itſelf augmenting by the ratio of the product ariſing.

CHAP. XX.

An Engliſh Farm eſtabliſhed in France.

AMONG the moſt intereſting obſervations which the Duke of Liancourt had made, in the various viſits he paid to England, was that of the ſuperiority to which the induſtry of that kingdom was carried beyond the practice of France; and above all, to what a degree of perfection agriculture had attained, founded on experiment, and manifeſt in an infinitely greater production of corn and of live ſtock than is to be found in almoſt any other country, extent and quality of ſoil confidered. Impreſſed with this fact, he had long cheriſhed the hope of introducing into his own country this ſource of increaſing wealth, flowing as well from the augmentation of produce, as from that of the people employed to raiſe it; but fenſible, at the fame time, that the moſt uſeful innovations could be introduced by example only—a truth the more applicable to agriculture, from being practiſed by men of fmall fortune, little or no education, and confequently full of prejudices, and unequal to the purſuit of any practice, but that of the *beaten track.*—he determined to attempt, as foon as it was in his power, an eſſay of Engliſh agriculture; but as he was defirous of having his example followed, it was neceſſary that theſe eſſays ſhould be fo conducted as to enfure fucceſs.

His friend, Mon. de Lazowſki's refidence during three years, in England, whither he confented to accompany the fons of the Duke, facilitated theſe means. Monſ. de Lazowſki, whom I had the pleaſure of knowing intimately, acquired that knowledge in agriculture, which much inquiry, aſſiduous application, and frequent converfation with the beſt farmers, could give to a mind very capable of, and much accuſtomed to obfervation: he was likewiſe no

T 2

ſtranger

ftranger to the projects of Monf. de Liancourt; and in this inftance, as on every
occafion, his unexampled friendfhip made him eager to fecond his views.

In 1789, Monf. de Liancourt, on becoming the proprietor of a large eftate,
fituated at thirteen leagues from Paris, refolved immediately to execute the plan
he had fo long projected: he accordingly engaged an Englifh farmer to come
over from Suffolk, with his family, and a common labourer; this Englifh
colony carried with it every kind of farming implement; they had with them
likewife five oxen, a bull, and five cows, from Suffex, to perpetuate that breed,
if the country into which they were tranfported would admit of it; to thefe were
added a Suffolk polled bull and five cows.

The farmer was placed in a farm that had hitherto yielded about two hundred
pounds a year; the land was in fome parts good, in others bad; it was fo divided in quality and in fituation, as to render one part fit for the reception
of fheep, and the other part for the feeding of cattle; thefe two objects were
thofe which Monf. de Liancourt was moft anxious to attain, in the agricultural
fyftem he was about to introduce; becaufe they were moft advantageous, in a
country furrounded by great markets, and very near to that of Paris; he added
a large extent of land to the farm, taken from his park, and from other farms,
confifting of about eight hundred arpents; two hundred and fifty of which were
appropriated to fheep, and the reft to the feeding of cattle; he defigned to have
made fuch additions to each part, as would have enlarged the whole to fifteen
hundred arpens; to which, in procefs of time, he would have nearly dedicated
the whole of his park. Whilft the Englifhmen were beginning their operations, and forming the labourers of the country to the ufe of the new fort of
plough imported from England, inftructing the common workmen as to the
conftruction of the new implements, and teaching the women fervants of the
farm the management of the dairy, the making of cheefe, &c. Monf. de Liancourt had fent two young labourers, out of the environs of Liancourt, to England, who, being placed by me with good farmers in my neighbourhood, qua-
lified themfelves to replace, at a future day, the Englifh family, in cafe thefe
fhould grow tired of living in France, or to affift them if, as Monf. de Liancourt hoped, they were difpofed to remain. The artizans of Liancourt learnt
to imitate the implements, the plough and the cart brought from England, and
made them very well.

To the cows, from England, were added twenty-four more from Normandy and Switzerland; the whole herd, a very fine one, amounted, in 1792,
to a hundred and five head, and hopes were entertained of increafing the number to three hundred, and of fupplying them completely with a fufficiency of
food. The young beafts were not then of an age to allow of any decifion

being

being made, whether the produce of the Suffolk or of the Suffex breed would beft fucceed, but the whole afforded the moft flattering hopes.

With regard to the flock of fheep—the Spanifh ram croffed with the ewes of Berry and the Spanifh ewes, and the Berry ram with the Flemifh ewes, were the two breeds defigned to be eftablifhed and improved; an Englifh ram from Romney Marfh was alfo croffed with the Berry ewes, all of which anfwered perfectly well: the lambs were fine, but as this branch of bufinefs had been began later than the other, the profpect of its fuccefs, although well founded, could not be entirely afcertained.

The lands had been put into excellent condition, in a country where inclofures were unknown; every field of the farm was inclofed by deep and broad ditches, with well planted hedges; gates were erected in all; the dry lands were irrigated, and the marfhy meadows drained, by cuts underground; old lands, for ages paft, judged incapable of yielding any produce, were burnt and rendered fruitful; the buildings on the farm were modelled to the new fyftem, and to the management of the culture that was introduced. The two young French labourers were returned from England, and the Englifh farmer (Mr. Reeve), an excellent one, and a very honeft man, fatisfied with his fituation, with his fuccefs, and with the treatment he met in the country, thought only of continuing his employment, of increafing his fuccefs, and of feconding the intentions of his mafter. He was ordered to keep an exact and daily regifter of all the bufinefs tranfacted on the farm, to fhow it to whoever chofe to fe it, and to anfwer all their queftions with truth, mildnefs, and patience, but not to intice any perfon to undertake an imitation of the Englifh method of farming; Monf. de Liancourt thinking, that in every innovation, nothing lefs than felf-conviction ought to actuate thofe who attempt it; and that by raifing their expectations too highly they rifk the fuccefs, which fooner or later would not fail to attend their efforts. The cows of the diftrict were covered by the bulls of the farm whenever they were brought, and the produce from them was already found, by the people of the country, to be much finer; the culture of turnips and of cabbages, for the feed of cattle, abfolutely unknown before in the diftrict, began to be introduced; fome proprietors inclofed their fields; feveral others had made, for their own ufe, farming implements after the Englifh model, and found them anfwer beft the purpofe; many more hands were employed, of all ages and of both fexes, in the farms; the Englifh were received with pleafure in the country, and treated in the moft cordial manner; every thing fucceeded to the utmoft wifh, and thefe fucceffes were, in great meafure, due to the indefatigable and enlightened vigilance of Monf. de Lazowfki, whofe heart is equal to his capacity.

The

The events of the 10th of Auguſt added the cruel neceſſity of forcing Monſ. de Liancourt to renounce the hope of being uſeful to his country, as he had every reaſon to expect from theſe eſſays, to the other misfortunes he has experienced from the ſame cauſe.

Agriculture was not the only object of improvement he ſought to tranſ-ſport out of England into his country; he had likewiſe began to eſtabliſh the ſpinning of cotton, a manufactory of linen, a ſtocking manufactory, and the fabrication of cards; he had engaged the different artiſans in each branch from England, conſtructed buildings, and ſacrificed his gardens to theſe various eſta-bliſhments; which, in 1792, already employed more than a thouſand people in the diſtrict of Liancourt; and, although yet far from having attained to per-fection, they were productive of the moſt ſalutary effects to the lower ranks of people. As theſe manufactures have remained in the poſſeſſion of an Iriſhman, whom he had taken as an aſſociate, Monſ. de Liancourt conſoles himſelf with the idea, that the conſiderable ſums of money it coſt him to form theſe eſtabliſh-ments, were not wholly loſt to the country he was ſo anxious to enliven and to enrich by induſtry. Theſe eſtabliſhments naturally recall to mind what the Mar-quis de Mirabeau, in his book *De l'Ami des Hommes*, relates of the Duke de la Rochefoucauld, the granfather of Monſ. de Liancourt, having, in 1754, made a ſacrifice of one of the fineſt orongeries in France, and part of his park, to the inhabitants on his eſtate at Verteuil, in Angoumois, for the purpoſe of planting mulberry-trees, and raiſing of ſilk-worms, the cultivation of which was at that time ſcarcely known at Verteuil. This benevolent man had, before his death, the conſolation of ſeeing many good intentions crowned with ſucceſs; Monſ. de Liancourt, on the contrary, has the ſenſible mortification of ſeeing the good he intended to do, and which he had ſo happily began, deſtroyed by thoſe very people for whom it was undertaken; and who, by a fatal error, in thinking to hurt him, whoſe ſole endeavours tended to their advantage, have hurt them-ſelves, by deſtroying an eſtabliſhment that would have been a germ of national proſperity, and was unique in France.

The deſtruction brought upon ſuch eſtabliſhments, by revolutionary anarchy, is one, among a thouſand leſſons that teach the danger, to the deareſt intereſts of the people, flowing from popular commotions. Little more remains of theſe agricultural eſtabliſhments, than the merit of having made them a ſource of heart-felt ſatisfaction to a worthy and patriotic individual. That he may be ſpeedily reinſtated in a property, which he lived only to improve and to adorn, is the ſincere wiſh of that gratitude and friendſhip which pens this faint ac-knowledgement of merit.

ITALY.

NOTES

ON THE

AGRICULTURE OF LOMBARDY.

ONE of the moft interefting countries in Europe, for the practice of various branches of rural œconomy, merits a much clofer and more minute detail than is poffible for a traveller to give, who, from the nature of his purfuit, can do no more than retain a few of the principal features, to point out thofe circumftances which demand the moft ftudious attention: fome of thefe are fo valuable, that years would not be mifpent in acquiring a complete knowledge of them. On every fubject, except what refpects directly practical hufbandry the fmall number of my inquiries is of lefs confequence, while the pen is in the hand of my efteemed friend, Mr. Profeffor Symonds, whofe elegant memoirs upon Italian agriculture * are fraught with information of unqueftionable utility. I fhall arrange the minutes I made in Lombardy under four heads, which will include all that I think worthy of the reader's confideration.

I. General circumftances of the hufbandry.

II. The management of grafs lands.

III. The management of arable lands.

IV. The encouragement or depreffion which agriculture receives from various caufes.

* Inferted in the *Annals of Agriculture.*

CHAP. I.

General Circumstances of the Husbandry of Lombardy.

LOMBARDY is one of the richeft plains in the world; for fertility of foil, united with the ufe that is made of it by watering, it much exceeds every other in Europe; but for mere natural fertility, I take the plain which extends from Holland to Orleans to confift of a richer foil, and it is alfo of a greater extent. From the foot of the Alps, near Suza, to the mouths of the Po, are about two hundred and fifty miles; and the breadth of this noble plain varies from fifty to one hundred, containing, probably, about fifteen thoufand fquare miles. The Po bends its ftately courfe through the whole extent, its branches ramifying, in innumerable ftreams, from the Alps on one fide, and from the Apenines on the other; the prodigious extent of the former range, covered with eternal fnows, afford a vaft fupply of water; preferved moft conveniently in thofe im- menfe refervoirs the Lago Moggiore, Lugano, Como, Ifeo, Guarda, whofe waters are the origin of the greater part of the irrigations of Lombardy. But in the Appenines there are no fuch refervoirs, nor any extent of fnow fimilar to that of the Alps. Thus the fpace watered to the north of the Po, is probably ten times more confiderable than that to the fouth of the fame river.

The foil of Lombardy is, wherever I viewed it, either fand, gravel, or loam. I met with none, or at leaft, with very little clay (fpeaking always as a farmer, and not as a naturalift), and no chalk.

Under this head I fhall infert the notes I took concerning—1, foil; 2, cli- mate; 3, inclofures; 4, farms and tenantry; 5, rent and price of land.

SECT. I.——OF SOIL.

PIEDMONT.

After paffing the Alps from Niece, and defcending towards Coni, in the level and fertile vale of Piedmont, the foil is every where a rich fandy loam, with fmall appearance of clay. Wherever rivers, or rather torrents are found, we fee great tracts of ftone and fhingle, which were brought by the water from the mountains. The Dora Baltia offers this fpectacle; from that river to Ciglione, are plains and wafts of gravel. The rice country of Verceil is a fandy loam. The diftrict of the Sefia is gravel. The Tefin is the fame. The gravels of Pied- mont are all full of round ftones, from the fize of an egg to that of twice a man's fift.

MILANESE.

MILANESE.

In the way from Milan to Pavia, great tracts of gravel, which would not be very valuable without water. To the north of the city, about Mozzata, &c. they have two foils chiefly,—a ftrong loam, a little clayey, blackifh, and free from ftones: and a gravel mixed with loam, fome blackifh, dries quickly, and always loofe. The Lodizan is a loamy fand, or loamy gravel *.

STATE OF VENICE.

The whole way from Vaprio to Verona, there are very great tracts of gravelly loams; there are alfo fome fandy ones; the foil naturally is not deep or rich, though there are tracts that merit both thofe epithets. The territory of Verona is, in general, indifferent, and would not be of great value, were it not for water, and much induftry. The beft meadows and rice-grounds are not more than nine inches deep on ftone and gravel. For fome miles from Verona, the ftoney gravel continues; but towards Vicenza, much fine red and brown, deep, friable, fandy loam, with few or no ftones.

ECCLESIASTICAL STATE.—FERRARESE.

In the Ferrarefe, between Paffo Siene and Bologna, the foil is two feet deep; of a brown fandy loam, with a yellowifh hue, under which is one foot of fand, and then blue clay, apparently ferruginous. In cutting, not long ago, through a field, for raifing a bank, they met with a heap of antient bricks, five feet deep. From Ferrara to Bologna, the foil is, to all appearance, the richeft I ever beheld; deep, friable, and with that degree of tenacity, which marks great fertility; it feems to be entirely a depofition of waters, that have brought thofe fine particles which are held fufpended, and which render that fluid turbid: thofe almoft impalpable particles which are long in fubfiding.

TUSCANY.

All I faw of this territory, is a rockey ftone brafh, or gravel. The loams are compounds of it, with more or lefs vegetable mould; I faw fcarcely any tracts, large enough to be worth mentioning, that are exceptions. It is, upon the whole, though improveable, not a fertile foil; and, if olives were not well adapted to it, would be productive of little befide fheep-walk; to which ani-

---

* The Lodizan foil is termed, by the Italian writers, *oriola*; a blackifh fand, mixed with clay. The Gera d'Adda of *gerivo*, a gravel, compofed of fand and reddifh gravel, with a little clay. The Cremonefe, a red feruginous earth. Sand and gravel every where. *Atti di Milano*, tom. ii. p. 163.

mal,

mal, all I faw of this country, is admirably adapted, and would, I doubt not, produce as fine wool as Spain itfelf.

MODENA AND PARMA.

A rich fandy or gravelly loam is predominant through thefe dutchies; in many tracts it is deep, moift, and friable, as I faw in the lands which were receiving their autumnal preparation for beans in the fpring. In fome diftricts it is of a firm texture, but not clay. Much the fame foil, but not equally deep, is found in the ceded provinces of Vogara, Tortona, and Alexandria; but parts of the laft more tenacious, and to be ranked among the ftiffeft I met with in Lombardy.

SECT. II.—CLIMATE.

On the climate of Lombardy, Mr. Profeffor Symonds is fo full and fatisfactory, that the reader can be no where fo well inftructed.

PIEDMONT.

The great complaint in Piedmont, is the exceffive heat in fummer; equal, I was affured, to almoft any that is felt on the globe, and of a fuffocating quality; while the frofts in winter are as fevere, in the contrary extreme. The peftiferous climate of Sardinia is known to every body; though between 39 and 41 degrees latitude; in the fouthern part of the ifland, they are not forwarder than in the Milanefe: they cut their corn in the north part in July: in the Milanefe before the end of June *.

MILANESE.

The moft remarkable circumftance in the climate of the Milanefe, is the mildnefs and warmth of northern and mountainous tracts, and the feverity felt in the plain. This fact is found particularly around the lake of Como; upon all the weftern coaft of that lake, which is about forty miles long, the *agrumi*, as the Italians call oranges, lemons, &c. are found, expofed to the open air, in good perfection; yet the whole of the lake is bounded by the high Alps, which, immediately to the north, are covered with eternal fnows. On the rich plain of Milan, and thence to the Apenines, no fuch plant can be left expofed; olives are not feen, and oranges, lemons, and bergamots, muft be covered in winter. Thefe *agrumi* are found chiefly on the weft coaft of the lake, but fome are fcattered on the eaftern. It is the fhelter afforded by the mountains, in peculiar pofitions, that has this effect. The fame circumftance is found in the Lago Maggiore, where the famous Borromean Iflands are covered with *agrumi*.

* *Riferimento della Sardegna*, tom. i. p. 155.

In

In all the Milanese, dry summers for corn (I believe it is the same every where in Europe), are most productive *.

In an experiment made at Vicenza, in the Venetian State, by the Accademia Agraria of this city, they sowed wheat October 18, 1787; came up the 28th; the ears appeared May 2, 1788; the flowers May 13; reaped June 19.

TUSCANY.

I was at Florence the beginning of November, and the ice was four inches thick; a severity never yet known in England. The English were, at the same time, skating at Rome.

One-fifth of all the productions of the earth are calculated to be destroyed by hail and other accidents.

PARMA.

In the management of the vines in the Parmazan, there is a practice, which shews the constant dread of severe frosts. All the vines are now (in November) turned down, and the end shoots buried † in the earth to preserve them; yet in a wet season they suffer by this treatment, as well as in all seasons, by being stript from the trees, in order to undergo this operation.

Mr. Professor Symonds, in the excellent paper quoted above, removed the common erroneous idea of the fine climate of Italy: I made many inquiries con-

---

* The same remark was made long ago, in 1540;

MDXL Extructum

Annus his bissextilis fuit, et luminare majus

Fere totum eclypsavit

A septimo idus Novembris ad septimum usque Aprilis idus

Nec nix nec aqua visa de cœlo cadere

Attamen, præter mortalium opinionem, Dei clementiâ,

Et messis et vindemia multa.

It is extraordinary, that in 1779 there was an almost total eclipse of the sun, followed by a fine winter, the same as in 1540. There was a small eclipse on the 7th of April, 1540, but an almost total one the 15th. of April, 1539, and which, for quantity and duration, was very much like that the 24th. of June, 1779. The crop was abundant, as it appears by the prices of the year, in the Ledger of the Cistersian Monks. Wheat, 1539, the moggia, 5 liv. In 1540, ditto, 4 liv. In 1541, ditto, 6 liv. The ducat of gold, or zecchin, then at 5 liv. 15 s. Campi (*Istoria di Cremona*, anno 1540) speaks of the extraordinary dryness of this year, the abundance of crops, and subjoins, that the corn was cut the middle of May, and the vintage the beginning of August. This is the harvest near forty days sooner than at present, and the vintage two months. *Opusc. Scel.* tom. ii. p. 136.

† The same practice was known among the antients. See *Strabo*, lib. vii. and *Quint. Curt.* lib. vii. c. 3.

cerning the leading facts, and have every reason to believe that it is, in point of health and agreeableness, one of the worst climates in the world: with the views of a farmer, however, it must be confessed, that the productions which the whole peninsula owes to its climate are very valuable; to omit speaking of Sicily or Naples, I may remark, that planting the poor brashy hills of Tuscany with olives is an advantage unequalled by any thing to be met with in the north of Europe; that the produce of silk throughout Lombardy is an object of the first importance—That rice is found to be an article of almost unrivalled profit. —That the productive state of the meadows is indebted almost as much to the heat of the summers, as to the plenty of water; and, for any thing I know to the contrary, the admirable quality of the cheese also. These are all objects of great magnitude, and entirely derived from climate.

SECT. III.—INCLOSURES.

PIEDMONT.

It is not very easy, in many parts of Piedmont, to pronounce, on a superficial view, whether the country be open or inclosed; but, on a nearer inspection, the greater part by far found to be inclosed; generally by ditches, and, in many districts, with hedges also; which, in some places, are as complete as in the best English counties.

MILANESE.

Much the greater part of this territory is inclosed, either with hedges or by ditches, which serve as conductors of the water used in irrigation. These, in the Lodizan, and other districts to the south of Milan, are planted so thickly, with willow and poplar pollards, that the country looks every where like a wood.

VENETIAN STATE.

Much of the country, from Bergamo to Brescia, is very thickly inclosed with hedges. From Brescia to the Lago di Guarda it is the same; but from thence to Verona not equally so.

ECCLESIASTICAL STATE—BOLOGNA.

The whole Bolognese is inclosed. They make and plash their hedges with the nicest attention: made with dead stakes, about four feet high, and tied in cross lines, with great neatness and strength. This care is, however, exerted for the boundary of the farm only; subdivisions of this kind are rare.

TUSCANY.

TUSCANY.

There are no rights of commonage in all Tufcany; thanks to the wifdom of Leopold; every man has a right to inclofe his property as he pleafes. The Appenines, croffed from Belogna to Florence, are, however, moftly uninclofed, and almoft wafte.

MODENA.

From the city of Modena to Reggio, the inclofures are very neatly formed, of well made hedges without any ugly fprawling ones; but all either trimmed, or made fo often, that they are not fuffered to fpread.

PARMA.

To Firenzuola all the country is inclofed.

PIEDMONT.—*Tortonefe.*

The fences from the Dutchy of Modena hither are greatly declined: there are fome hedges every where; but many large fields all the way, with only bad ditches or banks.

Lombardy, upon the whole, muft be confidered as an inclofed country, and much of it clofely fo. It would indeed be a glaring abfurdity to keep land fo extremely valuable in an open ftate. The importance of inclofing is well underftood, and where not practifed in perfection, it arifes from caufes that form exceptions rather than effect the general rule.

SECT. IV.—OF FARMS AND TENANTRY.

The predominant feature in the farms of Piedmont is *metayers*, nearly upon the fame fyftem which I have defcribed and condemned, in treating of the hufbandry of France. The landlord commonly pays the taxes and repairs the buildings, and the tenant provides cattle, implements, and feed; they divide the produce. Wherever this fyftem prevails, it may be taken for granted that a ufelefs and miferable population is found. The poverty of the farmers is the origin of it; they cannot ftock the farms, pay taxes, and rent in money, and, therefore, muft divide the produce in order to divide the burthen. There is reafon to believe that this was entirely the fyftem in every part of Europe; it is gradually going out every where; and in Piedmont is giving way to great farms, whofe occupiers pay a money rent. I was for fome time deceived in going From Nice to Turin, and believed that more of the farms were larger
than

than is really the cafe, which refulted from many fmall ones being collected into one home-ftead. That belonging to the Prince of Corignan, at Billia Bruna, has the appearance of being very confiderable ; but, on inquiry, I found it in the hands of feven families of metayers. In the mountains, from Nice to Racconis, however, they are fmall ; but many properties, as in the mountains of France and Spain.

The Caval. de Capra, member of the Agrarian Society, affured me, that the union of farms was the ruin of Piedmont, and the effect of luxury ; that the metayers were difmiffed and driven away, and the fields every where depopulated. I demanded how the country came to have the appearance of immenfe cultivation, and looked rather like a garden than a farm, all the way from Coni ? He replied, that I fhould fee things otherwife in paffing to Milan : that the rice culture was fupported by great farms, and that large tracts of country were reduced to a defert. Are they then uncultivated ? No ; they are very well cultivated ; but the people all gone, or become miferable. We hear the fame ftory in every country that is improving : while the produce is eaten up by a fuperfluity of idle hands, there is population on the fpot ; but it is ufelefs population the improvement banifhes thefe drones to towns, where they become ufeful in trade and manufactures, and **yield a market** to that land, to which they were before only a **burthen**. No country can be really flourifhing unlefs this take place ; nor can there be any where a flourifhing and wealthy race of farmers, able to give money rents, but by the deftruction of metaying. Does any one imagine that England would be **more** rich and more populous if her farmers were turned into metayers ? **Ridiculous.** The intendant of Biffatti added another argument againft great farms ; namely, that of their being laid to grafs more than fmall ones ; furely this is a leading circumftance in their favour ; for grafs is the laft and greateft improvement of Piedmont ; and that arrangement of the foil which occafions moft to be in grafs, is the moft beneficial. Their meadows are amongft the fineft and moft productive in the world. What is their arable ? It yields crops of five or fix times the feed only. To change fuch arable to fuch grafs, is, doubtlefs, the higheft degree of improvement. View France and her metayers—View England and her farmers ; and then draw your conclufions.

The Milanese.

Wherever the country (**that I faw**) is poor and unwatered, in the Milanefe, it is in the hands of metayers. At Mozzata the Count de Caftiglioni fhewed me the rent book his *intendant*, (fteward) keeps, and it is a curious explanation of the fyftem which prevails. In fome hundred pages I faw very few names without a large balance of debt due to him, and brought from the book of the preceding

year ·

year: they pay by fo many moggii of all the different grains, at the price of the
year: fo many heads of poultry; fo much labour; fo much hay; and fo much
ftraw, &c. But there is, in moft of their accounts, on the debtor's fide, a variety of articles, befide thofe of regular rent: fo much corn, of all forts, borrowed of the landlord, for feed or food, when the poor man has none: the fame
thing is common in France, wherever metaying takes place. All this proves
the extreme poverty, and even mifery, of thefe little farmers; and fhews, that
their condition is more wretched than that of a day labourer. They are much
two numerous; three being calculated to live in one hundred pertichi, and all
fully employed by labouring, and cropping the land inceffantly with the fpade,
for a produce unequal to the payment of any thing to the landlord, after feeding themfelves and their cattle as they ought to be fed; hence the univerfal
diftrefs of the country. Thofe who are advocates for fmall farms, fhould come
hither, and fee how they infallibly generate poverty in every cottage. The
furplus of population is not demanded by manufactures, or by towns; the increafe, therefore, is only the divifion of a pittance of food amongft many mouths
inftead of a few. It is impoffible to prohibit procreation, or to force emigra-
tion; but it is in a landlord's power to introduce, gradually and prudently, a
different fyftem—to occupy a large farm himfelf, cultivated accurately, by day-
labourers, of all ages and fexes, well paid; and if this be not fufficient, to
eftablifh a manufacture of fome grofs and fimple kind, to employ the population already exifting; and, by a gradual alteration in his farms, to proportion
the food to the mouths that are to eat it *. There is at prefent an inducement
to fuch a change, that ought to weigh very ferioufly: the example of the French
revolution will fpread, and will be much more apt to take effect in countries
where there is nothing but the great land owner and the poor cottager, than in
others where there are intermediate ranks of men of fubftance, who have an
intereft in preferving public order. What a temptation to confufion and re-
bellion is it, to have a country full of miferable metayers, all deeply indebted
to the feigneur? Nine-tenths of the people, in fuch a cafe, have an immediate
iutereft in burning his caftle and his account-books, for he ftands fingle, on one
hand, againft all the people, fwarming on the other; but in the watered plain,
where the farms are large and not populous, from fo much being in grafs, there
is every where a race of wealthy farmers, who have an intereft in keeping the
people quiet,—who are united with the landlord.—and who, paying their men
in money, without thefe long and dangerous accounts, have not the temptation to
revolt; or even if they were tempted, they would not have the difproportion of
numbers to render it equally dangerous. The great object of men who have

* But inftead of the number of farms decreafing, they are increafed, as we learn from Sig. Lavizari,
Annot. ful Mitterpacher, tom. i. p. 221.

property, is at prefent to fecure it—and they can have no fecurity, while they fill the country, by metaying, with fwarms of a ftarving and indebted peafantry. It fhould be remembered, that the mifchievous confufions, plundering, and burnings, in France, were not in **the Pays de** Beauce, nor in Picardie, nor in Artois, where metayers are unknown, and the farms large; but in the Maçonnois, in Breffe, in Sologne, where all are in the hands of poor miferable metayers; an inftance, furely, exprefs to the purpofe; and which fhould have its weight with Italian landlords. But to work a change in this pernicious fyftem, demands a refidence on their eftates in the country, inftead of abandoning them to the rapacity of ftewards; it is not by living in the frippery of great cities, that their landed property is to be arranged on fafe principles *.

In the watered parts of the Milanefe, great and rich farmers are found. Here are the particulars of a farm, I viewed, between Milan **and Pavia; viz.** 3100 *pertichi*; 1600 of rice; 200 flax; 450 perennial grafs; 450 clover; 400 arable crops, wheat, rye, maiz, millet, oats, &c.; 12 horfes; 8 oxen; 55 cows; 2 bulls; 40 labourers; rent 20 liv. the pertica; the whole capable of being watered. And at Codogno the following are the particulars of one, where 100 cows are kept: 2000 *pertichi*; 100 cows; 1 cazaro; 1 fotte cazaro; 6 others; 9 for corn; 1 agent; 1 guard againft thieves, and thofe who fteal water; 1 waterman. To ftock fuch a farm 50,000 liv. neceffary. By means of fuch farms they have rich farmers; fome worth 100,000 liv. The general idea of profit, in thefe dairy diftricts, is 10 to 15 per cent.; fome dairy farms are occupied by proprietors, but the number is inconfiderable.

Venetian State.

All the lands in the Brefcian and Veronefe territory are let at half produce, *à la meta*; even vines: but fome meadows are ufually referved, and alfo woods. The proprietor pays the land-tax, and the farmer provides live ftock, and pays the taxes on it.

Sig. Locatelli has a farm of 100 campi, within two miles of the city, which yields him 250 zecchini nett; this is fomething more than 30s. an acre. He has alfo another farm more diftant, of 600 campi, which yields 650 zecchini nett; on which there are 8 cows, 22 oxen, and 150 fheep.

In the Vicentine †, rent, when calculated in money, 2½ zecchini per campo. They have farms fo large as 2000 campi.

---

* This whole paffage is left as originally written; before French horrors rendered French politicks objects of deteftation rather than example.

† Particulars of a farm of 120 campi: 20 of meadow, not watered; 90 of corn; 10 of clover; 15 oxen and young cattle; 3 cows; 2 horfes; 4 hogs; 7 men; 4 ditto, with oxen; 4 women; 2 children.

In the Paduan, 100 campi are a large farm; common 60; fmall 40; and they reckon fmall ones the beft cultivated; if this be fa{\(\)}, and not a matter of opinion in the gentleman, my informant, it fhews that their hufbandry muft certainly be efteemed bad; it is, however, queftionable, for the reafon added was, that there were more people on fmall farms; a fure proof that the progrefs of improvement has not been carried far. To ftock a farm, of a hundred campi, 1000 ducats are neceflary, reckoning the ducat at 3s. which is not exact; this is a poor ftock, for it does not exceed 33s. the Englifh acre. The arrangement of the farms, in the Paduan, may be guefled at, in fome meafure, from the following particulars; there are found, in the whole diftrict, 288,300 fouls; 49,943 cows and fatting cattle; 41,000 plough oxen; 102,000 fheep; 16,598 hogs; 731 mules; 2381 afles. One Profeffor informed me, that, in his opinion, the great mifchief of the country is, that of great land proprietors letting their eftates to undertakers or middle-men, who will hire to the amount of 10,000 ducats a year; and in re-letting to farmers will fqueeze them fo, that they cannot live, to the great degradation of the country. Another profeffor faid, that the diftrict of Padua is not fo well cultivated as the Vicentin, by reafon of the greater poverty of the farmers and peafants, who are miferable, and have no power to make the land yield well. Indeed I learned, from very good authority, that the Paduan is not equal to the Vicentin, except in the mountains, where the peafants are much more at their eafe than in the plain.

ECCLESIASTICAL STATE—BOLOGNA.

Eftates here are very generally let to middle-men, who relet them to the farmers at half produce, by which means the proprietor receives little more than one-half what he might do on a better fyftem, with a peafantry in a better fituation. The whole country is at half produce; the farmer fupplies implements, cattle, and fheep, and half the feed: the proprietor repairs. Silk, and even wine on the fame tenure.

Particulars of a farm (Sig. Bignami's) of 600 tornature; 360 on the hills; the reft on the plain: 6 metayers; 36 working oxen; 12 cows: 70 young cattle; 100 fheep. Produce, 2000 corbi of wine; 3 to 400 corbi wheat.

TUSCANY.

Letting lands, at money rent, is but new in Tufcany; and it is ftrange to fay, that Sig. Paoletti, a very practical writer, declares againft it *. A farm in Tufcany is called a *podere*: and fuch a number of them as are placed under the management of a factor, is called *fattoria*. His bufinefs is to fee that the lands

* *Penfieri*, &c. p. 162. 164.

X 2

are

are managed according to the leafe, and that the landlord has his fair half. Thefe farms are not often larger than for a pair of oxen, and eight to twelve people in one houfe; fome 100 pertichi (this meafure is to the acre, as about 25 to 38), and two pair of oxen, with twenty people. I was affured that thefe metayers are (efpecially near Florence) much at their eafe; that on holydays they are dreffed remarkably well, and not without objects of luxury, as filver, gold, and filk; and live well, on plenty of bread, wine and legumes. In fome inftances this may poffibly be the cafe, but the general fact is contrary. It is abfurd to think that metayers, upon fuch a farm as is cultivated by a pair of oxen, can be at their eafe; and a clear proof of their poverty is this, that the landlord, who provides half the live ftock, is often obliged to lend the peafant money to enable him to procure his half; but they hire farms with very little money, which is the old ftory of France, &c.; and indeed poverty and miferable agriculture are the fure attendants upon this way of letting land. The metayers, not in the vicinity of the city, are fo poor, that landlords even lend them corn to eat: their food is black bread, made of a mixture with vetches: and their drink is very little wine, mixed with water, and called *aquarolle*; meat on Sundays only; their drefs very ordinary. Yet in all thefe particulars they were in a worfe fituation before the free corn trade. The richeft peafants are in the Valdichiano. The moft common agrement is, for the landlord to furnifh all the cattle and fheep, and to pay the taxes, except the capitation on the peafants family of 3 liv. for all above three years old. In a confiderable *fattoria* of 18 poderi, at Caftello Villa Bali Martelli, the largeft is 200 ftiori (36 acres, at $5\frac{1}{2}$; $28\frac{1}{2}$, at 7), and 70 the fmalleft. Particulars of one of 190 ftiori; 1 pair of oxen; 2 calves; 1 horfe; 1 mule; no cows, fheep, or hogs; 14 people, of all ages and fexes; taxes, before the grand Duke's redemption, 80 pauls, now 15; tithes 15 pauls, half paid by landlord, half by peafant; this is 6s. 8d. in the whole for about 30 acres. Produce corn, 180 fcudi; filk, $6\frac{1}{2}$; wine, 58; oil, 60; in all 85l.; the half, or 44l. is the landlord's receipt for thefe articles, or above 1l. 5s. per acre, at $5\frac{1}{2}$ ftiori to the Englifh acre, and 1l. 11s. if at 7. No fmall proprietor.

Villamagna.

Sig. Paoletti, rector of this parifh, and author of fome valuable works on agriculture, which I have had occafion to quote, was fo obliging as to give the following detail of the 3 poderi belonging to his living, from which the arable œconomy of this part of Tufcany will be well underftood.

Three

Three Poderi; three Families.

Seed *sown.*—48 ſtaji of wheat —— 168 *ſtiori of land.*
    3 ditto   vetches —— 7½
  24 ditto beans   —— 28
   6 ditto oats   —— 10
Artificial graſſes ; viz. clover,
  great millet, vetch, and
  oats, all for forage   -   -   24
Wood,   -   -   283

The ſtajo of wheat, of 40 lb. Engliſh (52 lb. to 55 lb. Tuſcan), ſows 3½ ſtiori, and yields eight or nine times as much ; vetches four times the ſeed ; beans three times ; oats ſeven times ; the wheat is a tolerable crop ; all the reſt miſerable. If the farms, immediately under the eye of this able writer, yield no more in this *metà* ſyſtem, we may ſuppoſe the poverty of the common producꞈs ; we have, on the worſt lands in England, no idea of ſuch crops as theſe of vetches, beans, and oats. There are further on the 3 poderi, 36 ſheep ; 1 mule ; 6 oxen ; and 4 cows ; alſo 50 barrels of oil, at 5 ſcudi ; and 380 barrels of wine, at 10 liv. the barrel, vintage price, but at a year old 15 liv. or 16 liv. ; in ſilk 25 ſcudi ; and in wood 10 ſcudi, for three-fourths of the woods are in a ſtate of deſtruꞈion. Theſe poderi are let *a la metà* ; repairs are done by the proprietor ; live ſtock belong to the incumbent, and neither to the church nor to the peaſants ; implements belong to the tenants ; feed wheat, three-fourths to them, and one-fourth to the owner ; of ſpring corn, all to the latter ; alſo all ſorts that are put in with the vanga (ſpade), as the land is ſo much the better laboured. Let it be remembered, that the ſpade being preferred to the plough, is the moſt deciſive proof that tillage is in a ſtate of mediocrity, if not barbariſm.

MODENA.

In the mountains there are many peaſant proprietors, but not in the plain. A great evil here, as in other parts of Lombardy, is the praꞈice of the great lords, and the poſſeſſors of lands in mortmain letting to middle-men, who re-let to metayers ; under which tenure are all the lands of the duchy. The tenant furniſhes one-half of the cattle, and the landlord one-half. To Reggio the number of ſcattered houſes very great ; good ; and with neatly hedged home-ſtalls : apparently there is not a labourer's houſe in all the country ; all metaying farmers.

PARMA.

PARMA.

Appearances from Reggio to this place are much inferior to thofe from Modena to Reggio; the fences not fo neat; nor the houfes fo well built, white, or clean. All here metayers; the proprietor fupplies the cattle, half the feed, and pays the taxes; the peafant provides the utenfils. In the whole dutchies of Parma and Piacenza, and indeed almoft every where elfe, the farms muft be very fmall; the practice I have elfewhere noted, of the digging the land for beans, and working it up with a fuperfluity of labour, evidently fhew it: the fwarms of people in all the markets announce the fame fact; at Piacenza, I faw men, whofe only bufinefs was to bring a fmall bag of apples, about a peck; one man brought a turkey, and not a fine one. What a wafte of time and labour, for a ftout fellow to be thus employed.

SAVOY.

All the peafants are proprietors. So long ago as theyear 897, lands were let on leafe for twenty-two years, and not only for a payment of fruits or fervice, as in all the northern parts of Europe, but partly at a money-rent. This fhews how vaftly more forward Italy was in thofe early periods, than the reft of Europe *.

It is faid, that in 1464 began the cuftom of letting lands on a three years leafe †.

SECT. V.——RENT AND PRICE OF LAND.

This, as I have endeavoured to explain already, in the cafe of France, is one of the moft important inquiries in rural œconomy. The vulgar notion is, that nothing raifes the value of land, but trade or manufacture. If the refult of my travels, were only to produce facts fufficient to overturn fo falfe a theory, my time would not be altogether loft.

PIEDMONT.—*Cbentale.*

Land, in general, is fold at 800 liv. or 900 liv. the *giornata*, which is to the Englifh acre as 7440 is to 7929. (*Paucton*). At a diftance from towns, 600 liv.

* ————Uncerto Donno, **che cerca da P Abate** di S. Ambrogio a nomo di livello, per ventidue anni, **alcune terre** nel Contado **di Brefcia,** ch'erano del moniftero d'Orona; promettando di pagare a fitto cioè per fiffa annuale **penfione** tanta quantità di generi, e di denaro. Secala modia decem, Seligine ftaria duodecem, faba, &c. &c. Giulini goes on; "Qui chiaramente si comprende, che s'ingannò il Mattioli il quale credette, che la fegale foffe la filigine degli antichi." *Memorie della Citta e della Camp. di Milano.* Giulini, parte ii. p. **62.**

† **Caronelli** *fopra l' Inftituzione Agraria della Cirventu.* 4to. 1789. P. 58.

to 850 liv. Some at 1000 liv. (53l. 6s. per Englifh acre.) Good watered meads, 1000 liv. to 1200 liv.

Turin.

The price of land in the environs of Turin, as may be fuppofed, is very high. Four miles from the town, fome is fold, without water, at 1200 liv. the giornata: with water, it depends on quantity, and the value is immenfe. Land that has one hour a week of fuch a ftream as will water five giornata in that hour, fells at 1500 liv. (79l. 19s. per Englifh acre); if it waters two giornata, 1000 liv.; and if three, 1200 liv. And fuch watering adds, at leaft, one-third to the value of the land. At Cambiano, five miles from Turin, arable land fells at 3000 liv. but this is uncommon. Near the town, fuch prices as 3000 liv. and 4000 liv. are known. But, in general, arable watered, near Turin, fells at 1000 liv.; at a diftance, and not watered, 200 liv. to 550 liv. If a general average were to be made, of all forts of land, except the very fineft, it would be about 500 liv. In regard to rent, but little is let for money; chiefly at one-half produce; but fuch meadows as would fell at 1000 liv. would let at 70 liv. to 75 liv. If two-thirds are arable, and one-third meadow, 40 liv. will be about the rent in good lands. In the territory of Turin, arable lets at 30 liv.

Vercelli.

Rice-grounds, 500 liv.; good wheat land, 800 liv.; watered meadow, 600 liv. and 700 liv. per giornata.

MILANESE.

The price varies from 15 liv. for the pooreft waftes, to 1000 liv. the pertica * ; but from 600 liv. to 1000 liv. more common. As the livre is 7¾d. Englifh,
1000 liv.

* The difficulty I have met with, in afcertaining the contents of a Milanefe pertica, is ftrange. Paucton, in his *Metrologie*, makes it to the Englifh acre, as 0.14727 is to 0.7929, by which proportion, it fhould contain 8090 feet, or about 5 1-3d perticas in an acre. Count Alexander Cicogno, in the Memoirs of the Patriotic Society of Milan, vol. ii. p. 304, fays, that if feeds are planted at fifteen oncie one from another, 1479 will plant a pertica. As the oncia is two inches Englifh, this makes 9243 Englifh feet in a pertica.

Monf. de la Lande fays, that it takes more than five perticas to make an arpent de Paris: now as that arpent is to the Englifh acre, 0,6694 is to 0,7929, there are confequently 36,775 Englifh feet in that arpent; at five perticas, it would confift of 7355 Englifh feet, or about fix to an acre.

In the notes to the new edition of the *Venti Giornata* of Gallo (1775), this pertica is faid to contain 6152 French feet, which will not differ materially from De la Lande.

Count Carli, who was prefident of the fupreme council of Finances at Milan, and has written intelligently on the *cenfiments*, fays, *L'arpent di Francia fta alla pertica Milanefe come 14 ad uno proffima mente.*

1000 liv. is 98l. 19s. 2d. per acre. It is ufually bought in fuch a manner as to pay 2½ to 3 per cent. for the purchafe-money.

Between Milan and Pavia, land rendered good by water, fome fells at 300 liv. to 500 liv. : at 300 liv. it lets at 12 liv.

From Milan to Mozzata, when you have paffed the watered plain, which is in a few miles, the rent, in general, is not more than 4 liv. or 5 liv. the pertica. In every new leafe, for a long period, fuch as eighteen or twenty-one years, there is always an augmentation of rent in every part of the Milanefe, and generally to a pretty confiderable amount. There is alfo an undoubted augmentation in the fpecie current in the country; and the prices of every thing have rifen at the fame time that money has increafed. It highly deferves noting, by the politician, that as the Milanefe fubfifts entirely by land produce, without trade (other than the fale of that produce), and without manufacture, it is remarkable that it has experienced an advance in its profperity, as well as countries that feem to engrofs both trade and manufacture; even at a period long after it had attained a height of cultivation and improvement, to which thofe trading countries have little to oppofe.

Lodi.

The beft land near this place, 600 liv. the pertica (59l. 8s. per Englifh acre); but farther off, 300 liv. to 350 liv. The *Spina*, a farm I viewed, belonging to the Caval. Don Baffiamo Bona Noma, lets at 30 liv.; others at 25 liv.; but the common price 12 liv. to 15 liv. The beft land and higheft rent is all for cows.

Codogno.

Watered lands fell at 300 liv. the pertica ; and let at 10 liv. (19l. 9s. per Englifh acre), nett rent, tenant paying cenfimento, &c.

mente. (Delle opere del S. Conte Carli. 8vo. 1784. Tom. i. p. 223.) The arpent of France being to the arpent de Paris as 48 to 32, there are 55,162 Englifh feet in it, and in the pertica (at 1½ to 1) 31,500 feet. But the fame author fays (p. 320) there are 4868 pertichi in a fquare Italian mile; if fo, there are 3628 in a fquare Englifh mile; this makes 5½ and 1-6th pertichi to an Englifh acre.

Finding fo many contradictions, I judged it neceffary to recur to different authority. The *oncia* of Milan is two Englifh inches; and the meafures thus arrange themfelves.

One pertica 24 tavoli.
One tavola 12 piedi.
One piede 12 oncie.

Of thefe the tavola and pertica are fquare meafures, the former containing 12 piedi *fquare*; this makes 576 Englifh feet, which, multiplied by 24, the refult is 13,824 feet for a pertica, or *about* 3 1-6th to an acre ; and by this eftimate I fhall calculate.

Rent

				liv.	*ſ.*
Rent nett,	-	-	-	10	0
Water-tax for diſtribution,		-		1	0
Cenſimento,	-	-	-	2	5
Total rent,		-		13	5

Venetian State—*Bergamo.*

Price of land near Bergamo, 80 ducats the pertica. The ducat is 8 liv. and 50 liv. the pound ſterling; and, if the editors of Agoſtino Gallo be not miſtaken, there are 6194 French feet in a pertica; on theſe proportions, land ſells at 78l. 8s. per Engliſh acre.

Breſcia.

The beſt ſells at 800 ſcudi; commonly from 300 to 500 ſcudi the jugero. This meaſure containing 4 pertichi, and the Engliſh acre 4¼, makes 400 ſcudi to equal 59l. per Engliſh acre, at 7 liv. the ſcudo. The beſt land, of 800 ſcudi, amounts conſequently to 118l. Rents, per jugero, 5 to 10 ſcudi; the mean, 7½ ſcudi, equals 22s. Engliſh acre.

Verona.

Land here commonly ſells at 70 zecchini the campo (44l. 6s. per Engliſh acre), and yields to the proprietor 3 to 4 per cent. I viewed an arable field eloſe to the city, yet ſowing with wheat, that would ſell for 100 zecchini per campo: and ſome other lands, juſt out of the Porta Nouva, that are exceſſively gravelly, would ſell for 15 zecchini; ſuch poor land, at a diſtance, would not ſell for more than 8 or 9 zecchini (5l. per Engliſh acre): it is, however, not ſo bad, but that good mulberry-trees are on it.

Vicenza.

The beſt watered meadows ſell at 2400 liv. to 3000 liv. the campo, which is about 65l. per Engliſh acre; the beſt arable is nearly as valuable. The worſt arable 300 liv.: in the beſt there are neither mulberries nor vines. Common price 900 liv. to 1000 liv.; and the produce 110 liv. per campo, about 55s. the acre. The higheſt rent in money is 3 zecchini the campo; common 1, 1½, or 2 zecchini. But, in general, land is let at half produce.

To Padua.

The beſt land ſells at 45 zecchini the campo: rice-grounds are at that price.

Padua.

The beſt arable land ſells at 200 ducats, of 6 liv. 4ſ. The campo is 840 pertiche quadrate, each of 6 feet, conſequently 30,240 feet; but the foot is 1 inch
longer than the Paris foot: it is, therefore, equal to about 35,280 Paris feet *,
or about ¹⁄₁₆th under an Engliſh acre. Middling land, 95 ducats; bad, 50 ducats; rice-grounds, and conſequently irrigated, 200 ducats; the ſame land, before
rice being planted, 100 ducats; watered meadows, 200 ducats; woods, 100 ducats; gardens, 400 ducats. Eſtates pay 5 per cent.

ECCLESIASTICAL STATE—*Bologna.*

Landlords are paid by half produce, which affords them about 1l. 6s. 5d.
per tornatura, of half an Engliſh acre, and as much is left for the farmer: this
is about 5l. 5s. an acre, groſs produce, on an average; but it is in the rich plain
only. Through all the country, and including good, bad, and indifferent, it
varies from 8s. 9d. to 26s. 5d. the tornatura, for the landlord's ſhare. The price
for ſuch land as yields the latter ſum, is 21l. 17s. 6d. Engliſh, the tornatura: in general, from 8l. 15s. to 13l. 2s. 6d. The return for the value of land
is 4 to 5 per cent. on the capital; but in farms on the mountains, 7 per cent.

TUSCANY—*Florence.*

The landlord's half of the produce, for all farms are let *a la metà*, is about
3 liv. nett (2s. 1½d.) per ſtiora on the plain (11s. 8¼d. per Engliſh acre) † : it is
2 liv. on the hills (7s. 8½d. per acre), and 1 liv. on the mountains. No other
proof is wanted of the poor ſtate of agriculture in this country, ariſing, doubt-
leſs, from ſo wretched a mode of letting land. What muſt it have been before
the time of Leopold, who has done ſo much towards the annihilation of its old
ſhackles?

Villamagna.

Three poderi, containing 200 ſtiori cultivated, and 283 of mountain wood,
would ſell at 12,000 ſcudi (3400.l) ; and, per ſtiora, for the whole, 7l. each : it
alſo yields a rent, by metaying, of 500 ſcudi; and land is commonly ſold to pay
3½ per cent. intereſt; but, more commonly, in other parts, only 3.

DUTCHY OF MODENA—*Modena.*

The biolca, which is here the meaſure of land, is 29 French toiſes, by 26. or
754; or, to the Engliſh acre, as 27,144 is to 38,300; or as 15 to 21. This

---

* Mr. Pauſton makes it more than an arpent of France, 1,0866. How he proves this, I am not
arithmetician enough to know.

* This at the ratio of 5¼ ſtiori per acre.

meaſure

meafure of arable fells from 500 liv. to 1200 liv.—the livre half that of Milan, or about 4d.; 800 would be 18l. an acre. Watered meadow fells at 1200 liv to 3000 liv.; the latter equals 70l. an acre. Such are mown thrice; the firft cutting yields 1 carro, of 100 poid, or 2500 lb. (the pound about 4ths of an Englifh pound); and the price of hay 3 to 4 zecchini per carro.

PARMA.

The beft land fells commonly at 50 zecchini the biolca (31l. 7s. per acre). To Firenzuola, the beft fells at 25 to 40 zecchini.

PIEDMONT—*Vogara.*

From St. Giovanni to Vogara, the price of the beft is 500 liv. the journal. After that town, 24 fcudi di Milano per tavola (about 20l. to 25l. per acre). From Vogara, to within a few miles of Turin, the average value of land is 500 liv. (26l. 13s. per Englifh acre.)

SAVOY.

At Montmelian, vineyards fet at 1000 liv. to 1200 liv. the journal, which about equals a French arpent. On the mountain fides to Chamberry, on a foil, to appearance, abfolutely ftones, that yield good wine, and fell as high as meadow. Cultivated land, at Modena, in the Haut-Savoy, at 1000 liv. Improved mountain fpots, 300 liv. to 500 liv.

The moft carelefs examination of the preceding prices, will be fufficient to fhew, that land is fold, at prefent, in Lombardy, fome ages after it has loft both its commerce and its manufactures*, at prices that ought to mark the direct influence of immenfe induftry; for it rifes from 30l. to 100l. an acre, through a territory not comparable for foil, naturally to many others. I will venture to affert, that the fame *land* in England, would not fell for half, perhaps, not for one-third of the money. And it is worthy of remark, that the cities which poffefs moft trade at prefent, as Leghorn, Genoa, and Venice, have little influence on the lands which fell at the prices here noted. It is not the competition of Venetian merchants that raifes the prices on the *terra firma*; and what have thofe of Leghorn and Genoa to do with the Milanefe and Piedmont? If Leghorn has not cultivated the Maremma, how was it to water the Lodizan?

---

* Every one knows, that, ftrictly fpeaking, there are both trade and manufactures in all parts of Lombardy; converting *raw* to organized filk, is certainly a manufacture; and making a few velvets at Genoa, or glafs beads at Venice, are manufactures; but, for all the purpofes of argument, Lombardy, when compared to fuch countries as England and France, muft be faid to be almoft deftitute of them.

Bologna

Bologna is, parhaps, the moſt manufacturing town in Lombardy; but has it drained the Commachio? If you recur not to preſent, but to antient wealth, you muſt turn to Florence *, Piſa, Genoa, and Venice; the two firſt are in one of the worſt cultivated countries in Italy; of Genoa I know nothing. but by reading; but I have read no author that ſpeaks of great cultivation in the Ligurian territory, *free from ſmall preſent proprietors:* and let it be remembered, becauſe it is a circumſtance that merits it, that great commerce and fabrics, eſpecially when depending on a *city* that governs a *territory*, have a direct tendency not to eſtabliſh, but to annihilate ſuch properties.

The effect of great wealth, flowing from induſtry, is to extirpate little properties, by the profits from trade being inveſted in their purchaſe; one country-gentleman, with half a ſcore farmers, and a hundred labourers, takes the place in countries, where the progreſs of wealth is in its natural courſe, of a number of little proprietors, who eat up all their produce, and yet are half ſtarving for want. Is this the caſe in the Genoeſe territory? I am ſure it is not at Venice.

The ſureſt proof of the want of diſſeminating wealth in the country, is the almoſt univerſal practice of cultivating the land by metayers; if trade and commerce did much for Italy, which cannot be doubted, you muſt look for their effects, not in the country, but in towns. Thoſe cities that poſſeſſed much induſtry (which I have named), carry ſure proofs of former proſperity: go out of their gates, and you meet with none—from what did this ariſe? Probably from thoſe cities being *ſovereign* ones, and ſhackling the country with every ſpecies of monopoly, in favour of themſelves. What is it, therefore, that will diffuſe wealth through all the claſſes, and give verdure to the fields, as well as luſtre to the towns? An equitable government. Whatever we poſſeſs in England, we owe to this origin; and it highly deſerves notice, that it is not a cultivation ſuperior to that of other countries, which diſtinguiſhes our iſland ſo

* For the immenſe manufactures and wealth of Florence, in the fourteenth century, ſee Giovanni Villani, lib. ii. cap. 93. " *In Firenze le Botteghe* (anno 1330) *dell'arte della lana erano dugento e più : facevano da ſettanta in ottanta mila panni di valuta di più di mille dugento migliaja di fiorini a'oro* (ſono a ſcudi fiorentini 22,860,000) *che bene il terzo e più rimaneva nella terra per coraggio ſenza il guadogno le'lanajuoli. Del detto coraggio vivevano più di* 30,000 *perſone.* Se per tutti i prodotti e manifatture dell'intera Toſcana preſentemente non entra più di un milione due centomila ſcudi; chiaro è, che tempo fa la ſola arte della lana in Firenze produceva venti volte più utile di quello, che preſentemente ne faccia tutto lo ſtato. *Carli Saggio Sopra* la Toſcana, op. i. p. 348.

A moſt ſingular law paſſed during the republic of Florence, that no man ſhould make proof of nobility, who was not able to deduce it from the manufacture of wool or ſilk. *Carli*, tomo v. p. 333. A more commercial idea could no where root itſelf.

much,

much, as the eftablifhment of a race of men generally found no where elfe ; a fubftantial and wealthy race of tenantry ; a race found in every corner of England : in Lombardy, you muft go for fuch, not to Florence and Genoa, but to the Lodizan.

CHAP. II.

Of the Management of Grafs Lands.

CATTLE and grafs lands are fo connected, that, I truft, it will not be deemed an impropriety to treat of them in the fame chapter, and as parts of the fame fubject. The obfervations I have made in Italy, will be divided eafily into—1, irrigation ;—2, live ftock.

SECT. I.—OF IRRIGATION.

If there be one circumftance which gives a fuperiority to Lombardy, over all the other countries I have feen, it is this, and therefore merits the moft particular detail.

PIEDMONT—*Nice.*

Such is the confequence of water here, that a garden of 4 feftaradi (a fquare of 12 trebucchi, *i. e.* 144 is a feftarada, and 400 trebucchi a giornata, which is to the Englifh acre as 0.7440 is to 0,7929), with a fmall houfe, lets at 20 louis d'or per annum, or about 15l. an acre.

Coni.

For the laft ten miles from Nice to Coni, the country improves continually. The foil, near the mountains, is ftoney, but is a good fandy loam lower in the vale. It is perfectly level, and watered with the utmoft attention, in a manner I had not noticed before; not, as in Spain, in beds, but the field is ploughed flat, fown with wheat, the clods broken with hoes and bufh-harrowed, and then great deep trenches ftruck with the plough, for letting in the water; thefe are 8 to 12 yards afunder. They are now (September) watering clover 8 inches high, by letting the water into thefe trenches, and conducting it in a fingular
manner.

manner. A man walking backwards, draws, by a line, a bunch of ftraw and weeds, juft large enough to ftop the water in the trench, and force it to over-flow on each fide. This is an expenfive and operofe method, and inferior to the Spanifh. The crops now on the ground are maiz; good, but not extraordinary: millet, and a little hemp; the male plants picked. A great deal of clover, but not much that is clean. But meadow abounds, which is the glory of Piedmont; and the conducting of the water, in multiplying conduits, feems well underftood, and practifed in great perfection.

Coni to Chentale.

In the watered meadows, much *chicorium intybus* and *plantago lanceolata*. Watered meadows are cut thrice commonly; but in fome feafons, four times.

Racconis.

The watered meadows are now mowing for a third time; the predominant plants—the *chicorium intybus, plantago lanceolata, acchillea millefolium,* and *trifolium pratenfe.*

To Turin.

From Coni to Turin, fomething more than half the country appears to be watered; poffibly two-thirds: and wherever the water is carried, it is apparently with great fkill. It is, however, rather fingular, that more trenches are not cut for taking the water off the land; the attention is chiefly paid to bringing it on; from which we may conclude, either that the heat of the climate renders fuch drains lefs neceffary than in England,—or that water is too valuable, from every one underftanding its ufe, to be brought on in the leaft fuperfluous quantity. The contrivance, towards Turin, for carrying the aqueducts of irrigation acrofs the roads, are beautifully executed: for convenience of diftribution, the water-courfe is raifed three or four feet, or more, above the general level: thefe aqueducts are brought to the fide of the road, and feemingly finifh in a wall, but really fink in a fyphon of mafonry under the road, and rife on the other fide, behind another fimilar wall. Seeing thefe buttreffes of mafonry, without perceiving, at firft, any water, I wondered, for a moment, to what ufe they could be affigned; but when I mounted the foot-way, this beautiful contrivance was, at once, apparent. Thefe are noble exertions.

Turin.

The irrigation in all this vicinity, is extenfive, and carried to great perfection. Water is meafured with as much accuracy as wine. An hour per week is fold, and the fee fimple of the water is attended to, with the fame folicitude as that of

the

the land. Rich meadows, without water, fell for 1000 liv. and 1100 liv. a giornata; and arable, worth 500 liv. without water, is, in many inſtances, worth 2000 liv. with it. Such a meadow as will fell for 1100 liv. or 1200 liv. per giornata, will yield, the firſt mowing, 115 rubbii of hay, worth 9ſ. to 10ſ. the rubbio; the ſecond, 90 rubbii, at 7ſ. to 8ſ. and the third, 80 rubbii, at 6ſ. to 7ſ.; the fourth growth is ſold, to be eaten by ſheep, at 5 liv. This produce amounts to 120 liv. or 6l. Engliſh, per giornata, which is under an acre. The intereſt of 1100 liv. being at 40 liv. or 50 liv. there remains a ſufficient profit, after all expences are paid. During the winter, as the meadows are commonly fed with ſheep, they do not water at all. Some experienced cultivators avoid watering in the ſpring, till the froſts are over, which happen here as late as the 10th, and even the 15th of May, as a ſtrong freſh vegetation is, in ſuch caſes, entirely cut off; but, in general, no attention is paid to this circumſtance; and watering goes on at all times, except when ſheep are on the ground. Thoſe who have water enough, let it on to their land once a week, during the whole ſummer; but if the weather is wet, once a fortnight; and a day or two before cutting, if the water is perfectly clear. In regard to the quality of water, they make no other diſtinction than that for mountains being cold; and that of the Dora, near Turin, being charged with ſo much ſand as to be bad. They attend to the cutting of weeds in the canals, that they may rot; and ſome good managers harrow the bottoms in the ſpring, to foul the water, which then acts more powerfully as a manure. Another practice, which tends alſo to prove what excellent farmers they are in all that reſpects meadow-grounds, is that of paring and burning, which they perform on pieces that have a bad herbage, or want of improvement; but do not ſow them with corn, or any other plant, except hay-ſeeds, in order to renew the graſs, with no other interruption. It is impoſſible to praiſe ſuch practices too much. They call this huſbandry *maſara*.

The power of effecting the great works in irrigation, which are viſible over this whole country, depends very much on the law, which ſuppoſes the right and property of all rivers to be veſted in the king; conſequently all canals taken from them, are bought of him; and this enſures another regulation, which is the power of carrying the water, when bought, at the pleaſure of thoſe who buy it, where they think fit; they cannot, however, cut acroſs any man's ground, without paying him for the land and the damage; but the law does this by regulations known to every one, and no individual is allowed a negative upon a meaſure which is for the general good. The purchaſers of water from the king, are uſually conſiderable land owners, or communities that have lands wanting water; and it is of no conſequence at what diſtance theſe lands may be from the river, whence the water is taken, as they have a right to conduct it where they chooſe, provided they do not cut through a garden or pleaſure ground.

ground. Nor can they carry the water *under* that of others, whofe canals are already made, as they might in that cafe deprive them of a part of their water; they are obliged to throw aqueducts *over* fuch canals. The benefit of water is fo great and well underftood, that nobody ever thinks of making objections; and in cafe their lands are not already watered, it is no fmall advantage to have a new canal brought through them, as they have the opportunity of buying water of the proprietors. It is fold per hour per week, and even half an hour, and down to a quarter. The common price of an hour per week, for ever, is 1500 liv.—At Gruliafcho, four miles from Turin, there are many Perfian wheels that lift up the water by bufkets; the wheels are double, with wafhers between for the ftream turning them; the buckets or boxes on one out fide only; they raife the water 8 or 10 feet, and about 2½ fhort of the full diameter of the wheel, and I could not perceive that they lofe a drop; none falls, except what adheres to the wheel itfelf. To fave the expence of multiplying fluices, for the occafional ftoppage of water, in carrier trenches, to force it over the land, they have a moveable board that fits the trench, which is placed occafionally where wanted, and anfwers the purpofe well. They have none of the ramifications of carrier trenches common among us; and not fo many drains for taking the water of as with us; and, on the whole, do not fhew any thing like our attention in the ufe of the water, though twenty, or rather an hundred times more in bringing it from rivers, and diftributing it about the country; and I could not but obferve, that their meadows have much bad herbage, and many places damaged by the water refting too long; this is more the cafe here than it feemed to be from Coni to Racconis, where the meadows carried a better countenance.

Turin to Chivafco.

Not one-third of this country is watered. At Chivafco but little alfo. After croffing the Dora Belta, there are foon two confiderable canals of irrigation; one made two years ago only, which is as great a work as a navigation in England.

Ciglione.

Little land watered in this country; but I obferved here fome meadows, with off channels, from the principle ones, for conducting the water, which I did not notice before; but very few drains. The new canal croffes a gravelly wafte, but none of it watered.

Trouchan.

A very rich country much watered; and many mulberries.

St.

St. Germano.

Mowing the third crop of grafs, and very poor; not more than 15 cwt. an acre, and yet watered. The glory of Piedmont is from Coni to Turin. Thofe who pafs Mont Cenis to Turin, and Turin to Milan, fee, on comparifon, nothing.

Vercelli.

The new canal, now making, for taking water from the **Dora** Baltia, and conducting it to the rice grounds of Vercelli, is done by the king, and will coft three millions; the water is fold to communities. The other I croffed near the Dora, at the fame time, was made long ago, and belongs to the Marquis de Bourg.

Milanese—*Buffalora.*

After croffing the Tefino, in feveral branches, and entering the Milanefe, we find a great fyftem of watering meadows to Buffalora, where that magnificent canal, the Navillio Grande is 20 yards broad, and though navigable, was originally made for irrigation alone.

St. Pietro Olmo.

Hence, for fome diftance, there is no watering; but then there is fomething in our Berkfhire method; the lands are arched up, and juft in the centre, on their crown, are the carrier trenches for conducting the water, and on each fide a row of low fallows; fome of thefe lands are two rods broad, and two feet higher in the ridge than in the furrow; the land firm and the herbage good: wherever the meadows feem good, there is abundance of *chicorium intybus, plantago lanceolata,* and *trifolium pratenfe.*

Milan.

As the irrigation of the Milanefe is perhaps the greateft exertion of the kind that ever was in the world, and certainly the firft that was undertaken in Europe, after the decline of the Roman empire; it merits every attention that a farming traveller can give; for it will be found, by very briefly recurring to records, which have been fearched, that great exertions (perhaps as great as ever known) were made in this country, at a period when all the north of Europe was in a ftate of barbarifm. In the year 1037, mention is made of the canal Vecchiabbia. In 1067, watered meadows were common, called *prato roco,* by Landolfo[*]. In 1077, there are notes of many ftreams ufed. In 1138, the

---

[*] *Giulini,* tom. iv. p. 122. 224. 225.

monks of Chiarevalle bought of Giovanni Villano some commons, woods, and meadows for 81 liv. under the contract (a parchment yet remaining) " ut monasterium possit ex Vectabia trahere lectum ubi ipsum monasterium voluerit et si fuerit opus liceat facere eidem monasterio fossata super terram ipsius Johannis ab una parte viæ et ab alia.... &c. possit firmare et habere clusam in prato ipsius Johannis, &c." There is a similar contract of the following year, and various others, until the beginning of the 13 century; from which, and others, it appears, that the Vecchiabbia was the entire property of the monastery, and confirmed in 1276 by the diploma of the Emperor Frederick II. The merit of these monks appears to have been great, for they gained such a reputation for their skill and industry, that they had many applications for assistance in directing works similar to their own upon uncultivated lands; and the Imperial Chancellor Rinaldo, in the time of the Emperor Frederick I. being appointed archbishop of Cologne, found the possessions of his see in such a deplorable state, that he applied for, and found the same assistance, as reported by Cesarior Eisterbacense. Their greatest exertions were in irrigation, which was so well known, that they sold their superfluous water, transferring the use and property of some by the hour, day, and week. In two centuries they came to be possessed of 60,000 pertiche, mostly watered: there is reason to believe that the practice, in the 13th century, did not materially differ from the present modes; because, in the papers of the archives of the abbey of that period, mention is made of *chiuse, incastri, bochilli, foratoi**, and other works, to distribute the water, and regulate the irrigation †. In 1164, the Emperor Frederick gave various rights, in certain rivers, to the people of Pavia, for the purposes of irrigation ‡. In 1177, the people of Milan enlarged and continued the Navillio Grande, from Abbiate Grasso to Milan, being 14 miles; it was brought from the Tesino, near the Lago Maggiore, to Abbiate Grasso, 20 miles, by the people of Pavia, long before the date of any records now known to remain §. In 1271, it was made navigable. It is thirty-two Italian miles long, and twenty-five bracchi wide, or forty-nine English feet. ‖

The second great work, was the canal called Muzza, which takes the waters of the Adda, at Cassano, and carries them to Marignano, there dividing and

* *Chiuse*, are sluices; *incastri*, are water gates, that are moved perpendicularly; *bochilli*, openings in the banks to distribute water; *foratoi*, discharges for carrying off superfluous water; the same as *scaricatori*.

† *Memorie Storica ed Economica sull'Irrrigazione de Prati.* Don. Ang. Fumagalli *Atti di Milano*, tom. ii. p. 215.

‡ *Gianni*, tom. vi. p. 330.

§ *Nuova Raccolta d'Autoriche trattano del moto dell'Acque.* Parma. 1768. 4to. Tom. vii. P. Piii. p. 97.   ‖ *Ibid.* p. 98.

watering much of the Lodizan. It was executed in 1220 *, and done in fo admirable a ftyle, that Padre Frifi, in the preface to *Modo di regolare i fiumi, &c.* fays,—" il meccanifmo d'irrigar le campagne è ftato ridotto all'ultimo grado di maeftria e di perfezione nel canale di Muzza †." And Padre Antonio Lecchi, another great engineer and mathematician, remarks,—" De'noftri trè celebri canali di Muzza, e de'due navigli qual altra memoria ci rimane ora, fe non fe quella del tempo della loro coftruzione, e d'altre poche notizie, niente concernenti al maravigliofo artifizio della loro condotta ‡."

In 1305, the canal of Treviglio was made, which takes the water from the Brembo, and carries it, for feveral miles, about twenty-five feet wide, and about three deep; it irrigates the territory of Triviglio and the Ghiara d'Adda. And, within four or five miles, there are five canals, taken from the Adda and the Brembo, all of great antiquity. In 1460, the canal de Martefano was begun, under Duke Francis Sforza I. ; it was twenty-four miles long, and eighteen braccia (thirty-five Englifh feet) wide; fince lengthened feven or eight miles more. It takes the waters of the Adda, a little before Trezzo, by means of a powerful wear *(chiufe)* founded upon the living rock; it is then fupported for five miles by a folid wall of ftone, forty braccia (eighty feet) above the bottom of the Adda, and parallel with it. At Gorgonzola, it paffes over the torrent Molgora, by a bridge of three ftone arches. At Carfenzago, it is croffed by the river Lambro, which enters and quits the canal with all its floods. And, in order to prevent the furplus of water, which this circumftance occafions, from breaking the banks of the canal, or overflowing them, there are nineteen fcaricatori in the canal, above, below, and facing the junction, which are fo calculated, that they have not only powers fufficient to take off the waters of that river, but alfo half of thofe of the canal itfelf. Thefe fcaricatori are canals which take the water, when fluice-gates are opened for that purpofe, and convey it, at various diftances, to the Lambro again; the fall in its courfe being confiderable enough to free the canal from all fuperfluity of water. Near Milan, this Navillio receives the torrent Sevefo; and, after furrounding the city, unites with the Navillio Grande and the Olona. The fluices which Bellidor fuppofed to be invented by the Dutch, were ufed, for the firft time, near Padua, in 1481, by two engineers of Viterbo, Dionifius and Peter Domenico, brothers §. Leonardo da Vinci profited immediately of this great invention, for

* Verri, Storia di M. t. i. p. 240.　　　　　　　　† Nuova Raccolta, tom. vii.

‡ *Ib. Piano, &c. de tre torrenti*, p. 141.

§ *Moto dell' Acqua*, vol. v. Parma, 1766, p. 359. Mentioned by Zendrini in the tenth chapter, *Sopra l'Acqua Corrente*. This is the common fuppofition in Lombardy, and is thus recorded; but it appears to be an error, by a paffage in *Giulini*, tom. xii. p. 332, where, anno 1420, mention is exprefsly made of them, *machinarum quas conchas appellant, &c.*

the

the union of the two canals of Milan; and finding between them the difference of the levels to be eighteen braccia *, he, with fix fluices, in the year 1497, under Ludovico il Moro, opened and facilitated the navigation from one to the other. The greateft *fcaricatori* † of the waters united at Milan, is the canal of Vecchiabbia, which, after having ferved fome mills and irrigation, falls into the Lambro near Marignano; and if this canal were made ftraight, and fupported by fome fluices, the navigation might be continued to the Lambro, and thence to the Po and the fea. Both thefe canals, the Grande and the Martefano, are fo contrived, as to be completely emptied once a year, for cleaning and repairing whatever accidents may have happened to any of the works.

I have entered into this digreffion upon a very curious fubject, little known in Englifh literature ‡, in order to fhew how well irrigation was underftood, and how admirably it was practifed, when the countries on this fide of the Alps were barbarous. At the fame time, however, that juftice is thus done to thefe great exertions, we muft bear in mind, that few diftricts in Europe are better, or fo well, fituated for irrigation. The lakes of *Maggiore* and *Como*, nearly upon the fame level, are three hundred feet (one hundred and fifty braccia) higher than Milan,— and that of Lugano two hundred feet higher than thofe, with a nearly regular declivity to the Po §.

There are authors who have afferted, that agriculture is improved in confequence of great trade or manufactures only; but the inftance of the immenfe irrigation in the Milanefe, effected by thefe and many other canals, too numerous to mention, will not allow of fuch a conclufion being general; and to fhew that my opinion is not without foundation, a very brief review of the ftate of Milan, fo far as it refpects thefe periods, will not be difpleafing to a reflecting reader.

In 1177, when the canal de Navillio Grande was made, the republic of Milan had been gradually forming for about two hundred years ‖; but thefe dominions were exceedingly confined;—Lodi, Pavia, Mantua, Verona, Crema, Tortona, Como, Bergamo, Brefcia, Piacenza, Parma, Genova, Afti, Vercelli,

* P. 98. *Frif.*

† The *fcaricatori* are what I believe we call wears in England; they are difcharges of fuperfluous waters. Mr. Brindley made them, in the Duke of Bridgewater's canal, circular, and in the centre of the river, to convey the water, as into a well; but in Italy they are cuts or openings in the banks of the canal, at places that allow a quick conveyance of the water; for inftance, where a canal croffes the bed of a river: their powers are calculated with fuch a mathematical exactnefs, proportioned to the quantity of water brought into the canals, by the rivers joining them, that no floods ever effect the furface, which is of an equal height.

‡ One would naturally look for fome knowledge of thefe facts in *Anderfon's Deduction of Commerce*; but we fhall look in vain.

§ *Verri, Storia di Milano.* 1783. Tom. i. p. 5.

‖ *Storia di Milano.* P. Verri. 4to. 1783. Tomo i. p. 142.

Novara,

Novara, Cremona, Ivrea, Padua, Alba, Trevifo, Aquileia, Ferrara, Reggio, Modena, Bologna, Imola, Cefena, Forli, Rimini, Fano, and Ancona,—were, at that time, independent republics*; which united againſt Milan, in 1162, with the Emperor Frederick I and befieged and deſtroyed it. This fingular fact that in fifteen years after one of the moſt fignal deſtructions that could be brought upon a city, there ſhould be found energy enough in a petty republic, to undertake a work which is, in the prefent age, regarded as an honour to Lombardy, muſt be admitted as a proof, that the trade and manufactures of that period could have been but very inconfiderable.

Milan, however, unqueſtionably aroſe to great power and profperity; and our bufinefs is to inquire into that period, whence we may judge how much its commerce might influence the perfection to which ſhe has carried her agriculture.

1042, Civil war; the nobility driven out by the people.

1056, The government changed.

1067, Meadows watered. *Guilini*, IV. 122.

1108, War with Pavia.

1111, Lodi deſtroyed by Milan

1127, Como deſtroyed by Milan.

1153, Frederic Barbaroſſa interpofes.

1162, Milan taken and deſtroyed.

1167, The people of Milan living in tents and cabins. To,

1183, War with Frederic

1177, Navillio Grande continued to Milan.

1191, Grant of waters to Pavia, for irrigation, by the Emperor Henry VI.

1204, The nobility expelled.

1210. The archbiſhop's revenue 80,000 fiorini d'oro, equal to 10 millions of livres now.

1216, A woollen manufacture.

1220, The canal of the Muzza made.

1221, The archbiſhop and nobles expelled.

1237, War againſt the Emperor Frederick II.

1240, Government reduced to pay in paper money; the origin of all that has paſſed fince in Europe.

1257, The nobility expelled.

——, The Navillio Grande begun to be made navigable.

1263, Factions of the Guelphs and Ghibellines now in full activity at Milan.

1271, The Navillio Grande navigable.

* Verri, tomo. i. p. 175.

1277, Civil

1277, Civil war;—Toriani and Visconti.
1281, Ditto.
1288, Milan buys wool from France, Flanders, and England.
1296, Decree, that gave to every one the power of conducting water across all
       great roads, provided stone bridges were erected.
1302, Revolution;—the Toriani get the better of the Visconti.
1305, Canal of Treviglio made.
1310, Revolution; the Visconti prevail.
1327. Violent factions of the Guelphs and Ghibellines.
1332, Grant of water for irrigation to the people of Treviglio.
1350—1385, Tyranny of the Visconti drives away the manufactures.
1395, Great Power of Milan over the cities of Lombardy.*
       Through every part of the 14th century, the passages in the Annals are
           numerous which prove how well irrigation was understood, and how
           highly canals of water were valued.
1421, Milan exports cloths to Venice. †
1457, Most of the conquests of Milan lost.
1460, Canal de Martesano made.
1481, Sluices invented at Padua.
1497, Leonardo da Vinci joins the canals at Milan.

It should seem, from this detail, that the exertions in irrigation were almost
purely agricultural; the benefit enjoyed by the people of Pavia, from the Navillio Grande, was a constant proof of the advantages to be derived from similar
canals; and they were executed at moments which will not allow us to attribute
them to the influence of manufacturing or commercial wealth.

* In 1378, Giovanni Galeazzo Visconti Conte di Virtu was declared Duke of Milan, his dominions then comprising Arezzo, Reggio, Parma, Piacenza, Cremona, Lodi, Crema, Bergamo, Brescia,
Verona, Vicenza, Feltro, Belluno, Bassano, Bormio, Como, Novara, Alessandria, Tortona, Vercelli,
Pontremoli, Bobbio, Serzana, Pavia, Valenza, Casali, Padua, Alba, Asti, Bologna, Pisa, Siena, Pe-
rugia, Nocera, Spoleto, and Assisi. *Verri.* p. 417.

† As this woollen manufacture is said to have been in the hands of an order of friars, the *frati
umiliati*, we have no reason to suppose it an object of great consequence; the expressions seeming to
imply its magnitude being applicable to a comparison with poorer neighbours. Count Giulini says,
on occasion of its being carried from Milan to Sicily, " *che tanto scriva fra noi*," (tom. viii. p. 585;)
but records do not explain the extent; though we are told that they worked up wool from France,
Flanders, and England, in 1288 (tom. viii. p. 399.); which trade had existed to some degree of
consideration in 1216. Count Verri uses the expression——" lavoro de pannilani la quale formò la
ricchezza cospicua di Milano," (*Storia di Milano*, tom. i. p. 357.) But it was Venice, Genoa, Pisa,
Amalfi, and Ancona that had the empire of the sea, which gave that author reason to say, " che tutto
il commercio dell' Europa era presso gl' Italiani." (tom. i. p. 465.)

To

To this may be added, that during the thirteenth and fourteenth centuries *, Italy was the perpetual fcene of bloody wars: the Venetians and Genoefe, the Venetians and the Milenefe, and, in their turns, the other republics, feem to have had no other bufinefs than that of cutting each other's throat. A perpetual ftate of warfare, and fo many revolutions as were taking place in the governments of the Italian cities, were little adapted to give a fecurity of poffeffion effentially neceffary to the eftablifhment of fuch manufactures and commerce, as fhall, by the overflowing of their furplus, ameliorate the agriculture of a country.

It was but fifteen years after the deftruction of Milan, that the Navillio Grande was made; and within three years after the lofs of all her conquefts, that the canal de Martefano was digged: thefe great undertakings were, therefore, executed at periods when commercial profperity could leaft of all effect them. There was no ftability in that profperity. It is alfo to be remembered, that throughout this period of Milanefe hiftory, that people, even at the height of their power, were never mafters of a commercial fea-port. It is true, that they twice took Genoa; firft in 1353, but kept it for a very fhort time; and again in 1421, when they were in poffeffion of it but fourteen years; and amongft all the dominions of Galeazzo Vifconti, Sarzano was the only port, and that never a commercial one; thus the fabrics of Milan were obliged to be exported through the Venetians or the Genoefe, who laid duties on the tranfport of their commodities.

The conclufion of the whole feems fairly to be, that we are not to attribute the irrigation of the country to wealth derived from foreign commerce; the fertility and excellent management of the lands fupported a great population, which proved as induftrious as public calamities and confufions would allow; but it does not appear that this induftry was ever continued through a long feries of peace and happinefs.

An other idea has been ftarted, that Lombardy owed her irrigations to the effect of the crufades; that the mad enthufiafts, who went upon thofe expeditions, brought home with them the art of cutting canals, for this moft beneficial purpofe; but hiftory does not give fufficient lights to allow of this conclufion. I have already remarked, that the Navillio Grande was made by the people of Pavia, long before thofe of Milan made the cut to that city; and fo long before, that no records in the archives were found of it by that moft

---

* In the preceding periods it was probably worfe. Count Verri obferves, " Dello ftato della populazione nel decimo fecolo—mi pare verofimile che doveffe effere mediocremente popolata Milano. Le terre erano coltivate parte da fervi e parte da liberti. Molte parti del ducato era bofco. In qualche luogo, che ora fi coltiva forfe, ancora v'erano delle acque ftagnanti." *Storia di Milano*, tom. i. p. 76.

induftrious

induftrious fearcher into antiquity, Count Giulini. This fact feems nearly decifive; for the firft crufade did not commence till 1096, nor terminate till 1100, before which period there is every reafon to fuppofe, the canal in queftion was cut as the refearches of Giulini go fo far back as 773. The crufades ended in 1291; and, had the effects been as great as poffible, yet they cannot be imagined to have taken place immediately; it muft be, after much confultation and long reafoning, that whole towns could be brought to co-operate in the execution of fuch plans for the common good, from mere reports of the effect in diftant countries and different climates. Another circumftance, tending to prove that irrigation in Lombardy was much more antient than the crufades, is that Theodoric, who began to reign in Italy, anno 493, publicly rewarded an African who had come thither, in order to inftruct the Italians in the art of irrigating lands, as Mr. Profeffor Symonds has explained, with his ufual elegance, in his moft agreeable paper on the effect of water in the agriculture of Italy *. Now if this art had been thus introduced, or, more properly fpeaking, revived in Italy above fix hundred years before the crufades were thought of, there connot be much reafon for attributing that improvement to the obfervations of thofe frantic enthufiafts. It is remarkable, that Count Verri, in his Hiftory of Milan, fays, he had long conceived, that their irrigations were to be afcribed to the Crufades; but, from paying more attention to the authorities quoted by Count Giulini, he gave up that opinion, and concurred in the idea of a greater antiquity †: for which alfo P. Frifi feems to contend, when he fays expreffly, that the canal made by the people of Pavia was more antient than 1177 ‡.

And here it may be worth remarking, that Pavia was the capital and refidence of Theodoric, whence there refults, at leaft, a prefumption, if he fent to Africa for a perfon to inftruct the Italians in irrigation, that here was the field of his exertions; and that this very canal was the work of that fovereign, not the lefs celebrated for thus laudably applying himfelf, in a barbarous age, to works that would do honour to the politeft.—But to return from this long digreffion.

The fame law that has been fo effectual in watering Piedmont, operates here alfo, and has done even greater things. He who difcovers a fpring, conducts

---

* Annals of Agriculture, vol. I. p. 421.

† Storia di Milano, tomo i. p. 354.

‡ Con tutte quefto però, fe imparzial mente fi vorrà avere riguardo al tempo, alle circonftanze, alla maeftria del lavoro, il naviglio di Milano che forma la communicazione del Tefino, e dell'Adda, potrà parlare per il capo d'opera, che abbiamo in quefto genere. Per quanto dice il Sigonio nel libro 14 del regno d'Italia all'anno 1179, pare che il primo tronco dello fteffo Naviglio, del Tefino ad Abbiate Graffo, foffe già dai tempi più antichi incominciato e finito dai pavefi per irrigare le vicine loro campagne. Fù nell'anno 1177 che i Milanefi conduffero lo fteffo cavo da Abbiate a Corfico, e a Milano. Nuova Raccolta, vol. vii. p. 97.

it where he pleafes, paying a fixed compenfation * for cutting through the properties of others. All rivers belong, as in Piedmont, to the fovereign, who fells the waters to fpeculators for this moft beneficial purpofe of irrigation. In the diftribution of it, by fale, **they do not meafure by the hour, as in Piedmont,** but by the ounce; 12 oz. are a braccio, or 22 inches: an ounce of water is a ftream that runs one braccio long and one ounce deep; and the farther the water has run, the higher is the price, as being more charged with manure.

As an example of the beneficial influence of this law, I was fhewn, between **Milan and** Pavia, a fpring that was **difcovered two miles** from the lands of the difcoverer, the properties of many perfons lying between **him** and the fpring. He firft bought the property of the perfon in whofe land it was fituated, which was eafily done, as it was too low to be there of any ufe; then he conducted it by a trench at pleafure the two miles, paying the fixed price **for** cutting through his neighbours lands; and, having gained it **upon his** own, prefently changed poor hungry arable gravel into a very fine **watered** meadow.

Near Milan, a watered meadow fells at 800 liv. the pertica (32l. 15s. the Englifh acre); and the rent of fuch is about 30 liv. (1l. 5s. the Englifh acre.) This muft not, however, be claffed high; for there are lands that rife to 4000 liv. (163l. the Englifh acre.). In land at 800 liv. or 1000 liv. water often makes half of the value; that is, the rent to the owner of the land will be 15 liv to 20 liv.; and as much to fome other perfon for the water.

In viewing a great farm, fix or feven miles from Milan, in the road to Pavia, I found that all the watered meadow was mown four times; and that what was watered in winter, *prati di mercita*, five times. Such is the value of water here, that this farm, which **watered is** rented at 20 liv. the pertica, would not let at more than 6 liv. without water, the foil being gravel. The irrigation of the *mercita* begins in October, and lafts till March, when it is regulated like all other meadows. All in general begin in April, and laft till September; and if there be no rain, once in feven to fifteen days. An ounce of water, running continually from the 24th of March to the 8th of September, is **worth, and** will fell for 1000 liv. When arable crops want water, it is always given.

Milan to Mozzata.

Every confiderable fpring that is found, becomes the origin of a new canal. They clear out the head for a bafon, and fink cafks, by way of tunnels, for the

---

* Thefe laws, relative to the conduct of irrigation, are as old as the republic of Milan; firft compiled into a collection of ftatutes and cuftoms in 1216 (*Verri*, p. 239.) They were revifed and collected, by order of Charles V. and are in full force to this day. *Conftitutiones Dominii Mediolanenfi Decretis et Senatus Confultis. Gab. Verri.* Follo, 1747. De aquis et fluminibus, p. 168.

water to rife freely, and without impediment from mud or weeds. There are ufually three, four, or five of thefe tunnels, at the bottom of a bafon of twenty or thirty yards.

Milan to Lodi.

Of all the exertions that I have any where feen in irrigation, they are here by far the greateft. The canals are not only more numerous, more inceffant, and without interruption, but are conducted with the moft attention, fkill, and expence. There is, for moft of the way, one canal on each fide of the road, and fometimes two. Crofs ones are thrown over thefe, on arches, and pafs in trunks of brick or ftone under the road. A very confiderable one, after paffing for feveral miles by the fide of the highway, finks under it, and alfo under two other canals, carried in ftone troughs eight feet wide; and at the fame place under a fmaller, that is conducted in wood. The variety of directions in which the water is carried, the eafe with which it flows in contrary directions, the obftacles which are overcome, are objects of admiration. The expence thus employed, in the twenty miles from Milan to Lodi, is immenfe. There is but little rice, and fome arable, which does not feem under the beft management; but the grafs and clover rich and luxuriant; and there are fome great herds of cows, to which all this country ought to be applied. I cannot but efteem the twenty miles, as affording one of the moft curious and valuable profpects in the power of a farmer to view; we have fome undertakings in England that are meritorious; but they fink to nothing, in comparifon with thefe great and truly noble works. It is one of the rides which I wifh thofe to take, who think that every thing is to be feen in England.

Lodi.

Examining fome watered meadows, in high eftimation, I found the following plants moft predominant, and in the order in which I note them :—1, *Ranunculus repens*; 2, *Trifolium pratenfe*; 3, *Chicorium intybus*; 4, *Plantago lanceolata*; 5, *Achillea millefolium* *; and about one fifth of the whole herbage at bottom feems what are properly called graffes. Thefe rich meadows about Lodi are all interfected by ditches, without hedges, but a double row of pollard poplars; all on a dead level, and no drains to be feen. They are now (October)

* There appeared but few figns of ray-grafs, yet it certainly abounds in fome of their fields : opinions in Lombardy differ concerning it; Sig. Scannagatta praifes it highly *(Atti di Milano*, tom. ii. p. 114); but one of the beft writers in their language, Sig. Lavezari (tom. i. p. 82.) wonders rather at the commendations given of it in other countries : he miftakes the French name, it is not *fainfoin*; the *bjeffa* of Lombardy, and the *ray-grafs* of England, is the *lolium perenne*; the French fainfoin is the *hedyfarum onobrachis*.

cutting

cutting the grafs and weeds in the ditches, to cart home for making dung.
The meadows are commonly cut thrice; but the beſt four times. The produce
of hay per pertica, 6 *faſſi*, of 100 lb. of 28 oz. at the three cuts. Price of the
firſt, 8 liv. per faſs; of the ſecond, 5 liv.; of the third, 4½ liv. They water
immediately after clearing, if there be no rain. Without irrigation, the rent
of the country in general would be only one-third of what it is at preſent. In
forming theſe watered meadows, they have very ſingular cuſtoms:—all are
broken up in rotation; flax ſown for the firſt crop, and their way of laying
down is to leave a wheat ſtubble to clothe itſelf; clover is prohibited by leaſe,
from an abſurd notion that it exhauſts the land; and that it is not ſo good as
what the nature of the ground gives; but on worſe land, the other ſide of the
Adda, they ſow clover.

Lodi to Codogno.

All this country the ſame as about Lodi; a dead level, cut into bits of from
three to ten acres, by ditches, without hedges, and planted with double rows
of poplars and willows, all young, for they are cut as ſoon as the ſize is that of
a thin man: here and there one is left to run up to timber. I remarked, in the
meadows fed, that the *ranunculus* is avoided by the cows as much as poſſible.
I expected, in one meadow, to find it the *acris*, but much of it was the *repens*,
All this country is alternately in tillage; ridge and furrow every where: no per-
manent meadow. After ſeven miles, the road being natural, ſhews the ſoil to
be a loamy ſand, binding with rains *.

Codogno.

Thirteen pertiche of watered land neceſſary for a cow; the hay of which is cut
thrice and it is fed once; ſuch land ſells at 300 liv. and lets at 10 liv. free from
tax. The whole country is ploughed by turns, being down to clover for the
cows four years.—1, Flax, and then millet; 2, maiz; 3, wheat and clover;
and reſts then for feeding cows; white clover comes, but it is bad for cheeſe.
The reader will note, that this opinion differs from that near Milan.

* As well watered as this country is, yet in the ſpring 1779 the ſeaſon was ſo dry, that, where the
Lambro enters the Po, men and women croſſed the Po itſelf on foot, as if merely a rivulet; the rector
of Alberoni himſelf paſſed it, and the water reached only to his middle. The damage was great
every where, but fatal in the Lodizan, where herds of cows were obliged to be ſent out of the country
to the paſtured: the miſchief the greater, as from 1774 to 1779 they had augmented their cows 5000,
(*Opuſcoli Scelti*, tom. vi. p. 56.) The climate has, however, in all ages, been ſubject to great
droughts. From May 1158 to May 1159, there fell no rain in Lombardy; wells and ſprings all
dried up. The Emperor paſſed the Adige, with his army, near Verona, without boats; and the
Count Palatine of Bavaria paſſed thus the Po, below Ferrara. *Giulini*, tom. vi. p. 175.

Codogno to Crema.

Crossing the Adda, from the Lodizan, there is more arable, and much fewer cows.

Milan to Vaprio.

In this line there are some dairies, but not many. Near the city there is much grafs, all cut into patch-work of divisions, and planted so as to seem a wood of willows; after that much tillage : though all is flat, and there are no great exertions in watering. But the road passes by that fine navigable canal de Martesano from Milan, which, at Vaprio, is suspended as it were against the hill, twenty feet above the Adda :—a noble spectacle.

Before we quit the Milanese, it will be proper to make a general remark on the conduct of their irrigation, that some evils are observed to attend the practice for want of a better foresight and more attention; particularly from the gradual enlargement of the carrier canals and ditches; they clean them with so much care, for the sake of obtaining the mud, as a manure, that these are every where become too wide for the quantity of water they convey. Sig. Bignami has written upon this point very rationally, in his dissertation *Sull'abuso di scavare i canali delle roggie ed i fossi nel Lodigiano*; where he asserts, that one-tenth part of their lands is occupied by canals and ditches. The evils are numerous; it is not only a confiderable loss of land, but it is an equal loss of water, for when an oncia of a given run of water is purchased, there is a great difference between its first fitting a great or a small channel, as in proportion to the size will be the quantity of useless fluid. The atmosphere is also proportionably contaminated; for this great breadth, either of stagnant water, when irrigation is not actually going on, or, what is worse, of mud, in so hot a climate, must be pestiferous; and to this have been attributed the distempers which have frequently made such havoc among their cattle. Another inconvenience is, the greater expence of all erections, bridges, sluices, &c. &c. which are in proportion to the breadth of the channels. The remedy is obvious; it is to forbear all cleansing for the sake of mud; to let all aquatic weeds, and other plants, grow freely *on the banks, edges, and sides* of the canals, and to clear them in the middle only. Such a conduct would, in time, quite choak them up, and enable the farmer to keep his canals exactly to their right width. All these plants covering the spaces, which, in canals often cleaned, are bare earth or mud, would be very beneficial towards preventing and decompofing that noxious, and mephitic, and inflammable gas, always issuing from such mud, which is so pestilential to animals, yet so salutiferous to plants; for mud, covered with plants that are ready to feed on its exhalations, is much less mischievous

than

than that which is expofed to the rays of a burning fun. Count Carlo Bettoni, of Brefcia *, has practifed a method which acts on fimilar principles; namely, that of burying or fixing willows or poplars to the fides of the rivers whofe banks he wanted to preferve, with the precaution only of keeping the ends of the branches out of water; he finds that they grow vigouroufly in this fituation, and, by flopping the mud of the current, form a folid bank; this, on a fmall fcale, might certainly be executed: alfo in the canals of irrigation, as it has been remarked, by the author already quoted, in the *Atti di Milano*.

VENETIAN STATE—*Vaprio to Bergamo*.

There is a mixture of watered meadow in this line, but the quantity is not confiderable. In fome which are old, I found a good fprinkling of *trifolium repens, chicorium intybus,* and *plantago lanceolata*; but alfo much *ranunculus* and rubbifh. In the plain clofe to Bergamo, they clean the irrigation-ditches at the end of November, and harrowing them with a faggot, to thicken the water, let it immediately on to their meadows, which is faid to enrich them much.

To Brefcia.

The Venetian State, thus far, is a confiderable falling off from the Milanefe, in refpect to irrigation; the country is not without canals, but neither the number, nor the importance of them, is to be compared to thofe of Milan. From Coquillio to Brefcia, there are many channels, yet the lands are not half watered.

Brefcia to Verona.

The road paffes, for fome diftance, by a very fine canal, yet the quantity of watered land in this route is but inconfiderable. Before we arrive at the Lago di Guarda, there are a few meadows never ploughed, that have a good appearance: but none from the lake to Verona. On the whole, thefe forty miles, for want of more irrigation, are not comparable to the Milanefe or to Piedmont. This route, fo much to the north, gives the traveller an opportunity of feeing a chain of confiderable cities, and of obferving the effects of one of the moft celebrated governments that has exifted; but a better direction for me, would have been by Cremona and Mantua.

* *Henfieri ful Governo de Fiumi.* Brefcia, 1782.

Verona,

Verona.

The meadows here are cut thrice, and fed once; are never ploughed, if good and well watered. Water for irrigation here, as in all Lombardy, is measured with great care and attention, by what is called the quadrata, which is a square foot (the Veronese foot is to the English about as twenty are to twelve). Twelve quadrate are sufficient to water five hundred campi of rice-grounds (about three hundred and eighty English acres), and the price of such a quantity of water, is commonly about three thousand *zecchini* (1425l. sterling). The wheels in this city, for raising water for irrigating the gardens, are very complete; they receive the water, as in Spain, into hollow fellies. There is one in the garden of the Daniele monastery, for watering about four campi, which are said to yield a revenue of three hundred zecchini; which is one hundred zecchini, of 9s. 6d. per English acre. The wheel raises the water about twenty-five feet, receiving its motion by the stream; a low wall crossing the garden, conveys the water in a trench of masonry on its tops; and a walk passing along the centre of the garden, the wall there is open, to admit the path; the water sinking in a syphon, and rising on the other side, to the same height, passes again along the wall, in the same manner as canals are carried under roads in Piedmont, &c. The wheel has double fellies, for giving water on both sides into troughs, which unite in the same receiver, and the washers for giving the motion are placed between the fellies. The whole apparatus, complete, cost three hundred zecchini.

To Vicenza.

There are in this tract of country, some perennial meadows watered, quite upon a level, which have a very good aspect: the existence of such should make us question the propriety of the Lodizan system of ploughing, where water is so regularly at command.

Padua.

The country, from Vicenza to this city, is not watered, like many other districts of Lombardy. The practice is very well known; and there are rice-grounds about Padua, but not nearly the use made of water which is found in the Milanese; yet the rivers in the Venetian state belong to the prince, as well as in other parts of Italy, and water is consequently to be bought: but there is not the same right to conduct it at will, and consequently the water itself might almost as well not exist.

To Venice.

In this tract I saw no irrigation, though the whole is very low, and quite level.

Venice.

Venice.

The same admirable law, that takes place in the Milanese, for enabling every man to conduct water where he pleases, is found in the Venetian state also, contrary to my information at Padua; but so many forms are necessary, and the person who attempts it, must fight his way through so much expensive litigation, that it is a dead letter, and nothing done in consequence. I was farther told, that it is a principle of the Venetian code, that not only all rivers, but even springs, and rain itself, belongs to the Prince: an idea worthy of this stern and tyrannical government.

ECCLESIASTICAL STATE.—*Bologna.*

I saw no watered lands.

TUSCANY.

I saw no irrigation in Tuscany; and, from the intelligence I received, have reason to believe, that the quantity is not considerable; some meadows, however, are watered after mowing. The best meadows I heard of, are about Poggio, Caiana, Villa Sovrana, ten miles from Florence.

DUTCHY OF MODENA.

The quantity of irrigated land in the Modenese, is but small; it does not amount to more than six biolche in eighty, nor have they more than fifteen perpetual water-mills in the whole territory. From Modena to Reggio, there is a sprinkling of these meadows, the canals for which, taken from the Lecchia, are not large; all, whether watered or not, are manuring, with black well rotted compost, and have a very neat countenance.

DUTCHY OF PARMA.

The country from Reggio to Parma, is not without watering, but the quantity is inconsiderable; there is, in this line of country, a great inferiority to that from Modena to Reggio; not the same neatness nor attention, in any respect; there are mole-casts in the meadows, a thing unseen before; and though there are much cattle and sheep, yet the features of the husbandry are worse. From Parma to Firenzuola, not an hundredth part of the country irrigated, yet there is a good deal of grass, and in some places in large pieces.

PIEDMONT.—*Pavese, &c.*

For some miles in the Sardinian territories, there are a good many meadows, but very few watered. I passed two small channels of irrigation, but the quantity was inconfiderable. If a map of thefe countries be examined, there is the appearance of many rivers defcending from the Appenines, and falling into the Po, but the ufe made of them is fmall. It is remarkable, that all the way by Tortona, Alexandria, &c. to Turin, the quantity of irrigation, till almoft clofe to the laft mentioned city, is quite inconfiderable, not one acre, perhaps, in a thoufand. What an idea can be framed of Piedmont, by thofe who pafs through it from Mont Cenis, and quit it for Milan or Tortona, without feeing it from Turin to Coni?

SAVOY.

In the mountains of the Alps, by Lanefburgh, &c. they mow their watered meadows once only, but in the plain twice.

From this detail of the irrigation of Lombardy, it muft be apparent, that, for want of laws fimilar to thofe which take place fully in Piedmont, and the Milanefe, and partially in the republic of Venice, no fuch exertions are ever likely to be made in a free country. We can in England form no navigation, or road, or make any trefpafs or private property, without the horribly expenfive form of an act of parliament; we cannot even inclofe our own property, without the fame ceremony. Nor is it only the expence of fuch applications, but the neceffity of them generates oppofition at every ftep, and a man muft fight his way through country-meetings, through attorneys, agents, council, witneffes, and litigation,—in a manner odious to every liberal feeling, and at a ruinous expence, before he is at liberty to improve his own eftate, without any detriment to others; every idea of fuch works, therefore, in England, as we have feen common in Lombardy, is vifionary and impracticable; and we muft continue to view, with eyes of envy and admiration, the noble exertions which have been made and perfected in that country, and which, in truth, very much exceed any thing we have to exhibit in any walk of agriculture in this ifland:—an example to hold up for imitation, and an ample field of practical ftudy.

SECT.

SECT. II.—OF CATTLE.

PIEDMONT—*Nice to Coni.*

In this part of the Alps, the breed of cows refembles the Alderney, in horn, colour, and fize. They are ufually cream-coloured, or pale yellow, but with black around their eyes; black tail, and fome of them legs alfo; like the Poictou breed in France.

Turin.

Price of a plough ox, 150 liv. to 300 liv. A good cow, 110 liv.

The method of fattening, in the plain, the cattle called *moggie*, from the mountains of Suza and Buffolino, as given by the Agrarian Society, deferves attention. They begin, by putting them in airy ftables, healthy, and well lighted; bleed once or twice; anoint the bodies of the cattle; drefs them well at leaft twice a day; give water mixed with rye-flour; in the evening, feed with a certain mixture called *condut*, compofed of elm-leaves, with fome hay of the fecond or third cut, or clover-hay; to which they join a mefs of well pulverized walnut-oil-cake : on this mixture they pour fome boiling water, well falted, and ftir up the whole together; and mixing, at the fame time, an ey-mena of bran, according to the number of *moggie*; the pap, thus prepared, is turned into a tub, and, fome hours after, it is given to the cattle, who eat it with an avidity that marks a delicious food; continuing this method fome time, they caft their hair, grow fmooth, round, fat, and fo improved, as to fell fre-quently at double the price *.

MILANESE—*Milan.*

Examining the ox-ftalls of a farmer near the city, I found his ftandings 6½ feet wide, and made almoft like my own at Bradfield; except that, inftead of a ftep and gutter, he has a trench at their heels, in the Dutch method. I thought the houfe too clofe and hot; yet there were air-holes, but all ftopped, the farmer faying, that a cow gives more milk for being kept hot; but in fummer the fheds are open, and quite cool. They begin to work their oxen at four years old, and continue till ten, fometimes till twelve, but after ten they do not fatten fo kindly. They all draw, as in Piedmont, by the withers; fine ones fell at thirty louis the pair A pair will draw 4000 lb. of hay, each pound 28 oz. on a waggon that weighs 1000 lb. more, with wheels not three feet high, and

* *Memorie della Società Agraria*, vol. I. p. 73.

wooden axles. 4000 lb. at 28 oz. Milanese, are 6777 lb. at 16 oz. Englifh; and three tons being only 6720 lb. this is a confiderable load, in fuch a vehicle, and fhould imply no bad method of drawing, yet I cannot like it fo well as by the fhoulders. They are never fhod, except on ftoney hills.

This farmer fattens his oxen in winter with lintfeed cake, giving 5lb. or 6lb. a day to each beaft, and as much hay as they will eat; the beft for them, that of meadows not watered. When it is fcarce, they fubftitute forage of maiz, fown thick for mowing; and this hay they cut in a chaff-box, to the length of one or two inches.

But the great object in the vicinity of Milan, as well as in the Lodizan, &c. is a dairy; I viewed feveral confiderable ones, from four to feven miles from the city, and had my inquiries very fatisfactorially anfwered. Some of the particulars deferve noting, for I fhould remark, that all the dairies of the Milanefe are very famous; and few produce cheefe, that is not fold under the general name of Parmefan. They buy in, about the end of October, Swifs heiffers, with calf, generally at two years and a half old, under contract, that if they do not calve, or do not give milk from four teats, the bargin is void: the price, on an average, 13¼ louis. They keep fo long as till fifteen years old, or fo long as they breed. Till the age of fix years, the milk augments annually, but afterwards diminifhes. They are fold lean at 15 to 36 crowns each, 6 liv. (at 8d.) The beft two or three cows, in a dairy of forty or fifty, will give thirty-two bocali of milk per diem; but, in common, twenty-four, or eighteen Englifh quarts. The cows are moftly of a dark brindled red colour, with fmall horns *; and it deferves noting, that the beft made cow in fifty-five, *quafi* fattening, was the beft milker.

In refpect to cheefe, a dairy of fifty-five, which I viewed, make three hundred and twenty in a year, at 40 lb. on an average, or 12,800 lb. or 232 lb, per cow (380 lb. Englifh), at 90 liv. per 100 lb.; in all, per cow, in cheefe, 7l. 10s. Englifh. The butter amounts to 12 lb. to every cheefe of 40 lb. at 26f. per lb.: 3840 lb. which, at 26f. are 4992 liv. (166l. 8s. Englifh, or, per cow, 3l.) The calf, at eight or fifteen days, fells at 72 liv. per 100 lb. nett, and being weighed alive, 28 lb. per 100 lb. is the deduction. I do not clearly underftand this note, on revifion, but as veal at Milan is about the fame price as in England, I fhall call the calf 10s. To fifty-five cows, feven fows and a boar are kept, which breed forty hogs that are reared; twenty fold in fpring, and twenty in autumn, average 1½ louis each; in all for hogs, 6ol. Englifh.

† It is remarked by an Italian writer, that in chufing cattle, the horns muft not be overlooked; the larger thefe are, the worfe. The Swifs cows that are reputed the beft, have fmall horns; and, on the contrary, thofe of Sardinia, that are poor milkers, have very long ones. *Elementi D'Agricoltura di Mitterpacher*, tomo ii. p. 257, notes.

Recapitulation,

		£.	s.	d.
Recapitulation, per cow.—Cheese,	- - -	7	10	0
Butter,	- -	3	0	0
Calf,	- - -	0	10	0
Hogs,	- -	1	2	0
		12	2	0

The account of a dairy taken next door to me, in Suffolk, is complex, and such as not one man in twenty keeps accounts particular enough to ascertain; it may, therefore, be easily supposed, that greater difficulties occur in a foreign country, through the medium, not only of a different language, but of different manners and customs. This account was given partly as an actual one of fifty-five cows, and partly by calculation; but in such a number of cows, there will be some dry; there will not be fifty-five calves sold from fifty-five cows; hogs must, for such a produce, have some corn given them, though not much; and I should consider this estimate rather as what a good cow ought to do, barring accidents and exceptions, than as a fair average of a large number.

The expences, however, are high, as well as the produce; among others, there are the following to this dairy of fifty-five:

		liv.
Chief dairy-man, the *cazaro*.—Wages,	- - -	130
Five moggii of maiz, at 20 liv.	-	100
One ditto wheat, at 34 liv.	-	34
Half ditto rye, at 18 liv.	-	9
One ditto of white rice,	-	44
One hog, of 120 lb. at 15 *s*.	-	90
Lodging, fuel, salt, and butter,		
The under dairy-man, *sotto cazaro*.—Wages,	- - -	127
Board in the farmer's house,		
Three men, at 70 liv. each,	-	210
3½ moggii maiz, at 10½ liv.	-	210
½ ditto rye, at 3½ liv.	-	63
¾ ditto rice, at 2¼ liv.	-	99
½ ditto mullet, 1½ liv. at 18 liv.		27
Towards board, 20 liv.	-	60
Land enough for their flax,		
Two children, for the hogs, at 30 liv.		60
Five faggots per diem, at 5 liv. the 100		
4 liv. if large,	- -	60
		1323

Here

Here are above 44l. Englifh, without knowing at what to calculate the three
other articles; probably they would raife it to above 20s. a cow. There is
likewife the wear and tear of the dairy implements, falt, oil, and many fmall
articles; befides hazard, and the lofs by difference between the fale of old cows
and the purchafe of young. In regard to the management of the cows, they
eat in winter, that is, from the middle of December to the end of March, nothing but hay, and the allowance is 21 lb. of 28 oz. each cow, per diem; this
is 2184 lb. of Milan, or 3559 lb. Englifh, or about 1½ ton. This fingle article
of expence, without any other confideration, would make a very great produce
neceffary, or the farmer could not live. They milk at break of day, and fometimes before it: in the evening, two hours before fun-fet: the quantity moft in
the morning. The beft cheefe is made when the cows feed on white clover,
which comes of itfelf the fecond year, where red clover was fown, which occafions a vulgar notion here, that red clover changes into white. This fecond
year's white clover is better than perennial meadows for cheefe. For one fortnight in a year, they foil their cows,—the laft half of March,—and the grafs
goes thrice as far as when eaten in the field; yet they never do it at any other
feafon. The moft fingular circumftance, is that of their ftalling their cows, to
empty racks, moft of the day and all the night; they are turned out at eight or
nine in the morning, for three or four hours, and all the reft of the twenty-four
they have nothing. I inquired particularly into the motives for this very extraordinary practice, and was affured, it was neceffary to make good cheefe; as
without it the milk would not have the requifite richnefs. During fome feafons of the year, and in very wet or bad times, they give them, during this faft,
a fmall quantity of hay; but the practice is confined to fuch times, and is an exception from the general rule, which is decidedly that the cows muft not eat
grafs at pleafure. It is fo very fingular a practice, as certainly to deferve experiment in England. The French practice, of milking thrice a day, is quite unknown.

The method of making the cheefe known in England by the name of Parmefan, becaufe the city of Parma was once the *entrepot** for it, was an object
I wifhed to underftand as well as poffible. The idea is, that all depends on foil,
climate, and irrigation; and the boafted account, that the Kings of Spain and
Naples, in order to make fimilar cheefe in their territories, at leaft for their own
tables, had procured men of fkill from the Milanefe for this purpofe,—contribute to give a readinefs every where in anfwering queftions, as they are all
very well perfuaded, that fuch cheefe can be made no where elfe.

* This is the general opinion, but a late writer has fhewn that it is an error, and that Parma and
Piacenza were once the country in which the beft was made.

In

In order that I might view the procefs to the beft advantage, the 'Abbate
Amoretti conducted me to the dairy in queftion, belonging to the houfe of Leti.
It is, in the firft place, neceffary to obferve, that the cheefes are made entirely
of fkimmed milk; that of the preceding evening, mixed with the morning's
milk: the former had ftood fixteen or feventeen hours; the latter about fix
hours. The rennet is formed into balls, and diffolved in the hand in the milk;
the preparation is made a fecret of, but it is generally known, that the ftomach,
of the calf is dreffed with fpices and falt. The rennet was put to the milk at
twelve o'clock, not in a tub, but in the chauldron or boiler, turned from off the
fire-place at ten o'clock; the heat 22 degrees of Reaumur's thermometer,
and common to 24 degrees (81¾ Fahrenheit's), the atmofphere being at the
fame time 16½ (70 Fahrenheit's). In fummer, the whole operation is finifhed
by eight in the morning, as the heat fours the milk if in the middle of the day.
At one o'clock the cazaro examined the coagulation, and finding it complete, he ordered his fotto cazaro to work it, which he did, with a ftick armed
with crofs wires, as defcribed in *Annals of Agriculture*; this operation is, inftead
of cutting and breaking the curd, in the manner it is done in England, free from
the whey. When he has reduced it to fuch a firmnefs of *grain* as fatisfies the
cazaro, it is left to fubfide, till the curd being quite funk, the whey is nearly.
clear on the furface; then the cauldron which contains it, is turned back again
over the fire-hearth, and a quick fire made, to give it the fcald rapidly; a
fmall quantity of finely powdered faffron added, the fotto cazaro ftirring it all the
time with a wired machine, to keep it from burning; the cazaro examined it,
from time to time, between his fingers and thumb, to mark the moment when the
right degree of folidity and firmnefs of grain is attained. The heat was 41 deg.
(124½ Fahrenheit), but it is often 44 (131¼ Fahrenheit). When the cazaro finds
it well granulated by the fcalding, he orders his deputy to turn it off the fire;
and, as foon as a certain degree of fubfidence has taken place, empties about
three-fourths of the whey, in order the better to command the curd. He then
pours three or four gallons of cold water around the bottom of the cauldron, to
cool it enough for handling the curd; then he bends himfelf into the veffel, in
a formidable manner, to view it, refting his feet againft the tub of whey, and
with his hands loofens the curd at bottom, and works it into one mafs, fhould
it not be fo already, that it may lie conveniently for him to flide the cloth under
it, which he does with much apparent dexterity, fo as to inclofe the whole in
one mafs; to enable himfelf to hoift it out the eafier, he returns in the whey,
and taking out the curd, refts it for ten minutes or a quarter of an hour in a tub
to drain. The vat, in the mean time, is prepared in a broad hoop of willow,
with a cord round to tighten it, and widens or contracts at pleafure, according
to the fize of the cheefe. Into this vat the curd is fixed, and the cloth folded

over

over it at top, and tucked in around. This is placed on a table, slightly inclining, to carry off the whey that drains from the cheese; a round plank, three inches thick, shod with iron, like the block-wheel of a barrow, is laid on the cheese, and a stone about thrice the size of a man's head on that, which is all the press used; and there ends the operation. The cheese of the preceding day was in a hoop, without any cloth, and many others salting in different hoops, for thirty or forty days, according to the season,—thirty in summer and forty in winter. When done, they are scraped clean, and after that rubbed and turned in the magazine every day, and rubbed with a little lintseed-oil on the coats, to be preserved from insects of all sorts. They are never sold till six months old, and the price 90 liv. the 100 lb. of 28 oz.

The morning's butter-milk is then added to the whey, and heated, and a stronger acid used, for a fresh coagulation, to make whey-cheese, called here *mascbo-pino*. Little ones are kept in wooden cases, in the smoke of the chimney.

Upon this detail I am to remark, that the rules that govern the operation of making cheese in the Milanese seem to be very different from those which are attended to in England. These are marked distinctions.

  I. Starving the cows during so large a portion of the day.
  II. Breaking and scalding the curd.
  III. Light pressing.

The mode of feeding, which these farmers pursue, they think essential to good cheese; and that if the cows were allowed to pasture all day long, it would be difficult, perhaps impossible, to make cheese of equal goodness. It would be idle to reason upon a proposition, which demands in other countries experiment alone.

The breaking of the curd and scalding is absolutely different from ours, and apparently a method infinitely superior; our breaking by the hand, and cutting into cubes and other ways, are gross, and render it difficult for the scalding whey to operate equally; but in the Italian method it is broken minutely; and, by keeping the heating whey constantly stirring, the scald is equal throughout; and, operating on the minutely divided curd, must take a more regular and a greater effect. I described to the cazaro the method used in England, and asked his opinion, on which he replied—" Il vostro formaggio in quel modo non puol'essere troppo buono: come è la grana ?" By referring to the grain of the cheese, it is plain he thought that the texture of it demanded this way of operating.

In regard to pressing; all with whom I conversed were much against any very heavy weights; and seemed of opinion, that a good cheese might be

pressed

ſpreſſed into a bad one. Firmneſs, weight, and ſolidity, they contended, ſhould ariſe from the right fabric of the cheeſe, and from adapting the fabric to the land and to the ſeaſon, but never from much preſſing, which would be a bad way of remedying either evils or miſtakes. Hoved cheeſes are very rare with them, which may poſſibly proceed not only from the granulation given by their method of ſcalding, but alſo from their moderate preſſing. However it muſt not be imagined that the excellency and peculiarity of Parmeſan cheeſe depend altogether upon the fabrication ; their own idea is probably very juſt, that ſoil, climate, and irrigation come in for their ſhare ; and that the abundance of certain plants has an influence ; but this laſt cauſe will not have much ſtreſs laid on it, ſince clovers are found to be the chief plants.

I ſhall not quit this moſt intereſting diſtrict, without recommending it ſtrenuouſly to thoſe who would wiſh to give themſelves a completely good farming education. For ſuch a purpoſe, Codogno would be a proper ſtation ; for it is ſurrounded by great dairies, and contains the largeſt magazines of cheeſe of any town in Lombardy ; the conſequence of which is, a regular intercourſe with all the dairy maſters of the Lodizan. Much uſeful knowledge might here be gained in irrigation, and in making cheeſe.

The oxen of this dairy farm begin to work at four years old ; and are ſold at eleven or twelve years old, from 9 to 12 louis each. A pair will plough eight pertiche a day ; and draw, waggon included, 3000 lb. of 28 oz. twenty miles.

Mozzata.

They practiſe a ſingular method of fattening oxen here. They put chopped ſtraw, a little hay, the leaves of maiz, and alſo ſome flour of it, into a tub, and pour in hot (not boiling) water ; and as they give this ſoup to the beaſt, they add for each a handful of oil-cake in powder, or, for want of that, of elm leaves in powder ; oak leaves they give green. Another food in uſe is, powdered acorns, which is given inſtead of oil-cake, and with good ſucceſs.

Lodi.

The cows here are generally of a blood red colour, long, lank, and ill made. In a dairy of ninety, they make, for one hundred and ſixty days, one cheeſe a day, of 60 lb. ; but in April and May it is of 70 lb. After St. Martin, the beginning of November, greater, but not every day : in ſeven months, 190 cheeſes ; and in the reſt of the year, 170 ; in all, 360 ; this is 240 lb. per cow. In feeding, they give the cows nothing from four in the afternoon till nine the next morning, unleſs the weather be very bad, and then a little hay. In making the cheeſe, I found very little variation in the practice from that already deſcribed.

fcribed. For the coagulation, or what our dairy-wives call *fetting*, they heat the milk gradually, and take care not to do it too much at once. In the great heats of fummer, they fet it without heating, and even put ice or fnow (with which every dairy is provided) to cool it; but they do not confider the heat at fetting to be a point of much confequence, as a little more or lefs heat makes no difference. The curd is broken exactly as defcribed before, with two machines, one of wood only, the other armed with fine wires, and the faffron added during that operation. Scald it as at Milan, and, upon doing this with fkill, they affert, that much depends; as by more or lefs fcalding they can remedy certain deficiencies in foils and plants. The reft of the operation is juft as already defcribed, and all the utenfils the fame; the weight fomething lefs than at Milan; and here as great enemies to much preffing. The cheefe made yefterday is all honey-combed in the coat, and as yellow as was, a pale yellow: whereas at Milan the new cheefes are quite white. Thefe honey-combs wear out by fcraping after falting, which is for thirty-fix or forty days; they are then coloured, and there is given to them an appearance of a whitifh cruft, or efflorefcence artificially. They are preferved by oiling, as at Milan. Good cows give about five gallons of milk per diem; the beft of all, fix. Sixty cows require 100 pertiche for fix months in fummer.

Codogno.

The produce per cow is here reckoned at 100 lb. of cheefe *, at 28 oz. at 22½ƒ. per lb. and 80 lb. of butter, at 24ƒ. The calf fells at 20 liv, at fifteen days old; and the produce of hogs, 12 fows to 100 cows, which pay about 10 liv. per cow.

Milanefe.	liv.	ƒ.	*Sterling.*	£.	*s.*	*d.*
100 lb. cheefe, at 22½ƒ.	112	10	—	3	15	0
80 lb. butter, at 24ƒ.	96	0	—	3	4	0
Calf, - -	20	0	—	0	13	4
Hogs, - - -	10	0	—	0	6	8
	238	10		7	19	0

Thirteen pertiche of land are neceffary to carry a cow through the year, which they cut for hay thrice, and feed once. Such land bought, fells at 300 liv.

* This is the general idea; but let it be noted, that the particulars of two dairies I took, one of which was near Milan, were different; one 232 lb. per cow; the other, near Lodi, 240 lb. per cow; yet there is, near Milan, a notion, that the produce is 100 lb. per cow. The difference, probably, is this, that upon a general calculation of all the cows of a diftrict, good, bad, and indifferent, dry, and giving milk, the quantity is 100 lb.; but in certain capital dairies, and reckoning only the cows in milk, it is more than double.

and

and lets at 10 liv. The greateſt dairy in the country, 110 cows, and the price
ten louis each. In ſummer, they milk at four o'clock in the morning, and at
ſun-ſet. Make the cheeſe at eleven in the forenoon ; in winter at any time.
Skim all the milk, and never ſet it for coagulation without heating it by fire.
In other reſpects, the manufacture is conducted as already deſcribed. They
colour the coats with earth, and the whitiſh effloreſcence is given with rye-meal.
When the graſs is oldeſt, it always give the beſt cheeſe, but the produce, after
being down four years, declines ſo much, that the almoſt general practice is to
plough it.

View the magazine of cheeſe, at Codogno, of Sig. Bignami, and of Sig Sta-
bilini ;—the latter are immenſe. Moſt of it is ſold in Italy, much in Spain, and
leaſt of all in France ; there is not a ſolid cheeſe in that kingdom that is eatable,
and yet they conſume little Parmezan !

Condogno to Crema.

Meſſrs. Bignami had the goodneſs to conduct me to a great farm, two miles
from Codogno, in the way to Crema ;—here I found, that coagulation takes,
according to the ſeaſon, from one to four hours ; in ſome parts of the Milaneſe,
the cazaro informed me, that they *ſet* the milk without warming : here never ;
always heat it by fire. The *caggio* (rennet) is in balls about twice as large as
a pigeon's egg, put in a linen coarſe cloth, and rubbed, holding it in the milk,
till it is diſſolved. In this dairy, after three hours coagulation, the milk was as
hot as if freſh from the cow. Quantity of ſaffron, ¼ oz. to a cheeſe of 60 lb.—
945 lb. of milk, of 28 oz. make a cheeſe of 60 lb. weighed ſix months after.
The ſame quantity of milk, in ſpring and in autumn, makes more cheeſe than
in ſummer. Beſt and moſt from old graſs, but a cazaro who really un-
derſtands his buſineſs, will make all alike ; and the idea here is that fabrication is all in all. A cheeſe of 30 lb. will be as good as one of 100 lb. The
ſcalding in their manner, is to granulate the curd, and, united with ſo ſmall a
preſſure, leaves cavities in the texture of the cheeſe, that fill with an oleaginous
liquid, and form the peculiar excellence of Parmezan cheeſe. With the methods uſed in England, ſuch cavities ſpoil a cheeſe. I muſt, however, remark,
that ſuch Parmezan as was common many years ago, in which theſe cavities,
and their contents were of a texture that would allow of drawing out like a
thread of glue, is not ſo common now. The ſolid cheeſe, without cavities,
common at preſent, is not much better than our North Wiltſhire, and is apt to
dry much ſooner, if equally kept. *Quere*, if this declenſion of quality is not to
be imputed to their ploughing all the country ? When their cheeſe gained its
great reputation, it was made from old meadows ; now all is from arable land.
Here it is kept five or ſix years,—never till ten. Walking with the farmer,

the mafter of eighty cows, into his fields (1750 pertiche), I begged him to pick the plants in the order of his eftimation for cheefe, which he did;—firft, *trifolium repens*; fecond, *trifolium pratenfe* and *plantago lanceolata* equal; third, *chicorium intybus*. Thefe he efteemed capital. The *ranunculus repens* bad; all the graffes, properly fo called, bad, on comparifon with thofe above; but *lolium perenne* the beft, if it come naturally; bad, if fown. *Gallega officinalis* bad. They fometimes do not fow any thing to make a meadow, leaving the wheat-ftubble to cover itfelf; a barbarous practice, fince they confefs, that in the firft year it yields little. There were dung-hills in moft of the fields, well mixed and rotten, to be fpread in winter. Feed the cows, in winter, only with hay, and 20 lb. of 28 oz. the daily allowance; the price now $7\frac{1}{2}$ liv. per. 100 lb. I forgot to remark, that all the milk-trays are of copper: and that ice is in every dairy, to put into the churns with the cream. The cows are here fed, as every where elfe in the Milanefe, but a few hours in twenty-four; yet longer than in fome diftricts, for they are abroad feven hours; they eat nothing while tied up in the fheds.

In 1733, there were in the Lodizan 197 dairies: in 1767, there were 236, each of which had 120 cows, on an average, making 290 cheefes each dairy per annum; in thirty-four years, increafe—39 dairies, 4680 cows, 11,310 cheefes, and value 848,210 liv.* This is Count Carli's account, but I fufpect an error †. as I heard no hints of any decline; and at Codogno, the dairies were calculated for me, apparently with attention, at 213 each, making 310 cheefes in a year, or 66,030 cheefes, of 50 lb. each, or 3,301,500 lb. of 28 oz. at 1 liv. a lb.; this makes 110,047l. and the account I received was, that, of this quantity, two-thirds were exported.

In regard to the origin of this cheefe, it deferves notice, that it is not three centuries fince this great advantage of irrigated meadows has been here known; and I may obferve, that the Cifterfian monk who has written fo well—*Sull'Irrigazioni de Prati*, in the *Atti della Societa Pat. di Milano*, feems to admit, that the original manufactures of Parmezan cheefe was in the territory of Parma; and refers to original papers for fhewing, that Milan was fupplied, three centuries ago, with this cheefe from Parma. A clearer proof of this cannot be produced, than that in the ledgers of the monaftery of Chiaravalle, there are entries of the purchafe of cheefe from Parma, which, moft affuredly, could not have taken place, if fuch cheefes had been made at home. And this feems to be confirmed by the account of the entry of Louis XII. into Pavia, in 1499, given by Francefco Muralto, juris confulto of Como, who fays,—" Multa

---

* *Carli*, tom. i. p. 317.

† It muft be a grofs error to calculate the dairies at 120 cows, *en an average*; for in all my inquiries, I heard but of one that reached 110.

fuere

fuere per Papienfes dono regi tradita et inter cetera formæ centum cafei Placentinæ civitatis." It is alfo worth obferving, that though they did not make good cheefe at this period (as we may judge, from their buying it elfewhere), yet fome cheefe was made at Tecchione, a farm belonging to them, of the weight of 14 lb. per cheefe, as it appears by their ledgers for the year 1494 [*].

Venice.

This city is fupplied with beef from Bofnia, Carinthia, Styria, and Hungary: at prefent the export from thofe countries is prohibited, on account of fupplying the Emperor's armies in Hungary. Mutton from Dalmatia, and Bofnia.

ECCLESIASTICAL STATE.—*Bologna.*

In their cow-houfes they have the fame ftep at the heels of the beafts as I have in my own, and which I copied from Mr. Bakewell many years ago; but they have applied it to their horfe-ftables alfo, which I never met with before; yet it is an obvious improvement, which well deferves imitation. The floors of their ftalls are level.

TUSCANY.

Though the quantity of cattle of every kind in this country is much inferior to what it ought to be, yet is the art of fattening an ox well underftood. In fummer they feed on mown clover and *faggina* (the great millet, *holcus forgum*); alfo on maiz, and a mixture of all forts of corn and pulfe, called *farrana*. Price of an ox, 45 fcudi (at 5s. 8d.); a cow, 30; a fheep 1; a horfe, 20; a hog, 7.

Account of a Dairy of Eight Cows, at Vilamagna, in Tufcany, belonging to Conte Orlando del Benino.

	Scud.	liv.	f.
Eight cows coft - - -	85	2	0
Produce, firft year, in butter and milk, -	83	4	2
Second year, value of the cows and 3 calves,	92	3	4
Produce.—Calves, - - -	44	3	15
Milk and butter, - -	78	6	9
	127	3	4
Cheefe, - - -	3	0	4
Value of the cows, - - -	84	3	4
	214	6	12

[*] *Atti,* vol. ii. p. 220, 221.

Expences.

Expences.

	Scud.	liv.	ſ.
Value of the cows,	92	3	4
Dairy man,	12	0	0
Bran and bull,	6	5	4½
Saggina and clover ſown for them,	3	0	0
Profit,	100	5	:½
	214	6	12
Which, on 8 cows, is per cow,	12	10	8
At 5 liv. 15ſ. the dollar, and 47d. a dollar ſterling	£. 3	3	6
Which is per week,	0	1	3

In which experiment almoſt the whole of this was profit, becauſe no fewer
cattle of any other ſort were kept; but it muſt be obvious, that 1s. 3d. a
week is, according to our ideas, a very poor return for keeping a cow*. I copy
this account from Sig. Paoletti, with whom I had the pleaſure of conferring
perſonally on agriculture, and who informed me, that at Villamagna they begin to work their oxen at two years and a half old; they change ſome every
year; and gain by their improvement, while worked, about 6 ſcudi (of 5s. 8d.)
the pair, on an average, per annum; buy at 70 ſcudi, and ſell at 76. Cows
give two fiaſce of milk per diem, during eight months; price 4ſ. each.

MODENA.

Regiſter of all the live-ſtock in the Dutchy of Modena, taken in June 1771:
—Oxen, 42,615; cows, 61,445; calves of one year, 24,172; calves, 21,326;
horſes, 8,313; mules, 836; aſſes, 11,543; hogs, 137,326; ſheep, 329,015;
goats, 35,518. Augmentation in the reſt of the year; great cattle, 12,000;
ſmall, 38,000.

PARMA.

Many and great dairies in the Parmezan; ſome to ſixty cows, and numbers
from twenty to thirty; and thoſe who have a few cows, carry their milk to
ſome neighbouring dairy, and receive cheeſes in proportion to the quantity; but
this cheeſe has not the reputation at preſent of being ſo good as that of the Lodizan. As this country gave its name to the beſt cheeſe in Europe, and once
certainly made the beſt, I was deſirous of knowing how far the mode purſued
in the manufacture, differed here from that of the Lodizan: in the dairy of a

farmer

farmer of the Count de Schaffianatti, I had this opportunity. The apparatus is nearly the fame, except that the ftick with which the curd is broken, and which in the Lodizan is armed with crofs wires, is here only a bufh, the branches of which are drawn a little together by a ftring; this is not fo effective as fine wire, and is a variation in a point of importance in giving a fine *grain*. I have remarked already, that the board which in prefling is laid on the vat, is in the Lodizan one and a half or two inches thick; here it is five or fix inches, and heavy; and the ftone ufed to prefs it four or five times larger, yet the cheefes here are not often more than half the fize of the others; this variation, in a circumftance that cannot be uneffential certainly deferves notice; if fo very light a preffure in the Lodizan is given, the cheefe which is fuperior to all others, it undoubtedly fhould lead the farmers of Parma to examine whether the inferiority of their cheefe does not arife wholly or in part from thefe variations; the country, it is true, is not watered to one-tenth of what the Lodizan is, and the cows feed in perennial meadows, inftead of the pafturage of arable land. The trays here are of wood, inftead of copper for the milk; and it is fkimmed, as at Lodi, before making the cheefe. The coagulation is made ufually in three quarters of an hour, if the milk be what they call wholefome; that is, if it have no particular quality that demands a variation, in which cafe it is coagulated in half an hour: they vary the fcalding alfo; for bad milk they fcald with a fierce quick fire, but good is done more gently. In managing the lump of curd, when fettled to the bottom of the boiler, they vary alfo; they prefs it with a circular board, fixed at the end of a ftick or handle, and then get a milk tray under it; and when they have hoifted it out, they leave it to drain in that tray about half an hour; at Lodi, ten minutes, or at moft a quarter of an hour. The common price of the cheefe 30 liv. (2½d.) the pefo (22 lb. Englifh.) I tafted it at the table of the Count de Schaffianatti, and alfo at Parma; and the inferiority to the Lodizan is great.

The attention of giving falt to cattle and fheep here, as in every other part of Italy, is regular; they even confider a plenty of falt as fomewhat effential to having proper ftocks of thofe animals; and gave me an inftance, which is remarkable. In the Coursi di Monchio, a valley in which the bifhop is the fovereign, there is no gabelle on falt, and therefore given much more plentifully to cattle and fheep; the confequence is, that the numbers of both are much greater, proportionably to all other circumftances than in any other diftrict.

SAVOY.

They reckon, at Lanefburgh, that three goats are equal to one cow; the price here is 11 liv. or 12 liv. At Ifle, in Alface, a good goat fells from 12 liv. to 30 liv. French, in common 20 liv. Some there are fo good that two equal a cow; but at Tour d'Aigues, in Provence, it takes four to equal a cow, the price 10 liv. or 12 liv. French.

S E C T.

SECT. III.——OF SHEEP.

Nice.

I here obferved, what appeared very fingular, a flock of fheep brought down from the mountains to drink the fea-water, which is, I fuppofe, to fave falt. The gardeners near the town generally keep a few weep, confined in fties, juft as hogs in England, and fed with the offal of the garden. I took a fpecimen of the wool of one of thefe ftie-fed fheep; more like goat's-hair than wool; it fells at 6*f.* the lb.

Turin.

The price of fheep from 10 liv. to 15 liv.   The fleece is 8 lb. at 5*f.* unwafhed.

MILANESE.

Throughout this country I fcarcely faw any fheep, and thofe few bad.

VENETIAN STATE.—*Bergamo.*

Here I met a flock; an ugly breed; large, long, and ill made; without horns; the wool coarfe and hairy; large hanging ears; and their throats fwollen almoft like wens. They have a fabric of woollen cloth here, but the wool comes from Apulia.

Brefcia.

The fleeces here are 4½ lb. (about 2¾ lb. Englifh,) and fell at 25 liv. to 30 liv. per peze, not wafhed, which is about 1s. Englifh the pound.

Verona.

Price 30*f.* the lb. of 12 oz. (1s. the pound Englifh.)

To Vicenza.

Meet feveral flocks; all are clipped twice a year; the breed polled, and much like thofe, but not fo large, as on the other fide of Verona.

Vicenza.

The forts of fheep known here, are *Gentili,* which live only in the plain, not being hardy enough to refift the mountain cold; their wool is longer than of the other forts. *Tofetti,* thefe refift the cold well; have fhort wool, clipped

twice.

twice. *Monte Padouana*, are of a much greater fize; the flefh excellent; are clipped twice. Price of wool, 2½ liv. per pound unwafhed (the ounce of Vicenza, 12 to the pound is to the Englifh ounce as 690 is to 480, as I found, by buying an ounce weight there); this price is equal to about 11d. the Englifh pound. It is remarkable, that they here feed their fheep in winter, with a mixture, made in a hole in the ground, trodden well in, of *zucca* (gourds) cut in flices; the mark of grapes, vine-leaves, and green grafs.—Price of wool here:—Gentili preparata, 6 liv.; Gentili non preparata, 5 liv. 5*f.*; Tofetta, 5 liv. to 6 liv.; Tefino, 2, liv. 10*f.*; Padouana, 4 liv.; all by the pound of 12 oz. The ounce is to that of England, as 690 to 480; the pound, therefore, equals 17 oz. Englifh,—5½ liv. is above 2s. 6d. Englifh.

Padua.

Price of fheep about 2 ducats. In common they clip but once a year; fleece 3 lb.

Ecclesiastical State—*Bologna.*

Price of a good fheep, 14 pauls (7s.) Produce, per fheep, of a flock;—lamb, 4 pauls; wool, 3½; cheefe, 4; in all 11½ (5s. 9d.) per annum; half to the proprietor, half to the peafant. The wool 3 lb. at twice fhearing, and at 13 baiocchi the pound (10 baiocchi to the paul, of 6d. lefs a fraction). It is wafhed on the back before fhearing. There are 25,000 to 30,000 fheep in the Ferrarefe.

Tuscany—*Bologna to Florence.*

Some flocks of fheep are fcattered on the Appenines, of a fmall and rather pretty hornlefs breed. Near Florence, they cut the lambs in June, and fell them in September, to thofe who keep them till March. Price, in September, 10 liv. (7s. 1d.) and in March, for 18 liv. (12s. 9d.); there are few, or none, of two or three years old. They clip but once; weight of the fleece 4 lb. at 1½ paul per lb.; wafhed before clipping (Englifh weight and money, the fleece is 3 lb. at 1s. 1d. per lb.) Wethers are, in fome places, fattened on oats, barley, and hay, and fometimes with a few raves.

Villamagna.

Thirty-fix fheep kept on 483 ftiori of land, each giving 3 lb. of wool (equal to 2¼ lb. Englifh), at this year, 1½ paul, and laft, 1½ (the paul 5½d.); clipped but once a year, in May, and wafhed before. Each fheep ¼ of a paul in cheefe. Thirty-fix bring, on an average, twenty lambs, which fell, at five or fix weeks, at 4½ pauls; at fix months, 7 or 8 pauls.

Two

Two hundred sheep from the mountains, that pass the winter in the Maremma, the expence 157 scudi, composed of twenty rams, fifty ewe hoggits, one hundred and thirty breeding ewes; fifty lambs kept for stock.

	Scud.	liv.
Fifty lambs for stock, - - - -	39	2
Eighty lambs sold, - - - -	12	0
Wool, 7 lb. the pair, at 10 scudi the 100 lb. - -	70	0
Cheese, 2½ lb. to each sheep, at 6 f. per. lb. - -	11	0
	132	2
Half to the proprietor - - - -	66	1

Expence.

Winter food in the Maremma, - - -	40	0
Two hundred sheep to a shepherd; 24 stari of corn for the winter,	12	0
Passes, charges, duties, regulated at 6 scudi the 100 sheep,	12	0
Expences of travelling, utensils, fees, &c. -	8	0
Pasturing in summer in the mountains, - -	4	0
	76	0
Half to the proprietor, - - -	38	0
Nett profit to proprietor, - - -	28	1

Which profit, being on a capital of 157 scudi, is 18 per cent [*].

It is an observation of Sig. Paoletti [†], that draining the Maremma, and cultivating it, have lessened the number of sheep in Tuscany considerably: great flocks, before that period, were kept in some mountainous districts in summer, and pastured in the Maremma in winter; but cultivation has changed this. He does not say that the people of the Maremma have sheep of their own, but observes, that it is a diminution in number. This is sufficient to prove, that the improvements in the Maremma have been on false and vicious principles; for, if they had been on just ones, sheep would have been increased instead of lessened.

Sig. Paoletti recommends that all sheep should have 1 lb. of salt in March, and 1 in October, which makes them healthy, and to yield more wool [‡].

---

[*] *Tramontani Del Accrisscimento Del Bestiam e Toscano*, 8vo. p. 96.

[†] *Pensieri*, p. 207. He mentions their being *prodigiosamente piu numerose*, a century before, p. 221.

[‡] *Pensieri*, p. 208.

MODENA.

Modena.

Wool here fells from 2 liv. to 3 liv. per lb. wafhed; equal to 12½d. per lb. Englifh. There are many fheep in the mountains, but miferable things; clipped twice a year.

Parma.

In going to Firenzuola, I examined the wool of a flock, and found it more like the hair of a dog than wool; and all I fee, which are but few, are alike hairy; moft of them polled, but fome with horns; not badly made, but feel worfe. Thefe are the flocks whofe wool, Monf. de la Lande fays, is eftimable!

Piedmont.—*Pavefe.*

On entering the King of Sardinia's country, and for many miles, fee little parcels, of from ten to twenty-five, of poor dirty houfed fheep, feeding on the young wheat. Afti was formerly famous for wool;—*nelli antichi tempi famofa per la fua lane**; but the country contains none at prefent, to fupport that character.

Savoy.

Unwafhed wool, 10 f. the lb. of 12 oz.; fleece 3 lb. to 6 lb.; it goes to France or Piedmont. Sheep, 9 liv. to 12 liv. each. Though cattle and fheep are the great riches of all Savoy, yet no care taken of the breed, and the wool all bad †.

The price of wool, regard being had to that only which is long, coarfe, and bad (but not the worft), may be ftated in Lombardy at 1s. Englifh, the Englifh pound; fuch would fell in England, I calculate, at about 7d. or 8d. per pound.

---

* *Giulini*, tom. xii. p. 19.

† I may here add a minute on goats: Marquis Ginori introduced the Angora goats into Tufcany, for making camblets, which manufacture has fucceeded fo well, as to be termed *rifpettabile manifattura* by Paoletti. *Penfieri*, p. 220. And it is obferved by another writer, that if they are not fuperior to the antient camblets of Bruffels, they are, at leaft, equal to them. *Ragimamente fapra Tofcana*, p. 167.

CHAP. III.

Of the Management of Arable Land.

THE minutes I took, concerning the conduct of arable land, may, for the sake of clearness, be thus divided :—1, Of the courses of crops. 2, Of seed and product. 3, Of the culture of certain plants. 4, Of implements. 5, Of manures.

SECT. I.——OF THE COURSES OF CROPS.

PIEDMONT.—*Chentale.*

A year of fallow common in five or six years, during which year the land is never watered, only exposed to the sun. Wheat is sown on fallow; on clover land; always after hemp, because the land is in high order; the same after maiz, if well manured; in which case also after millet sown in June, otherwise meslin or rye. The fallow for wheat, commonly follows buck-wheat, called here *fromentin*, or millet. Clover is sown among rye in March, never among wheat. Millet de cottura is sown in June; millet de restuba the end of July, after wheat; and then dung well for hemp.

Turin.

In some arable land I viewed, a few miles from this capital, the following most extraordinary course was pursued, and was mentioned to me as being not uncommon; 1, maiz; 2, wheat; 3, wheat; 4, wheat; 5, maiz; 6, wheat; 7, wheat; 8, wheat.

The year of maiz being considered as such a preparation, as to allow of three successive crops of wheat. The practice however is barbarous. Upon the farm of Sig. Briolo, the following is the course;—1, maiz; 2, wheat; 3, rye; and when the land wants repose, clover is sown upon a small part.

Vercelli.

Upon good wheat land; —1, maiz; 2, wheat; 3, wheat; 4, rye. And in the rice grounds;—1, fallow; 2, rice; 3, rice; 4, rice. They have here an excellent practice, and it extends, more or less, over all Piedmont, which is to

mow

mow clover by the 10th of May, and to plow the land and plant maiz, which succeeds greatly after clover.

MILANESE—*Milan.*

The arable lands never repose; but a quick succession is reaped. Two crops of bread corn are gained in one year, by sowing maiz in July, after wheat.

Milan to Pavia.

The course common in the rice grounds, is,—1, rice; 2, rice, 3, rice; 4, fallow, and dung; 5, wheat, clover sown, either with it in autumn, or upon it in spring; the former best; 6, clover; 7, clover; 8, clover; 9, flax, and then millet the same year: and then rice again, as above.

Also,—1, wheat; 2, clover; 3, clover; 4, clover; 5, clover; 6, flax, and then maiz; 7, wheat, and clover again. Sometimes after flax, colefeed for oil. Another course,—1, 2, 3, clover; 4, maiz; 5, rice; 6, rice; 7, rice; 8 fallow; 9, corn, and clover.

In the Pavese.

1, Rye, and then fallowed for, 2, wheat, sown with clover in February, mown with the stubble, and then fed; 3, clover, 4, clover; 5, clover; 6, flax, and then millet; or, instead of both, maiz; 7, wheat; 8, wheat, and left, then, sometimes, to pasturage under clover.

Mozzata.

A course common here,—1, clover; 2, winter flax; 3, lupines; 4, maiz, for forage; 5, colefeed; 6, cabbages; 7, panic; 8, hemp; 9, beans. This course will be found to occupy about twelve pertiche in one hundred, and to pass in succession over the whole, for the benefit of variation. Another,—1, wheat, and millet after; 2, common maiz; 3, wheat and millet; 4, common maiz; 5, rye and quarantino; 6, common maiz; 7, rye and quarantino; 8, common maiz. The assiduity with which they avoil a fallow, deserves attention; and it is here effected, as in the south of France, by means of a plant that is asserted by many to exhaust.

Lodizan.

1, Wheat, sown in October and reaped in June, and the land ploughed thrice, and manured for, 2, wheat again, and clover, called *spianata agostano,* which is fed till the following spring, but sometimes ploughed the end of autumn; 3, flax; 4, millet. Another course, called *coltura maggenga,*—1, break up the

layer

layer for flax; 2, millet; 3, maiz; 4, wheat, the stubble of which remains in *spianata agostano.*

Cremonese.

1, Wheat, sown in October, and reaped in June, the stubble ploughed thrice for, 2, wheat, upon which sow clover the end of February; 3, clover, ploughed in November for, 4, flax, and then millet; 5, maiz; 6, wheat.

Carpianese.

1, Maiz; 2, wheat sown in the spring with clover, which is mown with the stubble, and remains *spianata agostano*; 3, clover; 4, flax, and then millet; 5, rice; 6, rice; 7, rice.

VENETIAN STATE.—*Bergamo.*

The land here is constantly cropped;—1, wheat; 2, clover, mown in the spring once, in time for maiz; 3, wheat; 4, clover. Also,—1, clover, or millet; 2, maiz; 3, wheat. By which courses they have half or a third of their land in wheat every year.

Brescia.

1, Wheat, and 20 lb. of clover-seed in March, per jugero,—the clover cut in August with the wheat-stubble, and then pastured; in winter dunged: —2, clover, called this year *prato grasso,* cut thrice; first in May, called *il maggiatico* second in August, called *l'ostano*; third in September, *il navarolo :—* 3, in March sow flax, which is gathered in June; then plough and sow quarantino, amongst which, at the second hoeing, sow lupines for manure:—4, plough in the lupines and sow wheat in November, which is reaped in June; cut the stubble immediately, and sow lupines or coleseed for manure:—5, plough in October, and sow wheat mixed with rye; reaped in June, and then sow part with quarentino and part with panic :—6, if a crop of coleseed is taken, it is sown amongst the maiz while growing, which cole is ripe in spring, in time to clear the ground for manuring and sowing the common maiz; if cole not sown, remains fallow in winter, and sow *melica* in spring,—the great millet.

Verona.

Here, as in all other parts of Lombardy, the land is never fallowed;—1, maiz, called *grano turco :* —2, wheat, and, when reaped, millet, or *cinquantino*; this is the quarintino of the Milanese :—3, barley or oats, and, when reaped, some other second crop. Wheat is always sown after maiz, and that after barley

or

or oats. No clover ufed here, except in rice-lands. In the rice-grounds,—1, wheat, reaped time enough for a crop of cinquantino; 2, maiz; 3, clover; 4, rice, &c. &c. Beans are alfo fown inftead of maiz, and wheat after them, and prepare for wheat much better. On the dry lands, fuch as about the Lago di Guarda, &c. no clover, as the land is not good enough.

To Vicenza.

No fallow any where. There is a little clover, and very fine, but the quantity is fmall: all wheat and maiz, and fcarcely any thing elfe.

Vicenza.

Wheat is always fown after clover, and cinquantino after wheat; but nothing prepares fo well for that crop as beans, fo that they are called the mother of wheat, *madre della formento*. This idea, in Lombardy, is as old as Gallo, who remarks, that wheat fucceeds after nothing better than beans, which *in graffano maggiormente la terra, che non fa ogni altro legume* [*]; and this he refers to as a cuftom of the Cremonefe and the Mantuans. It is equally true in England; and fuch a combination of authority ought to convince fuch as yet want conviction, of the utility of beans as a preparation for wheat; more, perhaps, to be depended on than any other preparation whatever. A common courfe near this city, introduced as a variety, is,—1, maiz; 2, wheat and cinquantino. A farmer cultivated a field, during fome years, in this courfe,—1, maiz; 2, wheat; 3, clover: and to preclude the neceffity of dung, he ufed only the *vanga* (fpade): for five years his crops were good, but afterwards declined greatly, till he could not get even clover. They fow wheat in October, and the clover-feed over it in March, if there is rain; the end of June the wheat is cut; the end of Auguft the clover is mown for hay; and another fmall crop again in October: here is, therefore, within a year, one crop of wheat and two of clover. The grafs is cut again in May, or beginning of the following June; a fecond time in Auguft; and a third growth ploughed in for wheat, which is ufually a very great crop in this hufbandry.

Padua.

On all forts of land, the moft ufual hufbandry is,—1, dung for maiz; 2, wheat; 3, wheat, and then cinquantino or millet, &c. Clover is fown both in autumn and in fpring; if the froft is not very fevere, autumn is beft, but fpring the moft fecure. It is cut once after the wheat is reaped.

[*] *Le Venti Giornate dell' Agricoltura. Brefcia,* 1775. 4to. P. 59.

Venice.

Venice.

Sig. Arduino affures me, there is no fallow to be found in any part of the Venetian territory; they have not even a word to exprefs the idea—*l'anno di ri-pofo*, is a different thing, and always means clover, or a ftate of reft, without any tillage. That gentleman's expreffion pleafed me much,—*La jachere è una fciocca pratica in agricoltura.* The two great points on which the beft agriculture of the Venetian State turns, are maiz on clover, and wheat on beans. All thefe plants are equally neceffary upon a farm; and there is a peculiarity in clover, as a preparation for maiz, and equally in beans, as preparatory for wheat.

Bologna.

In a very rich field near this city, which I viewed, the courfe has been, in 1787, wheat, which produced 100 corbi, or twenty times the feed. In 1788, hemp 5000 lb. In 1789, it is now wheat, and perfectly clean. This courfe, of—1, hemp; 2, wheat, is, perhaps the moft profitable in the world,—and brings to mind the noble vale of the Garonne, under the fame management. If land will do for hemp, they never fallow, but have fome fields in the courfe, —1, fallow; 2, wheat, which ought to be confidered as a difgrace to Lombardy. 1, Maiz; 2, wheat, is a courfe not uncommon. On the fallowed lands they fow beans, provided they have dung. Very little clover, preferring fenugreek, which is fucceeded by wheat. Vetches they fow in autumn, and beans alfo, both for a crop, and alfo to plough in, in the fpring, as a manure for hemp. With equal quantities of manure, beans give better wheat than hemp. Beans, on Sig. Bignami's farm, are now (November) fix inches high on the tops of narrow ridges, but none in the furrows; thefe are for a crop, and infinitely too thick, I fhould apprehend. Lupines alfo, for ploughing in.

TUSCANY.

In the Valdarno di Sura, Colini, Sienifi, Pifani, Volterrana, they fallow, and their courfe is,—1, fallow; 2, wheat. After travelling fo long in Lombardy without a fallow, it hurt me to find them common here. Clover is ufually made a preparation for maiz in moft parts of this country; and beans, where fown, are reckoned the beft for wheat. At Martelli, &c. the courfe is, —1, beans, French beans, or maiz; 2, wheat; 3, wheat; 4, wheat and rye, and no after-crop. In the Valdichiana, the following courfe, I am informed, is purfued,—1, maiz and French beans; 2, wheat, and nothing after it; 3, wheat and then raves,—and, in fome places, clover added. At Villamagna, the courfe is,—1, *biade*, vetches, beans &c.; 2, wheat; 3, wheat; 4, wheat.

The

The firft wheat produces nine or ten times the feed, if after beans; the fecond fix or feven; the third three or four: —a degradation that ought to explain fully the abfurdity of fuch a fyftem. In fome diftricts the following is the courfe, —firft year, biadi, viz. beans, peafe, chick-peafe, French beans, tares, lentils, oats, maiz, the great millet, fmall millet, panic in part, clover and oats, and, after cutting for forage, plough for fome of the above. Second year, upon the land thus prepared, wheat is fown, called *groffo* and *ariftata* mucked; or with half *groffo* and half *gentili* (white wheat). Third year, gentili wheat.

MODENA.

The bad farmers in the Modenefe are fallowifts, and their courfe is,—1, fallow, ploughed firft in May or June, in Auguft the fecond time, and the third in October, for fowing, 2, wheat. But the better farms fubftitute beans, French beans, vetches, fpelt, maiz, particularly the laft inftead of a fallow. Upon foils that are very good, and manured, they have an execrable cuftom of taking three crops of wheat in fucceffion; fometimes throwing in clover with the wheat, which is ploughed up in June for wheat again. When beans are fown in autumn, and ftand the froft, they yield much more than fpring fown.

The hufbandry practifed by Sig. Bertolini, which is the beft of the country, is,—1, beans, fown in October, and harvefted in May: then French beans, or formentoni, for forage, or thick-peafe, or lentils; 2, wheat, the ftubble ploughed thrice for, 3, wheat; 4, maiz, fown in March. To Reggio they fallow fome of their land every third year; but more commonly fubftitute maiz, beans, or fomething elfe in lieu.

PARMA.

In the country about Vicomero, the common courfe is,—1, beans; 2, wheat; 3, maiz; 4, wheat.

PIEDMONT.—*Tortonefe.*

A common courfe here, is,—1, beans; 2, wheat. Alfo,—1, melga, (great millet); 2, wheat. But they have fome lands in fallow courfes.

SAVOY.

At Lanefbourgh, the common hufbandry is that of a crop and a fallow: they plough in May or June, and again for the feed in Auguft, when they fow the rye; and they have no wheat.

From thefe notes it appears, that there is fomething both to commend and to condemn in thefe Italian courfes. The rejection of fallows is pretty general; this is a good feature, and the great ftrefs they lay on beans, as a preparation for

wheat,

wheat, cannot be praised too much. On the other hand, there seems to be no idea of so proportioning the crops of a farm, as to make cattle and sheep (kept on arable land) the preparation for corn: the culture of clover is not unknown, but scarcely extends further than to produce some hay. I no where met with artificial grasses introduced on so large a scale as to support a good flock of sheep. In some districts, the great plenty of watered meadow explains this deficiency; but there are more where it will not afford an apology. This objection, however, does not hold good in the Lodizan, where their immense dairies are supported on arable land, and certainly form one of the most curious systems of husbandry that are to be met with in Europe.

SECT. II.——OF SEED AND PRODUCT.

That reader who thinks slightly of the use of collecting a great mass of facts in these inquiries, has not, it is to be presumed, reflected sufficiently on the great importance, in every science, of combining circumstances apparently unconnected, in order for mutual illustration. He who collects such facts, insulated for a time only, may not live to see the effect of such comparisons; but the gradation of knowledge is preserved without interruption, and the uses will undoubtedly be discovered.

Savigliano.

They reckon here, that a farm of 100 giornati, one-third watered meadow, should yield 2300 liv. clear of taxes, landlord's half.

PIEDMONT.—*Turin.*

Products of Sig. Briolo's farm:—Wood, eight giornata; meadow, four; wheat, five; rye, five; maiz, five. Yields to the proprietor, for his half,

Ninety mines of wheat, at 3 liv. 10 ſ. - -	315 liv.
One hundred and five ditto of rye, at 2 liv. 15 ſ. -	236
One hundred and forty ditto of maiz, at 2 liv. -	280
Wood cut, at seven years growth, - -	71
Vines planted about the farm, 45 brenta of wine, at 5½ liv.	247
For landlord's half, - - -	1149

Total, 2298 liv.
Wood,   71

2221 liv. product of nineteen giornata of arable and meadow, or 116 liv. per giornata (about 6l. per English acre); which is a very large produce. There

are

are also mulberries enough to pay taxes; this land cost 750 liv. the giornata, and the wood 250 liv.

MILANESE—*Milan to Pavia.*

The crops are—Wheat, seven or eight seeds.—Rye, eleven seeds.—Maiz, forty seeds.—Ditto quarantino, twenty seeds.—Millet, fifty seeds.

WHEAT.

PIEDMONT—*Chentale.*

A proverb in this country is, that a good peasant should finish his wheat sowing by the 19th of October. After hemp, clover, or fallow, wheat yields forty to forty-five mina per giornata, each mina 45 lb. to 52 lb. average 47 lb. and the common price 3 liv. to 3 liv. 10 *f.* but at present 3 liv. 15 *f.* But, including good and bad farmers, and all soils, the produce is not more than twenty-four mina; that is, twelve for the landlord and twelve for the tenant. They sow four to four and a half; the common produce is, therefore, six times the seed, which is miserable; the better crops between ten and eleven seeds. Allowing for the Piedmont pound, being about one-tenth heavier than the English (though only of 12 oz.), and that the giornata is not equal to an acre, their best crops, at forty-two or forty-three mina, will be near five quarters per English acre; and their average near three; which are not greater than might be expected. Their quantity of seed appears, however, to be immense, for it amounts to 199 lb. per giornata, which is extravagant: and makes it suspicious, that the giornata here is larger that the legal giornata of the principality.

Savigliano.

They sow here, of wheat, 3½ eymena, and reap eight times as much, in a good crop.

Turin.

They sow five mina, or nine rabbii, and 10 lb. to the giornata; of rye and oats, the same quantity; of hemp, three mina; maiz, one-half; millet, one-half. Wheat produces twenty-five mina; or five times the seed; rye, thirty; maiz, fifty to seventy; millet, twenty. The mina at 45 lb. the crop of wheat is about 5½ coombs per English acre. For their land and climate, a miserable crop; but as good, or better, than they deserve, when their course of crops is considered.

MILANESE—*Mozzata.*

Produce of wheat, eight ftajo per pertica on the beft land; five on middling, and three on the worft.

There is a fingular neglect in keeping wheat in this country: being fhewed the granaries at two houfes, in which the quantity was confiderable, I was furprized to find, that where fome of the windows were open, the room ftunk very much; the fcent particular; and examining the wheat, I found the furface all either covered, even to fhining, with the webs of the wevils, or elfe in ropes, hanging together by it, and the flies bufy; the wheat was two or three feet thick, and had not been ftirred. In a third granary, to which I went for fatisfying my curiofity, in the hands of the owner (for the other two belonged to noblemen, and were managed by intendants,) I found in the fame condition; and all agreed, that to ftir the wheat is bad, as it makes the whole heap alike: whereas, by not moving it, the furface only fuffers. On this, I thruft my arm into the heap, to examine the interior, which all ftunk dreadfully. Perhaps, neither the wevil, nor any other infect, may live deep in the heap; but, for want of airing, the wheat ftinks; not to mention the furface, which is a lofs of 5 or 6 per cent. A moft barbarous fyftem of management. It is worth remarking, that the only good way of keeping wheat is in the ftraw: ftacks fhould be built on capt ftones, to keep vermin out, and the corn threfhed as wanted.

Mozzata.

The product here, on the three divifions of foil, are, per pertica, the meafure the ftajo,—

	Good.	Middling.	Bad.
Wheat -	8	5	3
Rye - -	8	5	4
Millet -	8	5	3
Common maiz,	10	6	4
Ditto Quarantino,	6	4	2
Lupines, -	8	6	4
Panic, -	6	4	2

Clover hay, 350 lb. of 28 oz. per pertica,
  at 3 mowings; 1¼ ton per acre. In money
  by corn, without mulberries or vines, 24 liv.— 15½ — 9¼

For the landlord's fhare, I fuppofe. And, in refpect to the country in general, if four fquare miles be taken around Mozzata, of fix parts, three are good, two middling, and one bad. Average corn produce, 18½ liv. The common notion
is,

is, that two-thirds of the grofs produce go towards maintaining the farmer, fupporting the cattle, wear and tear, taxes, &c. and that one third is nett to the proprietor.

	liv.
Produce of 100 pertiche, at 18½ liv. - - -	1850
Vines, proprietor, - - - -	.150
—— tenant, - - - -	150
	—— 300
Mulberries, 2000 lb. leaves, at 4 liv. per hundred, - -	80
	——
	2230
Deduct one-tenth of corn product, damaged by vines, -	185
	——
	2045
Deduct one-eighth of corn, for damage by hail; the produce of vines is nett, this is allowed for, - - -	209
	——
Total nett produce, - - -	1836

Hence, therefore, it does not quite reach 18½ liv. on the average

Proprietor—one-third of corn, - - -	555
——————— vines, - - - -	150
——————— mulberries, - - - -	80
	——
	785

Or, per pertica, 7¼ liv. (31s. per Englifh acre, *)

Such land would fell for 145 liv. per pertica (28l. 16s. per Englifh acre).

Codogno.

The feed and produce of the crops here, are,—wheat, fow one ftara and reap fix times as much; maiz, fow one fourth of a ftara, and get twenty for one; millet, fow one eighth ftara, and reap fix ftara; rye, fow one-half ftara, the produce eight ftara; rice fow one ftajo, gain fixteen rough, or eight white.

A Bergamafque writer obferves, that wheat cultivated with the plough, commonly yields four, five, and fix times the feed; but, cultivated with the fpade, twelve, fourteen, and fixteen times that quantity †, and this of greater weight; a fure proof of their miferable tillage.

* At 6 1-6th pertica per acre Englifh, corrected from fome of the proceeding proportions, from intelligence very lately received.

† Cantuni, Inftruzioni Pratichi interno al Agricoltura. 8vo. 1788, Bergamo. P. 16.

Brefcia.

Brescia.

Arable products in this vicinity, are,—wheat, three facchi, of fourteen pezè each pezè 25 lb. being about fix feeds. The pezè, of 25 lb. Brefcian, being equal to 14¾ French, makes 206 lb. French per fack, or 224 lb. Englifh: the three facks, therefore, are 672 lb. Englifh, on a jugero of four pertiche; this is fcarcely twelve bufhels the Englifh acre, reckoning four one-fourth pertiche in that acre *. Maiz, fown in March, produces fix, eight, ten facchi, each twelve pezè of 25 lb. This is about twenty-eight bufhels to the Englifh acre, fuppofing a bufhel of maiz to be 50 lb.; but quarantino does not yield more than five fuch facks. Melico (the great millet), fifteen facchi, of ten or eleven fuch pezè. Flax, fix to nine pezè, at 20 liv. to 25 liv. the pezè; this is about 125 lb. the Englifh acre, and 170 liv. at 6d. Englifh, 4l. 5s. and per Englifh acre 4l. Millet gives three facchi, of eleven pezè. Clover, three hundred pezè of hay, at three cuts; meadows yield the fameas clover, but are paftured in autumn. Price of hay 70 liv. the *carro*, of one hundred pezè. Three hundred pezè equal 4827 lb. Englifh, and per Englifh acre, 4522 lb. which we may call grofsly two tons; a very poor crop for three mowings.

To Verona.

In this line of country, the Lombardy fyftem, of planting all the arable lands with rows of pollards, for training vines, is at its height. There is a good deal of it from Bergamo to Brefcia; and fome are feen in paffing from Vaprio to Bergamo, but not fo univerfally as here. It is a moft fingular fyftem; rows of maple, afh, or poplar, are planted, from four to feven yards afunder, and rows of vines at their feet, which are trained up thofe trees, and in feftoons from tree to tree; the fpace is cultivated for corn. They do not feem to approve of a fingle ftem for thefe pollards fo much as feveral, for they have three or four, about fix feet high; cropped every fecond year, to prevent too great a fhade. In fome places, mulberries are mixed with thefe common foreft trees: one mulberry, and then two afh or maple. In fome rows, beyond all doubt, the vines

* In the new edition of Agoftino Gallo, the editors give a line for the length of a Brefcian inch (*oncia*) ———————————— which is the length of 1 5-8th inch Englifh. Twelve of thofe oncia make one braccio, and fix braccia make one cavezzo; confequently there are 9¼ feet in a cavezzo. A pertica is an oblong fquare, twenty cavezzi long and five wide; now multiply 9¼ by 20 = 195; and multiply 9¼ by 5, = 48¼; and the one product by the other, = 9506¼ fquare feet for a pertica; and 4¼ pertiche equals an Englifh acre; perhaps the editors of that new edition have made an error, in ftating 30,709 French feet in their jugero of 4 pertiche.

are

are trained equally on the mulberries as on the other trees; but not generally, being faftened only to the ftems of the mulberries. The better the land, the farther afunder are thefe rows, even to fixty or feventy feet; but, in worfe land, much nearer. All the way, the foil is a ftoney gravel, of a different appearance in quality, but where holes are dug for trees, it looks better.

Verona.

Wheat here yields five or fix times the feed. They fow one hundred Veronefe pounds upon a campo of land, and reap five hundred and fifty, which is about two bufhels of feed per Englifh acre, and the produce eleven bufhels. We have not, upon the pooreft lands in England, fo wretched a crop: to what are we to attribute it, if not to general bad management, united with the execrable fyftem of incumbering their fields with pollards and vines. They fteep their wheat feed in lime-water twelve hours, to prevent the fmut.

Vicenza.

The thirty-two miles from Verona hither, are all, except a fmall quantity of irrigated land, lined into the fame rows, as already defcribed, from twenty-five to thirty yards afunder. Wheat is fown clofe under them; but with maiz, fix yards are left on each fide not cropped; and, in fome pieces, thofe twelve yards are fown thick for forage, as not equally wanting fun; a fure proof that they admit the damage of the trees, and provide againft it as well as they can. In fome grounds preparing for wheat, manure is fpread as far as the roots of the trees extend, but no further. What a fyftem, to give dung to elms and maples, and to force wheat to grow under their fhade!

Wheat has now (October 23) been fown a month or fix weeks; it is high, and thick enough to hide a hare. The borders of thefe fown lands are dug clean away, as deeply as in Effex.

Maiz produces about nine one-half facchi the campo. Inquiring here into the eftimated damage refulting to corn from the plantations of trees in arable land, I was told, that the lofs in one-tenth of wheat, and one-half of maiz, but to clover none. The trees here are all walnuts, for training vines to, the damage done by them, agreed to be very confiderable. Of wheat they fow three ftari, and the produce eighteen to twenty; of maiz one, and the crop thirty to thirty-five; of cinquantino, half a ftara, produce fixteen; of buckwheat one-fourth, the return fix. In the farms around the celebrated Rotunda, maiz produces five facks, each of 150 lb.: a fack is four ftari, and the ftara about three pecks; this is fifteen bufhels, and not fixteen, the acre. They are fometimes troubled with the fmut; Sig. de Boning, Prefident of the Academy

of

of Agriculture, has tried liming and lime water, as a prevention, but without
any fuccefs. Of maiz they have a new fort, that carries a male flower on the
top of the cone, and this fort always fills with grain to the very point, which is
not the cafe with other kinds.

In refpect to the exhaufting quality of crops, they reckon that the maiz which
carries the flower at top takes moft from the land: 2, millet: 3, common
maiz: 4, wheat. It feems remarkable, that they fhould confider the crops
which are preparatory to wheat as exhaufting, more than the wheat itfelf.

Padua.

Of wheat they fow three ftaji in middling land, two in fertile foils, and four
in bad ones, per campo: as the ftajo is equal to forty-one French pounds, and
the campo about one-tenth lefs than an Englifh acre, it makes three ftaji equal
to two and a half bufhels per acre, which is pretty exactly the quantity we ufe
in England. The crop is two mozzi on the beft land, and one and a half on a
medium: each mozzo twelve ftaji: this is about fifteen and a half bufhels the
acre or under feven times the feed. Thus thefe wretched products purfue me
through all Lombardy. Of maiz they fow three quarti, or three-fourths of a
ftajo, but if planted, two: the produce, good five mozzi, middling three, bad
one. Of lucern (the quantity very inconfiderable) and of clover they fow 12 lb.
groffo. This pound is to the French one as 9150 is to 9216; this is between
14 lb. and 15 lb. per acre. Clover gives three carri, each 1000 lb. at three cuts.
Lucern four carri, at four or five cuts. Almoft the whole country is lined into
rows of pollards, as already defcribed; yet they admit that every fort of tree does
very great damage to all arable crops; but to grafs the mifchief is not great.

To Venice.

The fame level at this city that reigns about Padua, equally enclofed and
planted; much of it arable, and almoft the whole cut into little fcraps of fields,
with many gardens. Near the Adriatic, a dead level marfh, covered with
marfh graffes.

ECCLESIASTICAL STATE.—*Bologna.*

In a famous field near the city, remarkable for yielding great crops of hemp,
wheat yields one hundred corbes for five of feed. In general, they fow two
and a half tornature of land, or one acre and a quarter, with a corba of feed,
or 150 lb. to 160 lb. (fomething under the Englifh pound); and in all the Bolognefe, on an average, the produce is about five feeds, fome only three; but
on

en the beſt hemp lands twelve to ſixteen, on a medium; but twenty for one are ſometimes known.

TUSCANY.—*Florence.*

In the plains, the general produce is eight times the ſeed; the whole dutchy through, not more than five or ſix: in the depoſits of rivers, or ſpots remarkably rich, twelve, fifteen, and even twenty. All theſe are wheat. Beans four and a half and five. On one ſtioro of land they ſow three-fourths of a ſtajo of wheat, which weighs 52lb. to 55lb. of 12oz. (this pound is equal to three quarters of a pound Engliſh.) On the hills they ſow one-fourth more. Suppoſing the ſtiora * to be, according to De la Lande, 7056 French feet, about 5⅓ make an Engliſh acre; three-fourths of a ſtajo therefore per ſtiora, equals 165 lb. per acre, or very near three buſhels.

* There are three accounts before me of the contents of a Tuſcan ſtiora. Monſ. De la Lande, tom. ii. p. 314. ſays, " le ſtiora = 196 toiſes quarrés en ſuperficie;" theſe are French toiſes, each ſix feet: this makes about 5⅓ ſtiori to an Engliſh acre; that is to ſay, 7056 French ſquare feet, of which 38,300 are an acre. In *La Squadra mobile l'Arithmetica e l'Agricoltura, del S. Sangiovanni,* 4to, Vicenza, 1759, p. 11. and 132. is the meaſure of the ſoldo of Florence, which equals 1 1-eighth inch Engliſh; the braccio is 20 ſoldi, or 22½ inches Engliſh, (by another account 23½; 6 braccia make a canna: and 8 canne long, by 6 broad, make a ſtiora. Hence there are 6075 Engliſh feet in the ſtiora; conſequently there are ſomething above 7 ſtiori in an acre. Monſ. Paucton, in his *Metrologie,* p. 794, compares it to the arpent of France of 48,400 French feet, and makes it to that arpent as 0.11461 to 1.0000; by this account it will be about 27,800 French feet, of which feet 38,300 are an acre, or above 1 1-third ſtiora. In the *Giornale Fiorentino di Agricoltura,* 1786, p. 253. "L'acre al noſtro ſtioro ſtà come 18,992 a 10,592;" by this ratio, an acre is about 1½ ſtiora. All theſe accounts differ therefore greatly. To compare other circumſtances---At Martelli, they ſow one-third of a ſtajo of wheat ſeed on a ſtiora; and at Villamagna, they ſow 3½ ſtiori with 1 ſtajo, which quantities nearly agree. By De la Lande's account, this will be per acre Engliſh 73 lb. which appears to be a ſmaller quantity than any where uſed. By Sangiovanni, it will be about 94 lb. ſtill under the common quantities. By Paucton, it will be about 17 lb.; a portion not to be named as the ſeed of an acre. And by the Florentine author, about 23 lb. which is almoſt equally abſurd. Seed wheat will agree with none of the meaſures; ſuppoſe they ſow 2¼ buſhels per acre, then there are 15 ſtiori in an acre. If 2 buſhels, then there are 12 ſtiori. All is confuſion.

At Villamagna, they ſow 24 ſtaji of beans on 28 ſtiori of land; this is about 3 buſhels Engliſh per 5½ ſtiori, which agees very well with an acre being 5½: they ſow alſo 6 ſtaji of oats on 10 ſtiori, this would be 2 buſhels on 5: they ſow oats therefore rather thinner, proportionably to the Engliſh practice, than beans.

Upon my getting a friend to write to Tuſcany for information, I received ſuch as proved of no uſe; ſimply this table,---1 *quadrato,* 10 *tavole;* 1 *tavola,* 10 *pertiche;* 1 *pertica,* 10 *deche;* 1 *deca,* 10 *braccia ſquadra.* This makes the *quadrato* under 40,000 feet Engliſh. But what is the *ſtiora?* Such are the endleſs difficulties in every thing concerning meaſures.

Where authorities, apparently good, differ ſo greatly, the reader will of courſe receive all eſtimations with many doubts.

But

But I found at Martelli, near Florence, that they fowed but one-third of a ftajo per ftiora, which would not be more than two bufhels per acre. Beans would be much more cultivated, but for the pernicious plant the *cufcuta*—a parafite that feeds on and deftroys the crop, fo that even the feed again is not reaped; in the old botany called *orobanchis ramofa*, and in Tufcany *fucca mala*, and *fiamini*. Of faggini they fow 1¼ ftajo of feed, and the produce fifty to fixty. Of formentone (maiz) they fow half a ftajo, and reap twenty-five.

On the plains in Tufcany, the chief product is wheat, the fecond wine, and the third oil; but on the fouthern fide of the hills, olives on fpots bad for them, and wine. Silk no where enough to be a chief object.

MODENA.

The country from Modena to Reggio conftantly improves in its features, and muft be reckoned among the beft cultivated in Lombardy; the fields are thrown into arched lands, like Flanders, about twenty-five yards broad, and fmall ridges on thofe: a row of trees is planted on the crowns of fome, and along the furrows of others: in fome there are neat grafs trenches; and as the fences are equally well made, and the meadows with a good afpect, the country carries the general features of being well cultivated. The appearance of thefe broad ridges, in two of the beft cultivated countries in Europe, Lombardy and Flanders, juftly gives a high idea of the practice.

PARMA.

From Reggio to Parma, there are many lands, three or four yards broad, now (November) deeply ploughed, and the furrows cleaned out by fpades, laid up in this manner, for planting beans in the fpring; excellent management. There are alfo a good many autumn fown ones, three or four inches high: produce in general, about Vicomero, wheat four or five times the feed, and beans five or fix. To Firenzuola this practice takes place yet more, and is better done. The merit of their hufbandry appears to be greater about Parma than at Piacenza; there is a vifible decline as you advance.

SAVOY.

At Lanefbourg, they fow only rye, which they harveft in July, the produce about fix for one.

If the intelligence concerning the produce of wheat be reviewed, it will be found, on an average, varying from five to feven and an half times the feed; generally between five and fix. Suppofe the latter number, and we fhall, with

reafon

reafon, be amazed at the miferable products of this rich plain, in every thing except grafs and filk. The average foil of England cannot be compared with the average foil of Lombardy, yet our mean produce is eleven times the feed, perhaps twelve. Every one muft be curious to know the caufe of fuch wretched crops: I attribute them to various circumftances—but the predominant caufe muft be fought for in the fmall farms occupied either by little peafant proprietors, or, what is more general, by metayers. This abominable fyftem of letting land is the origin of moft of the evils found in agriculture, wherever the method prevails. Such poor farmers, who, in every part of Italy where I have been, are fo miferable, that they are forced to borrow of the landlord even the bread they eat before the harveft comes round, are utterly unable to perform any operation of their culture with the vigour of a fubftantial tenantry; this evil pervades every thing in a farm; it diffufes itfelf, imperceptibly to a common eye, into circumftances where none would feek it. There are but few diftricts where lands are let *to the occupying tenant* at a money rent; but wherever it is found, *there* crops are greater; a clear proof of the imbecillity of the metaying fyftem. Yet there are politicians, if they deferve the name, every where to be found, who are violent againft changing thefe metayers for farmers; an apparent depopulation is faid to take place; and the fame ftupid arguments are heard, that we have been peftered with in England, againft the union of farms. Men reafon againft that improvement of their lands, which is the natural progrefs of wealth and profperity; and are fo grofsly abfurd as to think, that doubling the produce of a country will deprive it of its people.

SECT. III.——OF THE CULTURE OF CERTAIN PLANTS.

Gallega Officinalis.

Commonly fpontaneous in the fields, between Milan and Pavia, and whereever cattle have admiffion all clofely eaten.

Paliurus.

I know no plant that makes a better hedge than this in the north of Lombardy. Sig. Pilati, near Brefcia, has one of fix years growth, as good as an excellent white thorn one in England would be in ten.

Trigonella Fænum Græcum.

Cultivated in the Bolognefe in preference to clover; foil with it; and fow wheat on the land.

Sainfoin.

In Tufcany, the *coline di Pifani* are much under this plant, which is called *lupinello*; particularly about Caftel Fiorentino, where it was introduced about twenty years ago, by Sig. Neri; one of the good deeds which deferve a nation's thanks, better than a victory, or the taking of half a dozen towns. A thoufand facks of the feed were fent thence to Naples and Sicily. Will thofe kingdoms awaken at laft? Sig. Paoletti, at Villamagna, has a piece of good fainfoin on a fteep flope; but I found one-third of it burnet.

Larch.

In the Milanefe, at Mozzata, the Count de Caftiglioni having 200 pertiche of wafte heath, and a community 200 more adjoining, he took a leafe of it for ever; and ploughing the whole, fowed acorns, planting alder, larch, and other trees, which do well; but the fown oak, in eight years, exceeded every thing, and are beautiful trees: the foil a poor gravel. We have in England fo many prejudices, that a man who does not travel is apt to think that every thing Englifh is better than the fame things in other countries; and, among other follies, that for oak England is fuperior to all the world: but timber wants fun as much as wheat; and I have no where in England feen fuch a growth of timber, as in many places abroad. Larch abounds greatly in the mountains, and is reckoned an admirable wood for water-works; all pofts are of larch. I have read in fome writer, that there is a law, in many parts of Lombardy, which allows a land-proprietor, whofe eftate is entailed, to plant, on the birth of a daughter, a certain number of Lombardy poplars, which are her portion on coming of age, or being married, in fpite of any entail. I enquired, both in Piedmont and here, into the truth of this, and was affured there is no fuch law; nor did they ever hear of the cuftom, even when eftates have not been entailed.

In the arfenal of Venice, is fome quantity of larch, kept under cover; and valued greatly for all works expofed to water. They are not very large, but coft twenty-two ducats each. The mafts are very fine pine-trees, from the upper Trevifano; I meafured one thirty-eight yards long, and two feet diameter at the butt, and one foot at the other end.

Lucerne.

I mention this plant, for an opportunity of obferving, how very rarely it is cultivated in Italy: I faw a little near Padua; and there is an inconfiderable quantity in the Parmefan, where it is cut five or fix times; they find, that cows give more milk on it, than on any other grafs.

Raves.

Raves.

I was fomewhat furprized, to find turnips, or rather the French raves (for I fear they are not the genuine turnip), cultivated in Tufcany. I was affured, that in the Valdichiana there are many, fown immediately after wheat, but never hoed, yet come generally from 2lb. to 5lb. ; fome to 30lb. (20lb. Englifh), and that they are applied to the feeding and fattening of oxen, which fell at 140 *fcudi* the pair (39l. 13s. 4d. Englifh); nothing befide is given, except a little hay.

Cyprus Tree.

At Soma, near the Lago Maggiore, there is a very famous cyprus tree, which Corio, in his *Storia di Milano*, fays, was the place where the people affembled in congrefs in the thirteenth century; it was then the moft celebrated tree for fize and age in the whole Milanefe; and muft therefore be immenfely old at prefent. It is now in good health, except a few branches that have fuffered a little towards the top; it is nine *braccia* in circumference.

CULTURE OF SILK.

Nice.

Eight *roups* of cocoons, or 84 lb. make 24 lb. of filk (11½ oz.), which fells at 10 liv. 5f. the lb.; a *roup* of leaves fells at 20f. and 250 *roup* are neceffary for 8 oz. of grain (eggs).

Coni.

The whole country, after afcending the Alps, is planted with mulberries, around every field, and if large, in lines acrofs. I remarked great numbers from ten to fifteen years old.

To Chentale, 1 oz. of grain requires 360 *roup* of leaves; each *roup* 25 lb. and yields 4 or 5 *roups* of *bozzoli* or *cacata* (cocoons), and 1 *roup* of cocoons makes 3 lb. of filk. The price of organzine 20 liv. to 24 liv. per lb.; the offal pays the fpinning. Gathering the leaves cofts 2f. to 3f. the *roup*.

Chentale.

The feed of the mulberry is fown in nurferies, and the trees commonly planted out at four years old. The firft, fecond, and third year, they are pruned, for giving the branches the right form; the fourth, they begin to gather the leaves. Some which were fhewn me by the Count de Bonaventa, of eighteen years old,

give

give 6, 7, and to 8 *rubbii* of leaves each. One old tree, a very extraordinary
one, has given 53 *roups*. A large tree, of fifty or sixty years, commonly yields
25 *rubbii*. They never dig around them, nor wash the stems as in Dauphiné;
but they have a practice, not of equal merit, which is to twist straw-bands around
the stems, to defend them against the sun. For one ounce of grain 65 to 80
rubbii of leaves are necessary, which give 2½ *rubbii* of cocoons and sometimes so
far as four. One *rubbio* of cocoons yields 20 to 21 oz. of silk organzine, of the
price of 18 liv. per lb. For gathering the leaves, from 1 f. 8 *den*. to 2 f. the *rubbio*
is given. The offal *(morefca and chocata)* pays the winding and spinning. They
never hatch the worms by artificial heat; using only that of the sun, or of the
human body. The common method of carrying on the business is, to provide,
as in France, grain and mulberries, and to receive half the cocoons. The cultivation is so profitable, that there are many lands to which mulberries add a value
of 200 liv. or 300 liv. more than they would sell for if they contained none; and
it is farther thought, that they are but little injurious to corn, the shade not being so prejudicial as that of the walnut, and of some other trees. The common
estimation of profit is, that trees of all ages yield from the time of beginning to
bear, from 30 f. to 4 liv. each nett to the landlord for his half produce.

Turin.

One ounce of grain gives 2 to 4 *rubbii* of cocoons, and demands 120 *rubbii* of
leaves; 1 *rubbio* of cocoons will give 22 oz. of commonly well spun silk. The
price of grain 12 liv. the oz. when very scarce, but in common 30 f.; that of leaves
7 or 8 f. per *rubbio*. Cocoons 21 liv. per *rubbio*. When I asked the price of the
silk, the answer was, Oh! for that! it is the price the English choose to pay for
it. The common price of organzine, 16 to 20 liv. first quality; raw, 12 liv.
For gathering the leaves, 2 f. per *rubbio* is given. Of the different sorts of mulberry, the wild is the best, in point of quality of silk. A tree of twenty years,
will give 24 or 25 *rubbii* of leaves; some to 35 *rubbii*. The trees are grafted in
the nursery, and planted out at four years, at the beginning of April; price,
20 f. to choose out of many; and in four years after, begin to gather. When
planted in watered meadows, the gathering damages the hay almost to the value
of the leaves, yet many are so planted; and many peasants think they lose in
corn by the shade of the trees, as much as they get by them. From the 22d to
the 26th of April, is the season for hatching; never by fire; nor have they any
method of retarding the hatching, in case of a want of leaves. Endive, lettuce,
and elm leaves, have been often tried as a succedaneum, but always killed the
worms; such things must never be depended on. The peasants generally sell
the cocoons, not one in a hundred spinning. A chamber of twenty feet by
twelve

twelve feet is neceſſary for 3 oz. of grain; and ſix tables, one *trebucco* long and two-thirds wide.

Novara.

Paſſed this place towards Milan, which is a great tract of mulberries for ſeveral miles.

MILANEŞE.—*Buffalora to Manienta.*

Many mulberry hedges, but they are bad and ragged; ſome new planted in the quincunx poſition. For ſeveral miles, the country is all planted in rows of vines, at twelve, ſixteen, and twenty feet, and fruit trees among them, for their ſupport; among which, are many mulberries, and the vines running up them. This muſt be a moſt profitable huſbandry indeed, to have ſilk and wine not only from the ſame ground, but in a manner from the ſame tree. Between the rows, the ground is cultivated; millet, maiz (cut), *holcus ſorgum*, the great millet, lupines, with dung amongſt them, to be ploughed in for wheat, with young maiz, ſown thick, as if for fodder.

Citricho.

A beautiful mulberry hedge, and in good order; ſix to eight inches from plant to plant, and cropt at ſixteen or eighteen from the ground. It is clear therefore, that the plant will do, with care, for a good hedge. Towards Milan, mulberries decline, oak and other pollards being found in their ſtead.

Mozzata.

The culture of mulberries and making ſilk, being here much attended to, were principal objects in my inquiries. The fruit is well waſhed, the end of June, to make the ſeed ſink; it is then ſown in rows, in a bed of earth well manured, and finely laboured, in the rich nurſeries near Milan; covered very lightly, and the ſurface lightly flattened; ſtraw is ſpread to defend it from the ſun, and much water given. When the young plants appear, they are weeded by hand. The ſecond year, they grow to two or three feet high, and hoed and thinned. The third year, they are cut to the ground above the buds that are to puſh, and tranſplanted from thoſe nurſeries, in the vicinity of the city, to others that are ſcattered all over the country, in ground well dug and manured, and at two feet ſquare; here they are kept clean by hoeing. The fifth year, in the ſpring, they are cut again to the ground; they then ſhoot very powerfully, and attention muſt be given, to keep but one good ſhoot, and the ground is dug or hoed deeper than common, and alſo dunged. The ſixth year, thoſe that are high enough, are grafted; and the reſt, the year following. Thoſe that took

the

the fixth year, ought to reft in the nurfery three years, including the year of grafting, that is, the feventh and eighth year. They do not like to plant large trees, and have a proverb,

> Se vuoi far torto al tuo vicino,
> Pianta il moro groffo e il fico piccolino.

As to plant fmall fig trees is as bad as large mulberries.

The holes are made in winter for receiving them where they are to remain; thefe are nine feet fquare and two feet deep, and have at the bottom a bed of broom, bark of trees, or other rubbifh; then the beft earth that can be had, and on that dung, one load of fixteen feet to four trees; this is covered with more good earth, and this levels the hole with the reft of the field; then prune the roots and plant, fetting a pole by the young tree to the north, and a fpur poft on the other fide, to guard it from the plough. Twine no ftraw the firft year, becaufe of the infect *forficula auricularia*, L.; but in November bind ftraw around them againft the cold, or, as ftraw is dear, the *poa rubra*, which abounds. Never, or very rarely, water. Much attention to remove all buds not tending in the right direction.

The fourth fpring after planting, their heads are pollarded, in March, leaving the fhoots nine inches long of new wood, and feeking to give them the hollow form of a cup, and that the new buds may afterwards divide into two or three branches, but not more. The next year, they begin to pluck the leaves. They are attentive in pruning, which is done every fecond year, to preferve as much as they can the cup form, as the leaves are gathered more eafily. Thus it is about fourteen years from the feed before the return begins.

After gathering the leaves, a man examines and cuts away all wounded fhoots; and if hail damage them, they are cut, let it be at what time of the year it may. Old trees are pruned after gathering, but young ones in March. In autumn, the leaves are never taken for cattle before the 11th of November, as the trees after that time do not fuffer. The third year after planting young trees, they fow about a hat full of lupines around the ftem, and when about ten inches high, dig them in for manure. The opinion here is, that the mulberry does very little harm to rye or wheat, except that when cut the falling of branches and trampling are fomewhat injurious. Maiz, millet, and panic are much more hurt. A tree, five years after tranfplanting, gives 10 lb. of leaves, each 28 oz. At ten years, 18 lb. At fifteen years, 25 lb. At twenty years, 30 lb. At thirty years, 50 lb. At fifty to feventy years, 70 lb. There are trees that give 80 lb. and even 100 lb. The price of leaves is commonly 4 liv. per 100 lb. (28 oz.). For one ounce of grain 500 lb. of leaves are neceffary, and yield 17 lb. of cocoons; but among the rifings in the mountain of Brianza, 25 lb. To make a pound of filk, of 12 oz.

5 lb.

5 lb. or 6 lb. of cocoons, of 28 oz. are required. Price of cocoons, in the low watered country, 2 liv. per lb. (28 oz.). At Mozzata, 2¼ liv. At Brianza, 3 liv. The grain is hatched in a chamber, heated by a chimney, and not a ſtove, to 17 deg. of Reaumur (70¼ Far.); but before being placed in this chamber, they are kept eight days under a bed, with a coverlet upon them, in boxes covered with paper pierced: and when hatched lay the young leaflets of the mulberries on the paper, to entice them out. The method of conducting the buſineſs here is the ſame as in France, the landlord furniſhes half the grain, and the peaſants half, and they divide the cocoons. Price of grain, 2 liv. the ounce. Mulberries, of all ages, are pollarded every ſecond year; a miſchievous cuſtom, which makes the trees decay, and leſſens their produce; it is never done in Dauphiné, where the culture is ſo well underſtood.

Milan.

Sig. Felice Soave made ſome intereſting trials on ſilk worms.

At Lambrate, near Milan, 2 oz. of ſeed in rooms, kept to the heat of 23 and 24 deg. Reaumur, hatched well, and kept healthy: the 28th of April, the ſeed was placed in the rooms, and hatched in the third, fourth, and fifth day: the 21ſt of May, the firſt cocoon ſeen, and at the end of the month all were at work. The product gathered the 3d of June; the product 92¼ lb. cocoons (28 oz.); eighty-four of them having been ſpun from four and five cocoons, gave 20¼ lb. (12 oz.) of ſilk, ſtronger and more ſhining than common: the conſumption of leaves, 1420 lb. of 28 oz. Wood uſed for fire, 2800 lb.; but the two rooms would have ſerved for 4 oz. of ſeed. In the common method, without ſtoves, the conſumption of leaves is 500 lb. for an ounce of ſeed, and the medium product is not above 15 lb. of cocoons; and by this new method, the conſumption of leaves has been 710 lb. each ounce, and the produce 46¼ lb. cocoons. Sixteen or ſeventeen cocoons weigh an ounce in the common method, but in this only thirteen or fourteen. The ſilk cannot commonly be ſpun from five or ſix cocoons; theſe were ſpun eaſily from four or five, and might have been done from three or four. To gain a pound of ſilk, in common, 5 lb. of cocoons are neceſſary; but here the ſame quantity has been gained from 4 lb.

Lodi to Codogno.

In this dead level and watered diſtrict, there are very few mulberries; none except near the villages; many of them, not all, appear unhealthy; perhaps by reaſon of their not exerting the ſame attention as in Dauphiné, where there is, in irrigated meadows, mounds made to keep the water from theſe trees.

Codogno

Codogno to Crema.

Mulberry trees here have large heads, as in Dauphiné, inftead of being pollarded inceffantly, as to the north of Milan.

There is an idea in the Milanefe, that filk was introduced by Ludovico il Moro. Francefco Muralto reports, " Prædia inculta infinita duobus fluminibus ad novalia (Ludovicus), reduxit infinitas plantas Moronum ad conficiendas fetas, feu fericas plantari fecerat et illius artis in ducatu, primus fuit auctor *." It is faid to have been introduced into Europe by fome Bafilian monks, from Sirinda, a city of Indoftan, to Conftantinople, under the Emperor Juftinian, in the year 550, by one account † ; and by another, in 525 ‡. In 1315, the manufactory of filk was brought in Florence to great perfection, by the refugees of Lucca ‖ ; but during the fifteenth century, no filk was made in Tufcany ; for all ufed in that period was foreign, filk worms being then unknown §. In 1474, they had eighty-four fhops that wrought gold and filver brocaded filks, which were exported to Lyons, Geneva, Spain, England, Germany, Turkey, Barbary, Afia, &c. ** Roger I. King of Sicily, about the year 1146 ††, having conquered fome Grecian cities, brought the filk weavers from thence into Palermo ; and the manufacture was foon imitated by the people of Lucca, who took a bale of filk for their arms, with the infcription—*Dei munus diligenter curandum pro vita multorum* ‡‡. In 1525, the filk manufacture at Milan employed twenty-five thoufand people ; and it feems to have augmented till 1558 ‖‖. In 1423, the Republic of Florence took off the duty of entrée upon mulberry leaves, and prohibited the exportation ; and fome communities of Tufcany have records concerning filk anterior to that period §§.

In almoft all the diftricts of the Milanefe, mulberry trees are met with, very old, with towering branches ; among which are thofe of Sforzefca, planted under Ludovico il Moro *†, who lived at the end of the fifteenth century.

VENETIAN STATE.—*Vaprio to Bergamo.*

There are many mulberries, mixed with the cultivation of corn and vines, in this tract of country.

---

* *Atti Societa Patriotica*, vol. ii. p. 220.   † *Saggio fopra la Replicata Raccolta della Foglia del Gelfo*, 1775, p. 1.   ‡ *Dizionario del Filugello*, 12mo, 1771, p. 43.   ‖ *Ragionamente fopra Tofcana*, p. 49.   § *Decima*, tom. ii. fez. 5. cap. 4.   ** *Benedetto Dei.*   †† *Giannone Storia Civ.* Y. ii. lib. 11. cap. 7. p. 219. *Giulini*, tom. v. p. 461.   ‡‡ *Saggio*, &c. p. 56.   ‖‖ *Opufc. Scelte*, vol. vii. p. 12. *Bartolazzi.*   §§ *Corfo di Agricoltura Pratica. Laftri*, tom. i. p. 285.   *† *Elementi d'Agricoltura. Mitterpacher*, tom. ii. p. 513.

Bergamo.

Bergamo.

Four ounces of feed are here given to each poor family, which yield four *pefi* of cocoons.

Brefcia.

One hundred *pefi* of leaves are neceſſary to 1 oz. of feed; and four *pefi* of *boz-zoli*, or cocoons, are the produce of 1 oz.; and the *pefo* of cocoons gives 28 to 30 oz. of ſilk. Cocoons ſell at 45 liv. per *pefo*. Leaves at 1 liv.; and ſilk at 22 liv. to 24 liv. per lb. The trees are lopped every three years; yet ſome are known that give 20 *pefi* of leaves. Small ones half a *pefo* and one *pefo*.

Verona.

One ounce of feed demands ſeventeen or eighteen *facchi* of leaves, each one hundred Veroneſe pounds (or 74 lb. Engliſh). Twelve ounces of feed are given to each family; and each ounce returns 60 lb. of cocoons, at 12 oz. the lb.; the price 24 ſ. the lb. To each ounce of feed ſixteen to eighteen *facchi* of leaves, each 100 lb. of 12 oz. are neceſſary. The 60 lb. cocoons, at 24 ſ. are 72 liv. or 36s.; which is the produce of eight trees, or 4s. 6d. a tree, the half of which is 2s. 3d. It muſt however be remarked, that theſe prices of cocoons vary ſo much, that no rule can be drawn from them: this price of 24 ſ. the pound is very low, and muſt ariſe from ſome local circumſtance. One ounce of ſilk to one pound of cocoons. They are here, as in the preceding diſtricts, in the cuſtom of finding the trees, and half the feed, and the peaſants the reſt; and they divide the cocoons. A tree of forty years old will give four *facchi*; and if a plantation confiſt of one thouſand trees, they will, one with another, give two *facchi*. They make ſilk in the Veroneſe to the amount of a million of pounds of 12 oz. There are, near the city, ſome trees in a rich arable field ſeventy years old, that yield from four to ſix ſacks of leaves each; this is about 10s. a tree, at the loweſt price of cocoons.

To Vicenza.

There are many rows of mulberries in the meadows, that are never dug around, and yet quite healthy, which proves that they might be ſcattered ſuc-ceſsfully about graſs lands, if any proof were wanting of ſo undoubted a fact. In the arable lands, the ſoil all gravel, they are planted twelve ridges apart. Some of the trees are old, that ſpread ſeven or eight yards acroſs.

Vicenza.

The produce of filk amounts here to about 6 liv. the *campo*, over a whole farm; this is about 3s. an acre. The *facco* of leaves weighs 75 lb. and forty *facchi* are neceffary for one ounce of feed; which gives 100 lb. of cocoons, and 10 lb. of filk. One hundred trees, of twenty years old, yield forty *facchi*; price 3 liv. to 11 liv.; commonly 3 liv. Price of cocoons 30 f. to 50 f. the pound.

I was glad here to meet with fome intelligence concerning the new filk worm, faid to have come from Perfia, which they have had here eight years, but is in the hands of fo few perfons, that I could get none of the feed; and I fufpect that it is loft; for, on repeated inquiries, I was referred to other parts of Italy. While they had this worm, they had four crops of cocoons a year:— 1. In the beginning of June. 2. The end of the fame month. 3. The middle of Auguft. 4. In October. This worm is effentially different from the common ones in the circumftance of hatching: no art will hatch the eggs of the common fort the firft year, that is the year of the flies dropping them; they can be hatched the year following only; but of this new fort, the eggs will hatch in fifteen days the fame year, if they be in the proper heat. But it is to be obferved, that they ufe this fort of worm not really to command feveral crops in the fame year, for mulberry trees will not bear it without deftruction, but merely as a fuccedaneum to the common fort of worms, if by frofts in the fpring they be loft for want of food; this new fort is in referve, to apply the leaves to profit once in the year. Theoretically the plan is good; but there muft have been fomething in practice againft it, or we may conjecture that after many years the ufe of them would have been generally introduced.

This will not be an improper place to introduce fome remarks on this fubject, by an author much efteemed, but quite unknown in England. It appears from the work of Count Carlo Bettoni, of Brefcia, that the difcovery of the new filk worm arofe from experiments made with a view of finding out a cure for the ficknefs of mulberry trees, called *moria*; this was fuppofed to arife from ftripping the leaves in the fpring annually; it was thought, that if fome means could be difcovered of poftponing the gathering much later in the year, it would greatly favour the vegetation and health of the trees; an effect that could only take place by means of a worm that would hatch much later than the common one. In 1765, a fecond hatching of the eggs of the common worm is faid, by the fame author, to have been made; part of which were fed with the fecond growth of leaves, and part with the leaves of trees that had not been gathered in the fpring. Thofe fed with the old leaves gave a greater number of cocoons, and of a better quality than the others. Thefe experiments were repeated by many perfons; and it was found, that in the heats of July

and

and Auguſt the worms would not do well; but in September much better, and
that the trees did not ſuffer from having their leaves gathered in September.
The ſame author ſays, that the new worms (which he calls *foreſtieri*) will
hatch three times a year, and that no art will prevent it; no cellars, no cold
will keep them from it, though it may retard them ſome time, as he tried in
an ice-houſe, by which means he kept them inert till Auguſt. But, on the
contrary, the common ſort cannot in general be hatched a ſecond time the ſame
year, even with any heat that can be given; yet he admits, that they were
hatched by certain perſons in 1765. The new ones ſleep four times, like the
common ones, but begin to ſpin their cocoons five or ſix days ſooner: they eat
leſs in quantity, but give leſs ſilk; and as this defeἀ is balanced by the advantage in food, they ought not, ſays the Count, to be proſcribed. Their
cocoons are ſmall, but the conſiſtency is good and fine; and their ſilk is fine
and ſofter than the common: he ſold it for 4 liv. or 5 liv. a pound more than
common ſilk. There is, however, an evil attends them, which is the uncertainty of their hatching the ſecond and third time; ſometimes all the feed will
hatch, but at others only a part; even only the ſeventh and tenth of the quantity: but the firſt hatching is regular, like that of the common worms. A
circumſtance in the courſe of his trials deſerves noting, that he found the worms
of both the old and new ſorts would drink water when offered to them, and
that the cocoons were the larger for their having had the water.

They have had a ſort in Tuſcany that hatches twice a year; and the Count
writing thither for information concerning them, found that their ſilk was
coarſer than the common, and of leſs value; and he judges them to be a different kind from his own, which hatches three times. The Count concludes
nothing determinate concerning them; but reſolves to continue his numerous
experiments and obſervations. As there may be perſons who think, as I did at
firſt, when I heard of this ſort of worm, that if any ſucceed in England it
would probably be this; it is proper to obſerve, that Count Bettoni had nothing in view but the diſeaſes of the mulberry trees, and does not ſeem to have
had at all in contemplation the evils attending late froſts, depriving the worms
of their uſual food; and if the common ſort may be retarded in hatching
(which he ſhews) till Auguſt, equally with the new ſort, there does not ſeem
to be any extraordinary advantage in this ſort, for a northerly climate, more
than in the others. The Count's book * was printed at Venice in 1778.

Sig. Pieropan has made an obſervation, which deſerves noting; mulberries,
and likewiſe other trees, are generally found to ſucceed much better when
grafted a little before ſun-ſet than at any other time: the reaſon he attributes

---

* *Progetto per preſervare i Gelſi*, &c. Co. *Carlo Bettoni.* 8vo. Various paſſages.

to the heat of the earth after fun-fet; he kept a journal fome years, of the comparative heat of the atmofphere and the earth, at the depths of four, twelve, and twenty-four inches; and has found, that immediately after the fetting of the fun the mercury in thofe thermometers under ground had always rifen fome degrees gradually till the rifing of the fun, when it as regularly falls.

The following is the Account of the Profit and Lofs of Six Ounces of Seed, for Three Years, at Vicenza, by Sig. Carlo Modena.

1778.

	liv.	f.	den.
Expences.			
Semenza—feed, 6 oz.	36	0	0
Foglia—leaves, 26,475 lb.	1545	4	0
Spefa—gathering leaves and attendance,	868	16	0
Filare—fpinning 992 lb. cocoons, which give 159 lb. 5 oz. filk,	557	18	0
	3007	18	0
Produce.			
159 lb. 5 oz. of filk,	4144	15	0
Refufe ditto, 41 lb.	102	10	0
Seed, 55 oz.	330	0	0
	4577	5	0
Expence,	3007	18	0
Profit,	1569	7	0

1779.

	liv.	f.	den.
Expences.			
Seed, fix ounces, half given to the peafants, three ounces,	18	0	0
Leaves, 15,607 lb.	753	9	0
Spinning—the produce 446 lb. cocoons, half of which, 223 lb. to the proprietor, 29 lb. of filk,	101	10	0
	872	19	0
Produce.			
29 lb. of filk,	754	0	0
Refufe ditto,	21	2	0
	775	2	0
Lofs,	97	17	0

1780.

1780.—Upon his own account.

Expences.

	liv.	ſ.	den.
Seed, 6 oz.	36	0	0
Leaves, 370 ſacks,	957	13	0
Gathering and attendance,	1303	12	0
Spinning 910 lb. of cocoons,	265	0	0
Reducing 118 lb. 6 oz. of ſilk into organzine,	451	10	0
	3013	15	0

Produce.

	liv.	ſ.	den.
Refuſe ſilk,	116	4	0
118 lb. 6 oz. of organzine,	4325	5	0
Leaves ſold,	28	0	0
Silk kept for own uſe, 2 lb. 3 oz.	49	10	0
	4518	19	0
Expences,	3013	15	0
Profit,	1505	4	0

This year the profit would have been much greater; but through the negligence of the women in the night, not attending to the degrees of heat (from 25 to 27 deg. Reaumur), many were ſuffocated *.

To Padua.

One ounce of feed gives 60 lb. of *galetta* (cocoons), and 8 lb. to 10 lb. of *galetta* 1 lb. of ſilk: the ounce of feed requires ſixteen **ſacks of leaves,** of four **peſi,** each 25 lb.; and twelve ſmall trees yield one ſack, but one great tree has been known to yield ſix ſacks. Price of gathering, 20ſ. the ſack. **Expence of** making 60 lb. of ſilk, 250 liv. Spinning, 30ſ. the pound. Cocoons ſell at 30ſ to 36ſ. Silk this year, 25 liv. the pound, *fotile.*

Padua.

One ounce of feed gives in common 30 lb. of cocoons, and 8 lb. of cocoons 1 lb. of ſilk: twenty ſacks, of 80 lb. of leaves, are neceſſary to feed the worms of an ounce of feed. Price of gathering, 20ſ. the ſack. The greateſt trees give ten ſacks of leaves each; a tree of twenty years four or five ſacks. It is not

* *Opuſcoli Scelti,* tom. iii. p. 33.

the

the general cuftom to divide this bufinefs with the peafants. The common fort of filk worm is hatched about the 25th of April; the others the middle of June; but filk demands a more expenfive operation in the latter feafon.

Venice.

There are three forts of filk worms:—1. The common one, which cafts its epiderm, or fleep as it is called, four times. 2. A fort known at Verona, that cafts only three times; the cocoons fmaller than thofe of the other fort. 3. The new fort mentioned by Count Carlo Bettoni, the feed of which hatch two or three times a year; but the others only once. The feed of the two firft forts cannot be hatched the fame year it is dropped; but that of the third will hatch of itfelf, if it be not carefully kept in a cool place.

Bologna.

One hundred pounds of cocoons are made from 1 oz. of feed, and yield 7¼ lb. to 8¼ lb. of filk, of 12 oz. Price of cocoons, 20 to 25 *baiocca.* Silk, 34 *pauls,* at 6d. the pound.

Tuscany.—*Florence.*

Making inquiries here concerning the new fort of filk worm, I found that they were not, as I had been before told, a new difcovery in Italy, but known long ago; and, what is remarkable, is prohibited by law, in order to preferve the mulberry trees from being ftripped more than once. The filk made from them is not more than half as good as the common, and very inferior in quantity alfo. They affert here, that by means of heat they can hatch the eggs of the common fort when they pleafe, but not for any ufe, as they die directly; which is not the cafe with the new fpecies, or that as it is called *di trè volte.*

Their contrivance for winding filk is very convenient, and well adapted to fave labour; one man turns, for a whole row of coppers, the fires for thofe which are without the wall; and the clofets with fmall boilers of water, for killing the animal in its cocoon by fteam, are equally well adapted.

At Martelli, near Florence, on a farm of 190 *fiori* (34 acres) there are forty or fifty mulberries, enough for 1 oz. of grain, which gives 50 lb. or 60 lb. of cocoons, and 6 lb. or 7 lb. of filk. Price of cocoons this year, 2 *pauls* the pound; laft year 2¼; and in 1787 it was 3 *pauls.* In the culture of the trees they do not practife fuch attentions as the French in Dauphiné; they never dig about them, except when young; never wafh the ftems; they prune the trees when neceffary, but not by any rule of years. The beft fort is the wild mulberry, but it yields the leaft quantity; next, the white fruit.

In

In 1782, Sig. Don Gio. Agemi di Giun, prelate of the Greek Catholic church, on Mount Libanus, exhibited to the academicians Georgofili of Florence, the 4th of December, fome filk worms, in number thirty-eight, part of which had already made their cocoons, and part ready to make them, as accuftomed to do in his own country, with the leaves of the wild mulberry. The feed was hatched in October; the worms fed with leaves, procured from warm gardens; cocoons were made in November; mallow leaves were ufed alfo *.

MODENA.

The export of filk from the city 46,000 lb. at 38 liv. (4d. each); from the whole territory, 60,000 *zecchini.*

PIEDMONT.—*Pavefe.*

Immediately on entering the dominions of the King of Sardinia, within two miles of St. Giovanne, mulberries are found regularly every where, and continue to Turin. Seven-eighths of them are about twenty or twenty-five years old ; fome however are amongft the largeft I have feen.

LOMBARDY POPLARS.

They are very fcarce throughout Lombardy ; there is a fcattering between Modena and Reggio ; and Count Tocoli, five or fix miles from Parma, planted feveral thoufands along a canal, on the birth of his daughter, for her portion ; but there is not, in any part of Lombardy, any law which in fuch cafes fecures the property of the trees thus planted, to the child they are intended for ; it is merely private confidence.

CLOVER.

PIEDMONT.—*Chentale.*

Such is the power of climate united with the advantages of irrigation, that clover is here mown for hay once after harvefting the corn it grew with ; the hay is not of the beft quality, but ufeful.

MILANESE.—*Milan to Pavia.*

On the rich dairy farms, the cows are fed much on clover. The red fort is fown, which wearing out, white clover comes fo regularly, that the country people think the one fort degenerates into the other.

* *Corfo,* vol. iii. p. 123.

Vicenza.

They fow 12 lb. of feed per *campo* with wheat; it is cut twice the firft year, yielding 1 *carro* each cut; the fecond year it is mown thrice: price 44 liv. the *carro*, which is 100 *pefi*, of 25 lb.

Padua.

Sow 12 lb. *groffo* per *campo* (14 lb. or 15 lb. per Englifh acre) it gives three *carri*, each 1000 lb. at three cuts (1½ ton the acre Englifh;) but they have crops that go much beyond this.

FIGS.

PIEDMONT.—*Nice to Coni.*

On this range of the Alps, there are, in favourable fituations, a great quantity of fig trees; and the extreme cheapnefs of the fruit muft be of no trivial importance in fupporting the people, not only while ripe but dried.

HEMP AND FLAX.

PIEDMONT.—*Chentale.*

A *giornata* (to an acre as 7440 to 7929) produces 200 lb. for the proprietor, and as much for the farmer; and fome crops rife to 650 lb. They gather the female hemp from the 25th of July to the 4th of Auguft: the male the beginning of September. Of fome pieces I was informed that a produce not uncommon was 30 *rubbii* of female, and 17 of male, worth 4½ liv. to 5 liv. the *rubbio*, both of the fame price; and alfo 25 to 30 *mine* of feed, if well cultivated; but if not, 12 to 15. The *mine* 35 lb. and the price 4½ liv. to 5 liv. the *mine*. The common calculation is, that a *giornata* is worth 150 liv. to 200 liv. which may be called 10 l. per Englifh acre. Their contrivance for fteeping is very fimple and effectual: there are many fquare and oblong pits with pofts in them, with open mortifes for fixing poles to keep down the hemp, which is vaftly preferable to our fods and ftones.

Turin.

They fow 3 *mine* (45 lb. of wheat), and get 30 *rubbii*, at 4 liv. 10 f. to 5 liv. the *rubbio* grofs; but ready for fpinning 12 liv. 10 f. the fineft; the fecond quality is 7 liv. 10 f.; and the third 5 liv.; befides 3 *mine* of feed, at 2 liv. each. This product is above 8 l. the Englifh acre.

MILANESE.

MILANESE.—*Mozzata.*

Winter flax is here efteemed the properer for land that is not watered; they fow it the middle of September; they have had it in this country two years only, and call it *lino ravagno.* It gives a coarfer thread than fpring flax, but a greater quantity, and much more feed. The price of the oil 22 *f.* the pound, of 28 oz.; of the flax, ready for fpinning, 25 *f.* or 26 *f.*; of the thread, 4 liv. and 4¼ liv. A *quartaro* of feed is neceffary for a *pertica,* for which it returns eight times the quantity of feed, and 20 lb. of flax ready for fpinning, at 25 *f.* the pound.

Codogno.

When they break up their clover lands they fow flax on one ploughing, which is worth rent 20 liv. and crop 40 liv. per *pertica,* being 24 lb. of 28 oz. and feed three times more than fown. Much winter flax now green.

VENETIAN STATE.—*Bergamo.*

Winter flax green in October.

ECCLESIASTICAL STATE.—*Bologna.*

The territory of Bologna produces from 12 to 14,000,000 lb. of hemp. They manure for it highly with dung, feathers, the horns of animals, and filk worms refufe. The beft hemp-land is always dug; the difference between digging and ploughing is found to be very great. If ploughed, three earths are given; when the fpade is ufed, the land is firft ploughed and then dug. For this crop five or fix yards are left *unfown* under the *rows of trees.* The foil agrees fo well with this plant, that the crop rifes ten feet high; they gather it all at once, leaving only a few ftands for feed. It is watered in ftagnant pools. A good product is from 100 lb. to 200 lb. of 12 oz. per *tornatura,* of half an acre. The price of the beft is from 20 liv. to 27 liv. the 100 lb. At prefent 25 liv. (the Englifh pound one-fifth larger than the Bolognefe, and the livre of the Pope's dominions is ten to the *zecchin,* of 9s. 6d.) ready for combing. When ready for fpinning, the price of the beft is 12 *f.* the pound; and they pay for fpinning fuch 6 *f.* to 15 *f.* the pound. Near the city, I viewed a field famous for yielding hemp: no trees are planted acrofs it, which is fo common in the country in general; a fure proof of the pernicious tendency of that fyftem; fince in very valuable fields thefe people themfelves reject the method. Little or no hemp on the hills near Bologna, but fome autumnal flax for family ufe.

MAIZ.

PIEDMONT.—*Chentale.*

Maiz produces here 25 to 30 *mine*, which holds 47 lb. of wheat, and the price 2 liv. each. It is fown on three feet ridges.

Savigliano.

Maiz, in a good year, will yield three hundred fold, but in a dry one fome-times fcarcely any thing.

Turin.

Made every where the fallow, which prepares for wheat.

Chivafco to Verceil.

A great deal of maiz through all this country, and all foul with grafs and weeds, even to the height of two or three feet.

MILANESE.—*Milan.*

They fow much maiz, of the fort called *quarantino*, from its ripening in forty days (which however it does not). They fow it the middle of July, after wheat, which they cut the firft week of that month. If the common maiz were fown at this time, they affert that it would yield no ripe feed: this is a very cu-rious circumftance. The culture has been often recommended to England; if ever any thing were done, it muft affuredly be with this fort; but even with this I fhould put no faith in the power of an Englifh climate.

Mozzata.

They cultivate three forts :—1. *Formentone maggengo*, fown the beginning of May, and reaped in October. 2. *Formentone agoftano o formentone de ravettone*, becaufe fown after taking off the rave or colefeed for oil, the end of May, and harvefted the end of September. 3. *Formentone quarantino*, fown after wheat or rye, and cut the end of October.

Venice.

This plant was cultivated in the Polefine de Rovigo, towards 1560; and fpread through Lombardy the beginning of the 17th century *.

* *Agft. Gallo.* Notes, p. 534.

OLIVES.

OLIVES.

On the banks of the Lago di Guarda are the only olives I have seen since I left the country of Nice; but the number is not considerable, and most of them are dead, or nearly so, by the frost of last winter, which made such destruction likewise in France.

Tuscany.

Near Florence, at Martelli, the product of a farm of 190 *stiori* was as follows: in 1786, thirty *barrils*. In 1787, it was no more than three. In 1788, it yielded eight. In 1789, it was twenty-five; but on an average ten; for which produce there are two hundred trees. They are dunged every two or three years, and dug about once in three years. They are reckoned to lessen the product of corn one-fifth; this is a notion of the country, but I believe very far from accurate. The average price of oil is 5 *scudi* per *barril*, of 150 lb. (1l. 8s. 4d.); ten *barrils* amount to 14l. 3s. 4d.; and as there are about thirty-four acres in 190 *stiori*, the product of oil is 8s. to 9s. per acre: a sum that yields no very favourable impression of the culture:—and, divided amongst two hundred trees, it does not amount to 1s. 6d. a tree.

The plain of Florence is all lined into rows of these trees, with vines between and upon them; in some places, an espalier of vines between the rows of olives; and when all are well cultivated, the olives yield the greatest produce, next the wine, and then the corn. I viewed, near Florence, some fields, in which I found twenty olives on a *stiora* of land, but this is not common: and on a very bad stoney soil, though in the plain, I found that it took twenty trees, of twenty-five years growth, to yield a *barril* of oil. But in a fine soil, and with very old trees, a *barril* a tree has been known. Vines are suffered here also to run up the trees, but they reckon it a bad custom. The price of oil is more than doubled in forty years. Very few olives were lost by the last hard frost, but great numbers by that of 1709. Landlord's half produce, of some fields I viewed—oil, 10 *pauls*; grain, 7; wine, 1; in all, 18 *pauls* per *stiora* (2l. 5s. per English acre.)

This year, 1789, the Grand Duke, for the first time, has given a gold medal, of the value of 25 *zecchini*, for the greatest number of olives planted; no claimant to be admitted for less than five thousand: in consequence of this premium, above forty thousand trees have been planted. It will be continued annually.

H h 2

There

There is, in the Maremma, some remarkable inſtances of the vaſt age to which olives will attain: Sig. Zucchino, profeſſor of agriculture at Florence, informed me, that, upon examining the hills in the middle of that tract, he found in the midſt of woods, and almoſt over-run with rubbiſh, olives of ſo immenſe an age and magnitude, that he conjectures them to have been planted by the ancient Hetruſcans, before the Romans were in poſſeſſion of the country; there muſt, of courſe, be much uncertainty in any conjectures of this kind; but a great antiquity of theſe trees is undoubted.

R I C E.

PIEDMONT.—*Ciglione to Verceil.*

They are now threſhing rice with horſes, as wheat in Languedoc;—threſh as much in the night as in the day:—meet alſo gleaners going home loaded with it. About five miles before Verceil, the rice-grounds are in great quantities: their culture, however, of this crop ſeems to want explanations. Here is, for inſtance, a great field, which was under rice laſt year, now left to weeds, with hogs feeding.—Why not ſown with clover among or after the rice? They never plough but once for rice. The peaſants are unhealthy from the culture; yet their pay not more than 24ſ. to 30ſ a day. The ſoil of the rice-grounds here, is that of a fine loamy turnip ſand; there is a mound raiſed around them, for the convenience of flooding at will.

Vercelli.

Rice is here reckoned the moſt profitable of all the cultivation of Piedmont; for it yields a greater value than wheat, and at a leſs expence. It demands only one ploughing, inſtead of ſeveral. Seed only 4 *mine,* at 1 liv. Watering, at 2 liv. 5ſ. Cutting, the end of July, 10ſ. The product is 60 *mine* rough, or 21 white; the latter at 4 liv. or 84 liv.; and 4 *mine* of a ſort of bran, at 15ſ. or 3 liv.; in all 87 liv. (ſomething under 5l. an acre). It is ſown three years in ſucceſſion; and the fourth a fallow; during which the land is dunged. The price of theſe lands, 500 liv. or 600 liv. the *giornata.* As rice can be ſown only on land that admits watering at pleaſure, I do not fully comprehend this account. Why, for inſtance, is not the land laid down for meadow, which evidently pays much better; and ſells at a higher price? I ſuppoſe rice is ready money on demand, and meadows muſt be converted to caſh circuitouſly. Good wheat land ſells at 800 liv.

To

To Novara.

Paſſing the Seſia, which exhibits a bed of five times as much gravel as water, in three or four miles the quantity of rice is conſiderable : the ſtubble is green, and in wet mud ; the ſheaves thin. It extends on both ſides the road for ſome diſtance ; the whole incloſed by ditches, and rows of willow poplar pollards, as bad to the eye, as it can be to the health. One or two fields are not yet cut ; it looks like a good crop of barley, being bearded. After Novara, ſee no more of it.

Milanese.—*Milan to Pavia.*

The rice-grounds receive but one ploughing, which is given in the middle of March, and the ſeed ſown at the end of the ſame month, in water to the ſeedſman's knees, which is left on the ground till the beginning of June, when the crop is weeded by hand, by women half naked, with their petticoats tucked to their waiſts wading in the water ; and they make ſo droll a figure, that parties in pleaſantry, at that ſeaſon, view the rice-grounds. When the weeding is finiſhed, the water is drawn off for eight days ; and it is again drawn off when the ear begins to form, till formed ; after which, it is let in again till the rice is nearly ripe, which is about the end of Auguſt, when it is reaped, or in the beginning of September ; and by the end of that month, all is finiſhed. Quantity of ſeed, the eighth of a *moggio* per *pertica*, produce 25 to 30 *moggio* rough, or 11¼ or 12 white. Price 37¼ liv. the *moggio*, (17l. 8s. per Engliſh acre), which produce is ſo large, that this minute I ſuſpect the higheſt crop gained, and not an average one. The *moggio* of rice weighs 160 lb. of 28 ounces. The ſtraw is of uſe only for littering cows ; and the chaff, like that of all other grain, from a notion of its being unwholeſome, is thrown on to the dunghill. They ſow rice three years in ſucceſſion, and then a courſe of ſomething elſe. See *Courſes of Crops.* The rice is rendered merchantable by being pounded in a mill by ſtampers, turned by a water-wheel.

In the great road there is a ſtone, at five miles from Milan, nearer than which it is prohibited to ſow rice.

State of Venice.—*Verona.*

Of the produce of the rice-grounds in the Veroneſe, they reckon one-third for expences, one-third for water, and one-third profit.

Parma.

Count Schaffienatti has ſown rice, at Vicomero, eighteen years in ſucceſſion, on the ſame land, without any reſt or manure. Sow on 54 *biolcchi* 90 *ſtaji*;

and

and the produce 18 for 1. He digs the ground, as it is too marſhy to plough it well; this coſts 3000 liv. (each 2½d.) The ſtraw ſells at 80 liv. the load, of 80 *peſi*, of 25 lb. (¼ lb. Engliſh). Oxen alſo eat it. Rice is reckoned to yield four times over more nett profit than any other huſbandry; more even than watered meadows.

VINES.

PIEDMONT.—*Antibes to Nice.*

A ſingular cultivation of this plant ſurrounding very ſmall pieces from ſix to twenty perches, trained up willow trees; and the ſcraps of land within them cultivated. What a ſun muſt ſhine in a country where thick incloſures are counted by perches and not by acres.

Chentale to Racconis.

In rows at twelve to twenty feet, and appear like thoſe of hops in Kent, ſupported on willow poles, twelve feet high, ſome of which take root, but are afterwards pulled up.

Chivaſco.

Vines faſtened from mulberry to mulberry, but not running up theſe trees, only up willows, &c. that are between them.

MILANESE.—*Mozzata.*

Half this country is lined with vines, and it is reckoned that they will damage to the amount of one-tenth of the produce: each *pertica* of vines, in a common year, will give 50 lb. of grapes, worth 6 liv. the 100 lb. of 28 oz. hail allowed for; and of this half is the peaſants ſhare, for the expence of culture. At Leinate, I viewed ſome wine preſſes, which are enormous machines, the beam of one is forty-five feet long and four feet ſquare; and at the end, where the ſcrew is, a ſtone of vaſt weight, for which there is a paved hole in the pavement, that it may keep ſuſpended; the cuves caſks, and all the apparatus great: the quantity of vines 1000 *pertica*. The ſeeds of the preſſed grapes are kept till dry, and then preſſed for oil; the ſeed of the grapes that yielded 70 *brenta* of wine will give 10 lb. of oil: it is uſed for lamps. The poor people, who bring their grapes to be preſſed, pay one-twelfth of the wine. Price at preſent, 6 liv. the *brenta*; but only 3 liv for what is laſt preſſed. The firſt flow is trod out by men's feet. Common price, 10 liv. or 12 liv. the *brenta*.

VENETIAN

Venetian State.—*Bergamo*.

From entering the Venetian territory, near Vaprio, the country is almost all planted in lines of vines, and the spaces between tilled for corn.

To Brescia.

This country, inclosed with hedges, besides which it is lined in stripes of vines, that are trained to low ash and maple trees, with mulberries at the end of every row; but the vines are not trained up these trees, though fastened to their trunks.

Vicenza.

The country, for 32 miles from Verona to Vicenza, except the watered parts, which are not a tenth of the whole, is lined into rows of pollards, each with three or four spreading branches, and at the foot of each two vines, many of them very old, with stems as thick as the calf of a man's leg; and many of the elms, maples, &c. are also old. They stand about a rod asunder, and the rows from twenty-five to thirty yards; and around the whole mulberries. Where the vintage is not finished, the vines hang in festoons from tree to tree, garnished with an astonishing quantity of bunches of grapes.

Vines, near Vicenza, produce 2 *mastati*, each of 240 bottles, per *campo*; the price 16 liv. the *mastato*; the *campo* here is larger than at Verona, amounting to near an English acre; this is about 17s. an acre; a produce very easily lost, in the damage done to the corn.

Padua.

The same husbandry, of pollards and vines, continues hither. They reckon that vines pay better than mulberries; but in the districts of Verona and Vicenza mulberries are more advantageous than vines. This does not correspond with soil, for that of Padua is deeper and richer, for the most part, than the other, and therefore less adapted to vines. In conversation with Abbate Fortis, on the wine of the Paduan, &c. being so bad, he says, it is owing merely to bad management in making. They tread the grapes with their feet; put the juice in a great cuve; and will keep it fermenting there even so long as fifteen days, adding every day more and more, till the strength is exhausted, and the wine spoiled; no cleanliness, in any part of the operation, nor the least attention in the gathering, or in the choice of the grapes. He further added, that Sig. Modena, a Vicentino cultivator at Vancimuglio, adjoining the rice-grounds, and consequently as little adapted as possible to vineyards, provided the soil and

trees

trees were the caufe of bad wines, makes that which is excellent, and which fell fo high as 30 *f.* French per bottle : that Sig. Marzari, and Sig. il Conte di Porto, in the high Vicentino, with many others, as well as he himfelf, Abbate Fortis, has done the fame with raifins from vines that run up the higheft trees, fuch wine as fells from 20 *f.* to 35 *f.* French the bottle : and that fome of thefe wines are fo good, that the Venetian ambaffadors, at different courts, ufe them inftead of Madeira, &c. ; and the wines of Friuli as thofe of Hungary, which they refemble; yet thefe vines are all on trees. He alfo obferved, that it has been found, by experiment, that vines in thefe rich lands, trained near the ground, as in France, have yielded raifins and wine good for nothing; that the grapes even rot; that the land is too rich for the vines to have all the nourifhment, unrivalled by the roots of the trees. It is very much to be queftioned, if the experiments here alluded to, have been made with due attention: if the land is too rich for vines, plant them upon foils that are proper; and keep thefe low diftricts for grafs and corn; but that vines, hidden from the fun amongft the branches of trees, can ripen properly to give a well-concocted juice, appears very dubious; and the fact of all the wine, commonly met with in this country, being bad, feems to confirm the reafoning.

Ecclesiastical State.—*Bologna.*

All this country, where I have viewed it, is lined into rows of trees for vines, ten or twelve yards afunder, on the mountain, but more in the plain. But Sig. Bignami has his vineyards planted with *echalats* (poles), in the French way, about four or five feet fquare, and he finds that thefe always give better wine than the vines trained to trees; and the land by *tornatura* gives a great deal more wine; though each vine feparately on trees, gives more than each in this method. The object, in this inftance, was the goodnefs of wine; Sig. Bignami thinks the common method moft profitable. The vines are now (November) trained and pruned, and turned down five or fix feet and tied; if allowed to mount, they yield much fewer grapes. Vines on the mountains yield thrice the value of the wheat; and the double of all other productions, wheat included.

Tuscany.—*Bologna to Florence.*

Vines in this route are planted differently from any I have yet feen. Some are in efpaliers, drawn thinly acrofs the fields; others are trained to fmall pofts, through which, at top, are two or three fticks fixed to hold them up; others are in fquares of five or fix feet, and fix or feven high, without fuch pofts; but all in the arable fields are, generally fpeaking, in lines.

Florence.

Florence.

I here met with a cafe abfolutely in point, to prove how mifchievous trees are to corn, even in this hot climate.—A field under olives, which yielded in corn 6½ for 1 fown, was grubbed, after which the common produce was 14 for 1. Now, as the olive is by no means one of the worft trees for corn, this fhews the great lofs that accrues from the practices I have noted throughout Lombardy. Yet, in common converfation here, as elfewhere, they tell you the injury is fmall, except from walnuts, which do more mifchief than any other.

Modena.

It appears to be a fingular circumftance, that in the parts of this territory near the hills, corn pays better than wine; but in the plain, wine better than corn: I fufpect that fome mifmanagement occafions this apparent contradiction. From Modena to Reggio the country is planted in rows, as in the Venetian State, &c. and the trees that fupport the vines being large, the whole has the appearance of a foreft.

Parma

From Reggio to Parma, the fame fyftem holds, but executed in an inferior manner. And from Parma to Vicomero, the trees that fupport the vines are pollards, with old heads, like many we have in England; contrary to the prac-tice of the Venetian State, where they are kept young. To Firenzuolo, the vines are all buried in like manner; fome here are planted for props, and the poles which ferve as fuch are fet in rows: in both methods the fhoots are equally buried. A fcattering of golden willow in the rows, I fuppofe for attaching the vines to the props. From Borgo St. Domino to Firenzuola, there is a decline both of vines and wood; the country is not as hitherto, regularly lined, and many large fields are without any; this is the more to be remarked, as here begin fome inequalities of country, the gentle ramifications of the Appenines. To Caftel Giovanne, moft of the fields have no vines, only a fcattering; fhoots buried as before; but the inclofures have many pollards in the hedges, like the woodlands of Suffolk. From Piacenza, after paffing the Trebbia, the rows of vines are thirty to forty yards afunder, with heaps of props, ten feet long, fet like hop-poles; very few or no vines trained to trees.

Piedmont.—*Pavefe*[*].

The country is all the way hill and dale; the flat of Lombardy finifhing with the Dutchy of Piacenza. It is about half inclofed, and half with rows of

---

[*] The country ceded by Auftria to Sardinia, part of the diftrict of Pavia.

vines. There are also vineyards planted in a new method; a single row of vines, with a double row of poles, with others flat, so as to occupy four ridges, and then four to ten of corn. Some vine shoots buried for a few miles, but afterwards none. Near Stradella, the props appear like a wood of poles.

Savoy.

The vineyards of Montmelian yield 1¼ *tonneau* per *journal*, which sell at 4¼ louis the *tonneau:* all, not in the hands of peasant proprietors, is at half produce.

SECT. IV.——OF IMPLEMENTS AND TILLAGE.

Coni.

The ploughs have a single handle, twelve or thirteen feet long, which throws the ploughman to such a distance behind, that his goad is fixed in a long light pole. The oxen are yoked in the same manner as ours; but the bow is of iron under the neck, and the pressure is received by two bits of wood. Some ploughs drawn by a yoke, others by two yokes of oxen.

Chentale.

The names which are given to the parts of a plough here are,—long handle, of fourteen feet, *stiva*; beam, *bura*; head, *cannonl'a*; coulter rivetted to the share, *cultor*; share, *massa*; ground-rest, on which the share sheathes, seven feet long, *dentale*; earth-board, five feet long, *oralia.*

The Count de Bonaventa, in explaining to me their tillage, shewed the criterion, as old as Columella, of good ploughing, by thrusting his cane across the ridges, to see if rest-baulked. They plough mostly on the three feet ridge, forming and reversing at one bout; *i. e.* two furrows; the work strait. Use no reins, and have no driver, though the ploughman is above twenty feet from the oxen. Two small beasts cut a good furrow on the top of the old ridge, seven inches deep; and these ploughs, long as they are in the ground, certainly do not draw heavily.

The oxen, whether at plough or in the waggons, do not draw, as I conceived at first sight, by the shoulder, but in a method I never saw before, nor read of; they draw by pressing the point of the withers against the yoke, and not at all by the bows; and in examining them, the master and man contended that the strength of an ox lies there, and not in his shoulders, nor in his head,

or

or roots of the horns. It appears a ſtrange practice; but it is yet ſtranger, that yoke a beaſt how you will, he does his work, and apparently without diſtreſs.

Chentale to Racconis.

They have here a moſt ſingular cuſtom, which is that of ſhovelling all the moveable ſoil of a field, into heaps of a large load, earth, ſtubble, and weeds; they ſay, *per ingraſſare la terra*.

To Turin.

The lands ſown with wheat on three feet ridges, is worked fine with a ma-chine of wood, at the end of a handle, formed nearly like a hoe. Wherever one ſees theſe operoſe niceties, we may conclude the farms are very ſmall.

Turin.

Plough with a pair of oxen, no reins, no driver; go to work at five in the morning, and hold it till night, except 1½ hour at dinner; that is twelve hours work, and do a *giornata* a day, ſomething under an acre, one bout to a three feet ridge, reverſing.

Vercelli.

Price of a ploughing, 3½ liv. per *giornata*, this is about 3s. 4d. per Engliſh acre.

MILANESE.—*Milan to Pavia.*

Hire of a ploughman and pair of oxen, 4 liv. a day; but if no food for the oxen, 6 liv. The ploughs here vary from thoſe of Piedmont. The handles are not above half as long, and are called *ſtiva*; the beam, *buretto*; the coul-ter, *coltura*; the ſhare, *maſſa*; the earth-board, *orechio*; the land-board, *orechini*. There is a moſt groſs and abſurd error in all the ploughs I ſaw, which is the poſition of the coulter, 18 or 20 degrees too much *to the land*; every one who is acquainted with the right ſtructure of a plough, know that it ſhould juſt clear the ſhare; this great variation from the right line, muſt add greatly to the draft; and, in difficult land, fatigue the cattle.

Mezzata.

A light poor plough, the ſhare with a double fin, but ſo narrow as to cut only four inches of the furrow; the heel of the plough is nine or ten inches wide; the work it performs is mere ſcratching; and the land they were ſowing

with

with wheat, a bed of *triticum repens* and *agrostis stolonifera*. They have here a great opinion of digging; and a proverb, which says, *La vanga ha la punta d'oro*—The spade has the point of gold.

Codogno.

Here, as near Milan, the coulters are many degrees out of the line of the share; and the shares not more than four inches wide. Shocking!

Codogno to Crema.

The harrows in this country have handles to them of wood; I am amazed this practice is not universal; yet I never saw it before, except on my own farm.

Venetian State.—*Bergamo.*

In passing from Vaprio to this place, they are ploughing with a pair of oxen a-breast, and two horses before them in a line; wheel-ploughs; share five inches wide, and with a double fin. Near the town of Bergamo, I saw them ploughing a maiz stubble for wheat, as full of grass almost as a meadow: a lad drives, and another stout one attends to clear the coulter from grass, &c.; the plough low on the carriage, with wheels; the breast all iron, and not ill formed; the fin of the share double, and about eight inches wide; the coulter nearly in the same direction as the share, but clearing four inches to the land side; two short handles. The furrow full nine inches deep; but crooked, irregular, and bad work. Notwithstanding this depth, they are great friends to the spade. From four to six for one, are common crops with the plough, but twelve to fourteen for one, are gained by the spade. There must be an inaccuracy in this; the difference cannot be owing merely to digging. We may be certain, that the husbandry, in other respects, must be much better.

Vicenza.

They here plough with four oxen in harness; many of them are of an iron-grey colour, with upright thick ugly horns. Some, however, are fine large beasts. Their plough is a strange tool; it is two feet four inches of Vicenza wide, (their foot is above 1½ English): the share has a double fin, of a foot wide; consequently cuts half a foot in the furrow of more than two: has wheels, but no coulter. The land-board is called *fondelo*; the share, *vomero*; the earth-board, or breast, *arfedeman*; two short handles, the left *sinistrale*; the right *brancole*; the beam, *pertica*.

ECCLESIASTICAL

ECCLESIASTICAL STATE.—*Bologna*.

The coulter of the ploughs here ftand 16 degrees from the right line; an incredible blunder, had I not before met with it in the Milanefe. The beam, *pertica*; the handles, *ftiva*; the mould-board. *affa*; the fhare, *gomiera*; the ground-reft, *nervo del focco*; the coulter, *coutre.*

TUSCANY.—*Florence*.

Here the beam is called *ftanga*, and *bura*; the fingle handle, *ftagola*; the body of the plough, *chicapo di aratro*; the fhare, *vangheggiola*. The body is hewn out of one large piece of wood; the fin double, and feven or eight inches wide.—I fee no ploughing but on three feet ridge-work; reverfing. They are now fowing wheat among tares, about fix inches high, and plough both in together at one furrow, fplitting the ridges with a double-breaft plough. Oxen are ufed, that draw by the nape of the neck; then women, with a kind of half pick, called *marona*, work the ridge fine. No dreffing of the feed againft fmut, &c.

PARMA.

The plough here has wheels; a fingle-breaft, that turns to the right, and pretty well; a double finned fhare; and the coulter ftanding three inches to the left of the right line; drawn by two oxen, and two cows, with a driver.

SAVOY.

The oxen in the vale of Chamberry, draw not only by the horns, the yokes bound to them in the common way by leathers, but they have a double bar, one againft the fhoulders, as if the beaft might be able to draw by both at pleafure.

MANURES.

Nice.

There is here a greater attention paid to faving and ufing night foil, than even in Flanders itfelf. There is not a neceffary in the town which is not made an object of revenue; and referved or granted by leafe. In all the paffages between the walls of gardens, in the environs, are neceffaries, made for paffengers. The contents are carried away regularly in barrels, on affes and mules; and being mixed with water, is given regularly to the vegetables of the gardens. The laft winter having damaged many orange trees, they pruned off the damaged

branches;

branches; and, to encourage them to shoot again strongly, the roots are dug around, and at the foot of each tree, a good mess of this invigorating manure is buried.

MILANESE.—*Milan*.

Night soil is greatly valued; it is bought at a good price, and spread on sowing wheat.

STATE OF VENICE.—*Vicenza*.

Sig. Giacomello has tried gypsum with success, broken small and calcined in an oven; also in a lime kiln; pulverises it finely, and sifts it. He remarks, that this is the chief use of calcination. Uses it for clover, lucern, and meadows; sows it as a top dressing on those plants, just as they rise; never buries it; mixes with sand, in order to spread equally; best to sow it when the land is dry; never when the plants are high and wet: quantity, 140 lb. *grosso*, upon 1250 *tavoli* of Treviso. If the land is bad, 300 lb.; and on middling, 200 lb. The effect on perennial clover, upon good land, is such, that any greater crops would rot on the ground. The same quantity of meadow that gives, without gypsum, a *carro* of hay, will, with that manure, spread about the 11th of November, produce 2 *carri* the year following; 3 *carri* the year after that; and on some meadows even to 4 *carri*. On old poor meadows, full of hard and bad grasses, this manure does not take effect so soon, and require a larger quantity of gypsum. (*Modi di aumentare i Bestiami*, 1777, p. 9.)

Sig. Pieropan informed me, that this manure has been used here for eight years, with much success, especially on all dry lands, but is good for nothing on wet ones; it is supposed to act by attracting moisture; 400 lb. of 12 oz. are spread on a *campo*; best for clover, wheat, or natural grass. It is said to force land so much, that it demands more dung, than if no gypsum had been spread.

Parma to Piacenza.

The dunghills in this country are neatly squared heaps.

CHAP.

C H A P. IV.

Of the Encouragement and Depression of Agriculture.

IN every country, through which an inquifitive man may travel, there can be
no object of his inquiries more important than thefe—How far is government, and all the circumftances any way dependent on government, favourable
or unfavourable to the culture of the earth? In truth, this queftion involves
the whole circle of the political fcience. In fo immenfe a range, it is in the
power of an individual to give but a few fketches; which may afterwards, by
fome mafterly hands, be melted into one harmonious piece. All the writings
on political œconomy, which I have hitherto read, are filled too much with
reafonings; yet experiment ought to be the only foundation. The facts which
I have collected under this head, may be thus arranged:—1. Government.—
2. Taxation.— 3. Tythe.—4. Commerce.—5. Population.—6. Prohibitions.—
7. Prices of commodities.

SECT. I.—OF GOVERNMENT.

It is a vulgar error, of no inconfiderable magnitude, to imagine, as many
writers have done, that all arbitrary governments are the fame. Whoever travels into countries under various forms of dominion, will find, from innumerable circumftances, that ftrong diftinctions are to be made. The mildnefs of
that of France can never be miftaken, which was fo tempered by what *was* the
manners of the people, as to be free in comparifon with fome others. Among
the Italian ftates the difference will be found to be confiderable.

The dominion of the Houfe of Auftria has been, by fome, confidered as
hard, harfh, and unfeeling; till the admirable Leopold retrieved, by the
wifdom and humanity of his government, in Tufcany, the character of his
Houfe. By the conftitution of Milan, no new tax could be affeffed or levied without the confent of the States; but Mary Therefa, about the year
1755, abolifhed the States themfelves, which never were reftored till Leopold
came to the throne. It may eafily be conceived, that fuch a fyftem of
defpotifm, was followed by meafures that partook of its fpirit; the general
farms, by which I mean the farming of the taxes, which had from the beginning

ning of the prefent century been grievous to the people, became doubly fo
about the year 1753, when new ones were eftablifhed. The adminiftration of
thefe farms was cruel, or rather infamous; and the ruin brought on numbers,
for the fmalleft infraction of the regulations, fpread a horror againft the government through every corner of the Milanefe, and tended ftrongly to occafion a
declenfion in every fource of national profperity. The abolition of thefe farms,
was the work of the Emperor Jofeph; who heard fuch a reiteration of complaints againft the farmers, whofe great wealth * rendered them doubly odious,
that he made fuch reprefentations to his mother, as were effectual, and they
were abolifhed about eighteen years ago. The prefent Emperor no fooner came
to the throne, than he re-eftablifhed that conftitution, of which his mother
had deprived the Milanefe; the States and the Senate were reftored; and alfo,
the right of the States to appoint, what is called an orator to Vienna; in fact,
an ambaffador paid by themfeves, to lay their reprefentations before the court,
without the intervention of a governor; a right which cannot be deemed unimportant. So that at prefent, the government of Milan, though by no means,
fuch as can meet our ideas of freedom, is yet a kind of limited monarchy; for
affuredly, that government which does not poffefs the power of taxation, muft
be efteemed fuch.

Count Firmian, while prime minifter for the Milanefe, was the author of a
law, which, if it could be adopted in England, would be worth an hundred
millions to us. It obliges all communities, &c. that poffefs wafte or uncultivated lands, to fell them to any one that offers a price, in order to cultivate
them; but they have the neceffary liberty of publifhing the price offered, and
receiving propofals of a better; a fair auction takes place, and the lands become
cultivated. Such poffeffors of waftes, are even obliged to let them at an annual
rent *for ever*, by the fame procefs, if any offer of rent is made to them, be it as
low as poffible. And the effect of this excellent law, has been the cultivation
of many waftes, but not all; for, on returning from Mozzata to Milan, I
paffed a very extenfive one, highly capable of profitable cultivation.

VENICE.

The celebrated government of this republic, is certainly the moft refpectable
that exifts in the world, in point of *duration*; fince it has lafted without
any material change, and without its capital being attacked for 1300 years,

---

* One of them now living, *Count* de Crepy (what a plague have fuch fellows to do with titles,
unlefs to be written on the gallows on which they are hanged?) has between 20 and 30,000 *zecchini*
a year in land.   He was originally a poor boy, that fold cloth on a mule at Bergamo: one of his
commis made 100,000 *zecchini*.

while

while all the reſt of Europe, and of Aſia, has been ſubjeet to innumerable
revolutions, and the bloodieſt wars and maſſacres, even in the very ſeat of empire.   That duration is one of the firſt objeets of a government, can never
admit a doubt; ſince all other merit, however it may approach human per-
feetion, is nothing without this.   A well organized ariſtocracy, in which the
greateſt maſs of the wiſdom of the community, ſhall be found in a ſenate,
ſeems, from the vaſt and important experiment of this celebrated republic, to
be eſſentially neceſſary to ſecure the duration of any government.   But the duration of an evil, becomes a miſchief inſtead of an advantage; and that tyranny, which is ſo politically organized, as to promiſe an immenſe duration, is
but the more juſtly to be abominated.   The knowledge which will reſult from
long experience, may probably teach mankind the right compoſition of a
mingled form, in which the ariſtocratic portion will give duration and firmneſs; the democracy, freedom; and the conformation of executive power, energy
and execution.   Perhaps, the Britiſh government approaches the neareſt to ſuch
a deſcription.

The reputation of the Venetian government, is now its only ſupport, a reputation which it does not at preſent merit in the ſmalleſt degree:—but as this idea
is direetly contrary to the accounts given by many travellers, I feel it neceſſary
to premiſe, that I ſhould think it merely trifling with the reader, to travel to
Venice, in order to write diſſertations in my own name, on the government of
that republic; I do no more than hold the pen to report the opinions of Italians,
on whoſe judgment I have every reaſon to rely; and, as exaggerated panegyrics
have been publiſhed of the government of this State, it is fair to hear what
may be urged on the other ſide of the queſtion.

For twenty years paſt, there has been, in the republic, little more than a
multiplication of abuſes, ſo that almoſt every circumſtance, which has been
condemned in the arbitrary governments of Europe, is now to be found in that
of Venice.   And as an inſtance of the principles on which they govern their
provinces, that of Iſtria was quoted.   1. To preſerve the woods (which belong
to the Prince), they prevent the people from turning any cattle into them;
and if any man cut a tree, he is infallibly ſent to the gallies, which has driven
numbers out of that part of the country, where the woods are ſituated.   2.
There are great opportunities of making ſalt, and the pans might be numerous,
but it is a monopoly held by the State; they purchaſe a certain quantity, at
10ſ. French, per quintal, and if more than the ſpecified quantity be made, it
is lodged in their magazines on credit; and it may be two, three, or four years
before the maker of it be paid.   3. Oil is a monopoly of the city of Venice;
none can be ſold but through that city; by which tranſit, an opportunity is
taken to levy two ducats (each 4 liv. of France) per barrel, of 100 lb. and

five more *entrée* into Venice. 4. The coast abounds remarkably with fish, which are taken in almost any quantity; salt is on the spot, yet no use can be made of it, but by contraband, except for Venice singly. Thus a great trade in barrelled fish is foregone, in order to make a whole province beasts of burthen to a single city. 5. The heavy tax of a *stajo* of wheat, 130 lb. is laid on each head of a family, payable to the Venetian bailiff.

The practical result of such principles of government, confirms whatever condemnation theory could pronounce. Every part of the province, except a district that is more favoured than the rest in soil and climate, is depopulated; and so much are the woods preferred to the people, that parts, which once abounded with men, are become deserts; and the small population remaining in other parts, is every day diminishing. Dalmatia is in a yet worse state; for the greater part is a real desert:—in 1781 and 1782, no less than 12,000 families emigrated from the province. As I have not travelled in these provinces, I do no more than report the account given by well-informed Italians, though not residing in the territories of the republic. Before the government of this stern aristocracy is made the subject of exaggerated praise, let facts counter to these, be made the foundation.——But farther,

In the immediate operations of their government *at home*, the same weakness is found. Their poverty has increased with their revenue; they have raised the leases of the farmers general (for that odious collection is the mode they pursue) considerably: and near twenty years ago, they seized many of the possessions of the monks—that act for which the National Assembly of France has been condemned; but which, in the hands of numerous other governments, has either passed without animadversion, or has been commended. They did the same with the estates of some of the hospitals; but though such exertions have raised their revenue to 6,100,000 ducats, (1,054,000l.) yet they have found their affairs in such a situation, from bad management, that they have been obliged to sell the offices, which were in better times granted to merit; and committed a sort of bankruptcy, by reducing the interest of their old debts, from 5 to 3 per cent. Their credit is at so low an ebb, that, no longer ago than last June, they opened a subscription to fund 700,000 ducats; and, notwithstanding every art, could procure no more than about 300,000. Instead of their famous chain, which marked the wisdom of their oeconomy, their treasury is without a sol: and, to shew the apprehensions they have of provinces under their dominion throwing off their yoke, if they are at a small distance from the seat of government, the State makes a distinction in the political treatment of the Bergamasque and Brescian territories, from those nearer to Venice, in respect to privileges, punishments, taxes, &c.

No

No favourable feature of their government; and which shews that they think the people made for their city.

Perhaps, in the system of their finances, there is no circumstance that shews a decline of the real principles of their government, more than that of putting contraventions of the tobacco farm under the controul of the State inquisitors; which must have been done since M. de la Lande's second edition, as he mentions expressly their having nothing to do with the finances*. A conduct utterly ridiculous, in a State that once conducted itself with so much dignity.

Even in the delicate article of imparting the privileges of the aristocracy, to the nobility of Terra Firma, by whom they are in general detested, they have exhibited no doubtful symptoms of weakness, and want of policy. Reputation has been for many years the great support of their government; to manifest therefore such a want of policy, as strikes the most careless eye, is to suffer in the tenderest point. In 1774, they offered, gratis, a seat in the *consiglio maggiore*, to forty families, their subjects, who possessed 1200l. a year in land; provided there were four degrees of nobility, on the side of both husband and wife. Great numbers of families were eligible, but not ten in the whole would agree to the proposal. To offer a share in the legislature of so celebrated a republic, which in past periods would have been sought for with singular avidity, and to suffer the mortification of a refusal, was exhibiting a sign of internal weakness, and of want of judgment, adapted to reduce the reputation of their policy to nothing. The motives for the refusal are obvious: these families must of course remove to Venice; that is, to go from a city where they were old and respected, to another where they would be new and despised. Their estates also would not only suffer from their absence, but would be subject to new entails, and held by other tenures; no mortgage of them is allowable; and they are subject to peculiar laws of inheritance. In addition to these disadvantages, they are cut off from serving foreign princes; whereas the nobility of Terra Firma engage in such services. The Emperor's ambassador at Turin, is a subject of Venice; and one of the Pellegrini family, a field marshal in his army. Nor did the noblemen of Terra Firma refuse the favour, for these reasons alone; they dreaded the power which the State exerts over the noble Venetians, in sending them upon expensive embassies, in which they must spend the whole of their income, and, if that be not sufficient, contract debts to support themselves; for these reasons, and many others mentioned to me, which I did not equally understand, the government might have known before they made the offer, that it would subject them to the disgrace of a refusal. Long before the period in question, considerable additions had been

* *Voyage en Italie*, tom. vii. p. 7.

made to nobles of Venice, from the Terra Firma, but these honours were paid for, the price 17,000l. sterling; 7,000l. in cash, and 10,000l. lent to the State in perpetuity.

It is a curious circumstance, which marks undeceivingly the general features of the Venetian government, that about forty years ago, as well as at other periods, there were negociations between the Court of Vienna and the Venetians, relative to an exchange of territory; the district of Crema was to have been given by Venice, for a part of the Ghiara d'Adda; the rumour of which, filled the people of the latter with the greatest apprehensions; they felt even a terror, at the idea of being transferred to the government of Venice; knowing, certainly, from their vicinity, that the change would be for the worse. This ascertains the comparative merit of two governments, that one is less bad than the other.

Upon the whole it may be remarked, that the wisdom of the Venetian government flows entirely from its interior organization, which is admirably framed; but abuses, in spite of this, have multiplied so much, that the first real shock that happens will overturn it. The fall of a goverment, however, which has subsisted with great reputation so much longer than any other existing at present, ought to be esteemed a great political loss, since the establishment of new systems is not at present wanted for the benefit of mankind, so much as the improvement of old ones; and if by any amelioration of the Venetian aristocracy, the benefit of the common people could be better secured, it might yet last in enlightened ages, as well as through those of darkness and ignorance.

Bologna.

The government of the church, though in so many respects considered as one of the worst in Europe, ought not to be condemned too generally, for some discrimination should be used. Thus, in point of taxation, there are few countries that have less to complain of than this, as I have shewn in the proper place; and another circumstance was mentioned to me here, which proves that it is not the Pope's fault that it is not better—his Holiness was ready to abolish all fêtes, confining them to Sunday; and made the offer to the Senate of Bologna, if they would apply to him for the purpose; great debates ensued in that body, and it was determined not to make the application.

Tuscany.

The government of the Grand Duke is, as every one knows, absolute; it admits therefore of no other discrimination, than what results from the personal

character

character of the Prince. The circumftances I noted, during my refidence at Florence, will fhew that few fovereigns have deferved better of their fubjects than Leopold: the details, however, which I fhall enter into, will be very flight, not that the fubject wants importance, but becaufe many other books contain large accounts of this period; and efpecially the collection of his * laws, of which I wifh to fee a complete Englifh tranflation, for the ufe of our legiflators. The encouragements which this wife and benevolent fovereign has given to his fubjects, are of various defcriptions; to clafs them with any degree of regularity, would be to abridge that collection; a few, that bear more or lefs upon agriculture, I fhall mention.

I. He has abolifhed tythes, which will be explained more at large, under the proper head.

II. He has eftablifhed an abfolute freedom in the trade of corn.

III. He has for many years contributed one-fourth part of the expence of buildings, in the Val de Nievole, and the lower province of Siena.

IV. He has this year made the culture of tobacco free, and engaged to buy all that is raifed at 16 $f.$ the pound.

V. He has extinguifhed the national debt of Tufcany, which had exifted from the time of the republic; for it deferves noting (in order for fome future hiftorian of the † modern ages, to mark the fact that the richeft people run in debt the moft) that the republic of Florence was one of the moft commercial and rich in Europe. Two evils attended this debt, which the Grand Duke bent his operations to remove; *firft*, three or four millions of it were due to foreigners, particularly to the Genoefe, which carried much money out of Tufcany; and, *fecondly*, there were diftinct bureaus of collection and payment, for tranfacting the bufinefs of thefe debts. To remedy this double mifchief, he firft bought up all that part of the debt due to ftrangers, which he effected by the operation of a fteady and wife œconomy; he then called on the Tufcan creditors to liquidate their debts, in the ratio of 3 per cent.; thofe who had money did it; and to thofe who had none, he lent the neceffary fums: by this method, the diftinct receipt and payment were abolifhed; the accounts were melted into the land-tax; and a number of reve-

---

* *Collezione di Leggi,* 8vo. 10 vols.—Siena.

† There is no work in the whole range of literature, more wanted than a Modern Hiftory of Europe, written philofophically; that is to fay, with due attention to the progrefs of arts, fciences, and government; and with none paid to wars, battles, fieges, intrigues, generals, heroes, and cut-throats, more than briefly to condemn them: in fuch a work, the circumftance of the richeft countries in Europe, having plunged themfelves the deepeft and moft ruinoufly in debts, to fupport wars of commerce and ambition, fhould be particularly explained and condemned.

nue

nue officers, &c. were reformed: nine or ten millions of crowns were thus extinguifhed.

VI. He has abolifhed all rights of commonage throughout his dominions, and given the powers of an univerfal inclofure.

VII. He has fold a confiderable portion of the eftates belonging to the fovereign, which has occafioned a great increafe of cultivation, and the fettlement in his dominions of many rich foreigners *.

VIII. In levying taxes, he has abolifhed all the diftinctions of noble, ignoble, and ecclefiaftical tenures; and all exemptions are fet afide.

IX. He has built a magnificent lazaretto at Leghorn, and fpent three millions on roads; but it would be entering too much into detail to fpecify his works of this fort; they are numerous.

The effects of fuch an enlightened fyftem of government have been great; general affertions will not defcribe them fo fatisfactorily to a reader as particular inftances. Sig. Paoletti, who has been *curé* of the parifh of Villamagna forty-three years, affured me, that the forty farms, of which it confifts, have rifen in their value full 2000 *fcudi* each in that time, which is about *cent. per cent.* of their former value; this great improvement has been chiefly wrought of late years, and efpecially in the laft ten. It highly merits notice, that the countries in Europe, whofe whole attention has been given exclufively to their commerce and manufactures, and particularly England, where the commercial fyftem has been more relied on than in any other country, have experienced nothing equal to this cafe of Tufcany, the government of which has proceeded on a principle directly contrary, and given its encouragement *immediately* to agriculture, and *circuitoufly* to manufactures. In the tours I made through England, twenty years ago, I found land felling on an average at 32¼ years purchafe; it fells at prefent at no more than 28. While Tufcany therefore has been adding immenfely to the money value of her foil, without trade and without manufactures (comparatively fpeaking to thofe of England), we have in the fame period, with an immenfe increafe of trade, been lofing in our land. This fact, which is unqueftionably true, is a curious circumftance for political analyfis: it proves fomething wrong in our fyftem. Population in Villamagna has augmented about a feventh, in the fame period.

I fhall not quit this article, without giving the preference decidedly to Leopold, Grand Duke of Tufcany, as the wifeft of the princes, whofe power admits a comparifon in the age in which he lives: thofe are mean fpirits, or

---

* By the general regulations for the diftrict of Florence, of May 23, 1774, cap. 35. it is ordered, that all the landed property of the communities, kept in adminiftration, or let, fhall be fold or let on long leafe. *Paoletti*, p. 85.

fomething worfe, that will hefitate a moment between him and Frederic of Pruffia: a fovereign no more to be compared to him, than the deftroyers and tyrants of mankind are to be placed in competition with their greateft bene-factors*.

MODENA.

In an age in which the fovereigns of Europe are incumbered, and fome of them ruined by debts, a contrary conduct deferves confiderable attention. The Duke of Modena, for ten years paft, has practifed a very wife œconomy: he is fuppofed, on good authority, to have faved about a million of *zecchins*, (475,000l.) and he continues to fave in the fame proportion. This is a very fingular circumftance, and the effect of it is obfervable; for I was affured at Modena, that this treafure was much greater than the whole circulating cur-rency of the Dutchy; and they fpoke of it as a very mifchievous thing, to withdraw from circulation and *ufe*, fo confiderable a fum, occafioning prices generally to rife, and every thing to be dear. By repeated inquiries, I found this dearnefs was nothing more than what is found in the States around, which have all experienced, more or lefs, a confiderable rife of prices in ten years. But how could withdrawing money from circulation raife prices? It ought, on the contrary, in a country that has no paper-money, to lower them. That this effect did not follow, we may eafily conclude, from thefe complaints. But the very perfons who complained of this treafure could not affert, that money was more wanted in the Dutchy than before it was begun to be faved. They even gave a proof to the contrary, by affirming the rate of intereft to be at prefent 4½ per cent. only. Upon the whole, the effect is evidently harmlefs; and it is a moft curious fact in politics, that a government can gradually draw from cir-culation a fum that in ten years exceeded the current coin of the State, with-out caufing an apparent deficiency in the currency, or any inconveniency what-ever. Conclufions of infinite importance are to be drawn from fuch a fact; it feems to prove, that the general modern policy of contracting public debts, is abfurd and ruinous in the extreme; as faving in the time of peace, is clearly without any of thofe inconveniences, which were once fuppofed to attend it; and by means of forming a treafure, a nation doubles her nominal wealth, that fort of wealth, which is real or imaginary, according to the ufe that is made of it. The reputation, preventing attacks, is perhaps the greateft of all. How

* The conduct of this Prince in his new fituation, to which he acceded at a moft critical and dangerous moment, has been worthy of his preceding reputation, and has fet a ftamp on the rank in which I have fuppofed him. A few years more added to the life of Jofeph, would have fhivered the Auftrian monarchy to nothing; Leopold has, by his wife and prudent management, every where preferved it.

contrary

contrary to the funding fyftem, which carries in its nature, fuch a probability of prefent weaknefs, and fuch a certainty of future ruin!

PARMA.

The river from Parma to the Po has been furveyed, and might be made navigable for about 25,000l. fterling; but to the honour of the government which has been diffufed through fo many countries by the Houfe of Bourbon, no fuch undertaking can here be thought of. Don Philip's hiftory, it is to be hoped, will be written by fome pen that can teach mankind, from fuch an inftance, of what ftuff men are fometimes made, whom birth elevates to power. The prefent Duke fpends too much money upon monks, to have any to fpare for navigations.

PIEDMONT.

The Houfe of Savoy has, for fome centuries, poffeffed the reputation of governing their dominions with fingular ability; and of making fo dextrous a ufe of events, as to have been continually aggrandizing their territory. The late King was among the wifeft princes of his family, and fhewed his talents for government in the practice of an enlightened and fteady œconomy: it deferves no flight attention among the princes of Europe, in the prefent ferment of men's minds, whether there be any other criterion of a wife government. The late King of Sardinia faved 12,000,000 liv.; paid off a great debt; repaired all his fortreffes; adorned his palaces; and built one of the moft fplendid theatres in Europe; all by the force of œconomy. The contraft of the prefent reign is ftriking; his prefent Majefty found himfelf in poffeffion of the treafure of his predeceffor. He fold the property of the jefuits, to the amount of 20,000,000 liv.; he has raifed 7 or 8,000,000 liv. by the creation of paper-money; thus, without noticing the portions of the Queen and the Princefs of Piedmont, he has received 40,000,000 liv. extraordinary (2,000,000l. fterling): all of which has been lavifhed, and a debt contracted and increafing; the fortifications not in good repair; and report fays, that his army is neither well paid, nor well difciplined. Thefe features are not to be miftaken; the King, though free from the vices which degrade fo many princes, and poffeffing many amiable virtues, is of too eafy a difpofition, which expofes him to fituations, in which œconomy is facrificed to feelings—amiable for private life, but inconfiftent with the feverity of a monarch's duty.

It is a moft curious circumftance in the King of Sardinia's government, that there is in this court, a great defire to fell the ifland of Sardinia. A treaty was opened with the Emprefs of Ruffia for that purpofe, after fhe was difappointed

in

in her negotiation with the Genoese, in the projected acquisition of Spazzie, and of Malta : but in all these schemes of a Mediterranean establishment, she was disappointed by the vigorous and decisive interference of the courts of Versailles and Madrid. One cannot have any hesitation in the opinion, that to improve this island, by means of a good government, would be more political than so strange a measure as its sale *.

I shall

---

* It may not here be unuseful to the reader, if I note some minutes taken at Turin, concerning that island, one of the most neglected spots in Europe ; and which, of course, betrays the effects of a vicious system of government sufficiently, for conclusions of some importance to be drawn. The marshes are so numerous and extensive, that the *intemperia* is every where found; the mountains numerous and high; and wastes found so generally, that the whole isle may be considered as such, with spots only cultivated. Estates in the hands of absentees are large, the rents consequently sent away, and the people left to the mercy of rapacious managers. The Duke of Assinaria has 300,000 liv. a year : the Duke of St. Piera 160,000 liv. : the Marquis of Pascha as much ; and many live in Spain. M. de Girah, a grandee, has an estate of two days journey, from Poula to Oleastre. The peasants in a miserable situation ; their cabins wretched hovels, without either windows or chimnies; their cattle have nothing to eat in winter, but browzing in woods, for there are no wolves. The number of wild ducks incredible. Shooting them was the chief amusement of an officer, who was nine years in the island, and who gave me this account. Provisions cheap ; bread, 1 f. the pound; beef, 2 f.; mutton, 2½ f.; a load of wood, of 10 quintals, 4s. 9d. sterling. Wheat is the only export; in this grain the lands are naturally fertile, yielding commonly seven or eight for one, and some even forty. No silk; and oil, worse than easy to conceive. They have some wine almost as good as Malaga, and not unlike it. The great want of the island, is that of water : springs are scarce, and the few rivers are in low bottoms. To these particulars, I shall add a few from Gemelli.

Sardinia is a real desert, for the most part ; and where cultivated, it is in the most wretched manner : every thing consumed in the island (except the immediate food of the day), is imported, even their flax * and wood, from Corsica and Tuscany; the miserable inhabitants know not even the art of making hay ; their crops are destroyed by wild animals, for the very notion of an inclosure is unknown. Leases are annual †. The tunny fishery produces from abroad, 60,000 *scudi* ‡.

They have no mules ; and the cities, as they are called, have been supplied with corn from abroad ; with plenty in the island, which could not be brought, for want of mules to convey it ; insomuch, that a fourth part of the corn has been offered as a payment, for carrying the other three parts to the towns, and not accepted ‖.

In 1750, there were about 360,000 souls in Sardinia; in 1773, they were 421,597 ; so that in twenty-three years, the increase was 61,597 ; occasioned by an institution called *Monti Frumentarii*, which furnishes seed on credit to the poor farmers, who cannot afford to buy it §. Cattle in the island, in 1771 ; cows, &c. 1,710,259 ; oxen for work, horses, mares, and calves bred for work, 185,266 **.

* *Riforimento Della Sardegna Gemelli,* 4to, vol. i. p. 50. † *Ib.* p. 21 ‡ *Ib.* p. 54.
‖ *Ib.* p. 5. § *Ib.* p. 46. ** *Ib.* p. 350.

I shall not quit the subject of Italian governments, without remarking, that such deserts as Sardinia, under a despotic monarch, and Istria under a despotic aristocracy, are to be classed among political lessons. The tendency and result of such cases, are sufficient to shew the principles of government: the leaders should speedily correct the neglect of such systems. When people are well governed, THINGS CANNOT BE THUS. The wisdom applicable to the present moment, is to watch the colour and spirit of the age; to compound; and to yield, where yielding is rational.

Working oxen,	97,753
Cows in calf,	13,099
Calves, *ammonsite*,	8,080
Horses and mares,	66,334
Hogs,	152,471
Oxen and calves, *rudi*,	58,770
Cows and cow-calves, *rudi*,	166,468
Goats,	378,201
He-goats,	42,597
Sheep,	768,250
Rams and wethers *,	143,502
	1,895,525

The miserable state of this island, will best appear from calculating the number of acres. Templeman tells us, that it contains 6,600 square miles. England he makes 49,450; the real contents of which, in acres, are 46,915,933; Sardinia, in the same ratio, contains 6,261,782: the number of goats and sheep in the island, is 1,332,550; there is, therefore, about one sheep or goat to every five acres. Without viewing the island, I will venture to pronounce, that it would, without cultivation, support a sheep per acre; above six millions; and reckoning the fleeces at 3s. 4d. each, the wool only would produce one million sterling a year. It is said, the King of Sardinia offered to sell the island, to the Empress of Russia, for a million sterling. The purchaser of it would have a noble estate at twice that price, seeing the immense improvements of which it is capable. The fee simple of most of the estates are to be purchased at a very easy rate, as well as the sovereignty. The climate would admit of wool, as fine as the Spanish; if it were made into an immense sheep-walk, with culture only proportioned to their winter support, it would yield an exportable produce of full two millions sterling annually.

Gemelli mentions the island being capable of producing as fine wool as Spain; they rear them only for supplying their tables with lambs and cheese; and to have skins for dressing the people; and no attention whatever is paid to the quality of the wool, which is good for nothing; but to make the Sardinian serges.

* *Gemelli*, tom. ii. p. 145.

ACADEMIES.

ACADEMIES.

There is an agrarian fociety at Turin, which has publifhed four volumes of papers: a patriotic fociety at Milan, which has publifhed two volumes; neither of thefe focieties hath any land for trying experiments. At Bergamo, Brefcia, and Verona, there are alfo focieties,—without land. At Vicenza, the republic has given four *campi* for the purpofe of experiments. At Padua, I viewed the experimental garden, of about a dozen acres, under the direction of Sig. Pietro Arduino; the expence of which is alfo paid by the State. At Florence, a fimilar one, under the conduct of Sig. Zucchino; this was in good order.

Venice.

Perhaps no country ever had a wifer plan of conduct than the Venetians, in appointing a gentleman, fuppofed, from his writings, to be well fkilled in agriculture (Sig. Arduino), to travel over all their dominions, to make inquiries into the ftate of agriculture; its deficiencies, and practicable improvements; and the idea was, that the academies of agriculture, in all the great towns of the republic, would have orders to take fuch fteps to effect the improvements, as would moft conduce to national profperity. The plan was admirable; all, however, depends on the execution; as far as the academies are concerned, I fhould expect it to fail, for none of them are eftablifhed upon principles, that will allow us to fuppofe their members fkilled in *practical* hufbandry; and, without this, their ideas and their experiments would of courfe be vifionary.

It will not, perhaps, be improper to remark, under this head, that there is at Venice, an inftitution appointed by the State, which, though not an academy, has much the fame object, but with more authority, called the *Beni Inculti.* Their origin was about 1556, and in 1768 they added the *Deputati di Agricoltura.* I was informed, that they had once great power, and did much good, but that now there lies an appeal from their tribunal, to the council of forty, which is attended with a confiderable expence, and has done mifchief.

SECT. II.—OF TAXATION.

PIEDMONT.—*Chentale.*

The land-tax, near the town, is 6 liv. or 7 liv. per *giornata*, per annum, on such land as sells at 800 liv. to 1000 liv. ; which may be called about one-sixth of the rent, suppofing land to pay 5 per cent. The landlord, of courfe, pays his own capitation of 1 liv. for himfelf, and every one in family : and the tenant pays as much for his family, being more than feven years old. But what is abundantly worfe, he pays 25 *f.* a head for each cow, and 50 *f.* for each ox. Salt is a monopoly : the ratio per head, is 8 lb. for every one in family, after five years old ; 4 lb. for each ox and cow ; and 1 lb. for each fheep and goat ; and 1 lb. more per cow, for thofe that give milk : the price, 4 *f.* the pound.

Turin.

No capitation in Turin. The *entrées* are 8 *f.* the *brenta*, 50 bottles of wine ; 4 *den.* per pound, meat. Salt, 4 *f.* the pound. Hay, 1 *f.* the *rubbio*, to the Hotel de Ville, for lighting the city. No taxes except the *entrées*. The land-tax in common, is 4 liv. the *giornata*. Salt, 8 lb. each ox or cow, and 4 lb. each goat, fheep, or calf, at 4 *f.* ; and if they want more, the reft 2 *f.* the pound ; alfo 8 lb. per head of the family. Capitation in the country, 1 liv. per head, for all above feven years.

The following is a correct Detail of the Revenue of the King of Sardinia, which in 1675 *amounted only to* 7,000,000 *liv.* (306,250 *l.*)

	Liv.
Cuftoms—excife and falt,	14,000,000
Land-tax, which is between 7 and 8 per cent.	6,000,000
Since 1781, the clergy their thirds of the land-tax,	500,000
Addition to the land-tax, for the Nice road,	100,000
Contribution of the Jews,	15,700
Sale of demefne lands falling into the crown,	800,000
Fees in the courts of juftice,	110,000
Salt in the provinces of Alexandria and Novara,	65,460
Carry forward,	21,591,160

	Liv.
Brought forward, - - -	21,591,160
Enrollment of all public acts and contracts, - - -	276,100
Post-office, - - - - - - -	300,000
Lotteries, royal powder works, glass houses, mines, salines, &c. about	3,000,000
Total, exclusive of the last article, - -	* 22,167,260
Sterling, - £. 1,158,813

Expenditure.

Interest of the public debt, - - - -	* 4,738,840
Army, - - - - - - -	† 10,700,000
Carry forward, - -	15,438,840

---

* The following is another account:—

Sale,	3,504,233 liv.
Tobacco,	2,415,297
Dogana,	2,377,673
Carne,	1,240,230
Carta bollata,	249,103
Polveri,	215,788
Contravenzioni,	22,340
Gabella giaochi,	137,389
Reggio lotto del seminario,	388,487
Gran cancelleria,	162,537
Dritti insinuazioni,	44,647
Regie poste,	394,214
Domaniali,	442,884
Casuali,	1,449,548
	13,044,370

Sardinia, in 1783, produced 1,318,519 liv.; the population 450,000 souls.

* The debt amounts to 58,000,000 liv. originally at 4, now at 3½ per cent. and the fund is above par. There are 17,000,000 of bank notes, which at first bore 4 per cent. then 2, and now none.

† Guards,	1,397
Fifteen regiments of the line,	17,784
Twelve regiments of militia,	7,200
Legion,	1,718
	28,099
Invalids,	2,400
Sundries,	1,141
Infantry,	31,640
Cavalry and dragoons,	3,289
	34,929
Of which foreigners,	7,536

		Liv.
Brought forward, - - -		15,438,840
Ordnance, - - - - - - -		359,044
Fortifications, royal houses, and public buildings, - -		1,458,998
Houshold, - - - - - - -		2,500,000
Collection of the revenue, - - - - -		3,572,398
King's privy purse, - - - - -		711,425
		24,040,705
	Sterling, -	£. 1,202,035

If, as calculated, there are 2882 square French leagues in the King's continental dominions, the revenue amounts to 10,920 liv. per league; and as the population is 3,000,000, it is 8 liv. 2¼ ſ. per head. Savoy produces 2,432,137 liv. Piedmont, 11,444,578 liv.; and the provinces acquired by the treaties of Worms and Vienna, 1,972,735 liv.

Milanese.—*Milan.*

One liv. on the manufacture of each hat; duty of 7½ ſ. per lb. on the export of ſilk. There are *entrées* at the gates of Milan, upon moſt commodities. Wine pays 42 ſ. the *brenta*, of 96 *bocali*, of 28 oz. or ſomething under a common bottle. Salt in the city, is 12 ſ. the pound, and 11½ ſ. in the country. No perſon is obliged to take more than they think proper.

Mozzata.

The land-tax throughout the Milaneſe, is laid by a *cadaſtre*, called here the *cenſimento*; there was a map and an actual ſurvey of every man's property taken parochially, and a copy of the map left with the community of every pariſh. It was finiſhed in 1760, after forty years labour, under the Empreſs Maria Thereſa. The lands were all valued, and the tax laid at 26 *deniers*; 1 ſ. 6 *den.* per *ecu*, of the fee ſimple. There is at Milan itſelf, as well as in the accounts of travellers, ſtrange contradictions and errors about this tax; as ſoon as I arrived, I was told, even by very ſenſible men, that it amounted to full 50 per cent. of the produce. Monſ. de la Lande, in his *Voyage en Italie*, tom. i. p. 291, 2d edit. ſays, that it is one-third of the revenue, or half the *produit net*; this is the confuſion of the *economiſtes*, with that jargon which ſeems to have enveloped the plaineſt objects in a miſt; for one-third of the revenue, is not half the *produit net*. Monſ. Roland de la Platerie aſſerts, that it exceeds the half of the *revenu net*; but all theſe accounts are groſs errors. The inſtruction of the commiſſaries originally, who valued the country, was to eſtimate

mate it below the truth; of which thefe gentlemen feem to have known nothing. Nor do they take into their confideration, the improvements which have been made in near thirty years; for the *cenfimento* remains as it was, no alteration having been made in the valuation; when they talk therefore of 50 per cent. or a third, or any other proportion, they muft of neceffity be incorrect, for no one knows the value of the whole Dutchy at prefent; nor can tell whether the tax be the fifth or the tenth, or what real proportion it bears to the income. When I found the fubject involved in fuch confufion by preceding travellers, I faw clearly that the way to come at truth, was to enquire in the country, and not depend on the general affertions fo common in great cities. At this place (Mozzata) therefore, I analyzed the tax, and by gaining a clear comprehenfion of the value, rent, produce, and tax of 100 *pertiche*, was enabled to acquire a fair notion of the fubject. Under the chapter of *arable products*, I have ftated that 100 *pertiche* yield a grofs produce, in corn, wine, and filk, of 1836 liv.; of which the proprietor receives for his fhare, 785 liv. This land would fell for 128¼ liv. per *pertica*; or 12,833 liv. for the 100. Now this 100 *pertiche*, of fuch a rent and value, pays *cenfimento* 15½ f. per *pertica*, or 77 liv. This tax is paid by the farmer in the above-mentioned divifion; but if there were no tax, the landlord would receive fo much more as his portion; add therefore the tax, 77 liv. to his receipt, 785 liv. and you have 862 liv. for the fum which pays 77 liv.; which is 8$\frac{4:2:4}{}$, or 8l. 18s. per cent. or 1s. 9d. in the pound. So utterly miftaken are the people of Milan, and the French travellers, when they talk of 50 per cent, and one-third, and one-half, the *produit net* and *revenu net!* And it is farther to be confidered, that only half this payment of 77 liv. goes to the fovereign; for half is retained by the communities for roads, bridges, and other parochial charges; and in fome cafes, the partial fupport of the *curées* is included. When this happens, the payment of 1s. 9d. in the pound, is in lieu of our land-tax, tithe, and poor-rate; three articles, which in England amount to 8s. or 10s. in the pound. But though the burthen is nothing, compared with thofe which crufh us in England, yet 1s. 9d. is too heavy a land-tax—it is throwing too great a burthen upon landed property, and leffening too much the profit which fhould arife from invefting capitals in it; for it muft be remarked, that this proportion is that of the improvements included; this 1s. 9d. might probably, twenty-five years ago, be 3s. or 3s. 6d.: it is improvements which have lowered it to 1s. 9d. at the prefent moment. Thofe filent and gradual improvements, which take place from what may be termed external caufes, from the growing profperity, and rife of prices in Europe in general. Were 8¼ per cent. to be laid on new inveftments, not one livre would be invefted. Lands belonging to ecclefiaftics and hofpitals are exempted.

It

It muſt be ſufficiently apparent, that this *cenſimento* muſt vary in every pariſh in the dukedom; it varies proportionably to the variation, in the accuracy of the original valuation; and to the improvements that have been made; and to many other circumſtances. As it is at preſent, the land-owners are well ſatisfied, for the tax, though too heavy, is certainly not enormous; and it gives an accuracy and ſecurity to property that is of no ſlight value; as all mutations are made in reference to the parochial map of the *cenſimento*. They very properly conſider any alteration in it, as a certain ſtep to the ruin of the Milaneſe. It has been reported, that the Emperor has entertained thoughts of having a new valuation; but the confuſion and miſchief that would flow from ſuch a ſcheme, might go much farther than the court could imagine; and might be attended with unforeſeen conſequences. In theſe opinions, they are certainly right; for of all the curſes that a country can experience, a variable land-tax is perhaps the heavieſt.

Beſide the direct land-tax of the *cenſimento*, there is a capitation that is included in the roll, like the cuſtom in England, of putting ſeveral taxes into one duplicate or aſſeſſment. On 15,173 *pertiche* of land, at Mozzata, there are three hundred and eighty-two heads payable, and one thouſand three hundred fouls. It may be calculated, that 100 *pertiche* pay the capitation of three perſons, or 22¼ liv.

Codogno.

The watered dairy lands, taken in general, ſell here at 300 liv. the *pertica*; and lets, *net* rent, at 10 liv.; the tenant paying all taxes.—The account is thus:

Rent to landlord, - - - -	10 *liv.*	0 *ſ.*
Water-tax for diſtribution, - - -	1	0
Cenſimento to the prince and the community, -	2	5
	13	5

The 1 liv. we muſt throw out, being local, and then 12 liv. 5 ſ. pays 2 liv. 5 ſ. which is 18$\frac{11}{111}$ per cent. or 3s. 8d. in the pound; this is therefore doubly higher than in the poor country of Mozzata; one would ſuppoſe beforehand, that the caſe would be ſo. The improvements in the Lodizan are not modern; probably there are no other but ſuch as are common to the whole Dutchy, and which ariſe from the general proſperity of Europe, rather than from any local efforts in this diſtrict; but in much poorer countries, the improvement of waſte ſpots, and a huſbandry gradually better, are more likely to have this effect; the fact, however, is ſo; there was no ſuch difference as this, when the *cenſimento* was laid, which ſufficiently proves that the huſbandry of the poor diſtricts, has advanced much more in thirty years, than that of the rich ones,
which

which, once well watered, admitted of little more. We may remark, that
even here the accounts which Meffrs. de la Lande and Roland de la Platerie
have given, are grofs exaggerations.

Treviglio.

Upon 400 *perticbe* of land and fix houfes, the *cenfimento* amounts to 430 liv.
Rent, 7, 9, and 12 liv. the *pertica*, average 8 liv. or 3440 liv. about 12 per cent.
or 2s. 4d. in the pound.

Upon the land-tax in general in the Milanefe, I fhould obferve, before I quit
that country, that in 1765 it was calculated * that the Dutchy of Milan contained 14,000,000 of *perticbe*, and that lakes, roads, &c. deducted, there remained 11,367,287, of which 5,098,758 were arable. It has been further
ftated †, that the *cenfimento* of the Dutchy, raifed,

		liv.	f.	den.
For the Emperor,	- - - -	5,106,004	11	9
Suppofe as much more for the communities,	-	5,106,004	11	9
		10,212,009	3	6

Eleven millions of *perticbe*, paying ten millions of livres, is about 18 *foldi*
per *pertica* ‡.

In the *Epilogo della Scrittura Cenfuaria della Lombardia Auftriaca*, MS. fent by
Count Wilizek, prime minifter of the Milanefe, to the Board of Agriculture at
London, the general valuation of the territory, in the *cenfimento*, is thus ftated:

Milano,	-	-	-	40,139,942 *fcudi*.
Mantova,	-	-	-	14,487,423
Pavia,	-	-	-	6,173,740
Cremona,	-	-	-	15,112,042
Lodi,	-	-	-	11,014,562
Como,	-	-	-	2,153,626
Value of the fee fimple,		-		89,081,337

If therefore the tax produces but about ten millions of livres, it is not more
than 2 per cent. on the above capital.

---

* *Bilancio della Stato di Milano prefentato a S. E. Conte di Firmian*, 12mo.

† *Delle Opere del Conte Carli*, tom. i. p. 232.

‡ Upon the taxes of the Milanefe, it fhould be in general noted, that every father with twelve
children living, or eleven living and his wife with child of a twelfth, is exempted from all perfonal
taxes; and upon all others favoured 45 per cent. that is to fay, on all royal, provincial, municipal
impofts. *Delle Opere di S. Conte Carli*, 8vo, tom. i. p. 254.

STATE OF VENICE.—*Brescia.*

The land-tax amounts to 1½ liv. per *jugero*, about 7d. the Englifh acre; but there is a tax on all products, **viz.** wheat and rye pays the *foma* or *facco*, equal to 2 *ftara* of Venice, or 88 lb.; 11¼ *foldi* equal to 18 *foldi correnti*; this tax *(fenza portata in Villa)* is about 5d. Englifh the bufhel. Millet, maiz, &c. pays 12 *foldi* the *facco*, of or about 3½d. the Englifh bufhel. Hay, the *carro* of 100 *peze*, pays 12 *f.* 3¼ *den.* or about 6d. a ton Englifh.

Verona.

Meadows, throughout the Veronefe State, pay a tax of hay to the cavalry; furnifhing it at a lower price than the common one. The land-tax here, 24 *f.* for each *campo*, or about 10d. the Englifh acre; befides which, there are *entrées (dazio)* for municipal charges on all products, amounting to about 2 per cent. of the value; alfo others payable to the State. Hay pays 24 *f.* the *carro*: the fack of wheat, 10 *f.*: of maiz, 1½ *f.* There is a moft mifchievous tax on cattle; a pair of oxen pays half a *zecchin* per annum; cows fomething lefs; and fheep alfo pay a certain tax per head.

Vicenza.

Salt is 6 *f.* the pound: flefh, 3 *f.* entrée *(dazio)*: a fack of wheat, 4½ *f.*: of flour, of 180 lb. 3 liv. 2 *f.*: and every thing that comes in pays. Land-tax, 2 liv. the *campo*: and a poll-tax of 2 liv. a head, on all above feven years old.

Padua.

The land-tax, 20 *f.* the *campo*; and 10 *f.* or 15 *f.* for the expences on rivers; but this tax uncertain.

Venice.

No tax on cattle in the Polefine. The land-tax on all the Terra Firma; arable, 2 liv. the *campo*: meadow, 1 liv. 10 *f.*: woods, 10 *f.* The fale of meat in the city is a monopoly, no other perfons but thofe appointed being allowed to fell. *Entrées* are paid on every thing that comes in; on wine it is heavy. Tobacco is a monopoly, at a heavy price, referved by the State throughout all the Venetian territory, producing 50,000 ducats a month, and guarded by the fame infamous feverities, that are found in other defpotic countries. Salt the fame. Inheritances, except from a father, pay 5 per cent. on the capital; a woman pays this cruel impofition, even upon her receipt from a father, or a hufband. Infamous tyranny! The city of Venice pays about one-fixth of the whole revenue.

ECCLE-

ECCLESIASTICAL STATE.—*Bologna.*

Taxation, **at Bologna, is one** of the moft remarkable circumſtances I met in Italy. I had often read, and had been generally given to underſtand, that the government of the church was the worſt to be found in Italy; what it may be in the Roman State, I know not, but in the Bologneſe it is amongſt the lighteſt to be found in Europe. There **are four** objects of **taxation :**—1. The Pope. 2. **The municipal government of the city.** 3. **The** ſchools in the univerſity. 4. **The banks, &c.** of the rivers, againſt inundations. Of all theſe, **there is ſome reaſon to** believe that the Pope receives the leaſt ſhare. The common land-tax is only 2 *baiocchi* the *tornatura*; this is about 2d. the Engliſh acre. Lands ſubject to inundations, pay 5 *baiocchi* more. Among the impoſts levied in the city, wine only, and a few trifles, belong to his Holineſs. Salt, fiſh, **meat,** cocoons (for there is a ſmall duty upon them), and grinding **corn,** theſe are municipal; and among the heavieſt articles of the cities ex‑ **pence,** is the intereſt of about a million ſterling of debt. In general, the re‑ **venue of the** *dogana,* or cuſtom-houſe, is applied towards ſupporting the lectures in the public ſchools, and the botanical garden. There is a light capitation, which is paid in the country, as well as in the city. Upon the whole, the amount of the taxes of every kind is ſo inconſiderable, that the weight is felt by nobody, and was eſteemed to be exceedingly light by every perſon I converſed with.

TUSCANY.—*Florence.*

Every circumſtance concerning taxation, in the dominions of **the moſt en‑** lightened Prince in Europe, **muſt neceſſarily be** intereſting. If the reader is at all converſant with the works of the *economiſtes,* with which France was ſo deluged ſome years ago, he will know, that when they were refuted in argu‑ ment, upon the theory of a univerſal land-tax, to abſorb all others, they ap‑ pealed to practice, and cited the example of Tuſcany, in which dominion their plan was executed. I was eager to know the reſult; the detail I ſhall give, imperfect as it is, will ſhew on what ſort of foundations thoſe gentlemen built, when they quitted the fields of ſpeculation and idea. I was not idle in making inquiries; but the Grand Duke has made ſo many changes, no year paſſing without ſome, and all of them wiſe and benevolent, that to attain an accurate knowledge is not ſo eaſy a buſineſs as ſome perſons may be inclined to think. The following particulars I offer, as little more than hints to inſtigate other travellers, whoſe longer reſidence gives them better opportunities, to examine things of ſo much importance to the bottom.

The

The eſtimation on which the preſent land-tax is collected is ſo old as 1394; of courſe it can bear no proportion with the value or with the produce of the land; whatever improvements are made, the tax remains the ſame; much of it has been bought off in payments made by proprietors, who have paid at different periods certain ſums, to be exempted forever from this tax; a ſingular circumſtance, and which marks no inconſiderable degree of confidence in the government. That part of this tax which is paid to the communities for roads, &c. is not thus redeemable; and, without any breach of faith, the tax has received additions; it amounts to more than one-tenth of the net rent. A capitation from 1½ liv. to 4 liv. per head (the livre is 8½d. Engliſh). Every body pays this tax in the country, except children under three years of age; and all towns, except Florence, Piſa, Siena, and Leghorn, which are exempted, becauſe they pay *entrées*. Nothing is paid on cattle. Butchers in the country pay a tax of 1 ſ. per lb. (ſomething under ½d. per lb. Engliſh); in a diſtrict of ſeven miles long by four or five broad, the butcher pays 500 *ſcudi* per annum to the prince; as this tax implies a monopoly, it is ſo far a miſchievous one; and even a countryman cannot kill his own hog without paying 5 liv. or 6 liv. if ſold. Bakers pay none. Cuſtoms on imports, and ſome on exports, are paid at all the ports and frontiers; and the *entrées* at the above-mentioned towns are on moſt kinds of merchandize and objects of conſumption. Houſes pay a *dixme* on their rents. Stamped paper is neceſſary for many tranſactions. The transfer of land and houſes, by ſale or collateral ſucceſſion, pays 7 per cent. and legacies of money and marriage portions the ſame—a very heavy and impolitic tax. There is a *gabelle* upon ſalt, which however the Grand Duke ſunk ſix months ago from 4 to 2 *gras*; he, at the ſame time, made Empoly the only emporium, but as that occaſioned much expence of carriage, he augmented the land-tax enough to pay the loſs, by ſelling it to the poor only at 2 *gras*; the rich pay the ſame, but with the addition of carriage. Tobacco was alſo a revenue, and, with ſalt, paid 1 liv. per head on all the population of the Dutchy, or one million. The *entrées* above-mentioned are not inconſiderable; a calf pays 6 liv.; a hog, 5 liv. per 100 lb.; grain nothing; flour, 10 *ſoldi* (there are 20 *ſoldi* in 1 liv.); beans, 2 ſ.; a load of hay, of 3000 lb. 4 liv.; of ſtraw, under 2000 lb. 2 liv. Houſes are alſo ſubjected to an annual tax; Florence pays 22,000 *ſcudi* a year to it: it may be ſuppoſed to be levied pretty ſtrictly, as the Grand Duke ordered all his palaces, the famous gallery, &c. to be valued, and he pays for them to the communities. What a wiſe and refined policy! and how contrary to the exemptions known in England! When the capitation was increaſed in France, in a bad period, Louis XIV. ordered the Dauphin himſelf, and all the princes of the blood, to be rated to it, that the nobility might not claim exemptions. Lotteries, to my great ſurprize, I found eſtabliſhed here. The

domains

domains of the fovereign were confiderable. It was always a part of the policy of Leopold, to fell all the farms that could be difpofed of advantageoufly; he fold many; but there are yet many not difpofed of. I found it a queftion at Florence, whether this were good policy or not? A gentleman of confiderable ability contended againſt thefe fales, judging the poffeffion of land to be a good mode of raifing a public revenue. The opinion I think ill founded; if it be carried to any extent (and if incapable of being fo, there is an end of the queftion), the lofs by fuch poffeffions muft be great : every eftate is ill managed, and unprofitably, and ufually badly cultivated, in proportion to the extent.— And when this evil extends to fuch immenfe poffeffions, as are neceffary to conftitute a public revenue, the inquiry is decided in a moment; and it muft on all hands be agreed, that there cannot be a more expenfive mode of fupporting the fovereign.

From the preceding catalogue of taxes, which is very far from being complete, it may eafily be concluded, that Monf. de la Lande was not perfectly accurate in faying, " Le projet du gouvernement eft de réduire toutes les taxes dans la Tofcane à un impôt unique, qui fe percevra fur le produit net des terres." This is the old affertion of the *economiftes*; but if it be the project of government, it is executed in a manner not at all analogous to fuch a fyftem; for there is hardly a tax to be met with in Europe, which is not to be found in Tufcany. I was told, however, that the Grand Duke had formed an opinion, that fuch a fcheme would be beneficial if executed; but from his conduct, after a reign of twenty years, it is evident that his good fenfe convinced him that fuch a plan, whether good or bad in theory, is abfolutely impracticable. He may have made it a fubject of converfation; but he was abundantly too prudent to venture on fo dangerous, and what would prove fo mifchievous an experiment.

The Grand Duke gave to all the communities, the power of taxation for roads, bridges, public fchools, reparations of public buildings, falaries of fchoolmafters, &c. Among the long lift of taxes, however, there are no excifes on manufactures, fuch as leather, paper, &c.

The whole revenue of the Grand Duke may be eftimated at one million of *fcudi*, (5s. 8d. each), paid by about a million of fouls, fpread over a thoufand fquare miles of territory; or 283,333l.: this is the received opinion at Florence; but there are reafons for believing it under the truth, and that, if every kind of revenue whatever were fairly brought to account, it would amount to 400,000l. a year. At this fum the Tufcans muft be confidered amongft the lighteft taxed people in Europe; for they pay but 8s. a head. The people of England pay fix times as much.

MODENA.

MODENA.

The common calculation in the Modenefe is, that all taxes whatever equal one-fifth of the grofs produce of the land; as the duties are various, fuch calculations muft neceffarily be liable to a good deal of error. In the *cenfimento*, or *cadaftre* of the Dutchy, eftates are valued at the half of their real worth, and the tax is laid at 1 per cent. annual payment of their fee fimple; this amounts to 6s. in the pound land-tax; but it may be fuppofed that the real payment does not amount to any thing fo enormous as this. It appears by the *cenfimento*, that in the plain, there are 67,378 pieces of land, and 738,809 *biolca*. The total revenue of Modena at prefent amounts to 300,000 *zecchini*, (142,000l.); 200,000 of which go to the Duke's treafure, and 100,000 for rivers, roads, bridges, communities, &c. Among the taxes, many are heavy, and complained of; befide the land-tax above-mentioned, the general farms amount to 55,000 *zecchini:* all corn muft be ground at the Duke's mills, and 3 *pauls* paid for each fack of 300 lb. of 12 oz. There is a *gabelle* on falt; it fells, white, at 22 *bol.* the pound; black, 8 *bol.* Snuff is 1 *paul* the pound. They have ftamped paper for many tranfactions. Every horfe pays 20 *bol.*; each ox, 10 *bol.* Sheep and hogs, 4 *bol.*: and if any perfon be abfent from the State for the term of a year, he pays an abfentee tax. *Entrées* are paid by every thing that comes into the city; a load of wood, 20 *bol.*; a fack of wheat, 3 *bol.*; a load of hay, 20 *bol.*; of faggots, 20 *bol.* All meat, 4 *bol.* the pound. Wine, 14 liv. the meafure, of 12 *poids*, each 25 lb. of 12 oz. Coffee, $\frac{1}{2}$ *paul* per lb. The fale, &c. of land, pays 5 per cent.

PARMA.

The revenues of this dukedom are two-thirds of thofe of Modena. The land-tax is 50 f. the *biolca*, (about 9d. an acre). The peafants pay a capitation; this varies, if they are enrolled, or not as foldiers. A man pays 18 liv. (each 2½d.) per annum, if not a foldier, but 3½ liv. or 4 liv. if enrolled. A woman, not the wife of a foldier, 15 liv. Thefe foldiers, or rather militia-men, **pay** alfo 24 f. a month, as an exemption from fervice. He is enrolled for twenty-five years, after which he has the fame advantage. He pays alfo but half for his falt, 6 f. only the pound; others 12 f. A metayer, who is a foldier, pays all forts of taxes, about 60 liv.

SECT.

SECT. III.——OF TITHE AND CHURCH LANDS.

PIEDMONT.

Throughout this principality, tithe is an object of no account. I made inquiries concerning it every where: the greatest part of the lands pay none; and upon the rest it is so light, as not to amount to more than from a twentieth to a fiftieth of the produce *.

MILANESE.

In the country from Milan to Pavia, no tithe of any kind, but the *curées* are supported by foundations. In the village where I made inquiries into the dairy management,—the *curée* has 21 *stara* of rice, 12 *stara* of rye, 4 *stara* of wheat; 300 lb. of the best hay from one large farm; and he has some other little stipends in nature; the amount small, and never paid as a tithe.

At Mozzata, the tithes, as every where else, are so low as to be no object; grain pays, but not on all land; it is confined to the lands *antiently in culture* †; for even the ancestors of these people were much too wise, to allow the church to tax them in such a spirit, as to take tithes of new improvements. Never did such a measure enter their heads or hearts! The titheable lands are small districts; are near to the villages that have been in cultivation many centuries; and in some of these, tithe is not taken on all sorts of corn; only on those sorts antiently cultivated. The variations in this respect are many; but on whatever it is taken, it never exceeds a sixteenth, usually from one-seventeenth to one-twentieth; and of such as are levied, the whole does not belong to the *curée*, not more perhaps than one-fourth; one-half to the canons of some distant church, to which the whole probably once belonged; and one-fourth sold off to some lay-lord, with a stipulation to repair the church. The variations are so great, that no general rule holds; but they are every where so light, that no complaints are heard of them.

The church lands seized by the late Emperor in the Milanese, were of immense value. From Pavia to Plaisance, all was in the hands of the monks; and the Count de Belgiofo has hired thirty-six dairy farms of the Emperor, by

* Tithe in Sardinia is heavy. They pay one-tenth of the corn, and one-ninth of that one-tenth for threshing, and one-fifth of the one-tenth for carriage.—*Rifiorimente della Sardegna*, tom. i. p. 146.

† A remarkable passage in Giulini deserves noting here; under the year 1147, he gives *finalemente si prohibisce a ciascheduno effigere le decima dai terreni di nuovo coltivati*, tom. v. p. 459.

which

which he makes a profit of 50,000 liv. a year. The revenue that was feized, in the city of Milan only, amounted to above 5,000,000 liv.; and they fay in that city, that in the whole Auftrian monarchy, it amounted to 20,000,000 florins.

At Codogno, and through moft of the Lodizan, tithe is fo very inconfiderable, that it is not worth mentioning; the expreffion of the gentlemen who were my informants.

STATE OF VENICE.

In the diftrict of Verona, mulberries pay no tithe; wheat one-twelfth in fome places, in others lefs; maiz, millet, &c. from one-fifteenth to one-thirtieth; but if for forage only, they pay none, no more than vetches, chich-peafe, millet, &c. as it appears by a late memoir printed at Venice*. Meadows pay a light tithe, becaufe they are taxed to find hay for the cavalry at an under price. In the diftrict of Vicenza, tithe varies from the one-tenth to the forty-firft. About Padua, wheat alone pays the tenth: vines a trifle, at the will of the farmer: mulberries, fheep, and cows, nothing.

ECCLESIASTICAL STATE.—*Bologna.*

Tithes are fo low throughout all the Bolognefe, that I could get no fatisfactory account of the very fmall payments that are yet made to the church; every one affured me, that they were next to nothing; but that in the Ferrarefe they are high.

TUSCANY.

In many of the countries of Europe, the feizure of eftates and effects of the jefuits was a rapacious act, to the profit of the Prince or State; in Tufcany it was converted to a more ufeful purpofe. The Grand Duke fet afide thefe revenues for forming a fund, called the *Ecclefiaftical Patrimony*, under the management of a new tribunal, that fhould enable him gradually to abolifh tithes. This great reform, equally beneficial to every clafs of the people, has been in execution for many years: as faft as the prefent incumbents of the livings die, tithes are abolifhed for ever; their fucceffors enter into poffeffion of moderate falaries, payable out of thofe funds, or raifed by an addition to the land-tax; and thus an impoft, of all others the moft mifchievous, is fpeedily extinguifhing, and the agriculture of Tufcany improving in confequence; proportionably to fuch extinction of its former burthens. Many monafteries have been alfo fuppreffed, and their revenues applied, in fome cafes, to the fame ufe; but this

* *Raccolta di Memorie Delle Pubbliche Accademie,* 8vo, 1789, tom. i. p. 197.

has

has not been attended with effects equally good: the lands are not equally well cultivated; nor do they yield the same revenue as formerly; for the farms of the monks were in the best order, administered by themselves, and every thing carefully attended to. This was not the case, however, with **convents** of women, who being obliged to employ deputies, their estates were not **equally** well managed.

A proposition was lately made **by the court, to sell all the glebes belonging to the livings, and to add to the salaries of the** *curées* **in lieu of them ; but at a public meeting of the Academia di Georgofili, Sig. Paoletti, a** *curé* **in the neighbourhood of Florence, a practical farmer, and author of some excellent treatises on the art, made a speech so pointedly against the scheme, fraught with so much good sense, and delivered with so much eloquence, that the plan was immediately dropped, and resumed no more; this was equally to the honour** of Paoletti and of Leopold. When good sense is on the throne, subjects need not fear to speak it.

The lightness of the old tithes may be estimated, by **the** payment which **forty farms at** Villamagna yield to the same Sig. Paoletti, the *curé*, which is 40 *scudi* (each 5s. 8d.), and this is only for his life; to his successor nothing in this **kind will be paid. Having** mentioned Sig. **Paoletti, and much to his honour, I must give another anecdote of him, not** less **to his credit; after his Sunday's sermon, it has long been his practice to offer to his audience,** some instruction **in agriculture; which they** are at liberty to listen **to, or absent themselves, as they please.** For this practice, which deserved every **commendation,** his archbishop reproved him. He replied, that he neglected no duty by offering such instruction, and his congregation could not suffer, but might profit, and innocently too, by what they heard. A sovereign that receives so much merited praise as the great Leopold, can well afford to hear of his faults; first, why did he not reprove this prelate, for his conduct; and by so doing encourage an attention to agriculture in the clergy? secondly, why did he not reward a good farmer, and worthy priest, and excellent writer, with something better than this little rectory? Talents and merit in an inferior situation, which might be better exerted, are a reproach, not to the possessor, but to the prince.

The Grand Duke took the administration of the lands belonging to hospitals and the poor into his own hands also; but the effect of this has not, in the opinion of some persons, been equally beneficial; the poor remain as they were, but the revenue gone; this, in the diocese of Florence only, amounted, it is said, to three or four millions of *scudi*: if this be true, the mischief attending such revenues must be enormous; and taking them away, provided the *really useful* hospitals be supported, which is the case, must be beneficial. Too many and

great eſtabliſhments of this nature nurſe up idleneſs; and create, by de-
pendency and expectation, the evils they are deſigned to cure. Poverty always
abounds in proportion to ſuch funds; ſo that if the fund were doubled, the
miſery it is meant to prevent would be doubled alſo. No poor in the world
are found at their eaſe by means of hoſpitals, and gratuitous charities; it is
an induſtry, ſo ſteady and regular, as to preclude all other dependence, that
can alone place them in ſuch a ſituation, as I have endeavoured to ſhew in my
remarks on France.

The patrimony of almoſt all the pariſhes in Tuſcany, conſiſts in lands aſſigned
them : the rector is adminiſtrator and guardian of them; and, both by law and
his oath on induction, he is ſtrictly obliged to maintain and ſupport them; and
alſo to manure them, and to increaſe the produce *.

DUTCHY OF MODENA.

No tithe here; a voluntary gift only to the *ſub-curée*. The eccleſiaſtical
lands have been largely ſeized here, as well as every where elſe in Italy; but
the Duke gave them to the towns, to aſſiſt them in the expence of the municipal adminiſtration.

DUTCHY OF PARMA.

No real tithe; the payments in lieu very ſmall, and not proportioned to the
crop; a farm pays a *ſtajo* of wheat, (about 88 lb. Engliſh), two parcels of
raiſins, and twenty faggots, between the two *curées*.

Upon this detail of the tithe paid in Lombardy, &c. one obſervation ſtrongly
impreſſes itſelf, that the patrimony of the church is, under every government
in Italy, conſidered as the property of the State, and ſeized or aſſigned accordingly. It highly merits attention, that in the free countries of Holland and
Switzerland, (exempt at leaſt from the deſpotiſm of a ſingle perſon), the ſame
principle has been adopted; with what reaſon therefore can the *firſt* National
Aſſembly of France be reproached, as guilty of a *ſingular* outrage, for doing
that which every neighbour they have (England and Spain only excepted)
had done before them; and which may poſſibly, in a better mode, be followed in every country in Europe? They have in Italy rid themſelves of
tithes, though not half, perhaps not upon an average a third, of the burthen they amount to in England, where their levy has been carried to a

* *Pauletti Penſieri ſopra l'Agricoltura*, 8vo. Firenze, 1789. p. 50. 2d edit.

much

much greater height. If the legiflature of that kingdom would give a due encouragement, they will remove fuch burthens gradually, and with wifdom. All I converfed with in Italy, on the fubject of tithes, expreffed amazement at the tithes we are fubject to; and fcarcely believed that there was a people left in Europe, who paid fo much: obferving, that nothing like it was to be found even in Spain itfelf.

SECT. IV.——OF MANUFACTURES AND COMMERCE.

Piedmont.

Two-thirds of the rice raifed is exported: I met carts loaded with filk and rice on the great road to France; and demanding afterwards concerning this trade, I was informed, that the coft of the carriage was 30 f. per *rubbio*, to Lyons or Geneva, and 3 liv. to Paris.—The following are the principal exports:

				Liv.
Unwrought filk,	-	-	-	17,000,000
Damafks, &c.		-	-	500,000
Rice,	-	-	-	3,500,000
Hemp,	-	-	-	1,500,000
Cattle,	-	-	-	2,000,000
				24,500,000

Oil and wine from Nice; walnut-oil, cobalt, lead, and copper ore, add fome-thing. France commonly takes 10,000,000 liv. in filk, and England 5,000,000 liv. of the fineft fort. The balance of trade is generally fuppofed to be about 500,000 liv. againft Piedmont; but all fuppofitions of this fort are very conjec-tural; fuch a country could not long continue to pay fuch a balance; and, confequently, there cannot be any fuch. By another account, wheat exported is 200,000 facks, at 5 *eymena*; 5000 facks of rice, at 3 *eymena*; hemp, 5000 quintals; and 10,000 head of oxen.

Turin.

The Englifh woollen manufacturers having fworn, at the bar of the Houfe of Lords, that the French camblets, made of Englifh wool, rivalled the Eng-lifh camblets in the Italian markets, and even underfold them, I had previoufly

N n 2

determined

determined to make inquiries into the truth of this affertion. I was at **Turin** introduced to Sig. Vinatier, a confiderable fhopkeeper, who fold both. His account of the French and Englifh camblets was this; that the Englifh **are** much better executed, better wrought, and more beautiful; but that the French are ftrongeft. I defired to know which were the cheapeft. The Englifh, he faid, being much the narrower, it was a matter of calculation; but he fuppofed the confumers thought the Englifh cheapeft, as where he fold one French, he fold at leaft twenty-five Englifh. He fhewed me various pieces of both, and faid, that the above circumftances were applicable both to ftuffs mixed of wool and filk, and alfo thofe of wool only. I afked him then concerning cloths: he faid, the Englifh ordinary cloths were much better than the French, but that the French fine cloths were better than the Englifh. Thefe inquiries brought me acquainted with an Italian dealer, or merchant as he is called, in hardware, who informed me, that he was at Birmingham in 1786 and 1789, and that he found a fenfible diminution of price; and that the prices of Englifh hardware have fallen for fome years paft; and that, for thefe laft three or four years, the trade in them to Italy has increafed confiderably. He has not only bought, but examined with care, the fine works in fteel at Paris, but they are not equal to the Englifh; that the French have not the art of hardening their fteel; or if hardened of not working it; for the Englifh goods are much harder and better polifhed, confequently, are not equally fubject to ruft.

Milanese.

In the fifteenth century, the trade of this country was confiderable. In 1423, the territory of Milan paid to the Venetians:

Milan, - - -	900,000 ducats.
Monza, - - -	52,000
Como, - - -	104,000
Aleffandria, - -	52,000
Tortona and Novara, - -	104,000
Pavia, - - - -	104,000
Cremona, - - -	104,000
Bergamo, - - -	78,000
Parma, - - -	104,000
Piacenza, - - -	52,000
	1,654,000

And

And they ſent to Venice, at the ſame time, cloths to the following amount :

	Cloths.		Ducats.
Aleſſandria, Tortona, and Novara, at 15 ducats,	6000	-	90,000
Pavia, at 15 ducats, - - -	3000	-	45,000
Milan, at 30 ditto, - - -	4000	-	120,000
Como, at 15 ditto, - - -	12,000	-	180,000
Monza, at 15 ditto, - - -	6000	-	90,000
Breſcia, at 15 ditto, - - -	5000	-	75,000
Bergamo, at 7 ditto, - - -	10,000	-	70,000
Cremona, at 40¼ ditto, - -	40,000	-	170,000
Parma, at 15 ditto, - - -	4000	-	60,000
	90,000	-	900,000
Duties and warehouſes, - - -		-	200,000
Canvas, - - - - -		-	100,000

And at the ſame time the Milaneſe took from Venice annually :

Cotton raw, 5000 *miliari*, - -	250,000 ducats.
Cotton ſpun, - - - -	30,000
Wool of Catalonia, 4000 *miliari*, -	120,000
French wool, - - - -	120,000
Gold and ſilk fabrics, - - -	250,000
Pepper, - - - - -	300,000
Soap, - - - - -	250,000
Cinnamon, - - - -	64,000
Ginger, - - - -	80,000
Slaves, - - - -	30,000
Sugar, - - - - -	95,000
Materials for embroidery, - -	30,000
Dying woods, - - -	120,000
Indigo, &c. - - - -	50,000 *

The produce of ſilk amounts to 9,000,000 liv. ; nineteen-twentieths of which, at leaſt, are exported.

Count Verri, in his *Storia di Milano*, mentions that the Milaneſe, only ſixty miles by fifty, feeds 1,130,000 inhabitants ; and exports to the amount of 1,350,000 *zecchini* †, viz. ſilk, 1,000,000 ; cheeſe and flax, more than 200,000 ; corn, 150,000 (the *zecchini* being 9s. 6d. the ſum of 1,350,000 equals 641,200l.)

* *Giulini*, vol. xii. p. 362.　　　† *Verri*, tom. i. p. 236.

But

But this is changed much, for the export of cheese alone is calculated now at 9,200,000 liv. which is above 306,000l. sterling.

Bergamo.

The woollen manufacture at this place is of great antiquity, and it is yet confiderable. Its trade in filk is great; they buy from Crema, Monti, Brianza, Ghiara d'Adda, and in general the confines of the Milanese; this has given their filk trade a greater reputation than it deferves, for their commerce is more extenfive than their product. They have been known to export filk, to the amount of near 300,000l. sterling a year. Here alfo is a fabric of iron and fteel, of fome confideration in Italy; but none of thefe objects are in a ftile to be interefting to thofe who have been at all converfant with the fabrics of England. If, however, the manufactures of Bergamo are compared with thofe of the Milanefe, they will be found confiderable.

Brefcia.

This is a very bufy place; the city and the vicinity, for fome miles, abound with many fabrics, particularly of fire-arms, cutlery, and other works of iron. They have many filk and oil mills; and fome paper fabrics, that fucceed well. But their commerce of all forts has declined fo much, as not to be compared at prefent, to what it has been in former times.

Verona.

Here is a woollen fabric that ftill maintains fome little ground; though the declenfion it has fuffered is very great. I was affured, that 20,000 manufacturers were once found in a fingle ftreet; this, I fuppofe, may be an exaggeration, but it at leaft marks that it was once very great: now there are not 1000 in the whole city; in the time of its profperity, they ufed chiefly their own wool, at prefent it is imported.

In the Veronefe, they make one million of pounds of filk, of 12 oz.; and rice nearly to as great an amount.

STATE OF VENICE.—*Verona.*

Many years paft, the only great import of camblets was from Saxony; but after the war of 1758, the Englifh ones eftablifhed themfelves, and there is now no comparifon between the quantity of Englifh and French; of the latter, very few, but the import of the former is confiderable.

Vicenza.

Vicenza.

They fell nine pieces of Englifh camblets to one of French. A woollen manufacture was eftablifhed here three years ago, under the direction of Thomas Montfort, an Englifhman. It works up their own wool, and alfo Spanifh. Spinning a pound of fine wool, 50 f. and the women earn 15 f. a day; weavers, 2 liv. Count Vicentino has eftablifhed a fabric of earthen ware, with a capital of 9000 ducats; Mr. Wedgwood's forms (originally however from Italy) are imitated throughout. A good plate, plain, 12 f.; ewer and bafon, 12 liv.; fmall tea-cup and faucer, quite plain, 15 f.; tea-pot, 4 liv.; vaze, 18 inches high, with a feftoon and openings for flowers, 60 liv. It meets with no great fuccefs, and no encouragement from the government.

Venice.

In the fifteenth century, Venice employed 3345 fhips, great and fmall, and **43,000 failors*. The chief export** at prefent, is filk; the fecond, corn of all **forts; the third,** raifins, currants, and wine. Glafs is yet a manufacture of fome confequence, though greatly fallen, even of late years. Tuyan for beads, is, however, yet unrivalled. The glafs of Bohemia underfells, from the great cheapnefs of wood, and poffibly from that of provifions (my informant fpeaks), not only the glafs of Venice, but that of Carniola alfo. The chief export from Venice, of fabrics, is to the Levant; velvets and filks go there to fome amount. The **trade of the whole Venetian** territory, does not employ **above 250 fhips of national bottoms.**

Ecclesiastical State.—*Bologna.*

All the filk of the Bolognefe, is here made into crape and gauze; the crapes **are, perhaps, the fineft in the world,** price confidered. The gauzes alfo are **very beautiful: they meafure by the** *braccio* of forty inches; they fell at 26 to 36 *baiocchi* the *braccio*; (10 *baiocchi* equal 6d. Englifh). White handkerchiefs are alfo made of 7 liv. each. Crapes and gauzes employ feven or eight thoufand people.

Tuscany.—*Florence.*

The woollen manufacture was amongft the greateft refources of the Florentines, in the time of their republic.

---

* *Ragionamente ful Commercio, &c. della Tofcana,* 8vo, 1781, p. 21.—*Marino Sanudo tra gli Scrittori Italici del Muratori,* tom. ii.—*Conte Carli delle Monete,* tom. iii. dif. 7.—*Mebrgan Tableau de l'Hift. Moder.* tom. ii. epog. 7.

In

In 1239, the friars umiliate came to Florence, to improve the manufactory of woollen cloth. They made the fineſt cloths of the age; the beſt, of the wool of Spain and Portugal; the ſeconds, of that of England, France, Majorca, Minorca, Sardinia, Barbary, Apulia, Romana, and Tuſcany *. In 1336, there were at Florence, more than two hundred ſhops, in which woollens were manufactured, which made from 70 to 80,000 pieces of cloth yearly, of the value of 1,200,000 *zecchini*; of which, the third part remained in the country for labour; and employed more than 30,000 ſouls; and thirty years before that, the number was much greater, even to 100,000 pieces, but coarſer, and of only half the value, becauſe they did not receive, nor know how to work the wools of England. In 1460, they were augmented to two hundred and ſeventy-three, but the quality and quantity unknown †. From 1407 to 1485, was the period of its greateſt proſperity. In 1450, Coſmo of Medicis, was the greateſt merchant in Europe. From the year 1365 to 1406, the republic of Florence, in wars only, expended 11,500,000 *zecchini* ‡.

I was aſſured at Florence, but I know not the authority, that 1 ſ. a week, on the wages of the woollen manufacturers only, built the cathedral; and that at a ſingle fair, in the time of the republic, woollen goods to the amount of 12,000,000 of crowns have been ſold.

Giuliano and Lorenzo de Medici ſent into England Florentine manufacturers of wool, to exerciſe their trade, for the account of thoſe princes to take advantage of the cheapneſs of wool on the ſpot; from which circumſtance, the Florentine writer infers, that the Engliſh thus gained the art of making cloth §.

Theſe particulars, it muſt be confeſſed, are curious, but I muſt draw one concluſion from them, which will militate conſiderably with the ideas of thoſe perſons, who inſiſt that the only way of encouraging agriculture is to eſtabliſh great manufactures. Here were, for three centuries, ſome of the greateſt fabrics, perhaps the greateſt in Europe; and Piſa flouriſhed equally; and yet the eſtabliſhment and the ſucceſs of a vaſt commerce, which gave the city immenſe riches, the ſigns of which are to be met with at this day, in every part of it, had ſo little effect on the agriculture of Tuſcany, that no perſon ſkilled in huſbandry can admit it to be well cultivated; and yet the improvements in the laſt twenty years are, I am aſſured, very great. Here then is a ſtriking proof, that the prodigious trade of the Tuſcan towns had little or no effect in ſecuring a flouriſhing agriculture to the country. Theſe great political queſtions, are not to be decided by eternal reaſonings—it is by recurring to facts

---

** Ragionamente Sopra Toscana*, p. 39.

† *Ib.* p. 39, from Giovanni **Villani**, Franceſco Balducci, Giovanni da Uzzano Benedetto Dei.

‡ *Criſtofano Landino Apologia di Dante.*   § *Ragionamente Sopra Toscano*, p. 61.

alone

alone, that fatisfaction can be gained. No wonder that the rich deep foils of Lombardy and Flanders have been well applied; but the more ungrateful and fteril hills of Tufcany remain (at leaft what I have feen of them) wild and unimproved.

There is yet a woollen manufacture of fome confideration, and they make fine cloths of Vigonia wool; alfo hats; and various fabrics of filk.

The export of woollens from Tufcany in 1757, was 120,000 lb.; and in 1762, it was 180,000 lb.[*]

Among the filk manufactures, here are fome good, and pretty fatins, 18 *pauls* (the paul 5½d.) the *braccio*, (about two feet Englifh), the width one *braccio* four inches.

The filk fpun in Tufcany in ten years, from 1760 to 1769 inclufive, amounts to 1,676,745 lb.; or per annum, 167,674 lb.; and in the firft fum is comprifed 286,979 lb. of cocoons, bought of foreigners[†]. The filk manufacture amounts to a million of crowns, (7 liv. 10*f.* of Tufcany[‡]). Of oil, the export is about 100,000 *barrils*. The year following the edict for the free commerce of oil and grain, the export amounted to 600,000 *fcudi*[§]. Next to oil, hogs are the greateft export, to the amount of from 20 to 30,000 in a year.

The average of the quantity of filk made in Tufcany, and regiftered in the tribunal of Florence, from 1769 to 1778, was 165,168 lb.; and the import of foreign filk, 48,470 lb.; together, 213,649 lb. yearly[‖].

MODENA.

In 1771, the following were the exports of the Modenefe:

				Liv.
Brandy, 50,000 *poids*,	-	-	-	593,280
Wine, 150,000 ditto,	-	-	-	428,222
Oxen, 5,232 head,	-	-	-	1,569,600
Cows, 3,068 ditto,	-	-	-	613,400
Calves, one year, 500 ditto,	-	-	-	69,150
Wethers and goats, 23,500 ditto,	-	-	141,048
Hogs, 11,580 ditto,	-	-	-	347,280
Pigs, 21,900 ditto,	-	-	-	329,145
Linen, hemp, facks, &c. 1,800,000 *braccio*,	-	1,442,327
Carry forward,	-	-	5,533,452

[*] *Ragionamente Sopra Tofcana*, p. 183.
[†] *Penfieri Ap. Apol.* p. 56.　　[‡] *Ib.* p. 57.　　[§] *Ib.* p. 59.
[‖] *Ragionamente Sopra Tofcana*, p. 161.

		Liv.
Brought forward,	- -	5,533,452
Hogs salted, 1,900 poids,	- - -	24,479
Poultry,	- - -	24,342
Hats of straw and chip,	- - -	145,308
Ditto of woollen,	- - -	23,205
Grofs fabricks of wool,	- - -	83,362
Butter,	- - -	106,240
Hemp, fpun or prepared, 13,900 *poids*,	- -	348,000
Wax,	- - - -	74,400
Silk, 77,650 lb.	- - -	3,897,312
Honey,	- - - -	15,350
Cheefe,	- - -	98,556
Chefnuts,	- - - -	17,440
Fruit,	- - - -	81,320
		10,472,766

All thefe are by the regifters of the farms; the contraband is to be added.—
Exportation is now greater than in 1771.

PARMA.

The firft trade and export of the country is filk; the next cattle and hogs.

There is but one conclufion to be drawn from this detail of the commerce of
Lombardy, namely, that eighteen-twentieths of it confift in the export of the
produce of agriculture, and therefore ought rather to be efteemed a branch of
that art, than of commerce, according to modern ideas; and it is equally
worthy of notice, that thus fubfifting by agriculture, and importing manufactures, thefe countries muft be ranked among the moft flourifhing in the world;
abounding with large and magnificent towns; decorated in a manner that fets
all comparifon at defiance: the country every where cut by canals of navigation or irrigation; many of the roads fplendid; an immenfe population; and
fuch public revenues, that if Italy were united under one head, fhe would be
claffed among the firft powers in Europe.

When it is confidered, that all this has been effected generally under governments not the beft in Europe; when we farther reflect, that England has for a century enjoyed the beft government that exifts, we fhall be forced to confefs, perhaps with aftonifhment, that Great Britain has not made confiderable advances in
agriculture, and in the cultivation of her territory. The waftes of the three kingdoms are enormous, and far exceeding, in proportional extent, all that are to be
                                                                             found

found in Italy; while, of our cultivated diſtricts, there are but a few provinces
remarkable for their improvements. Whoever has viewed Italy with any degree of attention, muſt admit, that if a proportion of her territory, containing
as many people as the three Britiſh kingdoms, had for a century enjoyed as free
a government, giving attention to what has been a principal object, viz. agriculture, inſtead of trade and manufacture, they would at this time have made
almoſt every acre of their country a fertile garden; and would have been in
every reſpect a greater, richer, and more flouriſhing people than we can poſſibly
pretend to be. What they have done under their preſent governments, juſtifies
this aſſertion: we, bleſſed with liberty, have little to exhibit of ſuperiority

What a waſte of time to have ſquandered a century of freedom, and la-
viſhed a thouſand millions ſterling of public money *, in queſtions of commerce! He who conſiders the rich inheritance of a hundred years of
liberty, and the magnitude of thoſe national improvements, which ſuch immenſe ſums would have effected, will be inclined to do more than queſtion the
propriety of the political ſyſtem, which has been adopted by the legiſlature of
this kingdom, that in the boſom of freedom, and commanding ſuch ſums, has
not, in the agriculture of any part of her dominions, any thing to preſent
which marks ſuch expence, or ſuch exertion, as the irrigation of Piedmont
and the Milaneſe.

SECT. V.—OF POPULATION.

MILANESE.

In all Auſtrian Lombardy there are 1,300,000 ſouls.

In 1748, the population was about 800,000; and in 1771, it was 1,130,000.
The Milaneſe contains 3000 ſquare miles†. In 1732, there were 800,000
pertiche uncultivated; in 1767, only 208,000. In a ſquare mile, of ſixty to a
degree, there are, in the Milaneſe, 354 ſouls. There are in the Dutchy,
11,385,121 pertiche, at 4868 pertiche in a ſquare mile; and there are in the
State, excluſive of roads, lakes, rivers, &c. 2338 ſquare miles ‡, and 377 perſons per ſquare mile, which is certainly very conſiderable; and, that my
readers may have a clearer idea of this degree of population, I ſhall remark, that
to equal it, England ſhould contain 27,636,362 ſouls §.

* Sir *John* Sinclair's *Hiſtory of the Public Revenue*, vol. ii. p. 98.
† *Delle Opere del S. Conte Carli*, 1784, tom. i. p. 132.   ‡ *Ib.* p. 319.
§ At 73,306 ſquare miles each of 640 acres.

VENETIAN

Venetian State.—*Padouan.*

In the whole diſtrict of the Padouan, there were, in 1760, 240,336 ſouls: in 1781, they were 288,300: increaſe 47,914. There is probably no corner of Europe, barbarous Turkey alone excepted, in which the people do not increaſe conſiderably—we ought not therefore in England, to take too much credit for that rapid augmentation which we experience. It is found under the worſt governments, as well as under the beſt, but not equally.

Venice.

The population of the whole territory, 2,500,000: of the city, between 143 and 149,000, the Zuedecca included.

In Friuli, in 1581, there were 196,541; and in the city of Udine, 14,579. In 1755, in Friuli, 342,158; and in Udine, 14,729 *. The population of all the States of Venice, by another authority, is made 2,830,000; that is 600,000 in Bergamo, Breſcia, &c.: in the reſt of the Terra Firma, 1,860,000: in Dalmatia and Albania, 250,000: in the Greek iſlands, 120,000 †. In the time of Gallo, who died in 1570, there were ſaid to be in the Breſcian, about 700,000 ſouls; in 1764, there were 310,388 ‡.

Tuscany.

The progreſſive population of Florence is thus ſhewn, by Sig. Laſtri:

1470 §,	-	-	-	40,323
1622,	-	-	-	76,023
1660,	-	-	-	56,671
1738,	-	-	-	77,835
1767,	-	-	-	78,635 ‖

The total population of the Dukedom, is calculated at about 1,000,000 **. Two centuries ago, the population of the fields in the mountains, and on the

---

* *Gemelli*, vol. ii. p. 16.   † *Della Piu' utile Ripartizione de' Terreni, &c. San Martine*, 4to, p. 13.

‡ *Gallo Vinti Giornata*, Breſcia, 1773, p. 413.   § *Decima*, tom i. p. 232.

‖ *Ricerche ſull' Antica e Moderna Popolazione della Citta di Firenze*, 4to, 1775, p. 121. Sig. Paoletti is a ſenſible writer, and a good farmer, but he is of Dr. Price's ſchool,—" L' antica popolazione della Toſcana era certamente di gran lunga ſuperiore a quella de' noſtri tempi;"—from Boccaccio, he makes 100,000 to die in Florence, of the plague in 1348; yet, in little more than a century after, there was not half the number in the city; he admits, however, that this is *eſagerato. Penſieri Sopra l'Agricoltura*, p. 18.

** *Icure Mezzi Paoletti*, p. 58

ſea-coaſt,

fea-coaft, was little lefs than double what it is at prefent. And there is faid to have been the fame proportion in the cultivation and cattle [*].

MODENA.

State of the Dutchy in 1781:

Ecclefiaftics, - - -	8,306
Infants, under fourteen years of age, -	50,291
Girls, ditto, - - -	49,516
Men, - - - -	115,464
Women, - - -	124,822
Total	348,399

Marriages, 2,901; births, 12,930; deaths, 10,933. Multiplying the births therefore by 27, gives nearly the population; or the deaths by 41.—Of this total, the following are in the mountain diftricts:

Carrara, - - -	8,865
Maffa, - - - -	11,070
Garfagnana, - - -	22,242
Varano, - - - -	629
Caftel Nuovo, - - -	14,576
Frignano, - - -	19,526
Montefiorino, - - -	15,721
Montefe, - - -	19,694
Total	112,323

The reft in the plain.

PIEDMONT.

Subjects in the King of Sardinia's territories, 3,000,000. In Savoy, 400,000. In Sardinia, 450,000. In Turin, in 1765, 78,807. In 1785, it was 89,185. In 1785, births 3394; deaths 3537.

[*] *Differtazione fulla la Moltiplicazione del Beftiame Tofcani.* Andreucci, 8vo, 1773, p. 14.

OF THE POOR.

MILANESE.—*Milan.*

Charitable foundations, in the city only, amount to 3,000,000 liv. (87,500l. ſterling). In the great hoſpital, there are commonly from twelve to fifteen hundred ſick: the effect is found to be exceedingly miſchievous, for there are many that will not work, depending on theſe eſtabliſhments.

Mozzata.

The labourers here work in ſummer thirteen hours. Breakfaſt one hour; dinner two hours; merenda one hour; ſupper one hour; ſleep ſix hours. They are not in a good ſituation. I was not contented to take the general deſcription, but went early in a morning, with the Marquis Viſconti and Sig. Amoretti, into ſeveral cabins, to ſee and converſe with them. In this village they are all little farmers: I aſked if there were a family in the pariſh without a cow, and was anſwered expreſſly there was not one, for all have land. The pooreſt we ſaw had two cows and 20 *pertiche*; for which ſpace he paid five *moggio* of grain, one-third wheat, one-third rye, and one-third maiz. Another, for 140 *pertiche*, paid 35 *moggio*, in thirds alſo. The poor never drink any thing but water; and are well contented if they can manage always to have bread or polenta; on Sunday they make a ſoup, into which goes perhaps, but not always, a little lard; their children would not be reared, if it were not for the cow. They are miſerably clad; have in general no ſhoes or ſtockings, even in this rainy ſeaſon of the year, when their feet are never dry; the other parts of their dreſs very bad. Their furniture but ordinary, and looks much worſe from the hideous darkneſs from ſmoke, that reigns throughout; yet every cabin has a chimney. They have tolerable kettles, and a little pewter; but the general aſpect miſerable. Fuel, in a country that has neither foreſts nor coal-pits, muſt be a matter of difficulty, though not in the mountains. They were heating their kettles, with the ears of maiz, with ſome heath and broom. In the cold weather, during winter, they always live in the ſtable with their cattle, for warmth, till midnight or bed-time. For day labour they are paid 10ſ. a day in winter, and 12ſ. in ſummer. For a houſe of two rooms, one over the other, the farmer of 20 *pertiche* pays 24 liv. a year; that is to ſay, he works ſo much out with his landlord, keeping the account, as in Ireland, with a tally, a ſplit ſtick notched. They are not, upon the whole, in a ſituation that would allow any one to approve of the ſyſtem of the poor being occupiers of land; and are apparently in much more uneaſy circumſtances,

cumſtances, than the day labourers in the rich watered plain, where all the land is in the hands of the great dairy farmers. I drew the ſame concluſion from the ſtate of the poor in France; theſe in the Milaneſe ſtrongly confirm the doctrine; and unite in forming a perfect contraſt, with the ſituation of the poor in England, without land, but with great comforts.

STATE OF VENICE.

The people appear, in the diſtricts of Bergamo, Breſcia, Verona, and Vicenza, to be in better circumſtances than in the Padouan. And from thence to Venice, there are ſtill greater appearances of poverty: many very poor cottages, with the ſmoke iſſuing from holes in the walls.

Villamagna.

The peaſantry, a term which, in all countries where the landlord is paid by a ſhare of the produce, and not a money rent, includes the farmers, who are conſequently poor, live here better than in diſtricts more diſtant from the capital; they eat fleſh once a week; the common beverage is the ſecond maſh, or wort, of the wine; eat wheaten-bread; and are cloathed pretty well.

SECT. VI.——OF PROHIBITIONS.

PIEDMONT.

The exportation of the cocoons of ſilk is prohibited; and the effect highly merits the attention of the politician, who would be well informed, from practice, of the principles of political œconomy. It is a periſhable commodity, and therefore it is not at all likely, that if the trade were free, the quantity ſent out would be any thing conſiderable; yet, ſuch is the pernicious effect of every ſpecies of monopoly, upon the ſale of the earth's products, that this prohibition ſinks the price 30 per cent. While the cocoons ſell in Piedmont at 24 liv. the *rubbio*, they are ſmuggled to the Genoeſe at 30 liv.; which export takes place in conſequence of the monopoly having ſunk the price. The object of the law is to preſerve to the ſilk-mills, the profit of converting the ſilk to organzine; and for this object, ſo paltry on compariſon with the miſchief flowing from it, the land-owners are cheated in the price of their ſilk 30 per cent.: the State gains nothing; the country gains nothing; for not a ſingle pound would be exported if the trade were free, as the motive for the export would then ceaſe, by the

price

price rifing: the only poffible effect is, that of taking 30 per cent. on all the filk produced out of the pockets of the grower, and putting it into thofe of the manufacturer. A real and unequivocal infamy; which reflects a fcandal on the government, for its ignorance in miftaking the means of effecting its defign; and for its injuftice, in fleecing one clafs of men, for the profit of another. I demanded why the Piedmontefe merchants could not give as good a price as the Genoefe. *" They certainly could give as good a price, but as they know they have the monopoly, and the feller no refource in an export, they will have it at their own price; and if we do not give them this profit of 30 per cent. we cannot fell it at all."* What an exact tranfcript of the wool laws in England!

Another prohibition here, not equally mifchievous, but equally contrary to juft principles, is that of keeping fheep in fummer, any where in or near the plain of Piedmont; it is not eafy to underftand, whether the object of this law is, that the fheep at that feafon *fhall* be kept in the mountains, or that they fhall *not* be kept in the plain. In winter they are allowed every where. The fhepherds buy the laft growth of the meadows, at 5 liv. or 6 liv. per *giornata* for them; and pay for fuch hay, as may be wanted in froft or fnow.

Corn from Sardinia is not allowed to be exported, but when the quantity is large, and then paying a heavy duty, yet this is the only commodity of the ifland; and the execrable policy that governs it, has rendered it one of the moft wretched deferts that is to be found in Europe*. On account of this duty, they pay no land-tax †. No wonder that the authors of fuch a policy want to fell their inheritance!

MILANESE.

The export of cocoons are here alfo prohibited; and as it is rather more feverely fo than in Piedmont, the price is of courfe fomething lower. The duty on the export of filk, is 7½ ſ. per pound.

Keeping fheep in the vale of the Milanefe, every where prohibited by government, from the notion that their bite is venomous to rich meadows. The fame in the Veronefe; and there is a differtation in the Verona Memoirs in favour of them.

STATE OF VENICE.—*Brefcia*.

The cultivation of the mountains is every where prohibited in this republic, left the turbid waters falling into the Lagunes, fhould fill up thofe channels, and unite Venice with the Terra Firma. Mr. Profeffor Symonds has remarked

---

* *Riftoramento della Sardegna*, tom. i. p. 3.   † *Ib.* p. 147.

the

the ill effects of cutting woods on the mountains, relative to the mischief which rivers in that case do to the plains; it is suspected in Italy, that there are other reasons also; and they have observed in the territory of Aqui, in Piedmont, that hail has done more mischief since the woods have been cut down, in certain districts of the mountains, between the Genoese territory and Montferat *.

Verona.

The export of wheat is prohibited when the price exceeds 24 liv. the sack, of 11 *pesi*, of 25 lb.; 11 *pesi* are 205 lb. English; and therefore 24 liv. equals 26s. 6d. per quarter English, of 456 lb.; apparently a regulation that is meant as an absolute prohibition. The export of maiz is also prohibited, when it reaches a certain price, proportioned to this of wheat. The export of cocoons and unspun silk prohibited.

Vicenza and Padoua.

The export of cocoons prohibited.

Venice.

The export of wool, from the Venetian territory, has been always prohibited. The export of wheat is prohibited, when the price arrives at 22 liv. the *saccho*; but so much depends on the magistrate, that there is no certainty, and consequently the trade crippled. The *stajo*, or *staro Veneziano* of wheat, is 133 lb. *grosso*; 4 *stari* 1 *mozzo*. The sack of flour is 204 lb. to 210 lb. + The sack of wheat 132 lb. *grosso* ‡. As the Venetian pound is about one-twentieth heavier than the English, 22 liv. the sack about equals, not exactly, 36s. the English quarter, but the ratio of the price is of little consequence, in laws, the execution of which depends on the will of the magistrate ‖. Another prohibition, which marks the short and fallacious views of this government, on every object but that of their own power, is in the duration of leases; no person is allowed to give a longer one than for three years; which is in fact, to declare by law, that no renter shall cultivate his farm well.

ECCLESIASTICAL STATE.—*Bologna*.

The government of this country, in respect to taxes, is the mildest perhaps in Europe; but it loses much of its merit by many prohibitions and restrictions,

---

* *Memorie della Soc. Agraria*, vol. iv. p. 3.

‡ *Trattato della Pratica di Geometria Perini*, 4to, Verona, 1751.

‡ *De la Lande's Voyage en Italie*, tom. vii. p. 81.

‖ On this point, see Mr. Professor Symonds's excellent paper in the *Annals of Agriculture*.

which have taken place more or less throughout Italy. Silk cannot be fold in the country; it muft all be brought to the city. All wood, within eight miles of the fame place, is a fimilar monopoly; it can be carried no where elfe. The export of corn is always prohibited; and the regulation ftrictly adhered to; and, it may be remarked, that the price is never low; the natural, and probably the univerfal effect of fuch a policy, **muft be** a high price, inftead of that low one, which is the object of the State.

Tuscany.

In the States I have hitherto mentioned, to name prohibitions, is to exemplify their mifchief in the conduct of all the governments, through whofe territories I have yet paffed; **but in Tufcany the tafk is more agreeable—to give an account of prohibitions there, is to fhew the benefit of their reverfal, and of that fyftem of freedom, which the late beneficent fovereign introduced.**

In 1775, **an unlimited freedom in the export and import of corn was eftablifhed. The effect of this freedom, in the** commerce **of corn, has been very great;** in the firft place, the price of corn has rifen confiderably; and has **never for a** moment been low; the rife has been fteady; famines and any **great fcarcity** have been abfolutely avoided, but the augmentation of price on **an** average has been great. I was affured, on very refpectable authority, that landlords, upon a medium of the territory, have doubled their incomes, which **is** a prodigious increafe. This vaft effect has not flowed immediately from **the rife in the price** of corn, but partly from an increafed cultivation, in **confequence of that** price, and which would never have taken place without it. **On the** other **hand,** the confumers feel a very great rife in the price of every article of their confumption; and many of them have complained of this as a moft mifchievous effect. I was affured, that thefe prices have been doubled. Such complaints **can be** juft only with refpect to idle confumers, at fixed incomes; a penfion or an annuity is undoubtedly not fo valuable now, as it was before the free corn **trade; this is clear;** but it **is equally** certain, that landlords, and all the mercantile and induftrious claffes, profit greatly by the **general rife: this fact is** admitted, nor would the improvement of all the arts **of induftry; the fituation** of the poor moft highly ameliorated; and the increafe of **population, allow it** to be queftioned. Before the free trade, the average price was 5½ *pauls* (each 5½d.) per *ftajo*, of 54 lb.; now the average is 9 *pauls*. Here **is a** rife in the price **of** 40 per **cent.** Thofe whofe interefts, or whofe theories point that way, will contend that this muft be a moft pernicious evil, and that the confumers of corn muft fuffer greatly; it however happens, and well it deferves to be noted, that every **branch** of induftry, **commercial** and manufacturing, has flourifhed

more

more decidedly since that period, than in any preceding one, since the extinction of the Medici. This is one of the greatest political experiments that has been made in Europe; it is an answer to a thousand theories; and ought to meet with the most studious attention, from every legislator that would be thought enlightened.

No body can express himself better against the regulations in the corn trade, than Paoletti:—" Uno dei più gravi e dei piu solenni attentati, che in questo genere si sia fatto, è che ancora, da una gran parte dei politici governi si fà all' ordine naturale è certamente quello, delle restrizioni è dei divieti nel commercio de'grani. Non han conosciuto mostro il più orribile, il più funeste quelle sfortunate nazioni che ne sono state infestate. Le pesti, le guerre, le stragi, le proscrizioni dovunque aprirono il teatro alle loro tragedie non arrecarono mai tanti danni al genere umano, quanto questa arbitraria politica *."

It is remarked, by a very intelligent writer, that the early declension of Tuscan agriculture, was caused by the ill-digested and injurious laws of restriction and prohibition, in the beginning of the sixteenth century: the price of provisions was regulated, in order to feed manufacturers cheaply, not perceiving that the earth gave scanty fruits to poor cultivators; that exalting the arts by the depression of agriculture, is preferring the shadow to the body. Wool was wanted for the fabrics, yet no encouragement given to breeding sheep. Merchants and manufacturers composing the legislative body, whose interests were concentrated in Florence; all the other towns, and generally the country, were sacrificed at the shrine of the capital: they made a monopoly of the Levant trade, and even of ship-building; which had such pernicious consequences, that in 1480, they were obliged to lay open the remnants of trades once flourishing †. They shewed the greatest eagerness to encourage the planting of mulberry-trees; yet knew so little of the means of doing it, that they subjected the sale of cocoons to a multitude of restrictive regulations, and even fixed the price, and gave a monopoly of the purchase ‡; and even the power of fixing the price of silk was, by the government, given to four dealers; and in 1698, the whole trade was subjected to the price of one man; and such was the effect of these fine measures, that a law was passed *forcing* plantations of mulberries; four trees to every pair of oxen employed §. So utterly subversive of the intention will the prohibitory system always prove!

By the edicts of 1775, 1779, and 1780, of the Grand Duke, a multitude of restrictions, on the sale of cocoons and wool, and on the fabric of both silks

* *Iveri Mezzi,* &c. *Ap. Apel.* 1772, 8vo, p. 19.　　　† *Ragionamente Sopra Toscana,* p. 68.

‡ Cosmo I. first allowed the export of cocoons, February 22, 1545; subject to a duty of 18 *f.* the pound, of one sort, and 3 *f.* the other; augmented successively, and at last fixed to 2 liv.

§ *Ragionamente,* p. 83.

and

and woollens, were abolifhed.　A free trade in corn, oil, cattle, and wool, was given * about the fame time; as well as the rights of commonage deftroyed †. By the edict of March 18, 1789, the plantation and manufacture of tobacco was made free; and, that the farmers of the revenue might not be injured, the benevolent fovereign declares he will buy all cultivated on the ufual terms, till the expiration of the farmer's leafe ‡.

I am very forry to add to the recital of fuch an enlightened fyftem, a conduct in other refpects borrowed entirely from the *old fcbool:* the export of cocoons has been long prohibited; and even that of fpun filk is not allowed.　But what is much worfe than this, the export of wool, about fix months ago, was forbidden, under the fhallow pretence of encouraging manufactures.　Such a monopoly, againft the agriculture and improvement of the country, is directly contrary to the general fpirit of the Grand Duke's laws.　The fame arguments which plead in its favour, would prove equally in favour of prohibitions, and fhackles on the corn trade; he has broken many monopolies: Why give a new one?　The moft plaufible plea for this, is the example of England; but does he know that of all the fabrics of that kingdom, this of wool is the leaft flourifhing; and precifely by reafon of the manufacturers having the monopoly of the raw material, and thereby being enabled to fink the price 60, and even to 70 per cent. below the common rates of Europe?　The total failure of this policy in England, which cheats the land of four millions a year, in order not to increafe, but to hurt the fabric, fhould plead powerfully againft fo pernicious an example.　They fhould know, that the raw materials of our moft flourifhing fabrics, are exportable; fome free, and others under low duties; and that wool is an exception to all the reft; and at the fame time, the manufacture that has made the leaft progrefs ‖.

MODENA.

The export of wool is prohibited; wherever this is the cafe, it is not to be expected that any exertions can be made in improving the quality; and accordingly we find that all the Modenefe is miferably bad.　The meafure is intended as a gratification to the manufacture; and when that poffeffes the mo-

---

* *Leggi dei,* Sep. 14, 1774; Dec. 28.　Alfo, Aug. 24, and Dec. 11, 1775.

† March 7, and Apr. 11, 1778.

‡ *Della Coltivazione del Tabacco.* **Laftri.**　Firenze, 8vo, 1789, p. 40.

‖ See this point particularly explained in *Annals of Agriculture,* vol. x. p. 235, and in many other papers of that work.　Some of thefe memoirs were tranflated and publifhed in French, under the title of *Filature, commerce et prix des Laines en Angleterre,* 8vo, 1790; but fome of the beft papers, for inftance, that above alluded to, and others, were left out of the collection.

nopoly,

nopoly, the wool is fure to be worthlefs; which is the cafe here. They make in the mountains, fome coarfe things for the wear of the common people.

PARMA.

There is a fabric of earthen-ware at the city of Parma, to encourage which, the import of all foreign ware is prohibited; the effect is, that the manufacture is contemptible, without an effort of improvement; it has the monopoly of the home confumption, which yields a great profit, and further nobody looks. It was juftly obferved to me, that with fuch a favour no flourifhing manufacture could ever arife at Parma, as the advantage of the monopoly was greater. The policy of prohibitions has every where the fame refult.

SECT. VII.——OF THE PRICES OF PROVISIONS, 1789.

Nice.

Bread, 3 f. (the Piedmontefe *fol* is the twentieth part of a livre, or a fhilling, and the pound is about one-tenth heavier than the Englifh). Beef, 3 f. 8 *den*. Mutton, 4 f. Veal, 5 f. Butter, 12 f. Cheefe, 11 f. Bread, laft winter, 1 *piccolin* (one-fixth of a *fol*) cheaper. At thefe prices of meat, weighing-meat added.

Coni.

Bread, 2 f. 3 *den.*; for the poor, 1½ f. Beef, 3 f. 2 *den*.

Turin.

Bread, 3 f. Veal, 5 f. Butter, 9 f. Cheefe, 9 f. Brown bread, 2½ f.; for the poor, 1 f. 8 *den*. Nobody but the poor eats beef or mutton.

Milan.

Beef, 13 f. Cow ditto, 10 f. (the *fol* the twentieth of the livre, which is 7½d.; the pound *groffo* is to that of England, by Paucton, as 1.559 is to 0.9264). Mutton, 10½ f. Veal, 15 f. Pork, 18 f. Butter, 35 f. Cheefe, Lodizan, 42 f.

Codogno.

Bread, 4 oz. 1 f. Beef, 12 f. per lb. Veal, 12 f. Butter, 22 f.

Verona.

Bread, 5 f. per lb. of 12 oz. (equal to ¾ lb. Englifh). 20 Venetian *fols* equal to 6d. Englifh.

Vicenza.

Vicenza.

Beef, 14*f.* per lb. of 12 oz. *grosso*; this ounce is to the English, as 690 is to 480. Mutton, 13*f.* Veal, 16*f.* Pork, 17*f.* Butter, 30*f.* Cheese, 32*f.*; ditto of Lodi, 44*f.* Hams, 44*f.* Bread, by the ounce *sotile* (which is to the *grosso*, as 1 is to 1¼), 6*f.*

Padua.

Beef, 14*f.* per lb. of 12 oz. *grosso* (which is to the English pound, as 9966 is to 9264. Paucton). Mutton, 12*f.* Veal, 16*f.* Pork, 16*f.* Butter, 32*f.* Cheese, 24*f.*

Venice.

Beef, 15*f.* per lb. *grosso* (to that of English, as 9758 is to 9264. Paucton). Mutton, 13*f.* Veal and pork, 18*f.*

Ferrara.

Beef, 3¼ *baiocchi* (10 to a *paul* of 6d.) per lb. of 12 oz. Mutton, 3 *baioc.* Veal, 4 *baioc.* Butter, 9 *baioc.* Cheese, 8 *baioc.*

Bologna.

Bread, 2 *baiocchi* per lb. (to the pound English, as 7360 is to 9264. Paucton). Beef, 4 *baioc.* 2 *quatrini.* Mutton, 3 *baioc.* 4 *quat.* Veal, 5 *baioc.* 2 *quat.* Pork, 6 *baioc.* Butter, 10 *baioc.*; and in winter, from 15 *baioc.* to 20 *baioc.*

Florence.

The livre (of 8¼d.) is 12 *grazie*, or 20 *soldi*, the *sol* is 3 *quatrini*; and the pound is three-quarters English. Bread, 8 *quatrini* per lb. Meat in general, 7¼*f.* Butter, 1¼ *paul* (the *paul* 5¼d. English). Cheese, 10*f.*

Modena.

Bread, the best white, ¼ *paul* per lb. (the *paul* is 6d. English; and the pound is to ours, as 6513 is to 9264, or something under twelve of our ounces). For the poor it is cheaper. Bread is thus dear, owing to the *entrées* and *gabelle*; a sack of flour, of 70 liv. sells at 100 liv. Beef, 12 *bolognini* per lb. Mutton, ¼ of a *paul*, or 10 *bol.* Veal, 13 *bol.* Pork, 14 *bol.* Butter, 1 *paul.* Cheese, 40 *bol.*

Lanesbourg.

Bread, 4*f.* for 18 oz. Meat of all sorts, from 3*f.* to 3½*f.* for 12 oz. Cheese, from 4*f.* to 5½*f.* Butter, 6*f.* for 12 oz.

CORN,

CORN, 1789.

PIEDMONT.—*Coni.*

Rye, the *eymena* of 2 *rubbio,* or 50 lb. 3 liv.

Chentale.

Wheat, the *eymena* of 45 lb. or 52 lb. aver. 47, 3 liv. 15*s.* In common, 3 liv. 15*s.* Maiz, 2 liv.

Turin.

Maiz, 2 liv. Wheat, 3 liv. 10*s.* the *eymena* of 50 lb. Rye, 2 liv. 10*s.*

Milan.

Wheat, 34 liv. the *moggio* of 140 lb. 28 oz. Oats, 15 liv. Maiz, 20 liv. Miglio, 18 liv. Rice, 44 liv.

Codogno.

Rice, 5 liv. the *stara.* Willow wood, 14 liv. 6 *braccio* long and 3 *braccio* broad. Flax, 5½*s.* for 5 oz. ready for combing; 50*s.* per lb.

Verona.

Wheat, the export prohibited when it exceeds 24 liv. the fack, (26s. 6d. English quarter). Maiz, now 24 liv. the fack, of 11 *pesi,* of 25 lb. ; common price, from 20 liv. to 22 liv.; has been fo low as 6 liv.

Venice.

Wheat flour, 8½*s.* per lb. Bergamafque maiz, 24*s.* the *quarterole,* of 6 lb. Common maiz, 22*s.*

Bologna.

Wheat, the *corba,* 24 *pauls.* Maiz, 18 *pauls.* Oats, 12 *pauls.* Barley, 16 *pauls.* Beans, 18 *pauls.*

Florence.

Wheat, 9 *pauls* the *stajo,* which may in a rough way be called 1d. per lb. : this is 4s. 9d. per English bufhel, of 57 lb.; and 5s. per bufhel, of good wheat. Before the free corn trade, it was on an average, at 5½ *pauls.* Beans, now 5½ *pauls* to 7 *pauls.* Saggina (great millet), 4 *pauls* the *stajo.* Maiz, from 4 *pauls* to 5 *pauls.* Barley, 5 *pauls.* Oats, 4 *pauls.* French beans, 7 *pauls.*

WINE,

WINE, FUEL, HAY, STRAW, &c.

Nice.

Wine, 7 *f.* the bottle. Charcoal, 24 *f.* per 100 lb. Wood, 15 *f.* per 100 lb.

Chentale.

Hay, from 5 *f.* to 8 *f.* the *rubbio*, of 25 lb.

Turin.

Hay, 10 *f.* the *rubbio*. Straw, the same. Wine of Brenta, 7 liv. 10 *f.* the 36 pints, each 4 lb.; for the poor, 4 liv. Wood, 12 liv. the load, of 200 pieces, 3 feet long. Charcoal, 12½ *f.* the *rubbio*. Candles, from 9 *f.* to 10 *f.* Soap, 7 *f.* Lime, 5½ *f.* the *rubbio*. Bricks, 22 liv. per thousand.

Milan.

Iron, the pound of 12 oz. 5 *f.* Charcoal, 100 lb. of 28 oz. 3 liv. Bricks, 30 liv. per thousand.

Mozzata.

Wine, common price, 10 liv. or 12 liv. the **brenta**, now 6 liv.

Milan.

Hemp, ready for spinning, 1 liv. per lb. of 28 oz. Flax, ditto, 32½ *f.* Oil, linseed, per lb. of 28 oz. 26 *f.* Walnuts, 1 liv.

Verona.

Wood, 5 *f.* the *peso*, of 25 lb. (18 lb. English).

Vicenza.

Candles, 20½ *f.* Soap, 20 *f.* Dutch herrings, 3 *f.* each. Iron, 11 *f. grosso.* Charcoal, from 5 liv. to 8 liv. the 100 lb. Coals, from Venice, 4½ liv. the 100 lb. Wood, **the carro,** of 108 cubical feet, 22 liv.; of oppio, walnut, &c. the pieces the size of a man's arm. Sugar, from 25 *f.* to 35 *f. sotile.* Coffee, 3 liv. 6 *f.* Chocolate, 3½ **liv. or** 4 liv.; with vanilla, 6 liv. or 7 liv. By the ounce *grosso*, which is to the ounce English, as 690 is to 480, is weighed flesh, butter, cheese, candle, soap, &c. By the ounce *sotile*, is weighed sugar, coffee, drugs, rice, bread, silk, &c.; it is as 1 is to 1½.

Ferara.

Wine, 1 *baiecca* the *bocali*.

Bologna.

Bologna.

Wood, the load, 30 *pauls.* Faggots, 24 liv. per 200. No coal. Charcoal, 1½ *paul* the *corba.* Bottle of common wine, from 3 *baioc.* to 5 *baioc:* common price of wine, from 20 *pauls* to 30 *pauls* the *corba,* of 60 *bocali.* Sugar, 2 *pauls* 1 *baioc.* the lb. Coffee, 2 *pauls* 2 *baioc.* Of Moka, 3 *pauls* 5 *baioc.* Candles, 8 *baioc.* Wax ditto, 8 *pauls.* A footman, with a livery, 50 *pauls* a month. A man cook, from 20 to 40 *zecchins.* An English gentleman's table is served, nine in the parlour, and five in the kitchen, by contract, for 20 *pauls* a day.

Florence.

To plough a *ftiora* of land, 3 liv. Hay, 4 *pauls* the 100 lb. (about 2l. 15s. a ton). Straw, 3 *pauls* per 100 lb. Wine, 8 *grazie* the bottle. Charcoal, 100 lb. 4 *pauls.* Wood, the *catafter* of 6 *braccia* long, 1½ broad, and 2 high, 28 liv. Rent of a poor man's house, 18 *pauls.*

MODENA.

Wood, 45 liv. the load, of 3 *braccia* long, 3 high, and 3 broad. Wine, 40 liv. the 12 *pefi.* Candles, 20 *bol.* Soap, 15 *bol.*

PARMA.

Hay, 80 *pefi,* 150 liv. (the *pefi* 25 lb. each ¼ lb. English; and the livre 2½d. about 1l. 9s. per ton).

LABOUR.

Nice.

Summer, 30 *f.* (1s. 6d.) Carpenter and mason, 40 *f.* (2s.)

Coni.

Summer, 14 *f.* Winter, 10 *f.* (6d.) Mason, 25 *f.*

Savigliano.

Summer 12 *f.* Winter, 10 *f.* Farm servants wages, about 100 liv. (5l.) a year, beside their food, which consists of 3 lb. or 4 lb. of bread, according to the season, a soup maigre, a *polenta* (a maiz pudding), &c. &c. During the summer, they add cheese, and a little small wine, with a sallad; and in harvest time, a soup of good wine, which they call *merendon,* but they then work twelve hours a day.

Turin.

Summer, 11 *f.* Mafon, 25 *f.* Carpenter, 27 *f.*

Milan to Pavia.

Summer, 22½ *f.* (8d.) Winter, 10 *f.* (3½d.) Manufacturers, 40 *f.* Labourers pay 7 liv. (at 7d. English) for a cottage, and a very little garden.

Mozzata.

Summer, 12 *f.* Winter, 10 *f.*

Lodi.

Summer, 20 *f.* Winter, 12 *f.* Harveft, 30 *f.* Mowing, 20 *f.* a day; a good hand mows 5 *pertiche* a day.

Codogno.

Weavers, 20 *f.*

Verona.

Summer, 30 *f.* (9d.) Winter, 20 *f.* (6d.)

Vicenza.

Summer, 16 *f.* Winter, 14 *f.* Mowing, 30 *f.*

Padoua.

Summer, 25 *f.* and wine. Mowing, 2 liv. (1s.) a day: wheat, 3 liv. ditto. Winter, 16 *f.*

Venice.

Summer, from 30 *f.* to 40 *f.* Mafon, 4 liv.: the loweft in the arfenal, 3 liv. a day.

Ferrara.

Summer, 25 *baiocchi* (1s. 3d.) Winter, 12 *baioc.*

Bologna.

Summer, 12 *baioc.* and 2 *bocali* of wine, each 3 lb. 4 oz. Winter, 10 *baioc.* (6d.) In harveft, to 20 *baioc* Half a day, of 4 oxen and 2 men, 5 *paoli* (2s 6d.) Manufacturers earn from 5 to 20 *baioc.* a day. The women that fpin hemp, 3 or 4 *baioc.*

Florence.

In the filk mills of Florence, they are now (November) working by hand, for want of water. The men earn 3 *pauls* (1s. 4½d.) A girl of fifteen, 1 *paul* (5½d.) In the porcelaine fabrics of the Marchefe Ginori, common labour,

2 or

2 or 3 *pauls*. Painters, 4½ *pauls*. In fummer, 1½ *paul* and food. In winter,
1 *paul* and ditto. To plough a *ftiora* of land, 3 liv. Threfhing corn by the
day, 1 liv. and food. Cutting corn, 18 *grazie* and food.

MODENA.

Common labour, 1 *paul* and wine. Carpenter and mafon, 2 *pauls*.

PARMA.

Printer's men, 3 *pauls* a day, (16½d.)

Lanefbourg.

Winter, 10 *f.* and food. Summer, 20 *f.* and food.

POULTRY.

Nice.

Turkey, 7 liv. Fowl, 20 *f.* Pigeon, 20 *f.* Eggs, 12 *f.* the dozen.

Turin.

Turkey, 30 *f.* Fowl, 15 *f.* Duck, 25 *f.* Goofe, 25 *f.* Pigeon, 10 *f.* Eggs,
the dozen, 8 *f.*

Milan.

Turkey, 11 *f.* per lb. Fowl, 20 *f.* Duck, 32 *f.* Eggs, the dozen, 26 *f.*
Capon, 15 *f.* per lb.

Bologna.

Turkey, of about 4 lb. 3½ *pauls*. Pair of capons, 30 *baiocchi*. Eggs, 1 *baioc.*
each; in winter, 1½ *baioc.* Tame large pigeons, 24 *baioc.* the pair. Wild
fmall pigeons, 12 *baioc.* Eels, from 12 to 14 *baioc.* per lb. Tench, 10 *baioc.*
per lb. Pike, from 12 to 15 *baioc.* Sturgeon, 5 or 6 *pauls* per lb.

MODENA.

Capon, 1 *paul*. Fowl, 40 *bol.* Turkey, 4 liv. Duck, 4 liv. Twenty eggs,
25 *bol.* Pigeons, 1 *paul* the pair.

RISE OF PRICES.

Milan.

In 794, a decree of the Senate and Diet of Frankfort, canon 4, that corn should sell at the following prices, no regard to scarcity and abundance :— *Moggio* of oats, 1 *denaro*; one of barley, 2 *denari*; one of rye, 3 *denari*; one of wheat, 4 *denari*: proportion 1080 to 1.

In 835, hogs, 20 *denari*.

In 857, one pound of silver, *lira*, 20 *soldi* of 12 *denari*; one *denaro*, now at Milan, on comparison of an antient *denaro*, of half a *paolo*, was as 1 to 90; for 90 *denari* make half a *paolo*. The value of silver now, to that of antient times, as 1 to 12; therefore it is 1 to 1080 *.

In 975, *un stajo di vino*, 1 *denajo*; *un moggio di frumento*, 4 *denaji*; *un carro di legna*, 1 *denajo*, equal to 18 liv. at 1 to 1080 †.

In 1152, rye and panic, 3 liv. the *moggio*; 1 *denaro* equal to 130; consequently 3 liv. is equal to 13 liv. 10*s*. 10 *den.* ‡

In 1165, 500 hogs, each 6 *soldi*; which now we must call 65 liv. each ‖. Cart load of wood, drawn by a pair of oxen, 12 *denari*; equal now to 6¼ liv.

In 1272, 1 *moggio* of wheat, the common price, 19 *soldi*. Millet, 12 *soldi*; and this, to the money of the present time, is as a livre for a *sol*; that is, wheat, 19 liv. and millet, 12 liv. §

In 1315, 1 *soldo* for a mass, equal to 20 now; 1 *fiorino d'oro*, 30*s*. now 60 liv. as 1 to 40: the *fiorino d'oro* antient, and the present *zecchino*, the same thing. From this time to the present, the proportion of the money of those times to the present, is as 1 to 4 **.

In 1402, the *fiorino o ducato d'oro*, worth 42 *soldi*, equal to 16 liv. 8*s.* at present ††.

Bologna.

The prices of every thing are now, at Bologna, from 10 to 15 per cent. dearer than ten years ago; here attributed to the increased plenty of money, from a rise of the price of the products of the country, hemp and silk selling much higher. Twenty years ago, hemp was at 30 *pauls*, now at 50. And in Tuscany, the prices of every thing doubled since the free corn trade.

---

* *Giulini, Storia di Milano*, vol. i. p. 268.　　† *Ib.* vol. ii. p. 380.　　‡ *Ib.* vol. v. p. 527.
| *Ib.* vol. vi. p. 332.　　§ *Ib.* vol. viii. p. 254.　　** *Ib.* vol. x. p. 87.　　†† *Ib.* vol. xii. p. 63.

It is worthy of the reader's obfervation, that the general prices of provifions, and of *living*, as it may properly be called, have rifen, perhaps, as much in Italy, as in any country of Europe; certainly more than in England, as I could fhew by many details, if they were confiftent with the brevity of a traveller. A fact of fo much importance, would admit of many reflections; but I fhall obferve only, that this fign of national profperity, (and I believe it to be one), is not at all confined to the countries in the poffeffion of extenfive manufactures, and a great trade, fince we find it in thofe that have none.

I fhall not enlarge upon it, but barely hint, that the poffeffor of a landed eftate in Lombardy, has raifed his rents, to the full, as much in the laft ten, twenty, thirty, or forty years, as his brother landlord has in England, who has bleffed himfelf with the notion, that manufactures and commerce have done more for him, than for any other fimilar clafs in Europe. It is very common in the Englifh parliament, to hear the deputies of our tradefmen expatiate on what the immenfe manufactures and commerce of England have done for the landed intereft. One fact is worth an hundred affertions: go to the countries that poffefs neither fabrics nor commerce, and you will find as GREAT a rife perhaps in the fame period.

S P A I N.

SPAIN.

S P A I N.

CULTIVATION, &c.

THE vale of Aran * is richly cultivated, and without any fallows. Follow the Garronne, which is already a fine river, but very rapid: on it they float many trees to their saw-mills, to cut into boards; we saw several at work. The vale is narrow, but the hills to the left are cultivated high up. No fallows. They have little wheat, but a great deal of rye; and much better barley than in the French mountains. Inftead of fallows, they have maiz and millet; and many more potatoes than in the French mountains. Haricots (French beans) alſo, and a little hemp. Saw two fields of vetches and ſquare peaſe. The ſmall potatoes they give to their pigs, which do very well on them; and the leaves to their cows; but aſſert, that they refuſe the roots. Buck-wheat alſo takes the place of fallow, many crops of it were good, and ſome as fine as poſſible.

The whole valley of Aran is highly peopled; it is eight hours long, or about forty miles Engliſh, and has in it thirty-two villages. Every one cultivates his own land. A journal of meadow ſells in the valley for 800 liv. irrigated, but by no means ſo well as in the French mountains, nearly an arpent of Paris, which is ſomething more than an Engliſh acre. The lower arable lands are ſold for 500 liv. or 600 liv.; the ſides of the hills proportionably; and the higher lands not more than 100 liv. Their crops of all ſorts, vary from 2½ to 3 quarters Engliſh the acre. Hay harveſt no where begun.

---

* The route in which theſe obſervations were made, is marked in the journal inſerted in the firſt volume; alſo the dates.

The mountains belong, as in the French Pyrenees, to the parishes; each inhabitant has a right to cut what wood he pleases for fuel and repairs, in the woods assigned for that purpose; others are let by lease at public auction, for the benefit of the parish, the trees to be cut, being marked; and, in general, the police of their woods is better than on the French side; when woods are cut, they are preserved for the next growth.

Have scarce any oxen; what few they kill, they salt for winter. Taxes are light; the whole which a considerable town is assessed at being only 2700 liv. which they pay by the rent of their woods and pastures let: but if calculated by tailles, houses, &c. and including every thing, the amount would be about 3 liv. a year, on a journal of 600 liv. value. This is the proportion of an acre of land worth 30l. paying 3s. a year, in lieu of land and all other taxes.

Coming out of Veille, see to the right some of the most stoney land I have ever beheld, yet good hemp and buck-wheat were growing on it. In the hedges, many of the plants common to them in England. The pastures on the mountains good, quite to the snow; but the low meadows not watered with the attention given them by the French in their Pyrenees. Pass several of the thirty-two villages of the valley of Aran; population very great, for they croud on each other; and this results here from the division of property, and not from manufactures, which have more than once been supposed the only origin of great population.

Much millefolium here, and other plants common with us. Plough with bullocks; all we saw, pale reddish, or cream-coloured, and with horns.

No wood at the top, but pasturage and rocks of micaceous schistus; met a great herd of dry cows and oxen, cream-coloured. It is remarkable, that a pale reddish cream-colour holds from Calais quite across France hither, with very little variation.

Flocks of sheep, and a penn for oxen and cows—the latter milked for cheese. Plough with oxen in yokes and bows, as in England, and not yoked by the horns as in the south of France. Come to fallows (which is a point of worse husbandry than we have seen for some time), manuring by asses, loaded with baskets. The trees here (pines) are finer than on the French side; they are all cut for the Toulouse market, being carried over the mountains, and floated down the Garronne; from whence we may draw conclusions on the comparative demand of the two kingdoms. Land here sells from 400 liv. to 500 liv. the journal.

Come

Come to the valley d'Efteredano, where wheat and rye are cut. Every fcrap on the defcent is cultivated; an extenfive favage view of mountain, with patches of culture fcattered about the declivities: but fallows are found here.

Pafs Rudafe, on the top of a rocky mountain, come prefently to vines, figs, and fruit trees; fnow in fight. As we defcend to the vale, every fpot is cultivated that is capable of being fo.

Crofs the river to Realp; about which place is much cultivation, as the mountains flope more gently than hitherto. Hedges of pomegranates in bloffom. The town is long and has many fhops. Hemp is the great object in it; of this, they make ropes, twine of all forts, bags, and have fome looms for converting it into cloth. Corn and hay all carried on panniers.

Pafs Sort, a vale fpoiled by the river, which exhibited the depredations of the Italian rivers, fo excellently defcribed by my learned friend, Mr. Prof. Symonds.

Hitherto, in Catalonia, we have feen nothing to confirm the character that has been given of it; fcarcely any thing has a tolerable appearance. It is much to be queftioned, from the intelligence, whether they have any fuch a thing as a farmer who rents land: only patches of property—no maiz, and French beans very poor—fallows every where on the hills, and yet the rye after them miferable. Old vineyards, of late, quite neglected, over-run with weeds, yet the grapes of a fize that fhew what the climate is; they are now as big as peafe. In the towns every thing as bad; all poor and miferable.

Rifing up the mountain, which is all of pudding ftone, we find it is all cut into terraces, fupported by many walls, with rows of vines on them for raifins, not wine, mulberries, and olives: but here are fallows, and I thought I perceived traces of thefe hills having been formerly more cultivated than at prefent.

Pafs Colagafe. Come to a regular vineyard, the rows twelve feet afunder, the intervals alternate fallow and corn. The features of the country now begin to relax, the mountains are not fo high, and the vales are wider. The leaves of a good mulberry-tree fell for 44 f. or 22d. Englifh.

Many walnut-trees full of fruit. Much is tithed by the church: fee much corn threfhing every where.

Crofs two pieces that had rye laft year, left now to weeds, and will be under rye again next year; an extraordinary courfe. Mulberry-leaves never fold, but if fo, the price would be about 4½ liv. a tree. Cows all red. Land in the vale fells from 20l. to 25l. Englifh, the journal. The road leads up Monte Schia,

R r 2

the

the whole of which confifts of a white ftone, and argilaceous marl. Snow on the diftant mountains.

Look back over a great profpect, but totally to the eye without wood. Crofs a hill to another great vale, where is much, and fome rich cultivation, as the hills are not fteep, but floping.

Pafs in fight of St. Roma, near it the road leads by a fmall round lake, but it is on very high ground, no hills near it; it is faid to be very deep. Here they were hoeing a barley ftubble, juft ploughed, to form ridges, on which they fow French beans. This diftrict is called that of fhells: millet juft up; pafs a large wafte almoft entirely covered with lavender; corn on a part of it; but after a crop, they leave it to weeds to recover again. Here alfo they practife the alternate hufbandry of one bed, or broad-ridge, corn, and another fallow. Plough with cream-coloured oxen. In breaking up the waftes here, they cut the fpontaneous growth to dry, then pile it into heaps with the earth pared and placed on it; this is all burned; we faw heaps ready to be burned to the quantity of five hundred loads an acre: but the crops are wretched for many miles, fcarcely the feed again.

In our inquiries, meet with fome traces of what, in France, are called *Metayers*, that is, a fort of farmers who cultivate the land for half the produce; the landlord taking one half, and the tenant the other.

For two hours and a half, pafs a wafte mountain covered with fhrubs, and fcattered with ever-green oaks, and lower down, the evident remains of old terraces, which have once been cultivated, but now over-run with weeds. To Falca; the ploughs here have all long beams, as in the fouth of France, which reach to the yokes of the oxen, and confequently they have no traices; two fmall fticks form the mould-board; they plough all flat.

In this diftrict, not one acre in an hundred cultivated, all rocks, fhrubs, and weeds, with patches of wretched oats on the mountain fides. The road leads up one which is all of ftone, covered with rofemary, box, brambles, &c. As the top break at once on the view of a deep vale, or rather glen, at the bottom of which, a muddy river has fpoiled the little land which might have been cultivated. The hills are fteep, and all is cultivated there that could be fo, but the quantity very fmall.

Defcend into a very rich vale, and to the town of Paous. There we faw many perfons winding filk, the cocoons were in warm water, and wound off by a well-contrived reel, fomething different from thofe ufed in France.

Prices

Prices.

Bread, 3*f.* per lb. of 12 oz.
Mutton, 6*£.* per lb. of 48 oz.
Pork, 15*f.* per lb. of 48 oz.
Bottle of fweet white wine, 5*f.*
Bottle of fweet red wine, 2*f.*

Here they were threfhing, by driving mules around on a circular floor of earth, in the open air; a girl drove three mules round, and four men attended for turning, moving away the ftraw, and fupplying the floor with corn. Their crops are all brought home by mules or affes with panniers; met feveral; they each carried fix fheaves, equal to twenty common Englifh ones; where roads are bad, this is the only way in which it can be done.

Pafs a great wafte of argillaceous marl, in which are ftrata of talc:—much of it a foft white rock; the ftrata in fome places clear and tranfparent, fhining, break in thin flakes; the country for many miles wafte, fo that there are not more, I guefs, than one acre in two hundred cultivated.

More deferts for feveral miles. Some alternate fallow hufbandry between vines, and the crops fo contemptible, that they produce not more than the feed. Pafs fome vineyards furrounded on every fide by deferts; no water, and yet the vines and grapes are of the moft beautiful luxuriance; from which I conclude, that immenfe tracts of thefe wafte lands, might be applied with equal profit, if there were men and capitals enough in the country.

Meet a farmer, who pointed out to us a piece of land, containing exactly a Catalonia journal, from which, it appeared to be pretty nearly the fame meafure as an Englifh acre. They ftack their corn by the threfhing floor, drive mules, &c. around upon it, and draw the ftraw, when cleared, with ropes, by a mule to the ftack, in which it is depofited for winter ufe.

To Beofca, moftly defert hills, but fome broad vales, which are cultivated; about that place, many mulberries, vines, and corn, but all the laft gained by fallow. A farmer here, pays a feigneur, who lives at Barcelona, 2000 liv. a year for his farm, which is reckoned a large one. Through all this country, they collect from every wafte fpot, amongft their cultivated lands, fhrubby wood and weeds, with which they burn heaps of clods and earth, and fpread the afhes on the fallow as a manure for corn.

There feems every where to be inclofures fufficient for afcertaining diftinct properties, but not for fecurity againft any fort of cattle. No where any wood

to

to be feen, except fruit trees, olives, or ever-green oaks, which are almoft as fad as the olive; altogether, nothing for beauty of landfkip. The hills all rocks, and the vales vines, fcattered with thofe trees. Some new plantations of vines. Towards Toorà, the country is much more cultivated; the fides of the hills covered with olives. The vale has many mulberries, and much tillage; and for fome miles paft, there are many fcattered houfes, which has not been any where the cafe before: remarked one great improvement, which was a vineyard, with vetches fown in the alternate hufbandry between the rows, inftead of a fallow, to be followed by corn.

Leave Calaff.—Crop and a fallow; fome vetches; much cultivation; and better corn than we have in general met with; fome fown in fquares, as if in clufters, but could not learn the fact. In fome parts, many vetches inftead of fallow; they are planted by hand, and wheat fown after. The foil, a good adhefive loam, brown with a reddifh hue, better than the white land, which travelled with us fo long yefterday: moft of the corn cut.

Great wafte, and mount a hill, from whence an extenfive view; all the country alike, no wood; and not one acre in ten cultivated. Pafs four or five cream-coloured bullocks, and one or two blood-coloured. I note them, having feen fo few in fo many miles.

French beans, eighteen inches by twelve; a good deal of cultivation; but vaft waftes, and country of a rocky, favage afpect; many pines, but poor ones. Within four hours of Montferrat, vines at fix feet afunder, the firft we have feen planted in that manner, which fhews the proprietor content with having one product only on the ground.

Waftes continue; not one acre in a hundred cultivated. All broken country, and fcarcely any vales of breadth.

At the bottom we came again to olives. Meet two very fine cream-coloured oxen, which the owner fays would fell for about eighteen guineas; feeds them with ftraw, but gives oats or barley when they are worked; they are in fuch good order, that the ftraw muft either be much more nourifhing than ours, or their work very light indeed. From the marks in the pine-trees, conjecture that they draw refin from them.

Pafs Orevoteau, where is a hedge of aloes about four feet high. A gradual defcent, for fome time, on a wretched ftoney defert, of nothing but aromatic plants, thin, and fcattered with the difmal ever-green oaks, more dull and difagreeable, if poffible, than the olives.

Near

Near Efparagara, vines at five or fix feet, which cover the ground; red loam, mixed with ftones. This town is the firft manufacturing one we have met with, or which feemed to be animated with any other induftry than that of cultivation. The fabric is woollen cloths and ftuffs. Spinners earn 6*f.* a day, and food. Carders, 11*f.* They have alfo many lace-makers, who earn 9*f.* a day. Thefe are Spanifh money; their *fol* is fomething higher than the French, which is our half-penny.

Fallow every where, yet many of the ftubbles full of weeds. Corn yet in the field, and poor. Some vines promifcuous, at four feet; fome in rows at fix feet. Country difagreeable; many beds of torrents, without a drop of water, and fhocking to the eye. Apricots, plumbs, melons, &c. ripe, fold in the ftreets, from the open ground. A pair of very fine cream-coloured oxen, 24l. Englifh: the amazement is, how they can be kept in fuch order, in a country fo arid and defert, and that has not a pound of hay in it.

The country now is far more populous and better built: many vines and great cultivation, but with fallows. The foil all a ftrong red loam; a way cut through a vineyard of this foil, which fhewed it to be feven feet deep; at the bottom, was a crop of fine hemp; indeed, the foil to the eye, was as good at the bottom as on the furface.

They plough with mules abreaft, without a driver, having a line for reins, as in England; the beam of the plough is long enough to reach to the circular iron, about nine inches under the yoke, to which the mules are collared. The yokes are like thofe in which oxen are worked, only with collars inftead of bows. This method, which is very common in France alfo, has both its advantages and difadvantages; it will be a light draught, when the pitch of the beam is proportioned to the height of the mules, but if the fhare muft be raifed or lowered according to their height, it will be bad both for the land and the animals. To have the line of traction, from the draught to the body of the plough, is not quite correct, but it is much better than the common plough beams, made either too long, or too fhort: in this cafe, the length of the beams is afcertained: but the chief origin and intention of it, is cheapnefs. The mould-board of the plough here, has no iron on it, and is fixed to the left fide; the fhare is double, as if to work with a mould-board on either fide; this is a great fault; only one handle. It did its work tolerably. The wheat in fheaves is yet in the field, but the ftubbles all ploughed, a narrow flip only left, on which the wheat remained: this fhews good attention to the fucceffion of crops.

Prices

Prices of Provisions, &c. at Barcelona.

Bread, 4*s.* and a fraction, per lb. of 12 oz.
Mutton, 22½ *s.* per lb. of 36 oz.
Pork, 45*s.* per lb. of 12 oz.

That of the poor people, very little lefs; but they buy the foldier's bread, which comes cheaper; they live very much on ftock-fifh, &c.

Hams fometimes 3 or 4 *pefettos,* or fhillings, per lb. of 12 oz. Wine, 4*s.* or 5*s.* the bottle.

Common day wages, are 25*s.* French; fometimes rife to 33*s.*; the very loweft, 22½ *s.* Stocking weavers earn 33*s.*

Cream-coloured oxen in carts, their horns fawn off to the length of fix inches, two yoked abreaft, and one mule before. A pair of good oxen fell at 25l. Englifh. Vale from a quarter to half a mile broad.

All the corn in the country, is left in the field till it is threfhed, and they fay it never takes hurt. A hill cut through, thirty feet deep, for the road, and walled on each fide. The fea clofe to us on the right, all the way; and the vale I fpeak of, is between that and the hills: fome of them are fandy, and planted with vines, which yield, per journal, four charges, the charge felling at 13 or 14 *pefettos,* and a journal for 300 Spanifh livres; this is the journal, felling for 35l. 8s. 9d. and producing about 2l. 14s. very inadequate to the value of the land; there are great quantities of fruit-trees of all forts.

At Gremata; after which, a vale for a mile and a half, or two miles, the foil fandy; and much cultivation. On the hills, many vines. Some corn without fallows; it is all cut, but not carried, and the land all ploughed.—Vines.

A wheat ftubble ploughed up, and the land fown with buck-wheat, which is now up.

Part of a vale highly cultivated, but a great part wafte, though on the fame level to the eye, but much fpoiled by a torrent, for a quarter of a mile broad; it is entirely ruined, yet there is no water now, nor any channel, all being level; in fuch cafes as thefe, and indeed in moft others, induftry, united with good capitals, would remedy the evil. Eight men working a fandy field, by way of digging with an inftrument very common here, a fort of hoe, fixteen inches long, and nine broad, with a handle fo fhort, that the body is bent very much in ufing it. Vale two or three miles broad, and unites with an opening in the mountains. French beans often under maiz, but that crop much

thinner,

thinner, and nothing gotten by it. Some very fine orange-trees, near twenty feet high, large ftems, and thick round umbrageous heads. All this vale before Maturò, is under a very fine cultivation. They have much lucern; and an article of attention, I had not before obferved, was, tubs made on purpofe for carrying the riddance of privies and urine to their fields.

Hemp yields ten quintals the journal. Vineyards give three, four, and five charges of wine per journal, and fell for 200 or 300 Spanifh livres the journal: other lands, not irrigated, from 100 liv. to 150 liv. For above a league, vines on fand; very little other cultivation; the vale is two miles broad; fells at 150 liv. Spanifh, the journal; on the hills, and near the fea, vines; mountains cultivated, imperfectly, almoft to the top; but there is much wafte. Houfes fcattered every where.

The cultivators are *metayers*, that is, they pay a portion of the crop inftead of rent: the produce is divided into three parts; two for the farmer, and one for the landlord, in which cafe, the farmer is at every expence whatever. Some vineyards are let at from 15 to 40 *pefettos*; I have not met any where in France with vineyards let, for they are all in the hands of the proprietors. Land in general lets from 15 liv. to 35 liv.

Come to a great cultivated vale, but no water, or but little; maiz, fix inches to two feet high, in fquares, on land from which the corn has been cleared; the account we received. I fufpect the higheft to be previoufly fown in a bed, and tranfplanted as foon as the land was ready to receive it; millet alfo after corn; the foil a rich black loam.

Pafs Malgra. Vale two or three miles broad; vines and cultivation. A great deal of fine maiz, called, all over Catalonia, *Miliæ*. I found the fame name for it afterwards in Languedoc, where they fpeak the fame language as the Catalans. Lets for 15 liv. one with another. Maiz is fown, grain by grain, after corn; the foil a granite fand. A thick woodland, all inclofed. Pomegranates make very fine thick hedges. Much wood and vines—no watering nor fallows—houfes fcattered every where—foil fandy, but good. Very bad ploughing—cream-coloured oxen. Inclofures become ftill thicker. Poplars planted over fome fields, and vines trained to them, and from one to another: reading accounts of this hufbandry in books, I had formed an idea, that it muft be fingularly beautiful to fee feftoons of vines hanging from tree to tree, but there is nothing either pleafing or ftriking in it, and the wine is never good for want of fun, and owing to its being dripped on by another plant, which robs it alfo of its nourifhment; corn is fown under them, which is damaged ftill more. Broad flat vale, formed of the ruins of granite.

Pass for several miles in a vale, where the country has different features. It is all inclosed—much oak—a few vines, trained up trees. Soil bad. Two poor bits of meadow I noted, for they were the first I had seen bad in Spain. Many fields over-run with spontaneous rubbish. Maiz and harricots cultivated here together, as in many other quarters. Some scattered houses. Much waste on gentle hills that have vineyards on them, and would all yield that production, if planted. A sloping hill of granite sand, well cultivated. Vines, trained to oak and poplars, with many fruit trees. The price of wheat here is 15 or 16 *pesettos*, for the 3½ *quarterons*, weighing 5½ quarters, and each quarter 26 lb. ; this is 143 lb. of wheat, costing 15½ *pesettos*, which will be 50s. the English quarter. Barley half the price.

Come to a great waste, spreading over many hills, for several miles ; to northern eyes, a most extraordinary scene. It is a thicket of aromatic and beautiful flowering shrubs, with very little mixture of any that are common with us. Large spreading myrtles, three or four feet high, and covered with their sweet-scented flowers, jessamines, bays, and other shrubs, with which we croud our shrubberies, are here worse nuisances than heath with us, for we saw neither sheep nor goats. View after this, a large plain, bounded by mountains, and scattered every where with houses—a good deal of cultivated inclosure. But, on entering, find much waste in this plain. Vines now form hedges, and surround the fields. Come now to cattle, of which we have hitherto seen very little ; saw several small flocks of sheep, most of them entirely black, some without horns, others with, and curling round the ears. All the oxen cream-coloured ; except two, with the necks and end of their tails black ; all well made, and in fine order. Large breadth of corn, and some fields left apparently to grass. I suspect fallows.

The country still thickly inclosed, some pieces of grass, and a few of meadow, which are not burned, hot as the climate is. More cattle here than we have yet seen. They keep their sheep and hogs (all black) together, and the girls, &c. who attend them, spin hemp.

Pass Goronota ; and many wastes for some miles on gentle slopes ; the soil good, but covered with aromatic shrubs ; no cattle seen in any of them. Level vale with much culture, and much pasture : many large oaks on old double banks ; also tall poplars : all inclosed, and like many parts of England, as maiz and vines are not here ; a thick woodland. In this part, the soil is a deep, rich, brown, adhesive loam : the corn not carried, but the land ploughed and sown with French beans. They have pease, beans, maiz, hemp, &c. without watering, and, that circumstance considered, the crops are good. The

ploughs

ploughs are drawn by cream-coloured oxen, guided by a line, and without a driver. Some meadows without water; with many quails. They are *metayers*, paying the landlord one-third of the produce; but not of *phang*, which is for oxen; *phang* is their name for clover; and this the firſt time we met with any information about it. It puzzled us much to diſcover, what *phang* could be; but I found, by accident, a plant of *trifolium alpeſtre*, and ſhewing it to a farmer, found, by his deſcription, that it was clover *(trifolium pratenſe)* beyond all doubt. They were now ploughing a wheat ſtubble, in order to ſow it directly with *phang*. Their culture of it is ſingular, and very good; it is mown for hay once in the ſpring, yielding a fine crop; the land directly ploughed, and planted with *monget*, which is their name for fallow-hoeing crops, ſuch as French beans, millet, peaſe, &c. This *monget* is kept very clean, and wheat ſown after it, which is off ſoon enough for a ſecond crop of French beans. A courſe with them is,

  1. Maiz.
  2. Wheat, and ſown after with clover.
  3. Clover and French beans.
  4. Hemp and French beans.
  5. Wheat and millet.

Vines are here planted in eſpaliers; ſmall poles are laid on pegs driven into poſts, which ſtand at ſix or eight feet aſunder, and the vines trained to them; corn is ſown between the rows; good land, yet waſte join it. Many hedges are planted with the yellow-bloſſomed prickly acacia, which anſwers perfectly well for that purpoſe.

Within four miles of Gerona, huſbandry continues good. Trees have vines trained to them. Much cattle, mules, horſes, ſheep, and hogs, kept in the ſtubbles: fine cream-coloured oxen in the ploughs. The ſoil, fine deep reddiſh loam. Now reaping a crop of ſquare peaſe, three feet high, ſtout as lupines, with pods like that plant; all here, an incloſed woodland. Hemp, ſix feet high, and not watered. To the left of Gerona, mountain beyond mountain, branches of the Pyrenees, and very high; but ſeemingly a good deal of cultivation on them. Fine rich deep ſoil in the vale before Gerona; the ſame huſbandry—crops of corn, very fine, not carried, though all the land quite green with young millet; this extreme confidence in the climate, ſhews clearly what it muſt be.

A journal of the vale land ſells for 200 Spaniſh livres, or 23l. 12s. 6d. and lets at 8 liv. to 10 liv. that is, 1l. 1s. Engliſh; but none of it is irrigated. They do not tithe either lambs or other live ſtock.

Price

Price of Provisions at Gerona.

Bread, 3*f.* per lb. of 12 oz.; and excellent.
Beef, 10*f.*
Mutton, 6*f.*
Pork, 8*f.* per lb. of 16 oz.
Cheese, 20*f.* per lb. of 12 oz.

They have no mutton or beef, except what comes from France.

The poor live chiefly on vegetables, and a little pork: their labour, 20*f.* a day.

Leave Gerona.—Fine maiz, planted thin, with good cabbages under it: this is a fyftem which promifes well; but cabbages here, are only for the people, and not for cattle. Three meafures and a half make a journal, and a pair of oxen plough three meafures a day; buy their oxen in the French mountains, at a year old. Their hills are either wood, or cultivation, but mixed with part rocky wafte. Crofs fome hills, which contain a great deal of wafte, but fee a broad valley to the right; all inclofed, and well cultivated; to the eye rich; houfes fcattered.

At Marenia, iron, 4*f.* or 5*f.* per lb. of 16 oz. The road up a hill; twenty or thirty women giving it a winding direction, by levelling earth; on inquiry, find it is done by the communities, and that they earn nothing; hence it is by *corvees.* Enter a wood of cork-trees; many of them barked half way up; the texture of this tree is remarkable, it feems formed of layers of bark, one under another.

The country now generally cultivated; the fields ploughed, but have had a crop. Some well-planted olives, ploughed under. All the corn we fee is wheat; as to barley, it was cut and threfhed the firft week in June, and the land ploughed and fown with fomething elfe.

From Gerona to Calderoles, three hours and a half, generally cultivated; but waftes fcattered, and mountains every where in fight. The courfe here, is,

>　1. Barley, left to weeds, &c. for cattle.
>　2. Wheat and millet, or French beans.
>　3. Oats or barley, and maiz for cattle.

No fallow, or *phang*; French beans are called *phafols.*

Leaving Calderoles, the country all cultivated; many olives, and under them vines; all well inclofed; no wafte.

Pafs

Pafs Baſerà; a torrent has here deſtroyed a vale half a mile broad; paſs it by a ferry. Country now neither ſo rich, nor ſo well cultivated, as on the other ſide of that town. Maiz planted at ſix feet, and two rows; French beans in the intervals; olives ſcattered; but the maiz very poor under them. Country more poor and ſtoney, yet but few waſtes. Olives and many tall pines. Waſtes with pines; the ſea two miles to the right, and the ridge of mountains in the front, ſeems to end abruptly at it. Many vineyards, and planted with olives; all under culture, and well incloſed with acacia hedges; ſeveral with ditches to them.

The vale of Figuera bounded finely by the mountains; many olives and vines, and a good deal of corn; but neither ſoil nor cultivation equal to what have paſſed; the former is more of a ſtone braſh. Reach Figuera.

The 21ſt left Figuera, and breakfaſted at Jonquieras. Enter the bottom of the mountains very ſoon; paſs through many olive grounds; the trees are large, and ſtand about ſixteen feet aſunder; ſoil good red loam, but ſtoney; no watering. A quart of oil, 2¼ lb. of 12 oz. ſells, retail, for a *peſetto*. Olives bear only every other year. Our guide ſays, he knows a tree, in Arragon, which yields from 50 lb. to 80 lb. for a crop. In theſe twelve miles to Jonquieras, vines ſcattered all the way on the hills; ſome few olives; many cork-trees, latterly: much cultivation, but a good deal of waſte alſo. French beans in rows, and ploughed between with oxen. Soil all the way a granite ſand.

The firſt leading feature of the minutes, is the immenſe quantity of mountains, and other waſtes, which are found in every part of Catalonia. We travelled about three hundred and forty miles through the province, and may conclude, from what we ſaw, without any danger of being deceived, that not one acre in an hundred is under any ſort of cultivation; in ſuch groſs calculation, one would take care to be within the truth, and if I ſaid, not one in one hundred and fifty, I believe I ſhould ſtill be on the ſafe ſide of the aſſertion. When this fact is connected with the reputation which the province has, of being next to Valentia, the beſt cultivated, and, without exception, the moſt induſtrious in Spain, concluſions, very unfavourable to the ſtate and policy of that monarchy, muſt neceſſarily be drawn by every reader. The advantage of poſſeſſing the ſecond city of the kingdom, a place of great trade, and containing one hundred and twenty thouſand ſouls, is very conſiderable, and muſt have done much, to bring the province even to its preſent ſituation. At the ſame time, that theſe boundleſs waſtes were offending the eye, in every quarter, we could, in no part of Catalonia, condemn the people for want of induſtry; on the contrary, they ſeem very well to merit the character they have

gained:

gained: the activity which is seen through all the towns upon the coast, and they are very numerous, and very populous, can hardly be greater, in a country submitted to numerous festival days, by its religion: the fishery in all those places is confiderable, and attended to with an unabating spirit. The women and children make lace; and wherever the soil is good, or water conducted, cultivation is in a high state of perfection. Even in the interior country, we saw, every where, signs of much induftry; and, amidst a poverty which hurt our feelings, we generally saw something to convince us, that it was not the fault of the poor people, that greater exertions were not made. Those interior parts depend entirely on their agriculture; and the height to which they climb the mountains, in order to find a spot tolerably level for cultivation, fhews that their minds and bodies are ready for laborious exertions, whenever there is a profpect of enjoying the reward. With so much induftry among the people, to what are we to attribute the wafte state of their country? The inquiries neceffary for a complete inveftigation of such a queftion, were not to be made by travellers: a longer refidence would have been neceffary; but a few circumftances should be mentioned, which are, probably, connected intimately with it.

First, the poverty of the people in the interior country is ftriking; their towns old, ill built, dirty, and wretched; the people ill dreffed, and generally deficient in the wealth, beft adapted to such a country, cattle: in the higher Pyrenees, this is not so much the cafe; they have cattle, and are in every refpect in a better condition, owing to the plenty which great commons give in a country of good pafturage, and where wood is in profufion. The number of fheep we faw in general, was not the twentieth part of what the waftes, bad as they are for that animal, would maintain; and that of goats, so fmall, as to indicate the fame thing ftrongly. This poverty, not being the effect of a want of induftry, muft refult from a government inattentive to their interefts, and, probably, oppreffive; and from a total want of the higher claffes refiding amongft them. Till we came to the rich country, near Barcelona, that is to fay, in about two hundred miles, we faw nothing that had the leaft refemblance to a gentleman's country feat; thofe who have eftates let *in it are abfent*; thofe we heard of, live at Barcelona; and the whole country is thus abandoned to the very loweft claffes; and the wealth and intelligence, which might contribute to its improvement, diverted into diftant and very different channels; this is a great misfortune to the people, and which will long contribute to keep things in their prefent ftate. To the fame caufe it is owing, that the roads, so effential in the improvement of a country, are left in a ftate which precludes the ufe of wheel carriages; which, with the unnavigable flate of all

the

the rivers, except for rafters of timber grosly put together, cuts off that system
of reciprocal purchase and sale, that interior commerce, which is the best a
country can possess. These are also evils, which the residence of men of fortune is the most likely to correct; and much above the power of peasants and
mountaineers. With all these disadvantages, there are still circumstances which
make it surprising, that more land is not cultivated. Vines and olives succeed
very well on the poorest, and most arid soils; their growth and luxuriance, in spots
surrounded on every side with wastes, and in soils not better, yield a conviction, which leaves no doubt, that the adjoining lands would, if planted,
give a similar produce. The profit of doing it will not be suspected, if the
revenue and value of cultivated lands, on comparison with the wastes, be considered. Two points here, force themselves on our notice; first, the want of
capital for undertaking the work; and, secondly, the waste being in all probability in possession of absent landlords, who will not give sufficient encouragement to others to do **what** they neglect doing themselves.

Where cultivation climbs up the mountain sides, it is by small proprietors,
who purchase of the communities of the parishes the property of the land;
wherever the soil is in hands that will sell just the portion, which is in the
power of a man to buy, great exertions are sure to be the consequence. There
is no spur to industry so great, as the possession of a piece of land, which, in a
country where the means of subsistence are contracted for want of more diffu-
sive and more various employments, is the only comfortable dependence of a
man, who wishes to be the father of a family. The parish that will sell a
waste, at a moderate price, will be almost sure to see it cultivated; but the
great lord, who rarely, or never, sells any of his property, unless ruin forces
him to sell the whole, is equally sure of perpetuating the deserts, which are
the disgrace of his country. He would let them, and perhaps upon advantageous terms; but it demands considerable capitals, and a very enlightened
state of agriculture, for speculations of that sort to take place; the only capitals,
which can be found in Catalonia, for such a purpose, are the hands of men
willing to work; aided, perhaps, by some little savings, which have originated
from the view of wastes that are to be purchased. All that has been done, and
it is much in some districts, is to be traced clearly to its origin.

That these observations are just, will be confirmed by the prices of all the
necessaries of life in that province; they have nothing very cheap; every article of consumption is somewhat dearer than in France; and it is more than
once noted, that all the meat they eat comes from that kingdom. Their
mules are bred in France, and great imports of cattle and sheep are common.
This is a direct premium upon every species of rural industry, and its not
having

having operated greater improvements, muſt be owing to the cauſes on which I have touched.

To cultivate their waſtes, to ſpread irrigation wherever it is poſſible to carry it, are the two firſt objects in Catalonian improvement; all others are inferior; they have, however, ſome which ought not to be neglected. Their wine and oil are objects of the greateſt importance; for it is by theſe, probably, that all the lower waſtes ſhould be improved, which are not capable of irrigation; to improve the manufacture of theſe two articles, in ſuch a manner as to increaſe the demand for them, would be one great means of accelerating the cultivation wanted; they are both bad; the wine is thick, muddy, and poiſoned by the borachio; and the oil is generally rancid; both would otherwiſe be excellent; to remedy theſe defects, and force thoſe commodities, by their merit, into commerce, would tend powerfully to enrich the province; and to enrich it in the very beſt method, by one, which would, at every ſtep, accelerate its improvement. Wool is another commodity, which is of conſiderable value, and might be produced in an infinitely greater quantity than at preſent.

The reader will not expect from a traveller, who throws his ideas on paper amidſt the movements of a journey, that correct attention which leaves nothing untouched; I attempt no more than to glance at ſome prominent features, and to delineate them roughly; to draw into one point of view, the concluſions which ought to be the object of all uſeful travels, it would be neceſſary to ſee much more, to reſide longer, and to travel with greater advantages than I poſſeſs. This little journey has been very far from affording ſuch materials, but it has not to me been barren; it has removed many falſe ideas from my mind, which the writings of men, who have either been inattentive to, or ignorant of agriculture, had placed there, relative to this province; and I know better how to appreciate the praiſes or condemnation, which are given of this or other countries, in ſimilar climates.

There are many perſons who travel, for enjoying the beauty of proſpect;— and there are others, who ſeek for a reſidence better adapted than their own, to their health or their fortune; to ſuch I will add a few words.——To the taſte of a man that is fond of a country in a northern climate, there are few objects more pleaſing to the eye, or more refreſhing to the imagination, than the natural landſcape ſcenes of a well-cultivated and well-peopled country. Theſe have, in England, features that charm and inſtruct. Inequalities of country, not too abrupt; woods that preſent rich maſſes of ſhade; rivers that offer the contraſt of their ſilver boſoms, gliding gently through vales of conſtant verdure, which are neither hurt by their rapidity, nor rendered marſhy

by

by their fluggifhnefs; inclofures, which mark the value and the culture of the
foil; and fcattered habitations of the poor, clean and comfortable, mixed with
the houfes of farmers, in a ftate of eafe and profperity; and with the feats of
gentlemen, who find fociety and liberal pleafures, without deferting the fields
which gives them their fupport, for the profufion and wafte of a capital. No
philofophical eye can view fuch a fcene without pleafure, nor contemplate it
without inftruction. Such a fcene is not to be met with in Catalonia; the latitude
which fpreads over their heads a clear expanfe of blue, which lightens up in
their heavens a blazing fun, with rays of which we have no feelings, which
bids the perfumes of the caft breathe over their waftes, and gives to their gardens a profufion of moft delicious fruits, forbids it. Infinitely the greater part
of the province is rock or mountain, without verdure, and without other wood,
than ever-green oaks, olives, or pines; and no where, except in the Pyrenees, with any maffes of fhade that give effect to the profpect. The only
verdure in the country, tolerably durable, is that of the vineyards. Great waftes
are covered with fhrubs, which, however beautiful, when detached, have very
little effect in a general profpect. To look for neat cottages, or good farm-
houfes, is to look in vain; and to find the landlords of the country, you muft
go to Barcelona and Madrid. The deficiency of verdure, deftroys half the idea
of rural beauty; the eye, dazzled with the unvarying fplendour of the folar
beams, and tired with wandering over arid heaths, aches for cooler and more
quiet fcenes, and languifhes to repofe on the verdant mead. When watered,
where alone there could be verdure, all is a crowded fcene of trees, and corn and
hemp; of glorious fertility, but forming the good feature of a landfcape, only
when looked down upon from an eminence immediately above it. Hence, I
own, that in refpect of beauty of profpect, I muft prefer many parts of France,
and more in England, infinitely to any thing I faw in Catalonia, a country
whofe moft ftriking features are its rocks.

I take the climate to be equal to any thing that is known in the world; I
was there in the hotteft feafon of the year, and travelling twelve and fourteen
hours a day, yet bore it without any fuch oppreffion as could give an idea of its
ever being infupportable; and both men and women ftood their field bufinefs
through the day, except two hours, which they take for repofe. Suppofing,
however, that July and Auguft are efteemed much too hot, ftill the reft of the
year muft, from every circumftance we heard, be delicious—they fpoke with
rapture of the pleafantnefs of the month of May; and no doubt but the winter
muft be a charming feafon, where fuch vegetables as green peafe are gathered
through every month of it, from the open fields. In regard to wholefomenefs
for invalids, one circumftance fhould be confidered, which may be applied

equally to all watered arable lands : I fhould conceive, that they muft of neceffity, in fo hot a climate, be very unwholefome; and little better than rice-
grounds, which are known every where to be peftiferous. The land is kept
conftantly watered, it is therefore little better than an earth fponge, or mafs
of mud; innumerable fibres of vegetables are mixed with it; the heat, the
moifture, and the rich foil form a putrid fermentation, which gives health and
luxuriance to vegetables, but muft fill the air with phlogiftic effluvia, I fhould
apprehend far from wholefome to the human body. This is a confideration
for phyficians, and for thofe whom they fend to fouthern climates.

IRRIGATION.

THE profpects down the vale of Aran beautiful; it is without fallows, fine
hemp inftead of them. Look down on the town of Efteredano, around which,
culture rifes pretty high up the mountains. All the corn cut, is reaped, and bound
in fheaves—Walnuts. Defcend into the vale—Figs. Watered meadows. Ray-
grafs predominates; much common clover, white clover, trefoil, vetches, &c.
A caufeway for irrigation acrofs the vale; the meadows are uncut, and have
2¼ tons per acre, on an average; the corn all through, 3 quarters an acre.
Pafs a rich flat common; part of this vale fed by horfes, mules, hogs, affes,
and a few oxen.

Advancing—what meadows there are, are well watered; as are French beans,
hemp, and a fmall quantity of lucern.

Leave Poeblar; they have lucern, but not good; the gardens are all watered; mulberries; prices of filk this year, 18 liv. the pound. Cultivation all
around, among the olive trees; but it is corn one year, and fallow another.
Crofs the river, which is here fixty yards wide. Wheels for raifing the water
of it into the gardens, ten or twelve feet high; they are of a very fimple
conftruction; fomething like the common water-wheels of a mill, but made
very light; the fellies of the wheel are hollow in divifions, taking the water
in through holes at equal diftances, and as the ftream turns the wheel,
it delivers the water out of the fame holes at the top of its revolution, into a
trough, which conducts it where wanted; it is cheap, fimple, and effectual.
Many peach-trees fcattered about the gardens, &c. Mount the hills; pafs
two

two large tracts, of above one hundred acres, deftroyed by the torrents. Great quantity of pudding-ftones. The mountains around are of interefting and bold features. The country in general here has a great mixture of cultivation and wafte; it is for fome fpace pleafing enough to the eye, but the produce is, I believe, very low; we faw many oats, and fcarcely any that will produce more than a quarter an acre. They have no meadows; and I fhould obferve, that our mules have not found fuch a thing as hay; ftraw and barley are their food; in all thofe fpots which would give grafs, corn and legumes are fown, as more neceffary and more valuable; and this, I am told, is the cafe over, all Spain, lucern excepted.

Near Monte Schia—they have here poor crops of flat barley : of water, they know well the value, a fpring of any account being carefully conducted into a refervoir, and let out at feven in the morning and at night to water.

Advancing—there is fome good hemp, watered; and I fee enough of the country to find that water is all in all; where that is to be conducted, they get crops that pay well; but where no water, they have not the power or the know-ledge to turn the foil, however good it may be, to a profitable account; fallow the only effort, and the fuccefs every where miferable.

Crofs a fine ftream with many acres under it, yet no watering; the reafon I cannot tell, unlefs the land is common; if fo, it is eafily explained.

The foil ftoney; the large, of the pudding clafs; but, in the midft of this arid wretched defert, come to a fpring, which rifes out of the earth into a fmall refervoir, and is immediately ufed for irrigation; maiz, hemp, cab-bages, beans, and all fine; the contraft fhews the aftonifhing effect of water, and that in this climate, the foil is the leaft object—the fun and water do the whole.

Paffing Paous; every thing changes the features; the vale, on comparifon with thofe we have feen, is wide, and alfo flat, and water plentifully conducted in canals, which pafs every quarter, fo as to let into the field of every proprietor; having paffed above one hundred miles of dreary mountain, this vale, fo great was the contraft, had the appearance of enchantment; the care and attenton given to irrigation, cannot be exceeded. The land is prepared for it, by levelling with a nicety as curious as for making a bowling-green, and this (conducting the water excepted, which is common to every one), is the only expence: this general level is divided into oblong beds, from fix to eight feet wide, by little ridges of fine mould, drawn up nicely with a rake every time the ground is fown, in order that the water may not fpread over too much at once, in which cafe, the irrigation would be unequal; there would be too much of a **current** at the part where the water enters, a circumſtance of no great importance in watering graſs land, but which would be miſchievous in arable; ſmall trenches **take** the water from the carrier canals, and paſſing by the ends of thoſe beds, the farmer opens them at pleaſure, to diſtribute the water where wanted. As ſoon as the land is ſown, it is watered, and periodically, till the plants are up; moderately while they are young; but every day, and ſometimes twice a day, when full grown: the effect is ſurpriſing, and infinitely exceeds that **of the** very richeſt manures that can be ſpread upon any land. The rapidity of vegetation is ſo great, that there are but **few crops, which** demand all the ſummer for coming to perfection; I believe hemp is the only one; that plant is now five to ſeven feet in height, and of ſo thick a luxuriance, that nothing can be imagined finer. The rye ſtubbles are ploughed and ſown with French beans, which are up and watered. After hemp, wheat is the crop.

Watered maiz **here, ſeven** to nine feet high. Every **time** we ſee any irrigation, we are ſtruck **more and more** with the importance of water, even on ſoils which are apparently mere rock, and on the moſt arid deſerts, it gives at once the utmoſt luxuriance of vegetation. Vines and olives, however, ſtand in no **need** of it, but thrive admirably **on** the drieſt ſoils without **it:** not one acre, however, in twenty, is planted with them that might be.

Come to more watered grounds; gardening and huſbandry mixed; **peaches;** apples; ripe pears; pomegranates in the hedges, as large now as walnuts in the ſhell; onions and lettuces in great plenty. Some watered lands have been ſold at 1300 liv. the journal.

Near Martorelle is a fine irrigated valley; **French** beans, ſeven feet high. Good lucern, cut **three or four** times a year; onions, cabbages, and lettuces; but the hemp, every where **a principal crop, not great.** The land all formed into the beds for watering; which I have already deſcribed.

Exceeding fine hemp, watered. Maiz thick, and in ear. **Many fine and** tall poplars by the river.

They are now (July) ploughing their ſtubbles for French beans. Their courſe is,

  1. Hemp.
  2. Wheat; and after **wheat, French** beans.

Three crops are therefore gained in two years. The products good. Very fine mulberries. A journal, which is here alſo about an Engliſh acre, of rich land in the vale, not watered, ſells for 500 liv.: watered, for 1000 liv.

Leaving

Leaving Barcelona, enter immediately an extraordinary fcene of watered cultivation, and which muft have given the general reputation to the province.   Nothing can well be finer.   The crops in perpetual fucceflion—and the attention
given to their culture great.   Not the idea of a fallow; but the moment one crop
is off, fome other immediately fown.   A great deal of lucern, which is cut four,
five, fix, and even feven times in a year; all broadcaft, and exceedingly thick and
fine, from two and a half to three feet high, when cut.   It is all watered every
eight days.   We meet many mule loads of it going into the town, each 450 lb.
or 4½ quintals, which fells for 4 *pefettos*, or near 4s. Englifh; fuppofe it 4s. for
500 lb. it will not be difficult to calculate the produce of an acre.   All I faw
would yield 10 tons, green, per acre, at each cutting, and much of it a great
deal more; let us fuppofe five cuttings, or 50 tons per acre, at 16s. a ton, this
is 40l. fterling per acre.   It is to be remembered, that the growth we faw, was
the third, perhaps the fourth, and that the firft and fecond are in all probability
more confiderable, it will not, therefore, be thought any exaggeration to calculate on five fuch.   I by no means affert that lucern yields always, or generally fo, as I fpeak only of what I fee.   I have very little doubt, however, but
this is the amount of that portion, which is thus cut and fold to Barcelona;
poffibly one-third, certainly one-fourth, is to be deducted for the expence of
carriage; this is the moft difficult part of the calculation, for it depends on
how many times the mule goes in a day, which muft alfo depend on the readinefs of fale, and other circumftances.   The profit is, however, amazingly
great.   All the other lucern I have any where feen finks, in my idea to nothing,
on comparifon with the vaft and luxuriant burthens given by thefe watered
grounds.   The fineft crops I have known in England, are drilled, but there is
a fallacy to the eye in the drilled crops, in proportion to the diftance of the
rows; they appear thick while they are really thin, but in broadcaft ones,
which fatisfy the eye, there is no deception; and thefe immenfe burthens,
through which the fcythe is with difficulty moved, produce more at one cutting, than two feet drills would at three, with the advantage of the herbage being finer and fofter.   But weeds in England and Catalonia are two
very different things; it well deferves, however, with us, a better trial than
it has yet generally received; I have viewed broadcaft crops; particularly
Rocque's, on a very rich garden foil; and Dr. Tanner's, on a common turnip
loam, which, though not to be named with the Spanifh, were certainly encouraging.

Hemp, through all thefe watered lands, is the predominant crop, it is feven
feet high, and perfectly fine; fome of it is already harvefted.   I am forry to fee
that the watered part of the vale is not more than a mile broad.   Indian fig,
called

called here, *figua de maura*, grows fix or feven feet high, very branching and crooked, the arms at bottom as thick as the thigh of a common man; thofe and many aloes in the hedges. Every garden or farm has a fmall houfe, with a refervoir for water, which is filled in moft by a water wheel, with jars, around the circumference. The gardens between Barcelona and the fort, and alfo within the walls, are watered in the fame manner; the water is let into every little bed, in the fame way as I have already defcribed. They are crowded with crops, and kept in moft beautiful order; thofe in and clofe to the town, fcattered with mulberry-trees. But in the diftrict of which I am fpeaking at prefent, among the hemp and lucern, neither vine, olive, nor mulberry. Thefe watered lands belong generally to proprietors who live in Barcelona, and are let at 30 to 40 Spanifh livres the journal.

The valley, in its wideft part, is three miles broad. Here it lets at 34 Spanifh livres a year the journal, and fells from 600 liv. to 1000 liv.; each of thefe livres being about 54*ſ.*: (1000 Spanifh livres makes 2700 French ones). Taking the medium, or 800 liv. and the French livre at 10½d. this makes the price of a journal 90l. 2s. 6d.; and the rent of it 4l. The grofs rent of the land, therefore, pays nearly 4½ per cent.; but whether this is clear rent, the tenant paying all taxes, and doing the fmall repairs of his houfe, &c. or whether there are deductions on thefe accounts, are queftions which were neither forgotten nor refolved. To fhew the quick fucceffion of their crops, they have corn in ftooks on the borders of fome of the fields, and the land ploughed and fown with millet, which is already nine inches high. Many bleaching grounds.

Advancing—the irrigated land lets from 24 to 40 Spanifh livres: that not irrigated, at 15 liv. Water, therefore, here more than doubles the rent of the land; and in other places, we have found the difference yet greater. The foil all the way a red and brown deep friable loam, with a fufficient adhefion for any crops. They fow French beans after hemp, and then fow wheat.

At Ballalo, two hours from Barcelona, we meet with the firft vineyards, but the hills here come down to the fea; and where they do not, the vale is not more than half a mile wide. Lycium in the hedges; fome few mulberry-trees. Oranges in the gardens; a few palm-trees, with vines around them.

A journal of watered hemp, produces from 10 to 12 quintals; if not watered, the product much inferior; the price, 14 to 17 Spanifh livres the quintal, or 35s. Englifh, which makes 19l. 5s. an acre. This is, however, to be underftood of a very fine acre. The mountains are at half a mile diftant, and

partly

partly cultivated to the top. All the way inclofed, and the men mending gaps in their hedges.

Every fcrap of flat land well watered, from wells and refervoirs; the hill covered with vines.

Land, near Canet, well watered, fells for 500 Spanifh livres the journal; vineyards for 300 liv. They give, in good years, to 12 charges. Unwatered land, 100 to 150 liv.

Enter a flat vale, half a mile broad, not watered. Hemp, very poor; maiz, feven feet high. Vineyards, under regular plantations of olives; corn cut, in ftooks, and the land ploughed. A journal fells for 200 liv. and further on, where irrigated, for 1000 liv. which is an aftonifhing difference.

While the mountains and wafte parts of the province prefent an unfavourable profpect, the watered diftricts are, on the contrary, fcenes of moft exuberant fertility. To a perfon, from the north of Europe, there can hardly be a more ftriking fpectacle than the effect of watering in thefe fouthern climates; it converts an arid ftoney wafte, which would yield nothing but vines and olives, and on which every fort of grain would hardly return the feed, at once into fields, pregnant with the richeft harvefts; on fuch foils, it gives almoft the whole value of the land; and on the richeft, it raifes it, at the leaft, double; and, in fome inftances, five times. It enables the cultivator to have a fucceffion of crops, more important than any thing we know in the north. The reaping one crop is but the fignal for immediately putting in another; in doing which, they exert themfelves with the utmoft activity; ploughing univerfally as foon as the corn is cut; and are, by this means, enabled to have conftantly two crops a year. The extreme fertility of thefe lands has, however, led many travellers into great or ignorant exaggerations; they have afferted, that the land yields many crops at the fame time, one under another, which is both true and falfe. It is fact, that corn, wine, oil, and filk, are produced by the fame field, in fome few inftances; but it is not from hence to be concluded, that the goodnefs of the land, or the importance of irrigation, is at all fhewn by that circumftance. The fact is, that it is impoffible to raife one crop under another, without lofing in one nearly as much as you gain in the other; the olive, being a large tree, cultivation may be carried on under it, but the crop gained is poor, and fhews, that exactly in proportion to the fhade s the injury fuftained by the produce which is fhaded. If the trees are thick, the corn is hardly worth reaping; it is the fame in other cafes, and I was well convinced, from viewing their grounds with this defign, that the foil can

carry,

carry, profitably, but one crop at a time; feveral may be crowded on it, but
nothing is gained, with grafs under trees, this is not the cafe fo much in a hot
climate; but even grafs is damaged, and it is not the queftion, at prefent, as
they have none. A country to be fupported, and in a hot climate, without
meadows or **paftures,** founds very ftrange to Englifh ears, and it is among the
curious circumftances of this part, and I am told of the reft of Spain. If they
applied to grafs the land that is proper for it, they could not poffibly have bread
to eat; ftraw here is given inftead of hay, and entirely fupplies its place, and
the oxen and mules, which we faw, did not fhew in the leaft, by their looks,
any deficiency in nourifhment. Lucern is not at all common through the interior part of the province, and where they cultivate it, it is ufed green. Maiz
is fometimes fown merely for its herbage, as it might be, I believe, profitably
in England, late in the fpring, to avoid our frofts; it is one of the moft nourifhing plants in the world.

The confequence of water being fo apparent in the province, I could not but
attend particularly to their exertions in conducting it, and I concluded, that not
one acre in twenty, perhaps in forty, is watered, that might be. In the flat
vales, where canals of irrigation are made, at a fmall expence, a very good,
though by no means a complete, ufe is made of them; but on the declivities of
the mountains, it is neceffary to erect a mound of folid mafonry acrofs the river,
and to cut the canal partly out of rocks, and to fupport it by walls of ftone, as
I have feen in France; and having thus diverted a large portion of the water of
a river, to carry it on its level, along the fide of the mountain as far as it will
go; fuch exertions demand a much greater capital, than is to be found upon
the lands of Catalonia: it could be done only by a great lord, who knew the
importance of fuch undertakings, who refided on his eftate, and whofe income
was fpent in fomething elfe than the tafte and pleafures of a capital. But leaving fuch exertions to individuals, who either have not the money, or not the
will to employ it, is to perpetuate waftes. It is the King only who can
make thofe efforts; a monarch, who fhould be determined to improve his
kingdom, would prefently find the means of doing it. The importance of water is fo well known, that if a canal is made to conduct it, the proprietors,
or farmers of the lands below, would readily and fpeedily make ufe of it,
paying proportionably for the quantity they took; this is the fyftem in
Lombardy, and the effect is great. It would be the fame in Catalonia,
but the capital, for the great work of the canal, muft probably be fupplied
by the king, if not the whole, at leaft a confiderable portion. Such money
fhould be lent to undertakers, at a moderate intereft. Exertions of fuch a
nature, with a proper general attention given to thefe objects, would make

them

them fashionable among the great lords of the kingdom, and fertile provinces would soon be created out of barren and desolate wastes. Arbitrary power has been exerted for ages, in efforts of barbarity, ignorance, and tyranny; it is time to see it employed in works, that have the good of mankind for their aim. A beginning, and a very good one, is made in the construction of some great roads, on a scale of true magnificence, which is never exhibited with such effect, as in works of public utility; and whenever the importance of cultivation is well understood in Spain, and the right means of advancing it clearly analyzed, irrigation will then receive an attention that has not, hitherto, been given. Such is the necessity of water, for various productions in this climate, that rivers ought to be no more than infinitely multiplied channels, and collected in one stream only, as a reservoir for fresh, and repeated deviations.

SHEEP.

ON the northern ridge of the Pyrenees, bearing to the west of Bagnere de Luchon, are the pastures of the Spanish flocks. This ridge is not, however, the whole; there are two other mountains, in a different situation, and the sheep travel from one to another as the pasturage is short or plentiful. I examined the soil of these mountain pastures, and found it in general stoney; what in the west of England would be called a *stone brash*, with some mixture of loam, and in a few places a little peaty. The plants are many of them untouched by the sheep: many ferns, narcissus, violets, &c.; but burnet *(poterium sanguisorba)*, and the narrow-leaved plantain *(plantago lanceolata)*, were eaten as may be supposed, close. I looked for trefoils, but found scarcely any: it was very apparent, that soil and peculiarity of herbage had little to do in rendering these heights proper for sheep. In the northern parts of Europe, the tops of mountains half the height of these, for we were above snow in July, are bogs; all are so, which I have seen in our islands, or at least, the proportion of dry land is very trifling to that which is extremely wet: here they are in general very dry; now a great range of dry land, let the plants be what they may, will in every country suit sheep. The flock is brought every night to one spot, which is situated at the end of a valley on a river, and near the port or passage of Picada: it is a level spot sheltered from all winds. The soil is eight or nine inches deep of old dung; not at all inclosed, and, from the freedom from wood all around it, seems to be chosen partly for safety against wolves and bears. Near it is a very

Vol. II.   U u   large

large ftone, or rather rock, fallen from the mountain. This the fhepherds
have taken for a fhelter, and have built a hut againft it; their beds are fheep-
fkins, and their doors fo fmall that they crawl in. I faw no place for fire; but
they have it, fince they drefs here the flefh of their fheep; and in the night
fometimes keep off the bears, by whirling fire-brands: four of them belonging
to the flock mentioned above, lie here. Viewed the fheep very **carefully, and**
by means of our guide and interpreter, made fome inquiries of the fhepherds,
which they anfwered readily, and very civilly.

A Spaniard, at Venafque, a city in the Pyrenees, gives 6oo liv. French,
(the livre is 10½d. Englifh), a year, for the pafturage of this flock of two thoufand fheep: in the winter he fends them into the lower parts of Catalonia, a
journey of twelve or thirteen days; and when the fnow is melted enough
in the fpring, **they** are conducted back again. **They are the whole year kept in
motion,** and **moving** from fpot to fpot, which **is owing to the great range they
every where have of** pafture They are always in **the open air, never houfed,
or under cover, and never** tafte of any food, but what **they can find on the hills.**

**Four fhepherds, and from four to fix large Spanifh dogs, have the care of
this flock; the latter are in France called of the** Pyrenees **breed; they are
black and white, of the fize of a large wolf;** a large head and neck; armed
with collars ftuck with iron fpikes; no wolf can ftand againft them; but bears
are more potent adverfaries; if a bear can reach a tree, he is fafe, he rifes on
his hind legs, with his back to the tree, and fets the dogs at defiance. In the
night, the fhepherds rely entirely on their dogs; but on hearing them bark,
are ready with fire-arms, as the dogs rarely bark if a bear is not at hand. I
was furprifed to find that they are fed only with bread and milk. The head
fhepherd is paid 120 liv. a year wages, and bread; the others, 80 liv. and
bread. But they are allowed to keep goats, of which they have many, which
they milk every day; their food is milk and bread, except the flefh **of** fuch
fheep or lambs as accidents give them. The head fhepherd keeps on the
mountain top, or an elevated fpot, from whence he can the better fee around,
while the flock traverfes the declivities. In doing this, the fheep are expofed
to great danger in places that are ftoney; for by walking among the rocks, and
efpecially the goats, they move the ftones, which, rolling down the hills, acquire an accelerated force enough to knock a man down, and fheep are often
killed by **them. Examine the fheep attentively.** They are in general polled,
but fome have horns; which in the rams turn backwards behind the ears, and
project half a circle forward; the ewes horns turn alfo behind the ears, but do
not project; the legs white or reddifh; fpeckled faces, fome white, fome reddifh; they would weigh fat, I reckon, on an average, from 15 lb. to 18 lb. a
quarter.

quarter. Some tails left long. A few black fheep among them; fome with a very little tuft of wool on their foreheads. On the whole, they refemble thofe on the South Downs; their legs are as fhort as thofe of that breed; a point which merits obfervation, as they travel fo much and fo well. Their fhape is **very** good; round ribs, and flat **ftraight backs**; and would with us be reckoned handfome fheep; all in good **order and flefh.** In order to be ftill better acquainted with them, I defired one of **the fhepherds** to catch a ram **for me to feel, and examine the wool, which I found very thick and good of** the carding fort, **as may** be fuppofed. I took a fpecimen of it, and alfo of a hoggit, or lamb of laft year. In regard to the mellow foftnefs under the fkin, which is a ftrong indication **of** a good breed, with a difpofition to fatten, he had **it in** a much fuperior degree to many of our Englifh breeds, to the full as much fo as the South **Downs,** which are, for that point, the **beft** fhort-woolled breed which I know **in** England; the fleece was on his back, and weighed, as I gueffed, about 8 lb. Englifh; but the average, they fay, of the flock, is from 4 lb. to 5 lb. as I calculated by reducing **the** Catalonian pound of 12 oz. to ours of 16 oz.; and is all fold to the French, at 30 f. per lb. French. This ram had the wool of the back part of the neck tied clofe, and the upper tuft tied a fecond knot, by way of ornament; nor do they ever fhear this part of the fleece for that reafon; we faw feveral **in the** flock with this fpecies of decoration. **They faid that this ram would fell in** Catalonia for 20 liv. A circumftance which **cannot be too much** commended, and deferves univerfal **imitation, is the extreme docility they** accuftom them to; when I defired the fhepherd to catch **one of his rams, I fuppofed he** would do it with his crook; or probably **not be able to do it at all; but he** walked **into the flock, and fingling out a** ram and a goat, bid them **follow** him, which **they did immediately, and he** talked to them while they were obeying him, holding out his hand **as if to give** them fomething. **By** this method, **he brought me** the ram, **which I caught,** and held without difficulty.

The mountain paftures belonging **to the** Spaniards, not ufed by themfelves, **they let to the owners of** large flocks, **who** bring them from the lower part of **Catalonia, as** with the French mountains; thefe flocks rife to 4000 fheep; the **rent, in general, being** from 5 f. to 7 f. **a head,** for the fummer food. Every inhabitant poffeffes cattle, which he **keeps in** the common mountains in what **quantity he pleafes;** but others, who do **not** belong to the parifh, pay 5 f. to 7 f. **a head for the fheep, and** 10 f. **for a cow;** which difproportion they explain, **by** faying, that fheep muft have a much greater range.

They have good fheep in various parts of Catalonia, but all are fent to Saragofa or Barcelona.

The mountains and waftes in fome parts have no fheep; only goats.

Crofs

Cross great wastes, which in other countries would be sheep-walks; but none here; for five-sixths of the spontaneous growth are aromatic plants.

See two small flocks of sheep, exactly like those in the Pyrenees, described the first day of this journey.

A small flock of sheep, that give 5 lb. or 6 lb. of wool each.

Several small sheep-folds.——Such notes as these, shew how few they are, on comparison of what they ought to be.

In travelling over the lower mountains, after quitting the higher Pyrenees *, the deficiency of sheep struck me very much; the climate is too dry to think of a luxuriant vegetation of grass; but if the rosemary, lavender, and other aromatic useless plants were destroyed, and the land, by cultivation, properly adapted, was to be laid down to such plants as would feed sheep, fine pastures might not be gained, but much valuable sheep-walk would be created, and the quantity of wool increased an hundred fold. Such a system would unite well with olives, which might be thinly scattered over such improvements. To import immense quantities of sheep from France, and to take no steps to increase them at home, is a blind conduct, especially when it is considered, that in a proper system, they cannot be increased, without being at the same time, the means of improving fresh land.

Produce of the Kingdom of Valencia in 1787.

	Reals de Vellon.	English Money. £.	s.	d.
Silk, 2,000,000 lb. at 60 *reals*, - -	120,000,000 -	2,000,000	0	0
Hemp, 25,000 *quintals*, at 160 **reals**, -	4,000,000 -	66,666	13	4
Flax, 30,000 *quintals*, at 200 *reals*, -	6,000,000 -	100,000	0	0
Wool, 23,000 *quintals*, at 160 *reals*, -	3,680,000 -	61,333	6	8
Rice, 140,000 *cargas*, at 150 *reals*, -	21,000,000 -	350,000	0	0
Oil, 10,000 *quintals*, at 180 *reals*, -	1,800,000 -	30,000	0	0
Wine, 3,000,000 *arrobas*, - -	84,000 000 -	1,400,000	0	0
Dry raisins, 60,000 *quintals*, at 40 **reals**,	2,400,000 -	40,000	0	0
Figs, 60,000 *quintals*, at 32 *reals*, -	1,920,000 -	32,000	0	0
Dates and palms, - - -	1,200,000 -	20,000	0	0
		£. 4,100,000	0	0

* There is no line of boundary to be fixed, with any precision, to the Pyrenees; I am inclined to think, that all the mountains we saw, Montserrat perhaps excepted, are branches of that stupendous chain, uniting in some direction. The whole mountainous part of the province, that is, eighteen-twentieths of it, is properly the Pyrenees.

Prices

Prices at Madrid, 1788.

	Average	Eng. Money s.	d.
Beef, 14 to 15 *quartos* per lb.	15 *quartos.*	0	3½
Veal, 24 to 30 *quartos* per lb.	27	0	6½
Mutton, 15 *quartos* per lb.	15	0	3½
Fresh pork, 15, 17, to 20 *quartos* per lb.	17	0	4¾
Salted pork, 17 to 20 *quartos* per lb.	17	0	4¾
Ham, 18 to 22 *quartos* per lb.	20	0	5
Tallow candles, 15 *quartos* per lb.	15	0	3½
Soap, 16 *quartos* per lb.	16	0	4
Butter (Mantica de Flandes), 8 *reals* per lb.	8 *reals.*	2	8
Goat's milk, 6 to 7 *quartos* per *el quarto,*	7 *quartos.*	0	1½
Mancha cheese, 18 *quartos* per lb.	18	0	4½
Turkey, 12, 20, to 45 *reals* a piece,	25 *reals.*	8	4
Fowl, 8, 11, to 14 *reals* a piece,	11	3	8
Hare, 5 to 9 *reals* a piece,	7	2	8
Rabbit, 5 to 8 *reals* a piece,	6	2	0
Partridge, 4 to 8 *reals* a piece,	6	2	0
Pigeons, 5 to 6 *reals* a piece,	5	1	8
Eggs, 21 to 42 *quartos* a dozen,	31 *quartos.*	0	7½
Potatoes, 4 to 6 *quartos* per lb.	5	0	1½
Garvanzos (large pease), 10 to 12 *quartos* per lb.	11	0	2¼
Wheat flour, 13 *quartos* per lb.	13	0	3½
Rice, 11 to 12 *quartos* per lb.	11	0	2¼
Brandy, 2 *reals* per *el quarto,*	—	0	8
Common wine, 26 to 28 *r.* the *arroba* (about 18 bottles),	27 *reals.*	9	0
Valdefunas wine, 36 *reals* per *el quarto,*	—	12	0
Charcoal, 4 *reals* and 5 *quartos* the *arroba,*	—	1	5½
Wood, 3 *reals* the *arroba,*	—	1	0
Common bread, 6 *quartos* per lb.	—	0	1½
Pan candial, 6 *quartos* per lb.	—	0	1½
Common oil, 15 *quartos* per lb.	—	0	3½
Valencia oil, 4 *reals* per lb.	—	1	4
French oil, 7 *reals* per lb.	—	2	4
Coffee, 34 *quartos* per lb.	—	0	8½
Sugar, 30 to 38 *reals* per lb.	34 *reals.*	11	4
Chocolate, 6, 8, to 10 *reals* per lb.	8	2	8
Tea, 11 *quartos* per oz.	—	0	2¼
Hair-powder, 2 *reals* per lb.	—	0	8

MAJORCA.

M A J O R C A.

SOME circumstances relating to this island, which I procured from good authority at Barcelona, and at Bayonne, from Spaniards who had resided many years in it, I think too interesting to be omitted, as they may serve, if for no other purpose, at least, to point the inquiries of some future traveller, who shall have an opportunity **of visiting that island.**

Climate.

The most delicious that **has** been experienced by **various** persons well acquainted with France, Italy, Spain, and Portugal; and resulting in a good measure from the variety **of the** face of the country, which rises from some beautiful plains **to** gentle **slopes,** which, after many undulations of surface, finish in the mountains. **In the** greatest heats of July and August, the hills preserve the temperature almost vernal: nor **are** the heats ever suffocating in any part. The winters, **except on the highest** parts of the mountains, are mild and pleasant, as may **be gathered from** circumstances of vegetation, almonds blossom in December, **are in full** bloom in January; and many wild flowers **are in** all their beauty quite through the year. Spinnage, green pease, beans, **lettuce,** endive, cellery, &c. are in perfection the year round. In the depth of **winter,** ice is seen **to** the thickness of one-tenth of an inch, but melts before **the day is much advanced. No sharp** cutting winds are ever felt, either in winter or in spring; and a person who resided there sixteen years, never saw a fog. The houses have no chimnies; but when artificial warmth is wanted, almond-shells are burnt in *braseres.* This extremely agreeable temperature of the climate, was confirmed to me by General Murray and his Lady, who resided there many years; and the former mentioned a circumstance, which shews how erroneous it would be to judge of any climate by the latitude; Leghorn is nearly in the same parallel, but the severest cold he ever felt, in March, **was** at that place, **where, in washing, the water** became ice before a towel could **be well dipped in it.**

Culture and Products.

The hills are formed into terraces, and planted and cultivated with great attention. Olives are planted, and under them wheat sown; in the flats, many almonds and mulberries. Oranges and lemons are in such quantities, that they export many to **France.** They are in great profusion, and the most beautiful

to

[to be imagined. The mountains of Soleya are famous for peaches, and all forts of fruit. Hedges of pomegranates are attended with medlar and quince trees, alternately on one fide, and on the other mulberries; but the beft fence is the prickly pear, the fruit of which is ripe in July, which is eaten, both leaf and fruit, by cattle, and are fupported on it in fine order, when other things fail in the heat. Mufk and water melons are in great perfection.

Sugar-canes do well; but no fuch thing as rice, as neither fwamp, marfh, nor bog.

Irrigation is well underftood, and much practifed.

A common courfe of crops,

     1. Wheat.
     2. Barley.
     3. Beans.
     4. Peafe.

Capers (which are a weed), come up in the wheat ftubbles, which give a crop; then the ftubble and caper-bufhes are burnt, and the barley and legumes fucceed, and after thofe artichokes.

They plough with a pair of oxen, or mules.

The proprietors in general keep the land in their own hands.

Living.

This ifland, which, by every account, might be made a paradife, is one of the cheapeft fpots in Europe to live in; upon an income of 150l. a year fterling, men of the better fort live very comfortably, and bring up a family. Every vegetable production for the table, with all kinds of fruits, are not only in uncommon profufion, but excellent of their forts. Poultry no where better; turkies are kept in great droves, and driven to feed on berries, as regularly as fheep to pafture; they are fattened on myrtle-berries, and are not only of a delicious flavour, but a great fize, even to 36lb. weight. Mutton is excellent; fome fheep are fo fmall from the ifland of Yuvica, that three legs are fometimes ferved up in one difh.

All thefe circumftances united, feem to point out this ifland as an excellent winter refidence for thofe who can no longer refort to Nice or Hyeres, and is probably a better climate than either of them.

Produce

Produce of the Island of Majorca in 1786.

		Pesos.	English Money. £	s.	d.
Wheat,	475,336 *fanegas*	1,521,075	342,241	17	6
Barley,	152,880	300,664	67,649	8	0
Oats,	122,068	134,274	30,211	13	0
Pulse,	102,037	244,888	55,099	16	0
Almonds,	60,500	129,066	29,039	17	0
Oil,	193,030 *arrobas*	476,140	107,131	10	0
Wine,	1,665,660	322,829	72,636	10	6
Hemp,	24,446	83,180	18,715	10	0
Flax,	5,038	15,367	3,457	11	6
Carobs,	500,000	83,333	18,749	18	6
Figs,	175,000	62,000	13,950	0	0
Cheese,	-	25,000	56,250	0	0
Wool, 472,795 lb.		61,341	13,801	14	6
Straw of wheat and barley,		125,045	28,135	2	6
Silk, 5,347 lb.		24,061	5,413	14	6
Sweet oranges,		45,000	10,125	0	0
Fruits of all sorts,		170,000	33,250	0	0
Pimienta,		13,000	2,925	0	0
Capers,		4,500	1,012	10	0
Increase of sheep, by birth,		126,942	28,561	19	0
—— of goats,		31,430	7,071	15	0
—— of black cattle,		25,704	5,783	8	0
—— of hogs,		240,000	54,000	0	0
—— of horses, mules, and asses,	-	74,100	16,672	10	0
Many articles are not mentioned in this account, and are reckoned to amount (the specified produce comprised) to		4,983,326	1,121,248	7	0

The extent of Majorca is $123\frac{1}{4}$ square leagues, whereof twenty to one degree.

Majorca is reckoned to be the $\frac{1}{177}$ part of the continent of Spain; and the whole of Spain does not amount to 250,000,000 *pesos* per annum, according to the opinion of many well-informed Spaniards.

Majorca. 316,011 3 0
Spain. 55,933,988 17 0

I N D E X.

INDEX

TO THE SECOND VOLUME.

A

ACADEMIES, at Turin and Venice, 259
Agriculture, encouragement and depreſſion of, in Lombardy, 247. Effect of government upon it, *ib.*
Almonds, pay better than mulberries in Rouverge, 27. More ſubject to accidents than olives, 56. Yield a good crop only once in ten years, *ib.* Culture very hazardous, *ib.*
Arable land, management of in Piedmont, 202. 207. Milaneſe, 203. Venetian State, 204. Tuſcany, 206. Modena, Parma, Savoy, 207
Arabian horſes, imported into the Limouſin, 53. never ſaddled till the age of ſix, nor eat corn till five, 54
Auvergne noted for fine apples, grafted on crab ſtocks, 72

B

Beans, in the Soiſſonnois, 56. Drilled in Artois, Alſace, *ib.* The culture not ſo common as it ought, 57
Belleiſle (Duc de), experiments on ſilk in Normandy, 29
Bengal oxen travel ſix miles an hour in coaches, 53
Berry fine oxen, 42
Bologna, government of, &c. 252
Bretagne, famous for good dairy maids, 46. Three-fourths of it waſte, 92
Broom, cultivated in Bretagne and Bourbonnois for faggots, 57. Sown with oats, as clover in other places, *ib.* Improves land, *ib.* The principal ſupport of cattle in Bourgogne, *ib.*
Building materials, &c. 117

C

Cabbages, in Flanders, for cows, 59. Six feet in height in Normandy, *ib.* In Bretagne, Anjou, and Alſace, *ib.* The culture of, one of the moſt important objects in Engliſh Agriculture, 60

Capers in Provence, 86
Carrots for cows, in Flanders, 57 Stacked, againſt the froſt, 58. Cultivated with great ſucceſs in Suffolk, 59
Cattle, in France, 41. All cream coloured in Berry, *ib.* The importance of, well underſtood in Normandy, Bas, Poitou, Limouſin, Quercy, Guienne, and no where elſe in France, 52. Confined the whole year in ſtables, *ib.* Not one-tenth part of what there ought to be in France, *ib.* In Piedmont and the Milaneſe, 185. Tuſcany, 195
Cheeſe in the Milaneſe, 188
Cheſnuts, in Berry, Limouſin, boiled and made into paſte, good food, 61. For fatting pigs, *ib.* Diſtreſſing to the Poor when the crop fails, *ib.* Method of cooking, *ib.* Excellent timber, *ib.* The poor live on them in Poitou, 62. The Vivarais the greateſt region of, in France, *ib.*
Chicory, method of ſowing, 62. Luxuriance of, *ib.* Cut three and four times a year, 63. Loſes three-fourths by being made into hay, *ib.* Good for ſoiling, *ib.* Cows eat it greedily, *ib.* Not hurt by drought, *ib.* Laſts good, ten years, *ib.* The Author introduces it into England, and cultivates it with great ſucceſs, at Bradfield, *ib.*
Climate, of Piedmont and the Milaneſe, 148. Tuſcany and Parma, 149. Majorca, 334
Clos de Vaujeau the moſt famous of all the vineyards in Burgundy, 16
Clover, exhauſts land by bad management, 60. The proper method of culture, *ib.* In Piedmont and the Milaneſe, 231
Coals, in France, 103. Not half ſo good as Engliſh, *ib.*
Coleſeed, in Flanders ſown and tranſplanted on oat ſtubbles, 64. Method of culture, *ib.* More valuable than a crop of wheat, *ib.* Prodigious quantity cultivated near Lille, and Bailleul, *ib.* Never cultivated in France for coleſeed, 65. The proper method of culture, *ib.*

Commerce,

Commerce, of Piedmont, 275. Milanese, 276. Venice, 278. Ecclefiaftical State, 279. Modena, 281. Parma, 283

Corn, price in Piedmont and Tufcany, 295

Cows, fed with chick-weed boiled in bran and water, in the Pay de Beauce; and with weeds in Sologne, 41. Worked in Berry, 42. Goats and ewes milked for cheefe in Languedoc, 44. Fattened upon carrots in Picardy, 47. Bran and water their principal drink in Flanders, ib. Product of milk in Normandie, 48. Thrice milked, 50. Salt given them twice a day in Auvergne, 51

Crette de Palleuel (Monf. de), his chaff cutter a very powerful one, 54. His experiments on chicory, 62

E

Ecclefiaftical State, foil of, 147. Tenantry, 155. Rent, &c. 162. Seed and product of, 214

Economical practices, 117

Englifh hufbandry fupported by interweaving thofe crops which fupport cattle with thofe of corn, 52. Farm, eftablifhment of, in France, 139

F

Farms in Piedmont, 151

Fences, 118

Fern made into hay for horfes, mules, and young cattle in Gafcoigne, 45

Figs in Piedmont, 232

Fifh ponds well underftood in France, 119

Flax, in Picardie, 66. Languedoc, ib. Never watered, ib. A crop of, has fetched the feefimple of the land in Soiffonnois, ib. Has produced near 100l. per acre, 67. Great attention paid to the culture of, ib. Very fine in Artois, not watered, ib. Spread on grafs or ftubble, ib. Every where cultivated in Bretagne for domeftic purpofes, ib. Beans fown to fupport it, 68. In the Milanefe, 233

Fuel, price of in Piemont, Milanefe, Modena, and Parma, 296, 297

Fuller's thiftle very profitable, 65

Furz for horfes in Gafcoigne, 65. Sown with wheat and barley, ib.

G

Gallega officinalis, 217

Garonne, the vale of, the richeft diftrict in France, 66

Grafs, little underftood in French hufbandry, 53. Great importance of it as a preparation for corn, ib.

H

Hay, price of, in the Milanefe, Piedmont, Parma, and Modena, 296, 297.

Hemp in Quercy 66. In the Vale of the Garonne the moft productive in the Kingdom, ib.

Produce of, 66. Great Tracts in Guienne, ib. In Maine, 68. Much cultivated in Lorraine, ib. Chinefe hemp in Dauphiné, 69. Price of, at Marfeilles, ib. At Piedmont, 232. In the Ecclefiaftical State, 233

Hogs in Gafcoigne fed on acorns and fattened on maiz, 55. Which make the famous Bayonne hams, ib.

Horfes not fo applicable to the purpofes of hufbandry as oxen, 53. The beft light horfes from the Limoufin, ib. Bean ftraw excellent for, 54. Never give chaff to, in Saintonge, ib. Chaff the beft food, in the Ifle of France, ib. The fineft in Bretagne not worth two guineas and a half, ib. The Norman for draught, and the Limoufin for the faddle---the beft in the kingdom, 55. Great import from England, ib.

I

Implements of hufbandry, 122. Sort of, 130. In Piedmont, 242. Venetian State, 244. Ecclefiaftical State, Tufcany, Parma, and Savoy, 245

Inclofures in Piedmont, Milanefe, Venetian and Ecclefiaftical States, 150. In Tufcany, Modena, Parma, and Tortonefe, 151

Irrigation in Piedmont, 165. Of Piedmont the greateft exertion of the kind in the world, 169. Venice, 181. Spain, 322

L

Labour, price of in Piedmont, Milanefe, Venice, Tufcany, Modena, and Parma, 297, 298, 299

Languedoc, produce of filk in, 37

Larch in Normandie, 108. In the Milanefe, 218

Leaves for fheep, 120

Liancourt (Duchefs de) her dairy of Swifs cows, 46

Lime, 118

Limoufin, beft light horfes in France, 53. The breed much recovered by Arabians, ib.

Lodi, rent, &c. 160

Lombardy, notes on the agriculture of, 145. Poplar, 231. One of the richeft plains in the world, 146. Soil of, ib.

Looms (filk), number of in France, 37

Lyons, number of filk looms in, 37

M

Madder in Alface, 69. The culture not flourifhing in France, 70

Maiz, heat neceffary to the culture of, 70. Method of culture, 70. Highly manured, 71. The people live on it, ib. Mowed for foiling, ib.

Majorca, climate of, 334. Culture and products of, 335

Manufactures and commerce of Piedmont, 275. Milanese, 276. Venice, 278. Ecclesiastical State, 279. Modena, 281. Parma, 283.
Manure, 133. Of Piedmont, 245. Milanese, 246. Venice, ib.
Melilotus Siberica, its prodigious luxuriance, 86
Metayers in Piedmont, 151
Milanese, soil of, 147. System of farming, 151. Rent and price of land, 159. Irrigation, 169. Cattle, 185. Cheese and dairies, 186. Sheep, 198. Management of arable land, 203. Seed and product, 209. Silk, 221
Modena, soil of, 148. Tenantry, 157. Sheep, 201. Management of arable land, 207
Mulberries, 26. Produce of, 27. 34. Stripped for leaves four years after planting, 31. Sowing, transplanting, sort, and grafting, 32. Soil, planting, and cultivation, 33. Eggs of silkworms and hatching, 34. Feeding, 35. Impracticable to feed silk-worms with any other than mulberry leaves, 38
Mustard mowed in full blossom for cows, 72. Much in Artois, ib.

N

Normandie, large dairies in, 48. Finest pasture in Europe, ib. Expence and profit of an acre of pasture in, 49

O

Oil, the idea that those plants that produce it, combated, 77
Olives in Roussillon and Languedoc, 72. Dauphiné and Provence, 73. The largest trees near Antibes, 74. The best oil in Europe made in Provence, 74. The culture of, in a small part of France, ib. In the Venetian State, 235. Tuscany, ib.
Oranges at Hyeres, the only spot in France where they are cultivated in the open air, 74. Produce of the King's garden, ib.
Orchards in Normandie, 72. Damage the corn, ib. In Lorraine and Auvergne, ib.
Otter of roses made at Grasse, equal to that in Bengal, 86
Oxen, price of in Berry, 41. Food to fatten a pair, 42. Fattened with maiz in Quercy, 43. With hogs-grease, 44. Walnut-oil-cake the best food for fattening, ib. Method of shoeing, 45. Fattened upon carrots in Picardie, 47. Upon linseed cakes in Flanders, ib. Drawn by the horn in Bourgogne, 51. Fattened with the *lathyrus sativus* made into paste, in Provence, 52. Travel six miles an hour in coaches, in Bengall, 53. Comparison between oxen and horses, 128

P

Paliurus, 217
Parma, soil of, 148. Tenantry, 158. Irrigation, 183. Sheep, 201. Government, 256.

Parsnips for horses in Bretagne, 58. The people subsist on them, ib. The best of all food for horses, ib. Fatten bullocks faster than any other food, ib.
Pasture in the Pay d'Auge the richest in Europe, 48
Piedmont, soil of, 146. Farms, 151. Useful population, ib. Rent and price of land, 158. 163. Irrigation, 183. Cattle, 185. Sheep, 201. Management of arable land, 202, 207. Seed and product, 208. Silk, 219. Government, 256.
Pines in Gascoigne for resin, 75. In Guienne, Bretagne, and Auvergne, 76. The mountains of Provence covered with, ib.
Ploughing, method of in France, 125, 126, 127
Pont (Madame), her dairy of cows fed with lucern, 46. Method of making butter, ib. Pontoise veal the finest in France, 46. Why, ib.
Pomegranates in the hedges in Provence, 75. Produce, ib.
Poor, state of in the Milanese, 286. Venice, 287
Poplar, cut at twelve years growth, 108. Lombardy, 231
Poppies for oil in Artois, 77. In Alsace, ib.
Population of the Milanese, 283. Venetian State, Tuscany, 284. Modena and Piedmont, 285
Potatoes in Anjou, 77. Much cultivated in Lorraine, ib. Pare and burn for in the mountains of Alsace, 78. Produce, ib. In Dauphiné planted whole, ib. Cultivation of, not general in France, ib.
Prices, rise of, in the Milanese and Bolognese, 300
Prohibitions in Piedmont, 287. In the Milanese, 288. Venice, ib. Ecclesiastical State, 289. Tuscany, 290. Modena, 291. Parma, 293
Provisions, price of in Lombardy, 293
Prussia, King of, his exertions to produce silk in Germany, 38. His little success after forty years exertion, 39. His attempts a lesson to England, ib.
Pay d'Auge, the richest pasture in Europe, grazed by oxen, 48. System of, ib.
Pyrenees much covered with wood, 106. Great havock made of the beech there, ib.

R

Racine de disette, culture of, 79. Produce, ib. Cows and hogs it, ib. Culture of it common in Alsace, ib.
Raves, cattle fattened upon, in La Marche, Limousin, Languedoc, &c. 42, 43, 44, 45
Rent of land in Piedmont, 158, 163. Milanese, 159. Lodi and Codogno, 160. Venice, 161. Ecclesiastical State, Tuscany, and Modena, 162. Parma and Savoy, 163
Rice in Dauphiné, 79. Prohibited, ib. In Piedmont, 236. Milanese, 237. Venice and Parma, ib.

Saffron

S

Saffron in the Angoumois, **80.** Beft foil for it, *ib.*
Sainfoin in Tufcany, 218
Salt for cattle and fheep univerfal in France, 44
Savoy tenantry, 158. Rent, 163. Irrigation, 184. Cattle, 197. Sheep, **201.** Arable land, 207
Sheep in the Milanefe, **Venetian** and Ecclefiaftical States, Tufcany, 199. **Parma,** Savoy, and Piedmont, **201.** Spain, 329
Silk in Quercy, 26. Guienne, 27. Encouraged by government, **but** unfuccefsful, 29. In Normandie, Bourbonnois, Vivarais, 31. Culture more profitable than vines, *ib.* Silk the great produce of Dauphiné, *ib.* Import and price, 37. Home growth, and value, *ib.* Froft prejudicial to the culture, *ib.* Futility of the attempt to encourage the growth in England, 38. Culture in Piedmont, 219. Milanefe, 221. Venice, 224. Tufcany, 230
Soil of Lombardy, 146. Milanefe, **147.** Venice, *ib.*
Sologne, wretched ftate of, 87
Spain, cultivation of, 305. Irrigation in, 322. Sheep, 329
Straw, price of, in the Milanefe, Piedmont, Modena, and Parma, 296, 297.

T

Taxation in Piedmont, 260. The Milanefe, 262. Venetian and Ecclefiaftical **States, 267.** Tufcany, *ib.* Parma, **270**
Tenantry, 151. Of the **Milanefe, 152.** Venetian and Ecclefiaftical **States, 154, 155.** Tufcany, 155. Modena, **157**
Threfhing, 121
Tillage of France, **122.** Piedmont, **242.** The Milanefe, **243.** Venetian and Ecclefiaftical States, **244, 245.** Tufcany, Parma, and Savoy, **245**
Timber to build a man of war, 116
Tithe in Piedmont and the Milanefe, 271. Venetian and Ecclefiaftical States, Tufcany, **272.** Modena and Parma, 274
Tobacco in Flanders, 80. Artois, *ib.* Alface, *ib.* Inftead of exhaufting, improves land, *ib.*
Trigonella fœnum Græcum, **217**
Triticum repens in Guienne for horfes, **85**
Turbilly, Marquis de, his improvements, 92

Turnips in Guienne, **82.** Normandie, *ib.* The culture of, as practifed in England, the greateft defideratum in the tillage of France, 83
Tufcany, foil of, 147. Tenantry, 155. Rent, 162. Sheep, 199. Arable land, 206. Silk, 230. Government, 252

V

Valencia, produce of, in 1787, 332
Venice, foil of, 147. Tenantry, 154. **Rent,** 161. Irrigation, 181. **Sheep, 198. Arable** land, 204. Silk, **224**
Vines, cultivation of, 2. Vin de Grave, 3. Afferted to be the worft of all eftates, 8. Twothirds of the country round Epernay under vineyards, 9. The wine provinces afferted to be the pooreft, 12. **Burgundy, 16.** Clos de Vaujeau the moft famous of all the vineyards in Burgundy, 16. Great tracts of land **under** vineyards, too fteep for **the** plough, **21.** Generally fituated in the pooreft foils, *ib.* High amount of the product, *ib.* The reafons for afferting that the wine provinces are the pooreft combated, *ib.* The culture more profitable **than** fugar, 22. Great object of the home confumption, 23. Comparifon between beer and wine as a beverage, 24. Vineyards divided into unufual fmall property, productive of great mifery, which **is** the origin of the complaints againft them, **25. In** Piedmont and the Milanefe, **238. Venetian** State, 239. Ecclefiaftical State, **240. Modena** and Parma, 241
Vivarais, **the greateft chefnut** region in France, 62

W

Walnuts in Berry, **83.** Oil cake for fattening cattle made of it, in Poitou and Auvergne, 84
Waftes in Sologne, **87.** Languedoc, &c. 88. Vaft tracts in Bearne, &c. many miles in length, 90. Improvement **of in Normandie,** *ib.* Immenfe in Bretagne, **many leagues in** extent, 91. Amount of **in** France, nearly equal to the whole kingdom **of** England, 96. Method of improving fuggefted, 99
Wine, price of, in Piedmont and the Milanefe, 296.
Woods, 106. Produce of, 108, 109. Price, 110. Scarcity of very alarming, 113.

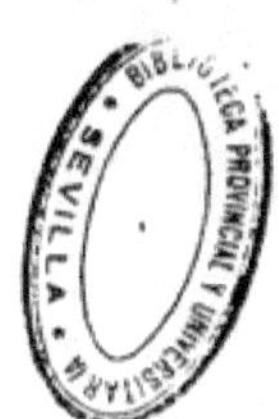

THE END.

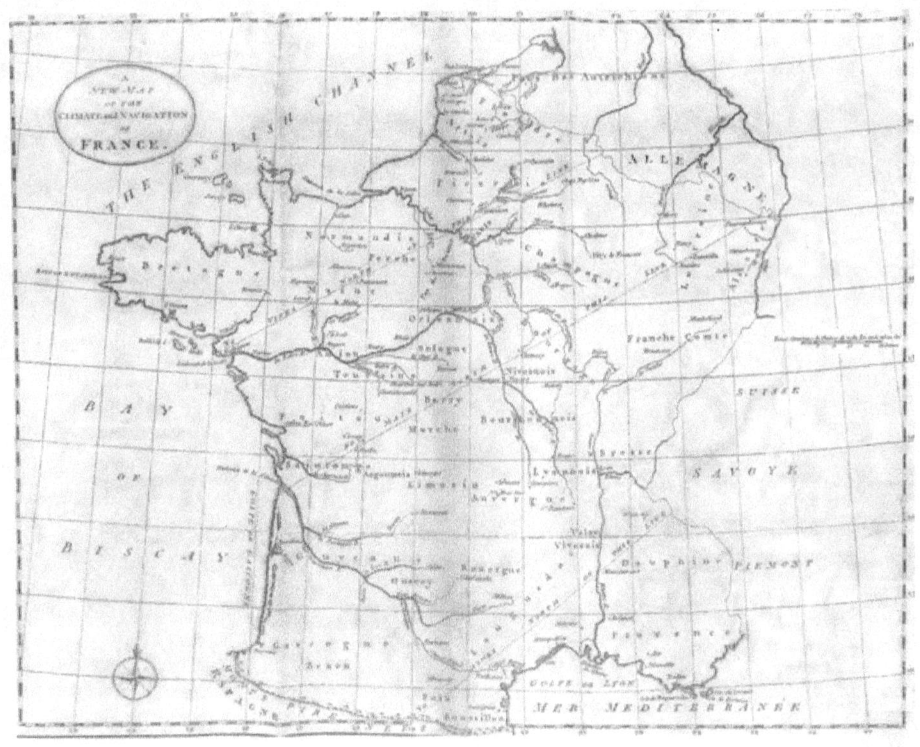
A NEW MAP OF THE CLIMATE and NAVIGATION of FRANCE.
THE ENGLISH CHANNEL
ALLEMAGNE
BAY OF BISCAY
Bretagne
Normandie
Perche
Maine
Picardie
Champagne
Orleanois
Franche Comte
SUISSE
Touraine
Nivernois
Berry
Bourbonnois
Marche
SAVOYE
Lyonnois
Limosin
Auvergne
Bresse
Rouergue
Querci
Vivarais
Dauphiné
PIEMONT
Guienne
Béarn
Provence
ESPAGNE
PYRENEES
Roussillon
GOLFE DE LYON
MER MEDITERRANÉE